Feminism and Fiction

India and Beyond

Feminism and Fiction

India and Beyond

Edited By

Shahram R. Sistani
Santwana Haldar

Prestige

an international publishing house

Published by
Prestige Books
New Delhi 110 058
Ph. 011-25507139
email: prestigebooks@gmail.com
website: asiabookclub.com

Associate Office
60/29-45 Parramatta Road,
Concord, NSW 2137
Australia

ISBN: 81-7851-078-2

Printed at Chaman Offset Press, New Delhi 110 002

Contents

Feminism and Fiction: India and Beyond: An Introduction
Santwana Haldar and Shahram Sistani 9

Freud's "Psychoanalysis": The Development of Feminity
Bhasker A. Shukla 21

Women's Education in the Victorian Era
Athokpam Elizabeth Devi 30

Treatment of Women Characters in Jane Austen's *Emma*
Reena Thounaojam 38

The Feministic Flare in the Novels of Virginia Woolf
Sarika Tyagi 43

Feminism in Egypt
Ahmed Syed 48

Gender and Politics in Naguib Mahfouz's *Miramar*
Abdulmomin Al-Rubiaee 62

A Study of Black Feminism and Womanism in Toni Morrison's *The Bluest Eye*
Fatemeh Azizmohammadi and Hamedreza Kohzadi 69

Identity in Alice Walker's *The Color Purple* A Postmodern Reading
Maryam Sarabi and Farzad Navabakhsh 84

Narratives of the 'Silenced Women': Victims of Violence and Sexual Abuse A Study of Fiction of the Indian Subcontinent
Tejinder Kaur 99

The Changing Position of Woman in Society: Shashi Deshpande's *That Long Silence* and Chandani Lokuge's *If the Moon Smiled*
Seema Suneel 111

Gita Mehta's *A River Sutra*: A Quest for Love and Redemption
Nanda Kishore Mishra 118

Nergis Dalal's *The Nude*: A Bonanza of Themes
Malti Agarwal 127

Theme of Rape in the Novels of Shashi Deshpande
Sunalini Kondapally 141

Reconstruction of a Powerful Myth: Feminist Intervention in Githa Hariharan's *When Dreams Travel*
Keisham Ragini Devi 150

An Interview with Manju Kapur
Deepa Diddi 159

Manju Kapur's *A Married Woman*: A Feminist study
Kamal Kumar Raul 166

Feminism and the Societal Set up: A Study of Manju Kapur's *Difficult Daughters*
Santwana Haldar 173

Feminism in Sujata Parashar's *In Pursuit of Infidelity*
Archana Singh 193

Maya and Men in her Life in
Anupa Mehta's *The Waiting Room*
Sagar Pandya 198

Cyclone as Metaphor in
Anita Nair's *Lessons in Forgetting*
Aroonima Sinha 206

The Unethical Politics in
Sivakami's *The Grip of Change* and
Arundhati Roy's *The God of Small Things*
A Comparative and Analytical Study.
S. Srinivas 213

Psychoanalytical Approach to the
Character of Manjari in Shashi Deshpande's *Moving On*
Bhavana Dwivedi 226

Equating Mythology with Emotion:
Marginalization of Women in
Githa Hariharan's *The Thousand Faces of Night*
Monika Gupta 233

Dialectic of Possession:
Kamala Markandaya's *Possession*
S.S. Gill 245

Bridging the Gap between the Two Cultures in
Kamala Markandaya's *The Coffer Dams*
Sangita Mehta and Suman Garg 251

Quest for Authentic Existence in Anita Desai
Jagdish Batra .258

Psychoanalysis of Anita Desai's *Fasting, Feasting*
in the Light of Humanism
Meenakshi Chaubey 266

De-masculinization of the Male in the Novels of Margaret Laurence and Anita Desai
Sarita Veerangana 272

Doris Lessing's Feminist Concern: An Analysis of *The Grass is Singing* and *The Golden Notebook*
Santwana Haldar 285

Doris Lessing's *The Cleft*: An Argument for Men by a Feminist
Dhananjay Tripathi & Krishan Rai 311

Gender Construction as an Emerging Trend in Margaret Atwood's *The Edible Woman* and Shashi Deshpande's *The Dark Holds No Terrors*
R.P. Mahto 317

A Journey into the Self: A Study of Margaret Atwood's *The Edible Woman*
V. Madhavi 326

Interrogating Culture and History in Buchi Emecheta's *The Joys of Motherhood*: A Feminist Perspective
M. Mani Meitei 335

Memoir as Literature: An Analysis of Fatima Bhutto's *Songs of Blood and Sword*
Jyoti Dahiya 361

Incarcerated Women in Modern Indian Fiction
Punita Jha 369

Feminism and Fiction: India and Beyond
An Introduction

SANTWANA HALDAR
F.M. University, Balasore
&
SHAHRAM SISTANI
Iran

The origin of Feminist Movement demanding for all women an equal status with men is traced to Mary Wollstonecraft's ground-breaking work *A Vindication of the Rights of Women* (1792) that launched a powerful attack on the second class status of women in the western society and was followed by the line of radical thinking as expressed in works like John Stuart Mill's *The Subjection of Women* (1869), Margaret Fuller's *Women in the Nineteenth Century* (1845), Virginia Woolf's *A Room of One's Own* (1929) and Simone de Beauvoir's *The Second Sex* (1949). All these writings form an ideology on which Feminism as philosophy is based. From sociological point of view, Feminism exposes the systematic social injustices caused by gender discrimination. An organized movement for women's right was, however noted in the USA. Since the Seneca Falls Declaration of Sentiments and Resolution was signed at the obscure village of Seneca Falls (near New York) in 1848, a continuous effort to gain the right for women's suffrage characterized feminist movement.

Historically, the first phase of feminist movement was over with the long-cherished victory on the issue of women's suffrage. The second phase, known as New Feminism, started as a part of Radical Movements against racial discrimination in America during the Sixties. These radical feminists believed that the most oppressed group in the western society was 'women.' They seriously meant a social reform in the society, not simply the elimination of differences between the sexes, putting emphasis on the individual's right to find out the kind of person he or she is and to strive to become that person. Gradually, Feminist theory that initially started with feminist ideologies included other issues related to postmodernism and post-structuralism which are found in the writings of Helene Cixous, Julia Kristeva, Luce Irigaray and a host of others. Postcolonial feminists point out that colonialism was a hyper masculine construct which celebrated specifically male qualities of valour, adventure, and resourcefulness and had rather overt sexual nuances. Thus colonialism was a qualitatively different experience for women, from what it was for men. In the late 1970s, a transformation from protest to self-realization was noted in the perspectives of feminism, as we note in the writings of Friedan.

Feminist literary criticism as well as feminist literary theory emerged as a dominating force in the arena of literary criticism since the 1980s. It is claimed that the patriarchal ideology having pervaded hitherto existing great literature, female characters were rendered as marginal and subordinate in those writings which need to be rewritten to do justice to female points of view. One of the most influential feminist critical writings, *The Madwoman in the Attic (1979)* by Sandra Gilbert and Susan Gubar, stresses what M.H. Abrams calls "psychodynamics of women writers" in the nineteenth century resulting in the creation of a monstrous counter figure to the idealized heroine, a figure like Bertha Rochester in Charlotte Bronte's *Jane Eyre.* Practically speaking, no classical work from Shakespeare to Sherlock Holmes has been kept out of the orbit of such criticism. Homi Bhabha and Gayatri Spivak further expanded the scope of feminist criticism with the inclusion of the theory of the Subaltern. 'Gynocritique' is a specialized discourse concerned with female creativity as well as the problem of a female language.

In fictional works by feminist writers, one finds the following characteristics: the introduction of feminine issues through women protagonists, rewriting the old classics from women's perspectives and attempts to bring the fiction close to the literary theories such as Gynocriticism and Ecofeminism. To start with the introduction of feminine protagonists and feminine issues, the trend was visible towards the end of nineteenth century, though there was hardly any attempt to criticize the gender discrimination and the specific role assigned to women by the society. The stress was on the sufferings of women at different stages of life but any thought of crossing the boundaries was strictly prohibited. Virginia Woolf's *A Room of One's Own* (1929) and other essays reveal her opinion in regard to the hindrances in the way of a woman's realization of her potential in a patriarchal society, but her novels are appreciated for the use of innovative technique and not for introducing feminine discourse.

Among the next generation British women writers Doris Lessing, the author of *The Golden Notebook* (1962), is regarded as the high priestess of Feminism. For her novels, Lessing chooses women protagonists with unconventional outlook to family and society. In her first novel *Grass is Singing* (1950), set in the backdrop of war-torn Rhodesia, the protagonist Mary faces psychological problems caused by the evils of colonial and patriarchal society. *The Golden Notebook* projects a galaxy of free women and explores the dilemmas of the independent, activist women in the British society. The central character Anna maintains four notebooks to keep things separate from one another. The first one is about Anna's relationship with her friend Molly who is separated from her husband and lives with her son Tommy. The second notebook, the Red one, shows Anna's analysis of the Communist party as an insider. The Yellow notebook looks like a manuscript of a novel about two women, Julia and Ella. The Blue notebook, again, is about Tommy. Political awareness and ideological commitment of women characters become strongly represented issues in Lessing's fictional writings. Instead of projecting some fixed standpoints in regard to the patriarchal society and emancipation of women—issues which are repeatedly focused by the feminist activists and theorists—Lessing views women as human beings, who may or may not be oppressed by the male-dominated society, but who necessarily get involved in all the significant issues they find around them and fight according to their might. After sixty years of a successful writer's career, Lessing comes to the conclusion that man-woman relationship is not a fixed one and that it is useless to fight just for feminist causes. "I hate talking about literature in terms of men and women. It isn't helpful," she says.

The feminist writers in the USA—particularly, the African-American women writers—are naturally drawn towards the triple jeopardy of race, class and gender that created a traumatic condition during the nineteen forties and fifties. Toni Morrison, the Nobel Prize winning author, is a female, black and a US citizen, all in one. The characters in her novels suffer from a double stigma of class and colour, often revealing the scars in their minds caused by sexual and racial exploitations. In *The Bluest Eye*, the tragic condition of the black women in racist America during the 1940s is portrayed in poignant terms from the perspective of nine-year old Claudia MacTeer, a young black girl in Lorain, Ohio. Claudia closely observes another black girl Pecola whose father Cholly, a violent and abusive husband and father, burned down their home leaving the family "outdoors." After facing a series of misfortunes, Pecola suffers from mental breakdown and Claudia sees in her misfortune a condemnation of the society in which she lives. The title *The Bluest Eye* is taken from Pecola's yearnings for blue eyes, the symbol of white women, which alone, Pecola thought, could remove the stigma attached to black woman and would help her survive.

Morrison belongs to the group of black women writers including Anne Petry, Gloria Naylor, Alice Walker and host of others who tried to trace the development of black women's image from invisibility to self-assertion. In *Sula* (1973), Morrison focuses on a risky contemporary reality through the exploration of a deep friendship between two black women, Nel and Sula. These two women found relief in each other's personality. "Because each had discovered years before that they are neither white nor male and that all freedom . . . was forbidden to them, they had set about creating something else to be" (52). There are differences in opinions among the critics in regard to Morrison's approach to 'lesbian' relationship between Nel and Sula. Without entering into the debate of whether Morrison intends to promote lesbianism, it can safely be observed that the writer shows the black women how to create their own space where they are safe from mental torture and day-to-day humiliations in the outer world. While black writers like Wright, Howe, Ellison, Hurston and others raised weapons of protest against racial oppression and gender discrimination, Morrison highlights "the tension between protest and transcendence, between suffering and strength, and between collective and individual identity."

Margaret Laurence, one of the prominent women writers in Canada, expressed typical feminine sensibilities nourished on Canadian culture in her novels, *The Fire-Dwellers, A Bird in the House, A Jest of God* and *The Stone Angel.* Hagar Shipley, the protagonist of *The Stone Angel* (1964), remembers her entire past life in bits at the age of ninety. Having lost her mother in her childhood and being brought up amidst two brothers, she was lonely while experiencing her biological growth. Though she was an obedient daughter of her father, she married Brampton, a widower, who was fourteen years older than her, against her father's will, asserting thereby her identity. Her matrimonial life with Brampton forms the second phase of her life. Much to her wonder and embarrassment, Hagar found him rough, uncouth and uncultured and yet tried to compromise with the situation. When her first son Marvin was seventeen and joined the army and her second son John was seven, she could no longer tolerate Brampton and left his home. She took John with her and got the job of housekeeper in the house of old Mr. Oatley. After a few years she was crestfallen to learn from John that he would go back to his father who was then living with a half-breed girl, that John and Marvin had been exchanging letters with their father. Hagar was thus forced to live without her husband and sons. After two years, John wrote to her that his father was very sick and would soon die. Hagar went back to her husband's home but felt no sympathy with him. After his death, Hagar tried hard to see John settled in life.

though it was clear that both the boys were like their father. Hagar's struggle to do something for John was futile as John met with an accident and died. Hagar came back to Mr. Oatley's house. At the time of his death Oatley left ten thousand dollars for her as a reward for her honest service with which she bought a house. As she became old and sick, she began to stay with Marvin and his wife Doris. A generation gap and clash of ideas with her son and daughter-in-law destroyed her peace of living in her own house, bought with her own earning. She was yet full of zeal for living till she faced her death in hospital. Her self-realization is revealed in the following sentence: "Pride was my wilderness and the demon that led me there was fear; I was alone, never anything else, and never free, for I carried my chains within me, and they spread out from me and shackled all I touched" (292). Hagar's self-analysis also reveals how a woman's sincere efforts to assert her individuality through acts of choice were foiled, thanks to the forces of patriarchal society. Hagar's father, her husband and her two sons represent the forces of patriarchy that dominated in Canada during the mid-twentieth century. While reading the novel, one is reminded of Derrida's views in regard to the liberation of our thoughts from binary opposition. While projecting feminist issues, Laurence rejects the thought of binary opposition and accepts multiplicity of truth and reality. Hagar did not like her husband and yet she spent so many years with him to satisfy her sexual urges. These urges are appreciated by the author who portrays Hagar as a person having human qualities. Hagar's life is suggestive of positive feminine sensibilities that can provide a better alternative to the existing system based on masculine or pro-masculine sensibilities.

Among a good number of classical writings rewritten from feminist perspective, Margaret Atwood's *The Penelopiad* (2005) may be taken into consideration. In Homer's account of Penelope in *The Odyssey*, we find a woman figure who is noted for conjugal fidelity and this mythical figure has been used as a salutary lesson through the ages. When Odysseus goes off to fight in the Trojan War after the abduction of beautiful Helen, a cousin of Penelope,

Penelope was left alone for twenty long years. In the face of scandalous rumours, she could manage to maintain the kingdom of Ithaca, keeping her suitors away, and took much trouble to bring up her wayward son. When finally Odysseus came back after a long voyage—he overcame monsters on the way and slept with goddesses for a long time—he kills her suitors and also twelve of her maids. Odysseus was never questioned why he killed the innocent maids. Homer did not think that a king should explain why he murdered his queen's maids. Atwood raises that question, which was ignored by Homer, in her dazzling, playful retelling of the story. In the 'Introduction,' Atwood writes, "I've chosen to give the telling of the story to Penelope and to the twelve hanged maids. The maids form a chanting and singing chorus which focuses on two questions that must pose themselves after any close reading of *The Odyssey*: what led to the hanging of the maids, and what was Penelope really up to? The story as told in *The Odyssey* doesn't hold water: there are too many inconsistencies. I've always been haunted by the hanged maids; and in *The Penelopiad*, so is Penelope herself." In section 26 of *The Penelopiad* that describes the trial of Odysseus, Penelope answers the Judge who wants to know why Penelope did not punish the impertinent maids. Penelope says, "I was fond of them. I'd brought some of them up, you could say. They were like the daughters I never had. (Starts to weep.) I felt so sorry for them! But most maids got raped, sooner or later; a deplorable but common feature of palace life. It wasn't the fact of their being raped that told against them, in the mind of Odysseus. It's that they were raped without permission" (146). Atwood gives Penelope new light and reality and offers us a unique feminist retelling of *The Odyssey*.

The western religions and cultures, particularly Judea-Christianity, had supported the male supremacy (Eve was created from Adam's ribs for accompanying him) and the women had always been subjugated and marginalized in society as well as myths and legends. To quote Simone de Beauvoir in this context, "She is defined and differentiated with reference to man and not he with reference to her; she is the incidental, the inessential as opposed to the essential. He is the subject, he is the Absolute—she is the Other" (*The Second Sex,* 16). Hence a western woman's demand for an equal status with man is quite a natural outburst of the oppressed and humiliated class. In India, however, women in general have experienced duplicity in the attitude of the male. Hindu myths are full of powerful goddesses who reign supreme in the hierarchy of thirty three crores of gods and goddesses and the Hindu male follow the tradition of worshipping these goddesses as their protectors. A newly wed bride is traditionally accepted as goddess Laxmi in her in-law's home. But in real life, the picture is often different. Besides the barbaric system of burning the wife on her husband's funeral pyre, the crudity of child marriage and the sufferings of the widows, the women hardly had decision-making powers in the family or in the society during the pre-colonial days. Yet, mother-worship was prevalent and sometimes an elderly widowed mother controlled her family, though such elderly women were supporters of patriarchy.

With the progress of western education and the emergence of national movements in colonial India, there developed a new patriarchy that strongly protested all sorts of barbaric customs inflicting tortures on women and allowed the new women an exposure to the outer world so long as it did not jeopardize her traditional place as a home-keeper. Women were given western education and were inspired to develop modernization without westernization, still modelling on the role of Sita in the epic *Ramayana.* Gandhiji, who materialized this emergence of new women through his call for Indian women to join freedom movement, maintained that the women should discharge their duties to their families first. In Raja Rao's *Kanthapura* (1938), for example, Rangamma and Ratna—the two Gandhian leaders who are rendered as the epitome of women's emancipation and this emergence of new women was associated with the historical goal of sovereign nationhood—follow the Gandhian precondition while advising the women volunteers to prepare meals for the family before coming to the meeting. This emergence of 'new woman' in pre-Independence days is ruthlessly criticized by Manju Kapur in *Difficult Daughters*

(1998), set in pre-Partition Amritsar and Lahore. Virmati, the protagonist of the novel, an educated and self-sufficient woman, is trapped in her own emotions as her education has prompted her to be true to her feelings. Her marriage with the married professor focuses on the difference between the status of an educated man and an educated woman during the Forties. Kapur brings the charge that education was thrust on women not for making them individuals but for satisfying the educated men's 'need' for educated companions.

The voice of protest against the existing status of women was not heard in women's fiction written just after Independence. In Kamala Markandaya's *Nectar in a Sieve* (1954) for example, the protagonist Rukmani is passive in spite of her immense strength to fight against the odds of life. Being a woman and a tenant farmer's wife, Rukmani is doubly marginalized, but Markandaya is least affected either by the feminist or by the Marxist discourse. The socio-economic factors in the lives of the peasants in colonial India are revealed as tragic forces in the life of Rukmani who faces all misfortunes in a calm and quiet way. Surprisingly, her devotion to her husband Nathan, an illiterate tenant farmer, was not affected after the revelation of Nathan's polygamy. Being the daughter of a headman, Rukmani was blessed with the opportunity of being literate, but her love for learning is not related to the renaissance of knowledge that demands new symbols.

Compared with Markandaya, Anita Desai is more concerned with the yearnings of her protagonist's inner self: Maya in *Cry, the Peacock*, Monisha in *Voices in the City*, Sita in *Where Shall We Go This Summer* have developed a sense of rebellion against the entire system of social relationships. None of them is a passive sufferer; yet the insensitive outer world labels them as mad, simply because they are in search of a deeper meaning of life that cannot be found within the creeds and conventions of the patriarchal society they have been forced to cope with. Desai's *Fire on the Mountain* (1977) depicts the loneliness and humiliation of Mrs. Nanda Kaul, the wife of the Vice-Chancellor Mr. Kaul, who continues his illicit relationship with the Mathematics teacher Miss

David throughout his life. Mrs. Kaul cannot revolt as she finds it impossible to deny the social status of being the wife of a dignified person, but after Mr. Kaul's death she finds seclusion on the mountain keeping her away from the male chauvinistic society.

Nayantara Sahgal, too, focuses on her women protagonists' intense mental pain caused by their insensitive life partners; but she prefers keeping balance between tradition and personal aspirations to rebellion. In *Rich like Us* (1985), Sonali appears confident as a New Woman, but her choice of a career and her keeping away from marriage indicate that Sahgal intended to create a virtuous woman, not a worldly woman of flesh and blood. Ruth Prawer Jhabvala also focused on a woman's growing awareness of herself as an individual and she was inclined to reveal a woman's rebellious nature. Amrita in *To Whom She Will* (1955) and Sarala in *Get Ready for Battle* (1962) are instances of Jhabvala's understanding of the limits of women in the convention-ridden Indian society.

The fictional works of Indian women writers in English (and also in Bhasha literature) during the 1980s and 90s indicate a clear transformation of ideas in regard to an Ideal Indian woman. The long worshipped models of Sita and Savitri are discarded, as conjugal fidelity is not considered to be the sole criterion to judge a woman's character. A noted Bengali poet and novelist Mallika Sengupta deconstructed the epic *Ramayana* and named it *Sitayana* in which all the events of the epic are rendered from Sita's perspective, revealing thereby the hollowness of the concept of a chaste woman. Shashi Deshpande's Sahitya Akademi Award-winning novel *That Long Silence* (1988) may be discussed in the context of a New Indian Woman's urge for searching a new role-model for emancipation. In an interview, Deshpande says, "The women in my books are people who come to realize what it is to be a woman in the process of their own lives and the situations they face. . . . I think feminism is an entirely personalized perception. It is when you start questioning preconceived notions about your roles. I don't think there is anything 'inherent' in a woman apart from the fact that she can conceive. All other things are equally important for them as they are for men" (*Times of India*, Nov. 1989). The protagonist Jaya in *That Long Silence* is a writer who realizes "what it is to be a woman" and a writer in the process of her own life. Once after her marriage she wrote a story about the man-woman relationship and her husband Mohan took it to be an insult to him after seeing it published. He behaved in such a way that Jaya was compelled to stop writing realistic stories and she started writing for the column of 'Seeta' in a woman's magazine much to her husband's satisfaction. After seventeen long years when Mohan is suspected by his office to be involved in a shady deal and takes shelter in their abandoned small flat to avoid inquiry and suspension and Jaya is compelled to follow him into 'exile,' following the footsteps of the mythical figure Sita, she realizes that Mohan is no more "a sheltering tree" for her because he has already accused her for extracting "comfort" from him as a result of which he was forced to be in corruption. The agonizing process of self-searching starts at this moment. Jaya asks her inner self, "What do you want? . . . Just to live. To know that at the end of the day my family and I are under a roof, safe, enclosed, in a secure world. If it is dark outside, what does it matter? I can close the door and windows, switch on the lights and the darkness will recede" (181-82). With this awareness, Jaya emerges out of her selfish existence to embrace the outer reality and confesses to herself that earlier she had not really cared enough to exercise freedom of choice and be an individual. One cannot dub *That Long Silence* as a feminist or psychological novel because labels are inadequate while confronting a work of art.

Shashi Deshpande's suggestion of a return to traditional mode of life with an acute self-realization is not accepted by other writers who prefer the feminist stand. Manju Kapur's *A Married Woman* (2002) is a "feminocentric protest against the phallocentric patriarchal culture." The protagonist Astha, who married a man of her parents' choice rejecting her boyfriends, is fed up with the materialistic outlook of her husband. She feels that he is a criminal destroying her life and ruining her happiness. After giving birth to children, she distances herself from him and struggles to be a painter and social activist. Kapur expresses her revolt against the patriarchal society through projecting Astha's lesbian relationship with Peepilika, the widow of Aijaz Akhtar Khan, the founder of the Street Theatre Group. Astha gets immense pleasure from the lesbian relationship and is aware of the traditional Indian society's disapproval of lesbianism. In a strange way she uses her satisfaction with the disapproved relationship as a weapon against her husband who fails to find in Astha's body the previous sensations with which he was habituated and thus he is denied sexual satisfaction. This peculiar way of protesting against her subordination under patriarchy exposes the existing irrationality in the patriarchal metaphysics in respect of women's status in the society.

Arundhati Roy's Booker-winning *God of Small Things* (1977) is a more severe attack on traditional Indian mindset. Against the rigid backdrop of gender patterns in India, Roy gives voice to transgression of 'Love-Laws,' "the laws that lay down who should be loved and how, and how much." Ammu's love relationship with the untouchable Velutha crosses the boundaries and is therefore sealed by death. Velutha dies in police custody and Ammu suffers the torture of death in life. Though the progressive Indian male may somehow tolerate such relationship, it is unthinkable for all of them to tolerate the incestuous love of Rahel and Estha, the twin issues of Ammu. These voices of rebellion indicate the inclusion of new feminist discourses in Indian novels in English.

The recent trends, however, pave way for a dynamic social order devoid of gender codes. This new social order with its positivist and holistic approach to life supports ethical values irrespective of sex. Madhu Kishwar, the editor of *Manushi: A Journal about Women and Society* (published from Delhi since 1978), strongly opposes established ideologies or 'isms' including 'feminism' and observes that these are time and culture-specific. Kishwar stresses on the capacity of choice, and this capacity alone, she believes, may give the women their desired goal. Most of the Indian women writers of these days like to follow the path suggested by Kishwar and hesitate to use the ideologies of western feminism.

Freud's Psychoanalysis: The Development of Feminity

BHASKER A. SHUKLA
Principal, S.D. Arts College, Mansa

Freud describes his theory of women's development in a series of articles written and published during the early 1920s to the early 1930s: "The Dissolution of the Oedipus Complex,"[1] "Some Psychical Consequences of the Anatomical Distinction between the Sexes,"[2] "Female Sexuality,"[3] Lecture 33 of the New Introductory Lectures.[4]

Freud developed his later theory in two stages. In the 1924 and 1925 articles, Freud begins quite explicitly from a male norm and compares female development to it. The foci of his discussions are female sexuality, her castration complex and the simplicity of her oedipal configuration. "The girl's Oedipus complex is much simpler than that of the small bearer of the penis; it seldom goes beyond the taking of her mother's place and adopting of a feminine attitude towards her father." Her castration complex—envy for the penis—leads up to her Oedipus complex; the Oedipus complex is never given up in as absolute a way as the boy, because she has no castration to fear.

This notable lack of active female sexual desire in normal femininity results from a sort of post-oedipal atrophy of desire. Indeed, female desire in this model remains only for the missing organ (the penis) rather than for the sexual object (the father or men more generally)

Freud thus explains most of what we conventionally mean, and what he explicitly means by femininity, both the girl's heterosexuality—she turns to her father to get a penis (=child)—and her maternal desires—her desire for a child (=penis)—as a secondary by-product of penis envy. He also introduced the problematic masculine outcome, that of the girl, who, when she must give up her father, identifies with him instead. "The girl makes her judgement and her decision in a flash. She has seen it and knows that she is without it and wants to have it. She develops, like a scar a sense of inferiority."[5] Both sexes develop contempt for women—the boy's horror of the mutilated creature or triumphant contempt for her, the girl, "the contempt felt by men for a sex which is lesser in so important a respect."

Freud discusses women as sex objects to men in "A special type of choice of object made by men (Contributions to the psychology of love, I)" (191oh, xi) and "On the universal tendency to debasement in the sphere of love (contributions to the psychology of love, II)" (1912d, xl), Freud's developmental account here implies that this universal 'tendency is found entirely in men.' Men, he suggests, split women symbolically and erotically into mothers, mothers and sisters, on the one hand and prostitutes on the other.

Freud gives us the psychodynamics of a split present in western culture, literature, and social organization. Indeed the wife setting her up as a sexual mother, as "a marriage is not made secure until the wife has succeeded in making her husband her child as well and in acting as a mother to him." The mother who signifies the limitless narcissism of childhood is the idealized mother, symbolized by her breast and her sometimes perfect love. Freud also claims that "sucking at the mother's breast is the starting point of sexual satisfaction."[6] Such sucking is gender free, but Freud later implies that the satisfaction at that time and its later sequel may be gender differentiated. It is hard to separate male wish-fulfillment from objective description of the female psyche when Freud tells us that "a mother is only brought unlimited satisfaction by her relation to son, this is altogether the most perfect, the most free from ambivalence of all human man relationships."[7]

In "The Taboo of Virginity," Freud suggests that women other than mothers, vengeful recently deflorated ex-virgins, might castrate a man or take his penis. In the ex-virgins' case, this would be revenge for their painful defloration. Whenever primitive man has set up a taboo, he fears some danger and it cannot be disputed that a generalized dread of women is expressed in all these rules of avoidance. The man is afraid of being weakened by the woman, infected with her femininity. The effect which coitus has of discharging tensions and causing flaccidity may be the prototype of what the man fears. Even worse, it seems, than the importance and lack of sexual desire that Freud suggests in the first two "Contribution to the psychology of love," is the possibility of total weakening and "infection" with femininity.

A final imagined version by the male psyche of woman as subject is, like the resentment of defloration presented by Freud as objective truth about women. Freud describes for us a variety of traits that characterize women and that he attributes entirely to penis envy and women's lack of a penis; shame at her body; jealousy, which results directly from envy itself; a lesser sense of justice resulting from the weak female superego that never forms because the girl does not fear castration and does not therefore give up oedipal longings or internalize sexual prohibitions; narcissism and vanity as the self-love the men centre on their penis becomes defensively diffused throughout the female body.

As Freud points out, feminists in his time and since have accused him of male bias in his views here. Freud as cultural man, then, seems to have borrowed a variety of (masculine) cultural attitudes about women whose origins he then coincidentally demonstrates to arise in female development.

We are led finally to the theory of femininity. At various points in his writings, Freud claims that activity-passivity are our best approximations of masculinity-femininity, but he is in fact much more focused on the distinction between phallically endowed or castrated: women are castrated men.

Freud's understanding about male attitudes toward women and femininity do not seem to be shadowy or incomplete at all. They are specific, informative, persuasive, precise and clear, covering generously a variety of sexual representational and neurotic formations. They illuminate for us with passion and empathy and in full daylight, the mysteries of the male psyche. We admire his clinical accounts and his forthright defence of hysterical women, and his condemnation of the conditions leading to repression and hysteria in women.

Freud's psychoanalysis has been an important milestone towards further debate/ discussion on the nature and understanding of masculine and feminine identities and in the development of feminist philosophy.

Many feminists however, disagree with Freud's biological determinism in the analysis of femininity. Particularly, the second wave feminists of the Sixties (which is, in popular culture, known as the bra-burning era), have denounced Freud's concept of penis envy, passivity, masochism, lesser rationality, and weaker superego in women as mere patriarchal viewpoints. Prominent among those who critiqued Freudianism include Kate Millett, Betty Friedan and Germaine Greer. However in *Psychoanalysis and Feminism* (1974), Juliet Mitchell made a solemn effort to defend and develop Freud's psychoanalysis for the feminist theory. Nancy J. Chodorow, in *Feminism and Psychoanalytic Theory* (1989), discussed how Freudian theory could be used to understand the nature of masculine and feminine identities and the cause of male domination over female. She regarded masculine identity as man's defensive strategy against the pressure of woman's mothering.

According to her, men are aggressive and resentful towards women and tend to be domineering because they experience and fear women as powerful and imposing mothers. Psychologically men seek some recompense for their matriarchal fears through domination over women. This was contradictory to Freud's considering woman as inferior, weak and.passive.

After Freud, there were two factions of psychoanalysts—one, the orthodox pro-Freud, biologists, and the other, the contra—Freud socialists, culturalists and anthropologists. Many of the post-Freudians like Alfred Adler, Karen Horney, Eric Fromm, Harry Stack-Sullivan and. Clara Thomson, with their socialist culturalist approach, questioned Freud's pontifications about inferiority of women. Karen Horney, who was previously an orthodox Freudian but later on shifted to the socialist group, in her works like *Feminine Psychology* (1973), regarded Freud's biologist determinism, sexual dualism and cordiality as anti-feminism. She expounded that the women's frailty, inferiority, ineptitude and passivity resulted from social oppression and denial of power and not from their 'penis envy' or castration.

Jacques Lacan modified/rewrote Freud's theory with his linguistic, structuralism and semiotic approach. He expostulated that the penis (the signifier) is the symbol of the Phallus/sexual power (the signified) of the father (and of all men). He regards the phallus as the key source of power in language and being, which treats man as the norm and women as 'the other.'

In a patriarchal system, it is in fact the 'law of the father' that represses femininity. Lacan mentions the feminine jouissance (the feminine pleasure/ enjoyment) which does exist but is not articulated within the patriarchal system of language discourse. Thus, according to Lacan, women are the victims of 'identity crisis' under the 'law of the Father.'

Jacques Derrida showed how meaning can be viewed neither stabilized in the signifier-signified relationship, nor in the centered system of relations, nor in the series of hierarchical oppositions, and therefore, proposed the term difference to suggest how meanings both depended on difference and were endlessly deferred.

A shift towards psychoanalysis within feminist theory during the 1970s was perhaps inevitable; psychoanalysis begins where cognitive-developmental and role-theory models of identity leave off. For feminism, the limitations of the rational explanations of the sources of women's oppression explored though consciousness-raising, clearly emerged since the mid-1970s. Feminist theory and practice revealed their interconnections; while alienation reduces the man to an instrument of labour within industry, it reduces the woman to an instrument for his sexual pleasure within the family.[8] The basis of one's subjectivity as masculine or feminine is formed out of one's consciousness.

Thus psychoanalysis is particularly well equipped to deal with this area of experience. "It is psychological problem which Marxists after World War I and feminists after 1960s, turned to psychoanalysis to solve,"[9] says David Ingleby.

Marxism, in particular had failed adequately to theorize the subject, and yet, as Janet Sayers points out, it is precisely women's subjective experience of the conflicting demands of home and work, of family and society that constitutes the major impetus of today's women's movement.'

Women writers in the 1970s discovered that deeper insights were needed, for example, into how women are positioned within sexual discourse whose repressiveness is often recognized, yet which offer such powerful emotional investments that resistance, proves virtually impossible: romantic love, the desire to conform to dominant images of feminine attractiveness, the misrepresentations of the experience of motherhood as simple joy.

The obvious problems for feminism in this account are those of sexist bias, universalism, biological determinism, ahistoricity, privileging of the visible. 'Both psychoanalysis and feminism attempt in different ways to make a science of subjectivity to make subjective experience itself the object of scientific or historical study and both lend themselves to normative or valuational thinking at every turn.[10] So Freud argues for the superiority of the penis, while Horney sees this as a rationalization of the male's envy of the womb. For women, in particular, psychoanalysis has served to reinforce myths of femininity and the naturalness of mothering.

'Women's liberation' in fact drew on a particular version of psychoanalysis in the 1970s which, in effect, simply reinforced the contradictions of the liberal definition of the subject. The theories of ego psychologists and the cognitive-developmental models of Erikson, Piaget and Kohlberg hover behind the pages of the novels of liberation and of feminist literary histories like Elaine Showalter's.

Most psychoanalytic theories of identity emphasize the urge for independence, autonomy, separateness, as the goals of maturity and specifically, the development of analytic and decision-making capacities.

A woman's different characteristics are produced not as a consequence of her innate narcissism or masochism but as a consequence of her history of economic dependency (necessitating her attention to physical attractiveness to secure a husband, compelling her to seek identity in definition or relationship through others). In existential terms her identity exists largely as being for others (needing to please, narcissisticity; mothering as institutionalized in western social practices; deriving security from intimate relations with others) rather than being-for-herself.

> Men act and women appear.
> Men look at women. Women watch
> themselves being looked at.

The surveyor of woman in herself is male: the surveyed female. Thus she turns herself into an object and most particularly an object of vision: a sight.[11]

According to most post-Freudian psychoanalytic theory, however female narcissism is a consequence of penis envy. The woman compensates for her lack by an over-estimation of or an excessive concern with her body, and through defensive displacements may thereby regain her wounded self-esteem.

For the fact of beginning life merged with a woman is potentially, a terrifying assault on masculine identity and involves the compulsion to project on to women aspects of their own experience which are regarded as displaying weakness. Woman will thus be seen as emotionally insatiable and voracious, scheming to trap men into commitments such as marriage and parenthood which threaten the independence, freedom, and self-expression of the male. As Len tells Peter in Atwood's *The Edible Woman*: "You have got to watch these women when they start pursuing you. They're always after you to marry them. You've got to hit and run. Get them before they get you."

If femininity is thus enveloping, threatening and possessing, then men are justified in their emotional distance, rationalism, and need for control of the female. Sartre, for example, says, "The obscenity of the feminine sex is that of everything which gapes open, it is an appeal to being as all holes are. Beyond any doubt her sex is a mouth and voracious mouth which devours the penis—a fact which can easily lead to the idea of castration. The amorous act is the castration of the man but this is above all because sex is a hole."[12]

Absence, lack, inchoateness, insatiability, nothingness, it is a monstrous image of the feminine, yet it is also astoundingly, the normative view presented in Freud (the castration complex), Lacan, Erikson (inner space) in Kersey's nurse, Roth's mothers, and Barth's female computer.

Freud argues for the superior abstract powers of the masculine superego, and Kohlberg argues that out of a possible score of six in moral reasoning, women tend to reason at three, while men reach a legalistic fourth stage superior in its abstraction and objectivity.

Masculine impersonality comes to be seen not only as superior, but as a necessary defence against the inferior feminine qualities of emotionality and subjective impressionism.

NOTES

1. "New Introductory Lectures on The Dissolution of the Oedipus Complex," S.E. (1924 d) X!X, 173-79.
2. "New Introductory Lectures" on "Some psychical consequences of the Anatomical Distinction between the sexes," (1925 j) S.E. XIX, 248-58.
3. "New Introductory Lectures on Female Sexuality" S.E. (1931 b) XX11, 225-43
4. "New Introductory Lectures on Psychoanalysis," S.E. (1933 a) XXII, 5-182
5. "New Introductory Lectures on Some Psychical Consequences of the Anatomical Distinction between the Sexes" (1925) S.E. XIX 248-58
6. *Introductory Lectures on Psychoanalysis* (1916-17) S.E. XV-XVI.
7. *Ibid.*
8. Ann Foreman, (1977), *Femininity as Alienation: Women and the Family in Marxism and Psychoanalysis*. London.

9. David Ingleby, (1984) "The Ambivalençe of Psychoanalysis," 15, pp. 39-71.
10. Jean Strouse, ed. 1974, *Women and Analysis*, New York.
11. John Berger, (1972), *Ways of Seeing*. Harmondsworth.
12. Jean-Paul Sartre, (1958) *Being and Nothingness*, trans. H.E. Barnes. London.

Women's Education in the Victorian Era

ATHOKPAM ELIZABETH DEVI
Manipur University, Canchipur

Rivalry of religious denominations proved to be a hurdle for the state to advance any rational system of education for a long time. In 1841 Sir James Graham wrote to Brougham: "Religion, the keystone of education, is in this country a bar to its progress." The state ventured in 1833 with a humble and inadequate grant of twenty thousand pounds a year towards the school buildings of the various voluntary societies. England then had a network of voluntary schools run on private subscription by societies with religious background and supplying the much-required primary education. For looking after the grant, there was an Education Committee of the Privy Council with a permanent secretary and a system of inspection of the state-aided-schools. The insistence on government inspection was a significant development. This was the humble origin of the Ministry of Education. Actually, the factory inspectors set up by the Factory Act of 1833, bred school inspectors; Mine Inspectors then followed:

> The English state gave the common people great political freedom and some share in government, but left them to be educated by private religious charity.[1]

By the Reform Bill of 1832, ten pound householders were given the voting right. The working classes of urban areas were enfranchised by the Reform Act of 1867. It was agreed by political leaders that a national system of education was a necessity but in the mid-Victorian period no government, Whig or Tory, could propose a national system of education at the public expense that would not have given harsh offence either to the Dissenters or to the Established Church.

Gladstone's Bill of 1870 marked the turning point in educational and therefore in English social history. It was the work of W.E. Forster, an ardent Churchman, though of Quaker origin. The Bill doubled the state grant to existing church schools and to the Roman Catholic schools, so as to enable them to become a permanent part of the new system, while it introduced publicly controlled schools to fill up the large gaps in the educational map of the country. The Board schools were to be governed by elected school Boards and paid for out of the local rates. Voluntary and church schools, National Schools (founded by the Anglican National Society and conducted on Church principles) which earlier supplied the primary education of the people were allowed to continue with Church teachings. But in the case of the New Board schools, there was a restriction for the use of catechism or formulary distinctive of any denomination in the religious teachings.

But unfortunately and to the dismay of the Dissenters, most of the villages had only one school to which all children go and it was the Church school, though in towns the voluntary schools and Board schools were available alternately. Thus the state seems to perpetuate the Church schools of the villages. However, by Balfour's Act of 1902, the Church schools had been brought under a considerable measure of control by Country Councils. This and subsequent decrease in hostility between the denominations had reasonably subdued the resentment.

Despite its drawbacks, the Act of 1870 provided a system of universal primary education without which England must have lagged behind among modern nations. Between 1870 and 1890, the average school attendance rose from one and a quarter million to four-and-a-half million, while the money spent on each child was doubled.

Balfour's Education Act of 1902 inspired by Sir Robert Morant, the great public servant, remedied some important defects of the Act of 1870. Some defects of the Act of 1870 were: the state's negligence of the secondary education, no sufficient school scholarships to the universities for the ablest children in primary schools as the new school Boards were charged with Primary Education only, the terms of the Act of 1870 and the Cockerton judgment by Law Courts in 1900 decided that the rate payers' money could not be spent on any form of secondary or higher education; and further Board areas being small confined to a single town education outlook became parochial in character causing unnecessary personal and intense feud between the Church and the dissent.

The measure of 1902 abolished school Boards and Country Councils were elected to provide both primary and secondary education. The councils established Country Education Committees with wider coverage and broader idea, an improvement benefiting both primary and secondary education and creating an effective ladder to the Universities.

A brief account of secondary education, meant to provide the essential leadership and management to handle the ever-growing power and wealth of England at home and overseas in the new century could be pertinent. The required secondary education unexpectedly was provided for by the 'Public school' system which itself underwent a remarkable development in the Victorian era. There were three kinds of secondary schools at the beginning of the century. First the fashionable 'Public Schools' (Private in reality) like Eton, Wincester and Harrow—a few in number and with a purely classical curriculum; the second kind was the unfashionable private Academies where dissenting middle class received a more scientific and modern education with better discipline; and the third kind was the old endowed Grammar Schools, many of which lost importance due to negligence and corruption inherent in the public institutions of the 18th century.

The govt.-endowed Grammar Schools, in the age of Reform and democracy, could have done better but these went to the contrary, losing their importance except the striking case of Manchester. Dissenting Academies, so useful in the previous century, similarly, petered out. But the unexpected 'Public schools' modelled on the old ideals of Eton, Westminister, Wincester and Harrow became fashionable and important. Rugby became the example with the great educational reformer of the 1830s, Dr. Thomas Arnold as its headmaster. Mr. Thomas Arnold emphasized religion (chapel services), monitorial system and succeeded in suppressing bullying, drinking profligacy and the worst indiscipline of the old 'bear garden' type of Public school.

'Organised games' became dominating, popularizing public school life—these went in due course to Oxford and Cambridge. In many respects the public schools successfully fulfilled their required part in providing secondary education. Though confined to the classics, in the new age of science and modernity, it provided the basis for a high development of literary culture at Oxford and Cambridge, and in Tennyson's England at large. The reformed public school catered to 'the middling orders of society'—the upper (landed gentry), the upper-middle (industrialists) and the professional classes and provided them with the opportunity to join the 'governing' class, thus forming, in due course, an enlarged and modernized aristocracy numerous and sufficient to meet the needs of Victoria's Empire. The public schools were one of the great institutions unconsciously developed by English instinct and character producing sufficiently numerous educated youths to fulfill the various requirements of government and leadership in Victoria's England.

The public school system of secondary education accentuated social segregation: it welded together the well-to-do and professional classes separating them from the rest of the population; thus further enhancing the geographic division of the various class 'quarters' in the urban areas. Again the expenses of a public school were relatively high and proved to be self-imposed burden on the middle class and professional families. It even caused a considerable decrease in the number of children in some of the best sections of the community at the end of the century. Opportunity for education of girls at the secondary level was even sacrificed for the expensive education of their brothers. Moreover, the secondary education for girls in the middle years of the 19th century, was ill provided. Matthew Arnold, son of the great educational reformer, Dr. Thomas Arnold, denounced the secondary system of education as "the worst in the world" and scorned its product, the governing upper class as "barbarians" to whom the public schools had tended to preserve both the virtues and limitations of "earth's primitive, vigorous sons."

Nevertheless, much of the success and much of the failure of modern England can be attributed to the Public Schools. Arnold himself was a poet and a cultural prophet of the age he denounced and in spite of his scorn, the fact remains that the higher culture of the nineteenth century was varied, solid and widespread over a large proportion of the English population.

Though religion had been an imposing fabric in the middle of the nineteenth century, there was a quasi-religious movement away from religion developed in literature and thought. It was the transitional period between the over-great strictures of tradition and the entire laxity of modernity. Sunday observances were gradually modified. Readings on Sundays not necessarily dwelt on religious books and besides great classical literature like the Bible, *Pilgrim's Progress* and *Paradise Lost*, more secular poetry and history had a chance of perusal. Again, scientific discoveries were certainly beginning to undermine the dogmas of Christianity. Charles Darwin's researches and conclusions, though he had no wish to be an iconoclast, were not compatible with the early chapters of the Genesis which were as much a part of "the English Bible" as the New Testament itself. There was this period of strife and change raged by the conflict between 'faith' and 'denial' throughout the 1860s, 1870s and 1880s. The intellectuals became more and more anti-clerical, anti-religious under the stress of the conflict. With much personal and family unhappiness and many searchings of the heart, the world of the educated (men/women) was marred by a real controversy which even the English love of compromise could not deny to exist. The feeling manifests itself in Tennyson's lines:

> Let knowledge grow from more to more,
> But more of reverence in us dwell;
> That mind and soul, according well,
> May make one music as before,

But faster.[2]

The materialism of scientist is felt to be as unsatisfactory as the literal truth of all parts of the Bible is felt to be untenable. The whole truth about the universe cannot be discovered in the laboratory or by the Church. Faith and Denial held different positions.

Though puritan in feeling and outlook, the Agnostics began to successfully attack the older and more definite religious beliefs. Matthew Arnold, the prophet of 'culture,' spoke of 'conduct' as 'three parts of life'—his idea was neither narrow nor purely negative. George Eliot's novels restated the moral law and process of soul-making, in terms more appealing and acceptable to the rationalist agnostic conscience. Vaguely but emphatically the prophetic utterance in Carlyle's *Sartor* supplied a creed to many like Darwin's militant champion Huxley. Passionate refusal to compromise with dogmas was rendered by John Morley, Leslie Stephen (who had once been a clergyman) and J.R. Green, the popular liberal historian, Lecky's *History of Rationalism* (1865) and Buckle's (rather over-confident materialism) *History of Civilization* (1857) manifested the strong current that carried men away from ancient faiths. Again, developments in Archaeology and History and discoveries began to shake the dogmatic assurance of orthodox beliefs. It was a time (later half of Victorian era) when Oxford and Cambridge were the uppermost in the public eye and an academic 'liberal' party of great intellectual distinction earnestly attempted and succeeded in freeing the two universities from the shackles of Church monopoly by the Test Act of 1871. The reform abolished the religious tests for academic posts. Following suit, Gladstone abolished patronage in all public offices and made competitive examination the normal entrance to the Civil Service. Trained intellect was henceforth the only passport, instead of social patronage, to joining the governing class. It was a compliment to the reputation of Oxford and Cambridge system of examination for degrees, and, in effect made closer than ever the connection of University men with public life. The liberal-minded and highly educated governing class of the Seventies was more closely affiliated to the Universities than the declining aristocracy or the rising plutocracy.

Relieved from Church monopoly, the 'dons' at Oxford or Cambridge were becoming less clerical and were even allowed to marry while continuing to hold their Fellowships. Besides older humanism and mathematics, physical science and history were being embraced as strongly in academic study. Maitland, the brilliant genius, was revelling in the common thoughts of medieval men through the harsh medium of their law while Arch-deacon Cunningham was founding Economic History. Cambridge was represented to the world by great men of science like Clerk Maxwell, Raleigh, J.J. Thomson, etc. in the last decade of the century. The atmosphere at Oxford was more of liberal and practical character being represented to the world by Jowett as Master of Balliol, the scholarship of Stubbs and Gardiner in repealing the growth of the English constitution and by the new scheme of the ethical philosophy of T.H. Green.

One remarkable achievement was the publication of the *Dictionary of National Biography*, an endeavour neither by a university nor by the state but unbelievably by a private individual publisher, George Smith by name. The dictionary is a monumental record of a nation's past and throws light on the business ability, the enlightened public spirit and widespread literary and historical scholarship of the Victorian Age at its final culmination.

Adult Education and Self-Education started in the early part of the century as an impact of the Industrial Revolution. Partly professional and utilitarian, partly intellectual and ideal, the movement arose from the desire of mechanics for general scientific knowledge on the one part and willingness of the middle class intellectuals to supply their demand on the other end. Started in Scotland in 1823 by Dr. Birkbed, Mechanics' Institutes spread throughout industrial England with Henry Brougham's organizing and advertising genius and his emphasis on the future and its needs. The efforts of the working class, crushed in the anti-Jacobean panic a generation before, rose attracting respectable looking students from garrets and workshops. In 1824, the *Me-*

chanics' Magazine sold 16,000 copies; and 1500 workmen subscribed a guinea a piece to the London Institute. Encyclopedic knowledge circulated in cheap books and periodicals received much attention of the workers. In 1827, non-conformist and secularists joined hands in founding an undenominational teaching centre, keeping theology off the curriculum and with no religious tests for the teachers or the taught and embracing modern studies, including science. The London University, thus, came into existence with its 'utility' principle appealing to the unprivileged population of the city. It was an educational event important for its spirit and inspiration, though the real significance got lost in sectarian and partisan recrimination of the time.

The modern system of education, despite its drawbacks, conferred great benefit to England. The reformed system of education certainly gave an edge to the country while competing with other modern nations. Further, an uneducated city population could have been barbaric and could have produced a far worse form of society than the uneducated rural population of earlier times—for in older times the mind and character of ploughmen and craftsmen alike were moulded by the influence of nature, the agricultural life and the old system of apprenticeship.

The system, no doubt, produced a vast population able to read but most of them were unable to distinguish what is worth-reading, falling prey to cheap appeals and sensations. The small highly educated class no longer sets the standards to the extent that it used to do and gets absorbed to the standards of the majority. In other words, lower forms of literature and journalism lured majority mass of the reading population. While the spread of education ushered in a scientific temperament amongst people, women's education received a great impetus in the process.

NOTES

1. G.M. Trevelyan, *English Social History* (India: Orient Longman, 1995), p. 518.
2. *Ibid.*, p. 564.

Treatment of Women Characters in Jane Austen's *Emma*

REENA THOUNAOJAM
Res. Sch., Manipur University

The last decade of the eighteen century had seen the rise of Feminism in England, if not as a widespread social movement, at least as a generally accepted ideal. There was a growing awareness of women's rights and women's need for rational education. This culminated in the 1790s in the works of Catherine Macaulay Graham and the much-discussed treatises by Mary Wollstonecraft. Jane Austen was not a social reformer, yet her novels constitute essentially a study in woman's psychology. "In her attention to the anonymous sex, and in her articulation of feminine ethos, Jane Austen was as revolutionary in her own way as Mary Wollstonecraft."[1] Jane Austen takes the woman as an individual and places her in a social setting, faced with a choice that is private and personal. A recurrent theme of her novels is the heroine's resistance to the efforts of the patriarchal community to force her into a social role at the cost of her own identity. She not only reveals "the influence and importance of women in her class, but also articulates the unspoken—for value of her sex."[2] However, Austen does not react against the place of women in the society; rather she reflects women's liveliness, intelligence, wit and significance as an active member of the society through her heroines. Her novels manifest the disabilities of women, their subordination to men, their lack of education, their economic dependence and resultant frustration, their pre-occupation with marriage and husband-hunting.

The accomplishments of Jane Austen's heroines and other female characters are strictly limited to what her own age would allow "a thorough knowledge of music, singing, drawing, dancing and the modern languages"[3] and Jane Fairfax who possesses all these accomplishments has only the choice of marrying Frank Churchill or becoming a governess, the only profession open to respectable and accomplished women of that age. Jane Austen portrays sympathetically the plight of such women and in keeping with the morals of her age is prudent enough to let her heroines hunt for husbands rather than look for jobs.

The gift of keen observation helps Jane Austen in realizing the characters in their complete psychological complexity so that we have 'three-dimensional' or 'round' characters that are living and life-like. *Emma* has a wide range of women characters. From the intelligent but deluded Emma to the simple, garrulous, foolish but kind-hearted Miss Bates, Jane Austen covers a wide spectrum of characters. Harriet Smith, Jane Fairfax, Mrs. Elton, Mrs. Bates, Mrs. Weston, Mrs. Goddard, Miss Bates, Isabella—all act as foils in some way or the other in highlighting the character of Emma, either through comparison or contrast. All the characters are sympathetically portrayed and each has a separate identity of her own.

Emma Woodhouse is a complex and unconventional heroine. She is independent and witty. Moreover, it is hard to grasp whether her thoughts and observations are correct or not owing to her excessive imagination. Yet Lionel Trilling states that the reader is inevitably attached to Emma since she impresses the reader by her energy, style and intelligence. Emma has the courage to reflect what she has in her mind without caring how the others might evaluate her. She possesses independent manners, which makes her quite a revolutionary unlike the conventional heroines of the 18th and 19th century English novels. In her conversation with Harriet about marriage, she reveals her female identity:

> If I know myself, Harriet, mine is an active, busy mind, with a great many independent resources; and I do not perceive why I should be more in want of employment at forty or fifty than one-and-twenty. Woman's usual occupations of eye, and hand, and mind, will be as

> open to me then, as they are now, or with no important variation. If I draw less, I shall read more; if I give up music, I shall take to carpet work.[4]

Emma's ideas vividly reflect that she has a belief in her feminine resources. She is aware of her mind and intelligence. She thinks that woman can use her energy and intelligence at any age.

It is clear that Emma encourages Harriet about gaining an identity of her own. She recommends Harriet not to worry about her breeding, rather she advises her to discover her own power.

> The misfortune of your birth ought to make you particularly careful as to your associates. There can be no doubt of your being a gentleman's daughter, and you must support your claim to that station by everything within your own power, or there will be plenty of people who would take pleasure in degrading you. (27)

Emma is indeed the most fallible heroine of Austen because of her excessive self-love. She perceives life only from her point of view. She is a snobbish person who likes to manage other people's life. But Jane Austen is able to retain our sympathy with the heroine by giving us an insight into Emma's psyche. Emma's agonized self-reproaches on discovering the error of her ways gives a psychological insight into her character and makes us sympathetic towards her situation.

Harriet's major contribution to the novel is helping Emma to realize her faults in life. According to Yasmine Gooneratne, Emma and Harriet's relationship clarifies certain features of Emma's personality. Their friendship exposes and indulges Emma's fondness for power and her desire to dominate all the people around her. The circumstances of Harriet's life—her illegitimacy and her lack of any accomplishments leave her no option but to be happy in the very sensible and appropriate match with Mr. Robert Martin. Harriet is a realistic portrayal of the simple, docile and somewhat stupid woman of poor circumstances. Yet she also functions as a foil. It is through her that much of Emma's cleverness, capacity to delude herself, high-handedness and snobbery are revealed to the readers.

Apart from Harriet, Jane Fairfax is another character who reveals a representation of female identity. Fairfax is dramatized as elegant, cultured and intelligent. She has talent in music and she has been educated to become a governess, one of the few jobs women were allowed to do in the eighteenth century. Her qualities are higher than anyone else in the novel. However, she is not as economically independent as Emma. Jane Austen points out that "very few hundred pounds which she inherited from her father made independence impossible" (142) for Fairfax. Therefore, although Fairfax deserves higher respect than Emma, she,cannot receive it. The characterization of Fairfax is indeed crucial in demonstrating the perception about women in conservative society. If a person, especially a woman, lacks society's standards such as money, it is really difficult for her to express her identity even if she is well-educated. Joseph Litvak observes that in Jane Fairfax's character, the readers can see the anxieties and pain of a single woman as governess. That is because female's education is considered as something, which aims at improving feminine qualities as wives.[5]

Women in this novel are more or less limited to drawing rooms, but men can walk in at all hours, and even go off to London for a haircut. Jane Fairfax is subject to a neighbourly inquisition when she is caught walking in the rain to the local post office on the chance of hearing from her beloved, but Mr. Knightley is free to ride through the rain all the way from London to attend to the needs of his.[6] Although Emma is usually playful about her entrapment in Highbury, she cannot bear to hear her relatives discuss the journeys they have taken: "I must beg you not to talk of the sea. It makes me envious and miserable; I who have never seen it! South End is prohibited, if you please." (94)

Jane Austen presents in some form or the other the deep-seated contradiction between the rational norm in eighteenth-century society and the standards to which women were, hypocritically, expected to adhere. Her novels conceal a tension between protest and acceptance, rebellion and conformity, held in equilibrium by the controlling device of comedy. "Without ruffling the smooth surface of her novels she managed to introduce in them some of the ideological debates of her time which questioned the implied assumptions behind the gender-based codes of conduct."[7]

Jane Austen was too genuine a creative artist to get involved in the contemporary social or political problems, but the disabilities that women of her times were exposed to, moved her very intensely. Although her characters are not reformists, there is an underlying disapproval of the circumstances which forced women towards subordination. The theme of her novels is the heroine's resistance to the efforts of the patriarchal community which force her into a social role at the cost of her own identity. On the surface, her novels may seem to be humbly submissive bourgeois conformist whose characters think only of ball room dances, picnics, gossips, love and marriage. The reader must be prepared to penetrate underneath the surface to see that Jane Austen portrays unconventional and non-stereotyped women characters, especially her heroines.

NOTES

1. Harish Trivedi, ed., *Jane Austen: An Anthology of Recent Criticism* (Delhi: Pencraft `International, 2006), p. 30.
2. *Ibid.*, p. 33.
3. Jane Austen, *Pride and Prejudice* (India: Surjeet, 2000), p. 28.
4. Jane Austen, *Emma* (India: Macmillan, 1994), p. 80.
5. Joseph Litvak, *Reading Characters: Self, Society, and Text in Jane Austen's Emma* (New York: Chelsea, 1987), p. 132.
6. Edward Copeland and Juliet Mc Master, ed., *The Cambridge Companion to Jane Austen* (London: Cambridge University Press, 1997), pp 68-69.
7. Meenakshi Mukherjee, *Re-reading Jane Austen* (India: Orient Longman, 1995), p. 2.

The Feministic Flare in the Novels of Virginia Woolf

SARIKA TYAGI
Inderprastha Engineering College, Sahibabad

It is rightly said that literature is the mirror of society. A remarkable correlation exists between literature and the social conditions and environment. It is inevitable for any writer to separate the two.

Virginia Woolf was born in 1882 as the third child of Julia and Leslie Stephen. Her parents were members of upper-middle class late Victorian society. Though her father was an intellectual person and encouraged his daughters to study at home but she was not permitted for school which upset her all through her life. It is a singular injustice which is often exercised towards women and that is to deny them higher education. Mary Robinson opines of building a 'University of Women,' where they should be politely and at the same time classically educated. Woolf was oppressed by the patriarchal society where women's intellectuality was condescended without any question:

> there was an enormous body of masculine opinion to the effect that nothing could be expected of women intellectually and the reading, even in the nineteenth century, must have lowered her vitality, and told profoundly upon her work. There would always have been that assertion—you cannot do this, you are incapable of doing that—to protest against, to overcome.

In Victorian England women were more controlled by space. The patriarchal structures enclosed women in the private space of home where they had inert and useless lives. According to Fordyce, women are created for domesticity and they are to be defined in relation to men. Woolf reacted: "I perfectly agree with you that no woman has any business to meddle with that or any other serious business, further than giving her opinion (if she is asked)."

Women were expected to take care of the household, and education was out of the picture. They were entrapped in a monotonous routine called home. Men constitute the society and they are offered the best of all educational opportunities. Woolf expresses her pain about it in a heart-touching way:

> One could not go to the map and say Columbus discovered America and Columbus was a woman; or take an apple and remark, Newton discovered the laws of gravitation and Newton was a woman; or look into the sky and say aeroplanes are flying overhead and aeroplanes were invented by women. There is no mark on the wall to measure the precise height of women. Few women even now have been graded at the universities; the great trials of the professions, army and navy, trade, politics and diplomacy have hardly tested them. They remain even at this moment almost unclassified.

In her writings one can clearly see her attitude towards the female role during her time. She shows the pathetic situation of women because she believes it is wrong and unfair:

> 'Wife-beating' was a recognized right of man, and was practised without shame by high as well as low. . . . Similarly the daughter who refused to marry the gentleman of her parents' choice was liable to be locked up, beaten and flung about the room, without any shock being inflicted on public opinion. . . . It was still the exception for women of the upper and middle class to choose their own husbands, and when the husband had been assigned, he was lord and master, so far at least as law and custom could make him.

She is depressed to see the double standards in society being exercised towards woman when she writes: "Why did men drink wine and women water? Why was one sex so prosperous and the other so poor? What effect has poverty on fiction? What conditions are necessary for the creation of works of art?"

She successfully reveals the injustice and the lack of educational opportunity for women. In a society, where the idea of an intellectual woman is unconceivable, and even unacceptable, Woolf makes a strong statement in *A Room of One's Own*: "Literature is strewn with the wreckage of men who have minded beyond reason the opinion of others" and "'Women live like bats or owls, labour like beasts, and die like worms." She became upset for not finding even a single book written by a woman when she visited a library: "But for women, I thought, looking at the empty shelves, these difficulties were infinitely more formidable. In the first place, to have a room of her own, let alone a quiet room or a sound-proof room, was out of the question, unless her parents were exceptionally rich or very noble, even up to the beginning of the nineteenth century."

Further, she gives a reason for woman's non-creativity: "that the middle-class family in the early nineteenth century was possessed only of a single sitting-room between them? If a woman wrote, she would have to write in the common sitting-room . . . 'women never have half an hour . . . that they can call their own'—she was always interrupted." According to her, "A woman must have money and a room of her own if she is to write fiction; and that, as you will see, leaves the great problem of the true nature of woman and the true nature of fiction unsolved." She departs from the old concepts of being purely feminine or masculine. She advocates that a man should be womanly and a woman should be manly in writing:

> Perhaps a mind that is purely masculine cannot create, any more than a mind that is purely feminine. But it would be well to test what one meant by man-womanly and conversely by woman-manly, by pausing and looking at a book or two.

Virginia Woolf is able to see into the life of things. She is supreme among the British writers and is one of the luminaries of world literature and thought. Her writings, although rather unpopular due to their depth and sincerity, have yet come to gain a secular place in the rich heritage of English literature. She has immensely influenced modern literature as well as thought. Her oceanic vision and all-inclusiveness distinguish her from her contemporaries.

More than any other writers of their time, Virginia Woolf clearly articulated feminist pacifism and figured the crisis of male impotence. She grew up with the suffrage feminism of the late nineteenth and early years of the twentieth century, and the struggles and debates of this period influenced all her writings. She has a sense of herself writing as a woman in a man's world. She creates a dialogue with reality. Part of her importance as a feminist is that she offered cultural and social explanations for this psychological handicap, which she perceived was not hers alone, but that of many women. The inhibition of a woman's sense of independent worth and identity she saw as the product of her education (or lack of it), family life and professional opportunities. This is the story she tells most explicitly in her polemical writings, but also, if less insistently, in much of her fiction. She turned to feminism because patriarchal Victorian society had crippled her own sense of humanity and dignity. With no robust ego, with no conviction of her own genius (compare her with some male writers of her time—Hemingway, Lawrence, Joyce, for example), she managed to create some splendid and original fiction, but the cost in suffering was high. She is deadly to a woman writer because she whispers in her ear, "you are writing about a book that has been written by a man. Be sympathetic; be tender; flatter; deceive; use all the arts and wiles of our sex. Never let anybody guess you have a mind of your own. Above all, be pure." And so the angel corrupts a woman's honesty and undermines her independence, whether the woman is trying to write the truth about another writer's work or about life itself.

Last but not the least, I would like to urge that the innocent souls, who are truthful, should not be suffocated to death. Life should not be made miserable for them. The "virginal girl" should not be compelled to make an end of her life. In spite of death the self of Virginia remained alive. She once said, "I am the thing in which all this exists." She kept herself inviolable and she is still alive in all of the women who are fighting for "a room of one's own."

Bibliography

Virginia Woolf, *A Room of One's Own* (London: Penguin, 2004).

Phyllis Rose, *Women of Letters—A Life of Virginia Woolf* (London: Routledge and Kegan Paul, 1978).

Najma Mahamood, *Virginia Woolf: Concept of Perfect Man* (Aligarh: Vision, 1998).

Maggie Humn, *Practising Feminist Criticism: An Introduction* (Great Britain: Prentice Hall/Harvester Wheatsheaf, 1995).

Daniel R. Schwarz, *The Transformation of English Novel (1890-1930): Studies in Hardy, Conrad, Joyce, Lawrence, Forster, Woolf* (Hampshire & London: Macmillan, 1995).

Laura Marcus, *Virginia Woolf.* (United Kingdom: Northcote House in association with The British Council, 1997).

Patricia Waugh, *Feminine Fiction: Revising the Postmodern* (New York: Routledge, 1989).

Feminism in Egypt

AHMED SYED
University of Mysore

Feminism in Egypt can be traced to the last decades of the nineteenth century, when Egypt was undergoing dramatic societal transformations and enormous changes in the lives of all classes and both sexes alike. Early in the century, Egypt was incorporated into the European-dominated world market system, and in 1882 had fallen under the British colonial occupation. The turn of the century saw a growing national consciousness. The overwhelming presence of Europe and the collapse of much of the traditional order led to a reconsideration of Egypt's own position and identity in relation to the west. National independence seemed to supply the answer to western domination. A growing dissatisfaction with Egyptian society began to emerge and with it came calls for reform. The improvement of the position of women was part of this reform. Since the end of the nineteenth century Egyptian Nationalists have claimed that there can be no improvement of the state without improving the position of women.

The British repression was the catalyst for change resulting in violent demonstrations. All classes of Egyptian society participated and it was the first time women were involved in such rallies. In fact "open political agitation and action on the part of women began with their participation in the Nationalist movement against the British" (Jeyawordena). The veiled gentlewomen of Cairo paraded in the streets shouting slogans for independence and freedom from foreign occupation. They organised strikes and demonstrations, boycotts of British goods and wrote petitions protesting British actions in Egypt. These demonstrations are believed to be what led to the emergence of the first phase of Egyptian feminism.

The new conditions under which women were starting to live, their new experiences, and comparisons with men in their families gave rise to a nascent feminist awareness. Women such as Aisha Al-Taimuriyya from the upper class and Zainab Al-Fawwaz from the middle class, who were both born in the middle of the century, were the first generation to reveal this through their writings.

Feminism in Egypt has two distinct phases. The first phase started particularly in 1890s, the tight grip of family patriarchy over women had been loosened by the projects and developments encouraged by the rise of the modern state, itself a new patriarchal formation. But while some forms of patriarchal control within the family were eroded, others tightened. At this historical moment, some women in the cloistered world of upper- and middle-class in Cairo and Alexandria deepened their feminist consciousness. This expanding awareness, which was invisible to the outside world, from the memoirs of Huda Shaarawi, who recalls the debates in the first salon for women presided over by Eugenie Le Brun, a French woman and convert to Islam, who, as the wife of an upper-class Egyptian, had been thrust into the segregated harem world. The women discovered that the veil and female seclusion were not required by Islam but were merely a function of patriarchal control. They also understood that they as women had rights within Islam which patriarchy withheld from them. This awareness was assisted by the Islamic modernist and the reformist Sheikh Muhammad Abduh had begun to expound earlier.

Simultaneous with the emerging feminism of upper-class women, middle-class women were also evolving a feminist consciousness shaped in important ways by their expanding formal education. They attended the new schools that had begun to open for girls in the nineteenth century. As early as the latter half of the 1880s, middle-class women began to be published in men's journals and in the early 1890s, middle-class women began to found and contribute to their own women's journals. The writings of many of these women reveal a feminist consciousness with a religious and nationalist dimension.

The decade after the emergence of a women's feminist consciousness saw the rise of social feminism. Upper-class women founded the Mabarrat Muhammad Ali (1909) to bring medical assistance and health instructions to poor women in their own neighbourhoods. Shaarawi and some other women explicitly placed this project in a feminist context, seeing it as the first step in the process of liberating the lives of lower-class women and, at the same time, expanding their own lives beyond the harem. Shaarawi's memoirs disclose the distinct nationalist impulse motivating her and other women to pioneer in public philanthropy. This, not the widely visible participation of women in the 1919 nationalist demonstrations, was the first time that upper-class harem women's unconventional, extra-domestic behaviour was legitimized as a nationalist act.

Women of the middle and upper classes came together in "public" that is, outside the harem but in places exclusively reserved for women like women's lectures given from 1909 to 1912 at the new Egyptian University and in the offices of the progressive paper *Al-Jarida*. Sponsored by upper-class women and given by middle-class women, Bahitha Al-Bad'iyya (Malak Hifni Nasif), Nabawiyya Musa, and Mayy Ziyada, a poet and writer of Lebanese and Palestinian origin, were among the speakers. In these lectures, feminist consciousness was further expanded and feminist bonds among women across class lines were forged.

Bahitha Al-Bad'iyya, whose untimely death in 1918 brought Huda Shaarawi to the podium for the first time to deliver a eulogy, was the first woman to make public feminist demands in Egypt. Because she was unable herself to appear before the all-male Egyptian Congress of 1911, a man presented her agenda, which included the demand that women be allowed into mosques as in early Islam, and have access to professions, especially those in which they could cater to other women. This, and her reluctance to favour unveiling, indicated her strategy of promoting women's development within the system of sex segregation, a stand shared at the turn of the century by Nabawiyya Musa, who, however, unveiled around 1909.

Nabawiyya Musa, a life-long teacher and school administrator and founding member of the Egyptian Feminist Union (EFU), argued for more education, appealing to upper-class women to finance schools for girls. She also called for better jobs for women both for their own welfare and as a nationalist strategy to reduce foreign workers and the loss of Egyptian capital. Both women argued for controls on men's tyrannical use of divorce and polygamy. These demands struck at an area of patriarchal control in the private sphere where family patriarchy stood firmest and women's family roles were most threatened. In this area, proponents of feminism and defenders of patriarchal principles have remained severely polarized in a century-long struggle.

While feminism in Egypt began with women in a world segregated by sex, its radical threat to patriarchy was hidden by the very barriers that obscured and obstructed its proponents. When a man, Qasim Amin, made public in a widely read book, *Tahrir Al-Mar'a* (The liberation of the woman, Cairo, 1899) what was the essence of Egyptian women's early feminism, patriarchal forces rose up in fury in a public counter-attack, for the moment missing the radical force evolving more invisibly.

The second phase began when middle- and upper-class women participated in the Egyptian nationalist movement (1919-22), in street demonstrations, political organizing, communications, and morale boosting, the patriarchy did not construe these as radical acts. On the contrary, the patriarchy considered women's unconventional behaviour as defensive national acts and as an extension of woman as defender of the home. Despite women's crucial roles which men needed and welcomed in the nationalist struggle, and male nationalists' liberation rhetoric and promises to women, when the militant struggle was over patriarchy hastened to consolidate its hold and expected women to retreat to the home. While women's nationalist experience did not, itself, produce feminism, it did give women valuable political experience, consolidated their claims on the nation, and quickened expectations. Women argued that patriarchal domination was akin to foreign imperialist domination and that national liberation was incomplete without women's liberation.

With the achievement of (partial) independence came a new constitution and parliamentary democracy. However, the electoral law denying women the right to vote and their prevention from attending the opening of Parliament except as wives of ministers and high officials which signalled to women that they were expected to retreat into the private sphere of house and family. Women might defend Egypt during times of crisis, but in "normal" times men must govern and command the public sphere. Egyptian women understood the message, and after several decades of hidden feminist evolution they were prepared to act. Huda Shaarawi and Saiza Nabarawi inaugurated the era of open feminist activism by removing their veils at the Cairo train station after returning from an international feminist conference, in a bold gesture declaring their determination to put a final end to sex segregation and female seclusion in the home. Shortly before, Shaarawi had led other upper- and middle-class women in forming the Egyptian Feminist Union (EFU). It declared an agenda for political, social, and economic transformation to integrate (urban) women into public life on a level with men and enhance women's lives in the private sphere. The feminists were aware that the lives of peasant women were not confined to the private sphere, and used the presence of these women in public space to argue their case. The EFU grounded its arguments for women's rights within the Islamic modernist and nationalist frameworks along the lines already worked out in the stage of unseen feminism.

The feminism of Huda Shaarawi, Saiza Nabarawi, and other EFU feminists can be called radical liberal feminism. The act of helping finally to dismantle the system of segregation and female seclusion through the dramatic gesture of publicly unveiling and by implication the ideology associated with this was clearly radical. The EFU feminist agenda called for political rights for women, changes in personal status laws especially for controls on divorce and polygamy, equal secondary school and university education for women, expanded professional opportunities for women in the fields of law, medicine, and education, and new work opportunities for women in factories and commercial establishments. It called for protective legislation for workers and support systems (childcare and health care), and also demanded an end to legalized prostitution.

By the time of Shaarawi's death in 1947, the EFU had witnessed successes for women in the public sector in education and work. Political rights were not achieved and women continued to be sexually exploited through legalized prostitution. The minimum marriage ages for both sexes were raised but there was no control over men's easy access to divorce and polygamy.

In the second half of the Thirties, the EFU members failed to respond to the initiative of Shaarawi and Nabarawi to serve the needs of a broader base of women and also displayed an elitist unwillingness to welcome the more active feminists of the middle class into their ranks. However, Shaarawi and especially Nabarawi were linked to a new populist feminism that the EFU itself was unable to disseminate within its own organization. With major achievements in the public sector, yet with so many pressing concerns ahead, the moment had come for a new thrust. This came from the populist feminists, predominantly middle-class women, who accelerated the campaign for political rights for women and conducted direct action among poor urban and rural women to help them achieve economic and social liberation. They also kept up the struggle to reform personal status laws.

Fatma Ni'mat Rashid, Durriyya Shafiq, and Inji Aflatun emerged as leaders of populist feminism. All three used their pens in the cause of feminism. Rashid and Shafiq founded organizations and their own journals. Aflatun wrote books and contributed to the journals of others. Fatma Ni'mat Rashid had written for the EFU's L'Egyptienne and had edited its Arabic journal, *Al-Misriyya*. She founded the National Feminist Party (NFP) in 1944, whose name indicated its conscious attempt to form, for the first time, a women's political party. Shafiq was far more successful than Rashid in rousing the women of the middle class. The Daughter of the Nile Union was the first feminist organization to establish a broad base in the provinces, where centers were opened for teaching literacy and hygiene to poor women. Shafiq herself was a far bolder leader than Rashid, and more directly confrontational than other feminists.

Aflatun used both direct action and her pen to further the cause of women's liberation. She also drew wider attention to the economic and social problems of workers and peasants and overarching patriarchal domination of women in the home and workplace in her book, Nahnu Al-Nisa' *Al-Misriyyat* (We Egyptian Women, 1949). She located class and gender oppression within the framework of imperialist exploitation. Like the other feminist leaders, Aflatun also insisted on political rights for women and on improved personal status laws. Although a communist, Aflatun situated her call for women's rights within an Islamic framework.

In the face of continued patriarchal domination, so unequivocally clear in the personal status laws, Nabarawi, Aflatun, and others formed the Ittihad al-Nisa' al-Qawmi, the National Feminist Union, appealing to a broad coalition of women across the political spectrum, but the government blocked their efforts by refusing the organization a permit. The government, which had finally granted women the vote in 1956, in the same year withdrew from them the right to organize politically. Feminist organizations and all other independent, political organizations were banned. The EFU was forced to confine itself to welfare work and to change its name and it became the Huda Shaarawi's Association; the word "feminist" was no longer acceptable. The following year Aflatun, as a communist, was sent to prison, where she remained for four years. Shafiq was under house arrest. Rashid's feminist party was dissolved. Nabarawi was silenced. Women's activist feminism inaugurated in the aftermath of the 1919 nationalist revolution was suppressed after three and a half decades of independent struggle. However, women kept their independent feminism alive behind the scenes in Egypt reminiscent of the early feminism of the harem, and their voice was heard internationally.

Feminism reappeared on the public scene at the beginning of the Seventies, coinciding with the coming to power of Sadat and the rise of Open Door (infitah) capitalism. It also coincided with the acceleration of the second wave of Islamic "fundamentalism" that had begun to make its appearance following the war in 1967 mainly among university students, women and men, of the lower middle class, many of whom had come from the rural areas. Among the women, resurgent Islamism took the form of a return to the veil (mainly a covering of the head and body but not face) and the home, an instrumental re-assertion of the essentializing notion of women's exclusive sexual and family roles.

At the moment when some women were returning to the veil, publicly calling attention to women as essentially sexual beings, women's bodies and female sexuality emerged as a feminist issue signaling the public re-assertion of feminism itself. The new feminist concern was expressed by a medical doctor and feminist, Nawal El Saadawi, in her book *Al-Mar'a wa Al-Jins* (Women and Sex), published the year after Sadat came to power (1972). In this book and subsequent writings, El Saadawi discussed in public what was most private and, indeed, taboo (1980). This took special courage and involved great risk; in fact, El Saadawi lost her job at the Ministry of Health and soon went into self-imposed exile. Not since Qasim Amin's *Tahrir al-Mar'a* (1899) had there been such an impassioned outcry from patriarchal forces. But, as before, there was also a positive resonance among progressive women. El Saadawi, in fighting against the practice of clitoridectomy among the issues she addressed, and Amin before her, in opposing the veiling of the face, she demonstrated that these practices had been falsely attributed to Islam and were simply forms of patriarchal control of women.

Earlier feminists had focused only upon the sexual exploitation of poor women as prostitutes but El Saadawi addressed sexuality more comprehensively. The sexual exploitation of women occurred in both public and family spheres and was not confined to a single (i.e., lower) class. El Saadawi located it in larger political and economic contexts. With the authority and clinical evidence of a doctor, and more particularly a woman doctor with a feminist consciousness, she attacked assaults on women's bodies connected with obsessive fears about female virginity and sexual purity and condemned both the public commercial exploitation of the female body and private forms of aggression against women's bodies. El Saadawi publicized the physical and psychological harm done to women's bodies by clitoridectomy, arguing for its eradication. She stressed that this extreme form of patriarchal control of female sexuality was wrongly sanctioned in the name of Islam. A number of feminists in Egypt struggled to wipe out clitoridectomy, but a similar campaign by feminists in Sudan has been far more visible and widespread.

El Saadawi pointed in public to the operation of a double standard whereby the Islamic prescription confining sexuality to the conjugal relationship was applied to women but not men. She exposed the sexual exploitation of women in the sanctity of their own homes with disturbing evidence that this was more widespread than commonly admitted. Like feminists before her, she decried the public marketing of women's bodies, but rather than focus more exclusively on matters of the law and policing, she exposed the roots of prostitution and its effects in her writings, most notably her novel *Woman at Point Zero*, based on a real-life case. El Saadawi bravely brought to light the subject of the sexual domination and abuse of women, placing the onus on men and society at a time when women were being increasingly told that the responsibility was theirs to cover (i.e., veil) themselves and distance themselves from the public arena to safeguard morality. Meanwhile, with open-door capitalism, women's bodies were being used for commercial exploitation as seen in blatant forms of advertising. El Saadawi forced the "private" subject of sexuality into the open and caused the matter to be looked at in new ways. The subject remains contentious and adversaries often allow themselves to misread the content and intent of feminists in issues of sexuality. During the Eighties, matters concerning sexuality became less visible but by no means insignificant and a new awareness had been raised.

In the Eighties, feminism in Egypt once again became public, visible, and organized. In 1985, Jam'iyya Taddamun lil-Mar'a al-'Arabiyya (the Arab Women's Solidarity Association, or AWSA), officially came into being, although the idea had first arisen earlier. The organization, under the presidency of Nawal El Saadawi, was headquartered in Cairo with branches in several Arab countries and in some Arab communities in the West. Egyptians as members of AWSA located their feminism within an Arab framework. AWSA feminism declared, "women's active participation in the political, economic, social, and cultural life of the Arab world is essential for the realization of true democracy in Arab society" (Badran and Cooke: 367). It demanded an end to gender discrimination both in the family and in society. The initial members of AWSA included a wide spectrum of feminists.

The rescinding of the liberal Personal Status Law of 1979, the first major revision since 1929, which was issued by a decree from Sadat (who had been pressured by his wife), galvanized a large number of women into action the first year of AWSA's existence. The 1979 law had given women more benefits in the case of divorce and had made it easier for them to obtain dissolution of marriage themselves. A broad feminist coalition formed the Lajnat al-Dif'i 'an Huquq al-Mar'a wa'al-Usra, the Committee for the Defence of the Rights of the Woman and the Family, to fight for the reinstatement of the law. They were successful, although the law was returned with certain restrictions.

While the broader feminist coalition subsequently fragmented, AWSA continued and strengthened itself institutionally. It conducted monthly seminars, organized international conferences held in Cairo, and in 1989 founded its own journal, *Nun*. AWSA feminism was highly visible and confrontational, and outspokenly critical of conservative Islamist positions on gender. In 1990 the government ordered *Nun* to cease, and the following year shut down AWSA itself. AWSA has taken the case to court and after many imposed delays on the hearings still awaits action. Other feminist groups were also formed in the mid-Eighties. These were informal groups. Two comprised women in their twenties and thirties who did not attempt to register under the Ministry of Social Affairs but coalesced more informally around their publications. A third included women in their forties and fifties who organized around a specific project.

In 1984, some women who had been active in the democratic student movement of the Seventies formed a study group in Cairo. Two years later the group started to issue *Majallat al-Mar'a al-Jadida* (The new woman magazine) to disseminate their feminist views. The group later formed committees to deal with various everyday needs of ordinary women in areas such as health, legal literacy, and income generation. The group announced their stand in a communication in 1990: "The New Woman Group is a progressive and democratic feminist group of women who believe that while Egyptian and Arab women share with men the hardships brought about by backwardness, dependence and economic crisis, they have to carry a double burden and suffer from a variety of forms of subordination, oppression and suppression arising specifically from their position as women."

The other group of women of the same generation sprang up in the provinces. In 1982 a number of women in Mansura in the Delta who had organized public protests against the Israeli invasion of Lebanon went on to form Jam'iy-yat Bint al-Ard, the Society of the Daughters of the Earth, and two years later brought out *Majallat Bint al-Ard* (The daughter of the earth magazine). The group works with women in the town of Mansura and in surrounding villages in feminist consciousness-raising and in practical, income-generating projects. The group works with local women within their own milieu dealing with needs the women themselves deem important.

Meanwhile, in the second half of the Eighties several professional women in their forties and fifties came together to work on a legal literacy project. Calling themselves the Communication Group for the Enhancement of the Status of Women in Egypt, they pooled their expertise to produce a booklet called *Al-Huquq al-Qanuniyya li al-Mar'a al-Misriyya bain al-Nadhariyya wa al-Tatbiq* (The legal rights of the Egyptian woman in theory and practice) to make women aware of the rights the law guarantees them.

By not being officially constituted, the informal groups do not risk being dissolved by the government as AWSA was. Other officially constituted feminist organizations may have survived; there simply are no cases to prove this. The contemporary climate, however, is not receptive to feminism. For reasons of expediency, and also because of uncertainties about meanings of feminism, many progressive women operate for the advancement of women within the context of their professions, eschewing labels and public identification with feminism. Thus, today in Egypt invisible and visible feminisms exist side by side.

The most striking feature of feminism in Egypt is that women have maintained the independent feminist tradition they initiated. The feminists, who started by understanding that patriarchy, not Islam, kept women down, have made the distinction between patriarchy and Islam in arguing their cause throughout the century. They have rejected the attempts of their opponents to impose restrictions on women in the name of Islam. This has been as true of the radical liberal EFU feminists as of the most leftist of the populist feminists. Women have not allowed their feminism and Islam to be polarized, and have certainly been aware of the political consequences of this. Women as feminists used Islamic arguments in the effort to end patriarchal tyranny in the private sphere and to legitimize their full entry into the public sphere. Both within the segregated system and outside it, women have conducted their own nationalist activities. When their nationalist activities caused them to contravene conventional behaviour, they stressed their nationalism to legitimize their actions.

However, during the period of nationalist militancy, women did not have to justify their unprecedented actions in the public sphere. There was a clear (political) crisis. Patriarchy, threatened on the national front, welcomed and encouraged women's actions. When efforts were later made to push women back into the private sphere, some women feminists marshalled nationalist arguments to justify their continued presence in the public sphere and their rights there. Throughout the entire century, feminists have placed their feminism within the nationalist context. In argument and by active agitation, they have defended the nation against foreign occupation and economic, political, and cultural imperialism.

The history of Egyptian feminism clearly demonstrates that, irrespective of political and economic formations and forms of imperialist presence and penetration, patriarchy survives and reshapes itself according to its own needs and the nature of its feminist opposition. Perhaps the most striking achievement of Egyptian feminism is that it has understood this well and has fought to maintain an independent tradition keeping alive its struggle for the cause of women.

At present, there are many different feminist groups within Egypt. Some of the movements are affiliated with the state in some way in that they are women's committees of political parties such as The Progressive Women's Union to the Women's Secretariat of the Labour Party. There are however also many independent feminist associations such as The New Woman Research Centre and Bint El Ard (Daughter of the Land) Association. Although the organisations have different goals in general they all entail the improvement of women's position in Egyptian by improving literacy, democratic and human rights, increasing women's participation in political life, and women's health.

Works Cited

Badran and Cooke, ed. *Opening the Gates: A Century of Arab Feminist Writing*. Bloomington: Indiana University Press, 1990.

Badran, Margot. "Dual Liberation: Feminism and Nationalism in Egypt, 1870-1925." *Feminist Issue* (Spring 1988): 15-34.

Coles, Juan Ricardo. "Feminism, Class and Islam in Turn of the Century Egypt." *International Journal of Middle East Studies* 13 (1981): 397-407.

El Saadawi, Nawal. *The Hidden Face of Eve*. 1977. Trans. Shreif Hetata. London: Zed Books, 1980.

Hijab, Nadia. *Women power: The Arab Debate on Women and Work.* Cambridge: Cambridge UP, 1988.

Huda Shaarawi, Harem Years: the Memoirs of an Egyptian Feminist. Trans. and ed. Margot Badran. London: Vigro, 1986.

Jeyawordena, Kumari. *Feminism and Nationalism in the Third World.* London: Zed Ltd, 1986.

Joseph, Suad. "Women and Politics in the Middle East." *MERIP* 1387, 16, 1 (Jan.-Feb.1986): 3-8

Khater, Akram and Cynthia Nelson. "The Women's Movement and Political Participation in Modern Egypt," *Women's Studies International Forum*, 2, 5 (1988): 465-83.

Tucker, Judith. *Women in Nineteenth Century Egypt*. Cambridge: Cambridge UP, 1985.

_____. "Insurrectionary Women: Women and the State in Nineteenth Century Egypt." *MERIP*, 138, 16, 1 (Jan.-Feb.1986):9-13.

Gender and Politics in Naguib Mahfouz's *Miramar*

ABDULMOMIN AL-RUBIAEE
University of Mysore

Naguib Mahfouz's *Miramar* is a novel of exiles—social and political—who take shelter in a pension in Alexandria. The pension, Miramar, becomes the site of conflicts between five male figures, each of whom stands for one aspect of the politico-historical context of Egypt. The men of the boarding house enjoy the company of the matron, a Christian old lady named Marianna, and Zohra, a maid. Narrating the events of the pension from the points of view of the male guests, Mahfouz makes his quartet an Interpretation of the androcentric society which reacts differently to the presence of the beautiful maid, Zohra, herself an expatriate like others. Notwithstanding her ostensibly marginal presence, Zohra plays a central role in the events of the pension. In the thus gendered atmosphere of Miramar, each narrator reveals his ideological standpoint; in this way Mahfouz fuses issues of gender and politics. This paper attempts to show how through different narrators' approaches to Zohra, who can be taken as the mother country, Mahfouz portrays the politico-historical scene of Egypt.

Zohra is a *fellaha*, an illiterate girl who has escaped from her village and the forced marriage with an old man, in need of a nurse. To Miramar, whose matron has been an old friend and customer of her late father, Zohra comes and works as a maid. Her physical attraction arouses the admiration of the male guests who approach differently her status both as an escapee and a female figure. In spite of her illiteracy and countryside origin, Zohra is fully aware of her gender in the patriarchal system; her determination to emancipate herself from the imposed subordination of society is the admired or resented point in her personality. Mahfouz depicts her as a strong and self-dependent figure. To avoid her brother-in-law's exploitation, Zohra used to farm her piece of land on her own and tried to "stand up to men like man" in the field or at the market (18). Unable to cope with the dominant conservatism of the village, she escapes to lead a life of her own in Alexandria. When her people come to take her back to the village, Zohra refuses partly because of her disapproval of the village life and partly due to her love for Sarhan El-Beheiry, one of the guests and narrators. On the same grounds, she turns down Mahmoud Abu el' Abbas' proposal for marriage, which arouses different reactions in the pension. To Amer Wagdi, the old journalist, Zohra mentions that the newspaper-seller, Mahmoud, has the same despising look about woman as her villagers; she has heard him saying: "All women have one thing in common. They're cuddly little animals without brains or religion, and the only way to keep them from going wild is to leather them every day!" (32). Zohra's opposition to the patriarchal society urges her to make sure whether her lover, Sarhan, considers her as his equal; it is the same motivation to be his equal that makes her get rid of illiteracy and learn a profession, some craft or trade. Although at the end, her lover betrays her, Zohra is still bent on continuing her education to secure a promising future. Mahfouz historicizes his novella by bringing to the scene two old men, whose contradictory political status stands for the politico-historical shifts the Revolutions of 1919 and 1952 have brought to the country.

Amer Wagdi is an old journalist whose pen has been at the service of the 1919 Revolution. As a national enthusiast, the ex-journalist represents the political scene of the old days of Egypt when Wafdism cried for independence and nationalism. Mahfouz symbolizes the decay of Wafdism both in the senile character of Wagdi and in his marginalized position as a journalist. For the old man there is no place among journalists who appear to him as "clowns . . . who got their training in a circus and then turned to journalism as the appropriate place to display their tricks" (4). In Miramar, he takes shelter to nourish his nostalgic desires. In the pension, the nationalist Wagdi comes across his political enemy, Tolba Marzuq, a King's henchman. The great landowner, Tolba, has been broken by the Wafdists' socio-economic reforms regarding the land-owning interest. Tolba's property has been put under sequestration and all his resources have been confiscated. These two old men, whose patriarchal outlooks have antithetical political bases, view Zohra and her gender differently. To the ex-journalist, Zohra is a strong graceful figure towards whom he develops "a surge of paternal tenderness" (16). The ex-lord Tolba, however, looks down on her both as a female figure and as a servant. When Zohra recoils from massaging his body he calls her a savage peasant, a wildcat. (20). Upon knowing Zohra's decision to educate herself, Wagdi foresees a promising future for Zohra. By contrast, Tolba expects her to become a prostitute or an actress. Whereas the reformist Amer Wagdi gives Zohra equal rights in the society, Tolba, based on his exploitative political stand, denigrates her as an object of desire. Zohra also detests the dethroned landowner who takes her escape from the village as an elopement.

Mahfouz, however, does not romanticize the new generation in the face of the old; this objective entails him to portray the "modernized" replicas of his historicized figures, Wagdi and Tolba. Hence, the quartet is politically dualistic; while Tolba's generation extends into the modern Egypt in such figures as Sarhan El-Beheiry and Hosni Allam, Mansour Bahy is the heir to Wagdi's Wafdism. In these doomed characters, Mahfouz posits his critique of the two contradictory political groups that have proved inefficient in recovering the socio-cultural predicaments in which exploitation and subordination pervade. Mansour Bahy views Hosni Allam's land ownership as the entrenchment of the old regime; Tolba's "withered glory had left . . . a nation of parasites. And Hosni is just a wing of this broken eagle" (68). However, unlike Tolba, Hosni has come late in an age when the society votes for education and the glory of having land is over. Thus Hosni, "A gentleman of property" (40), with no educational degree suffers the state of an exile. In the pension, he feels himself an outcast, like "the ineffable superiority of a Turcoman horseman, who finds himself living among sedentary trash" (44). To his counter character, Mansour Bahy, Hosni appears as "a lord without any real sovereignty or substance" (67).

Hosni's patriarchal stand is exactly the same as Tolba's. He regards woman as nothing more than an object of desire; he is seen making love with many different girls. Refused once by his cousin for his lack of degree and unable to find a suitable wife, Hosni permits himself to regard all women as his personal harem. To Hosni, Zohra is a first-class maid who can fill the vacancy in his future home. In his vain pride, he remarks: "She'll be grateful for the chance to play the lady without the trouble of child-bearing, nursing, and all that. She's beautiful. And she'll put up with my whims, my other love affairs. How could a girl from her background do anything else?" (45) For such a person Zohra's decision to educate herself sounds an annoying joke that gives his old wound a twinge (51). Like Tolba, he wonders at Zohra's refusal to marry the newspaper-seller. His assault on Zohra when he is drunk shows his exploitative approach to the "other" sex and represents the possessive nature of his economic fascism as Tolba's. In John Fowles' words, "the blind reaction of Tolby's generation turns into the freckless nihilism of Hosni's" (xi-xii). Mahfouz symbolizes this sense of nihilism in Hosny's maniac pleasure in roaming Alexandria in his car at high speed.

In the third voice, Mansour Bahy, Mahfouz posits Hosny-Tolba's counterpoint which resembles Amer Wagdi. While Hosni detests the old journalist calling him ironically Old Qalawoon or the Doddering Caliph, Bahy respects the Wafdist. Bahy is an announcer in the Alexandria Broadcasting Service. Unlike the bulky and huski figure of Hosni, he has delicate, feminine features. Being a man of degree is the main reason for Hosni's disgusting him since Bahy has the credit of what Hosni lacks and for that he suffers. Bahy who lacks neither education nor money is an expatriate in another way. A member of Marxist group, he has deserted his friends just before their arrest. With a brother as a high police officer, Bahy is suspected by his comrades as a traitor. His brother has placed him, and actually imprisoned him in Miramar under the care of Mariana. The critic, Moussa-Mahmoud, ascribes Bahy's state of introvert to his suffering "a Judas burden of guilt" (106) that detaches him from everyone in the pension except the matron, Zohra and Amer Wagdi.

Bahy, "A true child of the Revolution" (25), stands for the educated generation of the modern Egypt. As an intellectual, Bahy gives space to the marginalized other sex. His fractured androcentric status has turned into an androgynous one which welcomes the presence and progress of the woman in the society. Subsequently, he develops a more humane and sympathetic tendency towards Zohra. To Bahy, Zohra is a displaced figure, who is supposed to be "at the University . . . where she should have been, not running errands for the old lady" (64). Logically enough, upon knowing about her education, he admires her. Bahy's approval of Zohra's self-assurance contrasts Hosni's resentment that regards it an obstacle to satisfy his possessive desires. Bahy turns away from Tolba who appears to him as "old recollections, dreams of bloodshed, of classes in conflict, books and pamphlets studied in secret meetings" (68). Instead, Bahy is attracted towards Wagdi and feels sympathetic for the old revolutionary's state of callous neglet. Whereas the ex-journalist has his patriarchal reservations about Zohra's refusal to return to her village and to marry Mahmoud, his modernized replica, Bahy, appreciates Zohra. Himself in love with his professor's wife, Bahy sympathizes with Zohra but disappraves her lover, Sarhan. When Zohra is betrayed and left alone in her helpless situation, Bahy sees her as the mirror of his own plight and thus hates the traitor as much as he hates himself (77). As a result, he decides to kill Sarhan and get rid of an image of himself—a traitor to his friends and to his beloved. John Fowles views Bahy a victim of "a sort of narcissistic no-man's land" (xii). In this narcissism, Mahfouz locates the doomed failure of the rising intellectual wave in the politico-cultural sphere of the society.

In Sarhan El-Beheiry, the author hybridizes Zohra's peasantry origin, Bahy's educated status and Tolba-Hosni's ambition and opportunism. Making him speak of himself as the representative of the 1952 (98), Mahfouz renders Sarhan the representative of the present context of Egypt; thus in Sarhan's opprtunism and failure, Mahfouz critiques the political basis of the post-Revolution generation. As a man with few *feddans*, and some commitment at home, Sarhan is an economically troubled man. He is the Deputy Head Accountant at the Alexandria Textile Mills, and someone whom Hosny calls "educated rabbler," but with an ambitious nature. Unlike Bahy, Sarhan is attracted towards the "gentleman of property," Hosni Allam. In Hosni's state, Sarhan finds his own dreams: "handsome, tall and powerfully built, just what we'd all love to be" (103). Sarhan's utilitarian socialism puts him in contrast to Bahy's Marxism and Wagdi's Wafdism. He proves to be an ambitious opportunist whose sole aim is to get promotion in class by any means. He befriends people as a utilitarian. Looking for money in his relationships, he is attracted for some time towards Tolba whose ignorance discourages his hopes for partnership in business. He tries to keep good company with Bahy whose brother as a high police officer may be useful in lots of situations. Knowing about Hosni's plans to start a business, Sarhan tries to find himself a part to play in his project; but Hosni is mercurial, always dreaming and dashing around in his car.

For Sarhan the institution of marriage is a means to achieve his ambitious dreams; such values as high family, education and money are his criteria. His love for Zohra has just physical basis and it is a pity for him that Zohra lacks her teacher's status. Realizing that mariage with Zohra does not give him a push up the social ladder, Sarhan turns towards Zohra's teacher who is a career girl, with salary, elegance and education but no beauty. Zohra's love for Sarhan has motivated her to educate herself, but he regards her education as a waste of time and money. As an opportunist, he seeks a prosperous future through suitable marriage. Sarhan's dreams are, however, smashed as Zohra puts to task her teacher's family about their engagement. Also his complicity to steal a lorry of yarn and sell in the black market, as an easy way to get rich fails. Rebuffed by his fiance's family, having lost Zohra's love, and the failed theft, Sarhan commits suicide. In his frustrated ambition, Sarhan represents Mahfouz's dark vision of the present conditions of his country.

In this way, *Mirmar* becomes the battlefield for different politico-historical ideologies for which each narrator speaks. Taking Zohra the focal point of the narrative as the country—Egypt—Mafouz's narrative strategy interweaves the issues of gender and politics. Zohra can be the newly emergent female figure who tries to resist the subordinating patriarchy; she can also stand for the country that sets aside the agrarian lifestyle and tries to cope with the demands of modernity in its educated and developing form. The fact that the young narrators, each fails, bespeaks Mahfouz's critique of the post-Revolution generation, which is either fascistic like Hosni—a mirror of Tolba's old regime—or is too much abstract in its narcissism as Bahy, or fall a victim to its thirsty ambitions for bourgeois standards, like Sarhan.

Works Cited

Mahfouz, Naguib. *Miramar*. Intro. and trans. John Fowles. London: Heinemann, 1978.

Maussa-Mahmoud, Fatma. "The Outsider in the Novels of Naguib Mahfouz." *Bulletin* (*British Society for Middle Eastern Studies*) 8.2 (1981).

A Study of Black Feminism in Toni Morrison's *The Bluest Eye*

FATEMEH AZIZMOHAMMADI
HAMEDREZA KOHZADI
Islamic Azad University, Arak Branch, Iran

Set in Toni Morrison's hometown of Lorain, Ohio, Morrison's first novel, *The Bluest Eye* was published in 1970. The novel is the story of a young African American girl and her family who are driven in every direction by the white dominant culture that says to them "You aren't beautiful, you aren't relevant, you're invisible." In the novel, Pecola Breedlove is the protagonist of the novel who is victimized because of her blackness. Thus the blackness of her skin gradually disgusts her and leads her to embrace white beauty standards. She is trapped in white culture and white superiority. She believes that if she had blue eyes, she would be loved and her life would be transformed. More than anything she wants to be loved because she is constantly abused and tormented by her family and an abusive community available to her. But eventually her total submission to white beauty standards has a disastrous outcome for her and it shows nothing but her insanity.

Alice Walker in her collection of essays, *In Search of Our Mother's Gardens* (1984) writes innumerable passages about the situation of black women. First of all, Walker clearly recognizes the bipartite identity of black women. As she says, "it is the black woman's words that have the most meaning for us, her daughters, because she, like us, has experienced life not only as a black person, but as a woman" (275). Secondly, Walker makes clear that because of their double identity, black women are the victims of both sexism (sexual discrimination) and racism (racial discrimination). This leads her to say that the black woman is "oppressed almost beyond recognition—oppressed by *everyone*" (149). Expressing it with a folkloristic image, she says:

> Black women are called, in the folklore that so aptly identifies one's status in society, "the *mule* of the world," because we have been handed the burdens that everyone else—everyone else—refused to carry (237).

It is evident that *The Bluest Eye* reveals discrimination on the basis of gender. The characters candidly make known their lived experiences of sexism. In the novel, Pauline (Pecola's mother) recalls how she was treated by the doctors at the hospital where she gave birth to one of her children. One of the doctors was instructing other student doctors: "When he got to me he said now these here women you don't have any trouble with. They deliver right away and with no pain. Just like horses" (97). Thus, to the white doctor, as to the white community at large, the black woman has less worth than other humans. About the sexism among blacks Alice Walker writes:

> I tell [Coretta King] how important I feel this is: that black men not take out their anger and frustration on their wives and children. A temptation that is all too obvious. Coretta's face is thoughtful as she says, Maybe I shouldn't say this, because I don't *know* it, it's just a feeling I have . . . but few black men seem to feel secure enough as men that they can make women feel like women. (151-52)

In *The Bluest Eye,* Cholly is an abusive and alcoholic man who takes out his past and present frustrations on his wife, Pauline, and his children, Pecola and Sammy. On the one hand Cholly's past frustrations caused by orphanhood and the encounter of the two white hunters making fun of him and his girlfriend Darlene in making love, leaves Cholly a traumatic bruise. On the other hand, Cholly's present frustration caused by unemployment in the North by which Cholly and Pauline are forced into a role reversal in which the wife is the primary breadwinner reminds Cholly of his weakness and impotence and originate self-hatred and hatred toward his family members, especially toward Pauline and Pecola.

As a militant writer who is engaged in liberation struggles, Alice Walker feels that the cause of black male/female gender conflicts can be revealed if she focuses on the violent reality of what can be termed as the inhuman conditions of black women. In her insightful essay, *In Search of Our Mother's Gardens*, she explains the reasons behind her emphasis on black male/ female gender conflicts:

> Of course, the whites oppress us; they oppress the world? The white man, the rich man. But we also oppress each other and we oppress ourselves. I think that one of the traditions we have in Black Women's literature is the tradition of trying to fight all the oppression. (14)

And then, she adds:

> If someone is beating you at home, you don't then just sit in the room afterwards and write a novel about the white man's rule. I mean to deal with the guy who beat you up in your house and then see who's beating you up on the street (14)

In *The Bluest Eye*, black male/female gender conflicts are clear. With constant quarrelling and fighting over the material issues, Cholly and Pauline's loving relationship turns sour. Pauline starts considering herself a "Christian woman, burdened with a no-count man, whom God wanted her to punish" (30). Cholly as well turns to "Pour out on her the sum of his inarticulate fury and aborted desires" (30). Such hated marriage, of course, has great impact on family, or more specifically on their children: Sammy, who has "run away from home no less than twenty seven times" (32) and Pecola, who endures it with "a profound wish that she herself could die" (32). Except being a man of financial impotence, Cholly's childhood trauma that accompanies his adulthood altogether makes him a powerless yet dangerous man. Impotence and violence are the two sides of his character. After failing to appeal to and make the connection with his father, Cholly becomes a free man, and is "dangerously free" with destructive power piled up with the repressed pang and anger of being raped by the white (125). In indicating Cholly's freedom, the narrator (Claudia McTeer) hints that he is free enough to once defy against the white *sirs* and "killed three white men" (125). Yet, to be rid of his past childhood memories and frustrations, it seems that he needs to repeat the same pattern of sexuality abusing a person with lower social status, such as a girl like Darlene, as what he did as a helpless boy. The girl he chooses is no one else but a more distressed being, Pecola. Both Pauline and Pecola are victims of Cholly's abuse. They are both victims of discrimination based on gender. Alice Walker not only points the finger at black men, she also says: "It was at the Radcliffe symposium that I saw that black women are more loyal to black men than they are to themselves, a dangerous state of affairs that has its logical end in self-destructive behaviour" (318).

In *The Bluest Eye*, Pauline is more loyal to Cholly than she is to herself and this more loyalty as well as self-hatred eventually ends in her own and her daughter's destruction. She endures Cholly's wild and abusive behaviour despite the fact that she is often beaten up and abused by him. Religion becomes Pauline's means of controlling and using her family to boost her faltering self-esteem. Embracing the role of "martyr," Pauline resorts to Christian beliefs to justify the neglect of her own family: "Holding Cholly as a model of sin and failure, she bore him like a crown of thorns, and her children like a cross" (126-27). "She needed Cholly's sin desperately. The lower he sank, the wilder and more irresponsible he became, the more splendid she and her task became. In the name of Jesus." (42) One of instances which reveal Pauline's greater loyalty to Cholly is when Pauline gets angry with the first white woman she works for as a servant. The white woman is determined to persuade Pauline to leave Cholly. Upon the dilemma of leaving her abusive and alcoholic husband or leaving the white family that offers employment on the condition of Pauline's divorce, Pauline chooses to give up the job. Pauline contemplates on Mrs. Fisher and Cholly: "She said she would let me stay if I left him. I thought about that, but later on it didn't seem none too bright for a black woman to leave black man for a white woman" (94).

Pecola Breedlove as the protagonist undergoes a remarkable personal change. She evolves from an innocent little girl to becoming insane. An incident at Mrs. Breedlove's workplace starts Pecola's journey from being an innocent, troubled little girl to becoming insane. While Pauline is downstairs collecting the laundry, Pecola accidentally knocks over a blueberry cobbler. Instead of comforting Pecola, Mrs. Breedlove scolds her. She hits Pecola and calls her a crazy fool before she walks over and comforts the Fisher girl. Even the fact that the white girl can call her Polly while Pecola has to call her Mrs. Breedlove signals her mother's preference for the white girl. Furthermore Pauline does not seem to want to acknowledge that Pecola is her daughter:

> "Pick up that wash and get on out of here, so I can get this mess cleaned up." . . . As Pecola put the laundry bag in the wagon we could hear Mrs. Breedlove hushing and soothing the tears of the little pink-and-yellow girl. . . . "Who were they, Polly?" "Don't worry none, baby." She whispered, and the honey in her words complemented the sundown spilling on the lake. (85)

An already troubled girl, she once again gets proof that she is neither loved nor wanted. To be rejected by the person who should love Pecola the most must have had a detrimental effect on her already frail self-esteem. As a result of Pauline's indifference to Pecola, she aligns herself with white beauty standards to be loved by her parents and by black community. But what finally drives Pecola to insanity is being raped by her father and becoming pregnant by him. This rape of his daughter (twice) is linked with his childhood trauma, with being raped culturally by two white hunters. He takes out his childhood trauma on her daughter who is absolutely helpless and weaker than him. When Pecola has gone mad we learn that Mrs. Breedlove's betrayal may be equal to Mr. Breedlove's abuse. Pecola told her about the rape and Mrs. Breedlove did not believe her. Instead of helping, Pauline beat her and almost killed her. The audience realizes that Pecola was not just raped once, but that it happened twice. Pauline allowed the abuse to continue because she did not possess the ability to break away from her husband. She had no one to turn to and nowhere to go. Because of Pauline's compulsory loyalty to Cholly, Pecola speaks to her imaginary friend about it after she has gone insane:

> *I wonder what it would be like.* Horrible. *Really?* Yes. Horrible. *Then why didn't you tell Mrs. Breedlove?* I did tell her! *I don't mean the first time. I mean the second time when you were sleeping on the couch.* I wasn't sleeping! I was reading! *You don't have to shout.* You don't understand anything do you? She didn't even believe me when I told her. *So why didn't you tell her about the second time?* She wouldn't have believed me then either. *You're right. No use in telling her when she wouldn't believe you.* (158)

Racism is defined as discrimination or prejudice against a person or group based on their race. In *The Bluest Eye,* Pecola is victimized by different types of racism. In general sense of racism, she is pressed by white community due to her black race. For instance, when Pecola walks to the grocery store to buy Mary Janes candy, she encounters "the total absence of human recognition, the glazed separateness" (36). Mr. Yacobowski cannot acknowledge Pecola's presence as a subject because he simply cannot look at her, "How can a fifty-two-year old white immigrant storekeeper . . . see a little black girl?" (36)

Pecola is also victimized by internalized racism which results from the psychological programming by which a racist society indoctrinates people of colour to believe in white superiority. Pecola as a young black girl can't see her own beauty is trapped in this kind of racism. She believes she would be pretty, happy and loved if only she had blue eyes:

> Each night without fail, she prayed for blue eyes. Fervently, for a year she had prayed. Although somewhat discouraged, she was not without hope. To have something as wonderful as that happen would take a long, long time. Thrown in this way, into the biding conviction that only a miracle could relieve her, she would never know her beauty. She would only see what there was to see: the eyes of other people. (35)

One of the points Morrison is making is that the self-contempt and self-hatred cannot end until African-Americans view themselves differently. As long as Pecola achieves her value through the judgements of others she will feel like she is not beautiful and worthy. The novel demonstrates a remarkable attempt to tackle the complex symbolism behind this ritualized valuing of blue eyes and blonde hair. Through the tragic narrative of protagonist Pecola and her quest for blue eyes, Morrison explores damaging assumptions of immutable inferiority forcibly imposed upon the Black female body.

Alice Walker, in reaction to idealizing and valuing white beauty standards such as blonde hair, blue eyes and straight hair, says: "once you dread your hair, everything falls into place. I could not have written *The Temple of My Familiar* with straight hair, what I call 'oppressed hair.' I would like to say to other Black women looking at me and my hair. . . . You don't have to be afraid . . . you can just be free" (Byrd & Tharps, 127). Black women were expected to straighten their hair as a measure of white modernity and cleanliness. Alice Walker in her statement motivates black women to love themselves and their cultures and not to trap themselves in white beauty standards.

In *The Bluest Eye*, Pecola starts a process of enchantment with white beauty when she spends a short time in Claudia's family. She lives with the McTeers after her father sets the house on fire. At Claudia's house, Pecola's association with white supremacist aesthetic values and capitalist society's ideals begins with her admiration of young white artist Shirley Temple, whose beauty and blue eyes become extremely appealing to her. Claudia says: "we knew she was fond of the Shirley Temple cup and took every opportunity to drink milk out of it just to handle and see sweet Shirley's face" (23). Pecola's identification with Shirley Temple's beauty and blue eyes leads her to reach the dangerous conclusion that she and her family are ugly and that if she had blue eyes her life and her family would be beautiful. She feels so miserable that, in order to cease that distressing feeling, she will have to find a way to possess blue eyes. Claudia tells that it occurs to Pecola, from time to time, that if her eyes were different, beautiful,

> she herself would be different. . . . If she looked different, beautiful, maybe Cholly—her father—would be different, and Mrs. Breedlove too. Maybe they'd say, why, look at pretty-eyed Pecola. We mustn't do bad things in front of those pretty eyes. (46)

She takes solace in eating the candy, but more importantly, in symbolically digesting the smiling picture of the blue-eyed, blonde-hair little girl on the wrapper, "She eats the candy, and its sweetness is good. To eat the candy is somehow to eat the eyes, eat Mary Jane. Love Mary Jane. Be Mary Jane" (38). In this process, Pecola chooses and internalizes within herself the values of white superiority values. To Pecola, blue eyes, blonde hair and white skin stand for beauty, which leads to happiness. Thus she lives a life of self-hatred, and inevitable destruction. It is difficult to fault the young girl for this misinterpretation. In *The Bluest Eye*, Morrison presents the whole community as having taken the white criteria of beauty for their own.

> Adult, older girls, shops, magazines, newspapers, windows' signs, all the world had agreed that a blue-eyed, yellow-haired, pink-skinned doll was what every girl child treasured. (14)

Pecola is not alone in the internalization of the white-defined standard of female beauty. This phenomenon is also tangible in Pauline's preference for the little white girl to her own daughter, Pecola. Pauline gives up on her own family and takes refuge in the soft beauty surrounding the Fishers' home. When she speaks to Pecola and her friends, her voice is like "rotten pieces of apple, but when she speaks to the white girl, her voice is like honey." (78)

Internalized racism often results in intra-racial racism, which refers to discrimination within the black community against those with darker skin and more African features. We see this phenomenon illustrated in *The Bluest Eye* when Pecola is treated unfairly by other black children and even by her own mother for having darker skin, while another black child, the light-skinned Maureen Peal, is treated by the same black youngsters as if she were superior to them. Pecola's victimization stems from the inter-racial and intra-racial bias she has to face within her black community. Pecola's existence becomes severely complex because, on the one hand, she is oppressed by the white world and, on the other, the conflicting black community does not help her overcome her identity crisis.

Pressed by the two cultures, especially by the concept of beauty subscribed to by the black neighbourhood, Pecola's uncritical encounter with the two worlds intensifies her identity crisis. The instances of intensification in Pecola's identity, self and humanity crisis will be related to the intra-racial conflicts she has to deal with in her own black community. These problems derive from the wrong views these black people have of beauty, by means of which they judge others. For instance, at school, classmates and teachers ignore Pecola and antagonize her simply because she is ugly. Teachers do not look at her and, when schoolmates want to be particularly offensive to a boy, they say: "Bobby loves Pecola Breedlove" (46). On the street, Pecola is also insulted because she is not beautiful. For instance, beautiful young mulatto Maureen Peal cries at her: "and you ugly! Black and ugly e mos, I am cute." (73) Later, at Louis Junior's house, light-skinned Geraldine finds Pecola playing with her son and insults her because of her darker skin: "You nasty little black bitch. Get out of my house" (92). These light or dark-skinned blacks, the teachers, the boys, Maureen and Geraldine are also influenced by Anglo-American values and therefore, victimize Pecola and make fun of her ugliness, from the experience they have with white beauty. Thus, oppressed by the beauty conflicts she has to deal within the black community, Pecola, later, re-addresses her search for identity, self and humanity and naively aligns herself with the white world. As she does not find sensitive and civilized living within the black community, she embraces the white world, hoping she will find it there. In her mind, she wants something only the white world can give her: blue eyes, and the elimination of her ugliness. She believes that this sort of trade is possible, but this is not as simple as that. Pecola's submission to the Anglo-American ideals of beauty is neither a simplistic attempt to get rid of her ugliness, nor an emancipatory way to buy sensitive and civilized living, it is the way she trades identity, self and humanity for beauty. Finally, impressed by both inter-racial and intra-racial bias, she goes mad believing that she possesses blue eyes.

DuBois defines 'double consciousness' as a dual positioning—as Black and as American—a duplicated awareness loaded with the angst of living in the American world which "yields him no true self-consciousness, but only lets him see himself through the revelation of the other world" (364). He characterizes the Black two-ness as: "an American, a Black; two souls, two thoughts, two unreconciled strivings; two warring ideals in one dark body, whose dogged strength alone keeps it from being asunder" (364-65). The central point in DuBois' words is that the American Black wants to exist completely and live fully, as Black and as American, with no unbeatable constraints to professional gains, personal self-realization and emotional affirmation.

In the African-American literary tradition, writers in general, and women writers in particular, create special strategies to deal with the American Blacks' double-consciousness. In their works, Toni Morrison and Alice Walker associate the Black two-ness with womanism and its conceptual and practical implications. In her insightful essay *In Search of Our Mothers' Gardens* (1983), Alice Walker defines "womanism" as the way black women draw attention to their racial selfhood, identity and energies. She explains that "womanism" has to do with the black woman who displays "outrageous, audacious, courageous or willful behaviour," wants "to know more and in greater depth than is considered 'good' for one" and is "interested in grown up doings" (11). Walker also reminds us that a womanist is "a woman who loves other women, sexually and/or non-sexually. Appreciates and prefers women's culture, women's emotional flexibility, and women's strength, . . . Committed to survival and wholeness of entire people, male and female. . . . Loves struggle, Loves the Folk, Loves herself. Regardless" (11).

In this section, the article argues that whether or not in their specific moments of their lives, female Blacks, in their quest for self-realization behave as different stances of Alice Walker's womanistic ideals. In *The Bluest Eye*, Pecola represents the combination of womanistic two-ness with a personal search for identity, self and humanity. During her search, she develops an uncritical submission to the values of white beauty and abandons black culture. Her naive attitudes toward the ideals of the white world echoes the intellectual Blacks's deferential disposition toward the Western parent, the attitude West claims to be inadequate for a Black. Pecola aligns herself with whiteness and unwisely associates her search for identity, self and humanity with the aesthetic values of Anglo-American culture. She innocently believes that she can fuse white beauty with her black body and life simply through a strong desire to possess blue eyes. The result of her wrong aesthetic investment is the devastating consequence of her dream, which make her succumb to the damaging effects of the white values, which systematically deny black identity, self and humanity. In her quest for the ideals of the beauty sponsored by the white world, Pecola goes through a psychological imbalance and her madness defers her dream of building her own sort of identity, self and humanity. Though deferred and symbolized in a naïve womanistic "outrageous, audacious, courageous or wilful behaviour," (11) to use Walker's words, Pecola's dream of sensitive and civilized living, associated with an uncritical quest for beauty, does not seem to have been in vain, or useless, for those who know her in the black community, as Claudia wishes to tell us:

> All of us—all who knew her—felt so wholesome after we cleaned ourselves on her. We were so beautiful when we stood astride her ugliness. Her simplicity decorated us, her guilt sanctified us, her pain made us glow with health, her awkwardness made us think we had some sense of humour. Her inarticulateness made us believe we were eloquent. Her poverty kept us generous. (205)

What Claudia seems to be telling us is crucial: that Pecola's search for identity, self and humanity, the madness resulting from her tragic plight, and uncritical submission to the standards of beauty valued in black and white worlds, allow black community to re-elaborate a conscious evaluation of both Pecola's experiences and its own black image. Pecola strategically aligned herself with white supremacist ideals of beauty, assumed the spell of the blue eyes, was unable to integrate the black and white worlds and was used by her community as a tragic instance of black self-image.

Different from Pecola who perished under the enchantment of whiteness, Claudia and Frieda MacTeer strongly allied themselves with their Black culture and theology, sacrificed their insertion in the white world and, therefore, consciously refused to integrate the two worlds. Claudia and Frieda MacTeer are impulsive characters. They assert their beliefs rather than fawning upon others' fixed ideas. Claudia felt discomfort when she was given a blue-eyed baby doll because if she tried to take the role as a mother of the doll, it was so hard, sharp, and cold to hug or sleep with. However, she knew that all the other people believed that the doll was exactly what she wanted. So she was bewildered, frustrated and tried to "examine it to see what it was that all the world says was lovable" (21). She broke the doll apart to discover why everyone says, "pretty" to the doll or white girls but not to her. In other words, she dismembered the white baby dolls which represented not only the white standard of beauty but also the white domination of society over the black community.

When Claudia and Frieda see that Pecola is bullied by nasty boys, they fight against the boys without fear in a hand-to-hand battle, and then when they see Maureen harass Pecola, they join forces against her. Even though they are astonished by Maureen's devastating confidence in her own predominance, their self-esteem does not waver. On seeing that Pecola herself is just folding into herself and doing nothing, Claudia and Frieda feel irritated. While they grasp Pecola's grief, her pain antagonizes them and they "wanted to open her up, crisp her edges, ram a stick down that hunched and curving spine, force her to stand erect and spit the misery out on the streets" (73). Claudia and Frieda's anger stem from their self-love or self-affirmation and they believe these concepts should be equal among their folks. They believe in their value standards, and their own worth, so they try to analyze and fight against the absurd value standards of beauty and justice. They do not like Saturdays because they feel miserable when they have to take a bath. They were still in love with themselves at that time: "We felt comfortable in our skins, admired our dirt, and could not understand this unworthiness. Jealousy we understood and thought natural—a desire to have what somebody else had; but envy was a strange, new feeling for us" (4). In the novel, When Pecola's pregnancy reveals the cruelty and irresponsibility of the black community, Claudia and Frieda listen to any adult to express compassion or sorrow for Pecola,

> They were disgusted, amused, shocked, outraged, or even excited by the story. But we listened for the one who would say, "Poor little girl," or, "Poor baby," but there was only head-wagging where those words should have been. We looked for eyes creased with concern, but saw only veils. (190)

In their innocence, an innocence which they will lose, Claudia and Frieda decide to help Pecola. They are unaware of their powerlessness, "Our limitations were not known to us—not then" (191). They have developed strategies to deal with and defend themselves against the adult world: "we had become headstrong, devious and arrogant. Nobody paid us any attention, so we paid very good attention to ourselves" (191). They are also unaware that in helping Pecola and preserving her baby they are asserting their own value and their own beauty. To help Pecola and her baby, they agree to sacrifice something important to them, so they plant the money they collected and the marigold seeds, thereby giving up their hopes of getting a bicycle.

Claudia and Frieda can be considered as perfect examples of womanistic characters, as successful characters in following different instances of Walker's womanistic ideals. For example, the dismemberment of the white doll by Claudia, Claudia and Frieda's reactions to nasty boys as well as Maureen who bully Pecola, display Walker's womanistic ideal that both are "outrageous, audacious, courageous and wilful" in their behaviour. Their anger at Pecola's grief, their insistence on forcing her to be erect as well as their insistence on feeling comfortable in their skins represent Walker's womanistic ideals that both "love other women sexually or non-sexually" as well as both "Love the Folk, Love themselves." Their innocent act of burying the marigold seeds and money to save Pecola's baby denotes Walker's womanistic ideal that they are both "committed to survival and wholeness of entire people, male and female."

In opposition to Claudia and Frieda who were successful in following Walker's womanistic ideals to love both themselves and Pecola, Pauline Breedlove failed to follow Walker's womanistic ideals because she found no way to fight against the impoverishment and loneliness given by her idle and drunken husband, by her white hostess who owed her eleven dollars, by the community members' unfriendliness and by the white ideal she could never attain. Thus she could only hate herself, her husband and children. Pecola did not possess a mother who taught her self-love because even the mother was also the victim of her immediate environment, which finally pushed her to disguise her blackness by taking refuge in the white master's home. In short, both Pauline and Pecola were victimized by racist and sexist crises in the novel for defying Walker's womanistic ideals. In contrast, both Claudia and Frieda managed to survive the racist crises through their womanistic behaviour.

In *The Bluest Eye* Pecola aligns herself with whiteness and unwisely associates her search for identity, self and humanity with the aesthetic values of Anglo-American culture. She defies Walker's womanistic ideals and naively gives up her black body and life simply through a strong desire to possess blue eyes. The result of her wrong aesthetic investment is the devastating consequence of her dream, which make her succumb to the damaging effects of the white values, which systematically deny black identity, self and humanity. In contrast, Claudia and Frieda MacTeer in their quest for self-realization behave as different stances of Alice Walker's womanistic ideals. They assert their beliefs rather than fawning upon others' fixed ideas. Thus they can cope with problems and eventually survive.

Works Cited

Byrd, A.D., L.L. Tharps (2001). *Untangling the roots of black hair in America*, New York: St. Martin's Griffin Press.

DuBois, W.E.B (1993). "The Souls of Black Folk." In Krumholtz.

Morrison, Toni (1970). *The Bluest Eye*, New York: Plume, 1994.

Walker, Alice (1984). *In Search of Our Mothers' Gardens*. San Diego, New York, London: Harcourt Brace Jovanovich.

Identity in Alice Walker's *The Color Purple* A Postmodern Reading

MARYAM SARABI and FARZAD NAVABAKHSH
Islamic Azad University, Arak Branch, Iran

This paper will demonstrate that the traditional and highly valued frames of reference in terms of which people could define themselves and their place in society have been removed. Identity is now multi-faceted and constantly reconstructed by choice. This have increasingly resulted fragmented and unstable identities leading to an inevitable breakdown in social relationships and sanity. As it was seen in the novel, *The Color Purple*, there is a chaotic situation in which characters are wandering around and have no specific values to stick to. Within such community people are lost. Even, it was indicated that the family which is the basic constitution in the society is not worthy any more. Marriage has no more value like before because people are hollow and don't care; humanity is dead. Individuals' identities in traditional societies were fixed and stable, as Kellner states: "According to anthropological folklore, in traditional societies, one's identity was fixed, solid, and stable. In modernity, identity became more mobile but was still relatively substantial and fixed. Identity still came from a circumscribed set of roles." (126) Therefore, postmodernism has destroyed traditional identity and the notion of identity has differed a lot in postmodernism.

Modernism claims, what individuals call the self was seen as an independent or autonomous subject. Grenz states, Descartes himself ended by defining the human being as a thinking substance and the human person as an autonomous rational subject (83). Because individuals are related to others in social systems, they cannot be autonomous. They are social beings and can answer their needs by relationships. Middleton states: "Rising media's influence has created a situation where once proud self-centred ego is no longer that autonomous subjects, who can sovereignly, set processes in motion and who can also, at a moment of his choice, stop these processes again. Rather the modern self is now caught in the predicament of being managed rather than being the manager." (50) Therefore, individuals are caught in the network of rules they make; so-called modern folks have no way to escape the illusion of their own thoughts.

Individuals are drowned in a postmodern identity crisis of great scopes by the fall of the modern belief of the self and the loss of their fixed modern self-image. The traditional basis of identity was opinions, as Huntington states, "for people facing the need to determine who I am? Where do I belong? Religion provides compelling answers"? (97) Consequently, within such postmodern community, there is no truth, so, belief becomes a subject of individual choice and all beliefs become the same in significance. There is an anarchic condition in the novel, in which individuals are wandering around and have no specific values to stick to, and some individuals are lost and have no values to live for. People are detached from their origin and isolated from their society, since home is a transitory place with only short-term stability. Celie's sister Nettie, in the novel, *The Color Purple*, is a typical person who is separated from her own root and country. She runs away from home and comes to live with Celie and Mister. Nettie is very beautiful, and Mister finds her very attractive. He makes many passes at Nettie, but she simply ignores him. Finally, he kicks Nettie out of the house. She has joined a Christian missionary group that has gone to Africa to Christianize the natives. In fact, Nettie changed the route of her life.

Squeak's new identity was shaped partly due to the rape of warden, and her being lonely in such tough life. Even such a modern American society provokes women to get far from their human values and sell themselves at a really cheap price, and this is the cost of such avant-garde society of the new century. In the pivotal dinner scene, when Celie and Squeak announce that they have decided to forge new identities by leaving their husbands, they refuse to conform to the old patriarchal order. Celie stabs Mr.____ when he tries to slap her (271) and Squeak demands that she be called by her proper name: "Listen Squeak, say Harpo. You can't go to Memphis. That's all there is to it. Mary Agnes, say Squeak. Squeak, Mary Agnes, what difference do it make? It makes a lot, say Squeak. When I was Mary Agnes I could sing in public" (110). The final pages of the novel are spent in dramatizing the positive aspects of society, by incorporating and revitalizing the social values and institutions in light of the new order (Bloom 74).

Celie's new identity has been formed within the passage of time, and her experience, and the sort of people she had dealt with. When Shug asks her what she thinks, Celie's immediate response abnegates her previous annihilation and ignorance of her body: "It mine, I say" (80). In discovering and accepting with pride her own body, Celie initiates a desire for selfhood. Next she begins to find an identity through a network of female relationships with Shug, Nettie (whose letters she soon discovers), Sofia, and Mary Agnes. With her newfound identity, Celie is able to break free from the masculine prohibition against speech and to join a community of women, thus freeing herself from dependence on and subjection to male brutality (5-6).

To define identity, postmodernism has destroyed traditional identity. Postmodernism believes that there is no objective reality and with it the concept of an objective self. Because there is no truth, there can be no true me, just a version of me. Identity has become a matter of choice. Individuals can be whom they want at any given time or position. In a postmodern world, there is an anarchic condition which puts people under frustration. It was indicated in the novel that Celie did not even know what was done to her, not to mention discern the validity of what she was told by Pa after the rape, that her telling of what Pa had done to her would kill her mother. Fonso, Celie's stepfather, doesn't care about the life of his daughter. With Celie's first anguished letter to God, Walker enables the reader to enter into the private thoughts and emotional state of her traumatized, guilt- and shame-ridden, and depressed fourteen-year-old protagonist, who has been repeatedly raped and impregnated by the man (Alphonso) whom she believes to be her biological father: "Dear God, I am fourteen years old. I have always been a good girl. Maybe you can give me a sign letting me know what is happening to me." (1) Celie draws a line through "I am" and writes "I have always been a good girl," because the child victim of rape and incest often blames herself for her trauma; or, worse still, believes that this bad thing has happened to her because she is bad and therefore deserves it. Celie writes to God because she is ashamed of what is happening to her and because of the threat from Alphonso that immediately precedes Celie's first letter: "You better not never tell nobody but God. It'd kill your mammy." (1) (Bloom 93)

Individuals choose their identity by choosing an image, and images are associated with daily life. Though blood sister, Celie and Nettie are very different from each other in personality. Celie is uneducated, learns from experience, enjoys sewing and cooking, and is always associated with the image of the house, for example Celie writes to Nettie: "I sit here in this big house by myself trying to sew, but what good is sewing gon do? What good is anything? Being alive begin to seem like a awful strain" (262), while Nettie is intelligent, learns from books, enjoys reading and education, and is always associated with the image of the world. The pure pleasure Nettie derives from reading Blackness from a proper and sanctified point of view is the affective origin of the specifically nationalist politics previously repressed in *The Color Purple*: what hope and uplift can Africans all over the world take from their common field of history? (Bloom 33) And when Samuel and Corrine ask Nettie if she would like to join them in their African missionary enterprise, Nettie accepts, "But only if they would teach me everything they knew to make me useful as a missionary . . . and my real education began at that time." (138)

In the postmodern world, people have lost their identities, everything does not go as it ought to be, and everything is upside down. Since postmodern identity is about constructing an image by choice, it follows that individuals' identity is not fixed; since they are free to change their minds. To select a new image and adopt a new identity, as my identity does not represent a 'fundamental me; I can have more than one identity, depending on my thoughts.' Middleton claims, "We are inundated by a multiplicity of clamoring voices proffering alternative identities. This inevitably results in us making different choices." (50) Identity is frequently varying as Schrang declares, "The self is multiplicity, heterogeneity, difference, and ceaseless becoming" (37). According to Schrang, the story of the self is an upwarding story, a story subject to a creative advance, where the past stands open to new interpretations. Identity is not fixed but dynamic, ever changing to suit the fashions.

Identity provides an arrangement for individuals' associations with others. How they see themselves will affect how they relate to others. If individuals see themselves as weak; then they are more likely to allow others to oppress and manipulate them, then they would if they see themselves as strong. Individuals can identify their place in the society by knowing who they are. If this is uncertain, there is a threat that social order will collapse, which is possibly one reason that has led to the social breakdown clear at the end of the twentieth century.

As it was indicated in the novel, individuals are unaware of their real self, and this gives them a weaker understanding of themselves. Celie, the main character in the novel, is weak because she imposes weakness on herself and at those moments others such as Pa and Mister manipulate her. Kate, one of Albert's sisters, convinces him of Celie's need for clothes and takes her to a store to select cloth so that a dress can be made: "you got to fight them, Celie, she say. I can't do it for you. You got to fight them for yourself. I don't say nothing. I think bout Nettie, dead. She fight, she run away. What good it do? I don't fight, I stay where I'm told. But I'm alive" (22). This weakness is the result of people's failure in understanding their true position within the society they are dwelling. Individuals are psychologically distorted as the outcome of the nature of postmodern world, and they live in illusion rather than reality. They try to escape their distress in different ways such as drinking and smoking a lot of reefer; but, they do not seem to get a way out of it.

In *Discipline and Punish* and *The History of Sexuality*, Foucault examines identity and its relationship with the power. Foucault believes that power-knowledge's ubiquity avoids any expectation that the self can exist outside of it. Moreover, the self is frequently divided and formed by its procedures. Although, as power-knowledge encounters selves, it is in turn affected and redirected by them. Power is not wholly repressive and ruling, as the self cannot be a non-discursive unit that draws the unchanging result of discourse. Power comes from everywhere, and everyone in discourse. It is dispersed throughout the whole society. In the novel, power is omnipresent in the hands of every character; nevertheless, the ways individuals apply them are different. For example, Mister has his own way of applying power which is defined according to his situation in the public. The changeability of power relations and the probable system of different arrangements seem to all but hold the self from reflectively directing discourse. Foucault's given name for this prima facie inability to act as a unified, conscious self in power-knowledge is the 'docile body.' 'Docile body' asks for what kind of, and how much agency one may be capable. That is, every one can be simply controlled within the society and the network of relation (135-40).

Foucault asserts that discourse is both productive and oppressive. Since the conditionality of restrictions is related to changing shapes of discourse, he seeks to study the notion of aesthetics, an ethic of the self that is the method of fashioning oneself and studying knowledge. The self is what referred to as aesthetic practice. Because power is not something bad in itself from which one must free one's self (Simon 100). But if the individual understands that it is the process through which selves try to control and direct the actions of other selves, power is a relationship, and as a result changes in power as they might expect occur.

In the novel, Mister abuses power and makes power rather horrible and as power is a connection it changes with different citizens. By living in a society, their actions influence and control others automatically. The way Sofia deals Harpo gives another change in the method of the action of power. Celie is also attracted to her stepdaughter-in-law, Sofia, an Amazon who refuses to be dominated by her husband, Harpo. But an independent woman has a more difficult time than one who meekly accepts her meagre lot in life. Ironically, Harpo wants Sofia to act like the submissive Celie: "I want her to do what I say, like you do for Pa. . . . But not Sofia. She do what she want, don't pay me no mind at all. I try to beat her, she black my eyes. Oh, boo-hoo, he cry." (66) Even though he loves Sofia, Harpo's marriage is troubled because society has taught him that this is not the way a woman should behave (Bloom 72). People control and affect each other in both constructive and unconstructive ways.

According to Foucault, the practice of subjectification/ identity is dangerous because it most often leads to normative practices that regulate people, as they dictate limits and truth that should be disobeyed. He assumes, "we have to promote new forms of subjectivity through the refusal of these kinds of individuality." (1982: 216) Foucault refers to this disobedience as the practice of liberty. He shows that the subject is immanent within the limits of discursiveness, but irreducible to them. How people object to the society through their style of fashioning or art is a way for asserting their liberty.

Foucault's claim of selfhood, of displaying a degree of independence, as entangled in the actions of discursiveness, becomes even more apparent. Discourse and self influence each other too much in which the self is defined according to the discourse and it is discourse which gives value and meaning to the self. In fact, identity is not simply immersed in discourse but discourse is the condition of possibility of the self and the self is the condition of possibility of discourse. Therefore, it is meaningful to get them mutually and not independently. As it was seen in the novel, Mister has the kind of self which is defined according to the discourse of masculinity, but for Sofia the self is defined according to the discourse of feminism. Another instance is Fonso's self that is defined according to the discourse of patriarchy.

Foucault makes use of the insight of conditions of possibility and the insight of immanent irreducibility to assert that there is an essential causing of a self by virtue of a level of logically coherent conditions that can never logically be met and there are limits, as conditions of possibility, given rise to by the equation known as discourse. It is associated with an abstract domain of possible curves that can pass through a singular point. In fact, according to Foucault, the singular point takes the place of self, not in the sense of an atomistic metaphysical unit but an undefined nodule of activity and affectation. Therefore, the self is both a nodule of activity and affection. A nodule of affectation is suitable with what discourse does and what problems do. A nodule of activity corresponds more with solutions and theories. Individuals are supposed to keep in mind that problems are not merely negative. They identify the self with problems as they apparently identified the self with a solution.

The self is not just equivalent to a solution. As a solution, the self is always problematized. Certainly, situations have major function in defining self. In the novel, individuals go through different actions and their fortune is determined with the situations they are entangled in. Celie, Shug and Mary Agnus each separately have different selves and problems they face. It is these solutions which put them in special defined self. Individuals know that even problems make some people go in negative manners or some others in the positive behaviours. Celie goes the wrong way and Shug follows to satisfy her needs and desires.

Foucault makes declarations about relations of power/ knowledge without ever having to define exactly where and how far those relations broaden. A consistency of one or the other, equivalent to the self at one moment realizing all possibilities, forms at the same time a specific arrangement to discourse or the solution to the equation. That is, the relationship of power/ knowledge is changed into new possibilities for the self and guarantees its reality. By more entangling of power/ knowledge, the self turns into more restricted and dominated. By more power, knowledge can be made decisive, this makes the more possibilities for the self (Mills 67-79). Therefore, when the relationship of power and knowledge is too much fixed, individuals are more under observation and monitor. This is a reason for individuals to escape the stress of the public.

In fact, the self may become identified through its procedures and divisions with solutions more than problems. The method of the self contains a dialogic process whose usefulness is dependent upon the allegorical ability of a master, instructor, and the like. In this hermeneutical process are regulative ideas that fashion the self and involve it in games of truth and confidence. This regular dialogic process involves the frequent questioning and demanding of truths and limits. While the discourses change with each culture or situation, afterward, the limitations and margins change too. Therefore, individuals cannot expect a universally defined self, because the relations and problems vary from one society to another. In the novel, Celie's self in Memphis and her role and the kind of life she had there shows total differences of discourse or relations. Shug says that Celie will accompany her to Memphis; Albert forbids it and asks why, hurt that he is not going with Shug. Celie's pent-up wrath explodes at Albert:

> I thought you was finally happy, he say. What wrong now?
>
> You a lowdown dog is what's wrong, I say. It's time to leave you and enter into the creation. And your dead body just the welcome mat I need.
>
> Say what? he ask. Shock.
>
> All round the table folkses mouths be dropping open.
>
> You took my sister Nettie away from me, I say. And she the only person love me in the world. . . .
>
> Sofia so surprise to hear me speak up she ain't chewed for ten minutes. (181)

After this Celie and Shug go to Memphis, and Celie's business increases to the point that she is self-supporting and an employer. Albert pushes far past the point of rebellion; he does not count on the strength the women find through each other (Bloom 170-71).

Celie is surprised with her new freedom because she has been imprisoned by a patriarchal system all her life since her life has been in the serving position for years. Celie makes an attempt to accompany and help Shug during her singing tour. Again, Shug suggests that Celie sew some pants while she is gone. Before long, Celie is drawing much attention from people in the pants that she designs and creates. With Shug's support, Celie launches the enterprise called Folkspants, Unlimited. Through her successful business, Celie is able to gain her financial independence from Shug and Mr.______, despite his opposition: "All you fit to do in Memphis is be Shug's maid . . . you nothing at all" (212-13). Since it is believed that women are supposed to rely on men for everything, the fact that Celie is able to make her own money means that she does not need men anymore. It is through her pants business that Celie attains her full liberation from the patriarchal system. In addition, Celie's pants business also provides her with a new identity. As a successful entrepreneur, she is no longer seen as a submissive housewife, but she is now a master of something. She does not have to live with men and do what they tell her anymore.

In the postmodern world, there is no single absolute truth, only versions of truth. It has removed any sense of absolute truth and claimed that, what individuals believe to be true is only an interpretation of reality formed by their own perspective. For Nietzsche, there is no truth as such but only relative truths for a particular society. Since knowledge is a subject of perspective interpretation, every interpretation is a lie. Nietzsche believes that our world is a work of art that is frequently being created and recreated (Simon 325-26). Foucault claims that 'the truth' was simply a version of events preferred, indeed imposed, by the dominant or ruling group in society. Outside political contests and competing wills to power there was no such thing as truth, only different versions of events. Since there are no objective realities, only versions of reality, individuals miss any tangible worldview. The postmodern critique of modernism separates us from the enlightenment model of the individual identity. In the novel, the uncertainty of speech is observable between lies and truth. Fonso wants to convince Mister into marrying Celie instead of Nettie and describes Celie in the following way:

> She ugly. . . . But she'll make the better wife. She ain't smart either, and I'll just be fair, you have to watch her or she'll give away everything you own. But she can work like a man. . . . And another thing—she tell lies. (9)

Apparently, Celie's stepfather is telling the truth, emphasizing the consistency of his words by adding further to what he is believed to reveal—Celie is dishonest. The validity of this speech is controversial because its premises are false in the first place. Fonso's "lies" are covered up by his "truth-telling" and Celie is traded like goods, "circulated in place of words, [as] objects signified." (Tucker 84) In order to be free from the patriarchal field, the first step for Celie is to distinguish between "truth" and "lies." Kauffman believes that the "scene where Sofia confronts Celie marks the beginning of Celie's transformation, for she must confront her own rage." (198) Celie does not fight, because from her experience she knows that fighting is useless. Sofia causes Celie into the discovery of herself.

Postmodernist definition of self takes doubt and disbelief to the reality of self, which is called aporia. There is a coextension of the self and the aporia. It means the irreducibility and contingency of the self in relation to the irreducibility and contingency of aporia. But individuals should not equate them. An aporia cannot be set apart from the self because of the irreducibility of aporia. It is the product of the self. The self is an undecidable aporetic because it is quasi-existent. The self is not reducible to any of its not being able to decide in aporias. It is possible and results in its being aporetic. Aporia does not set the attributes of irreducibility and contingency. It is the discovery of the self, of irreducibility and contingency. The self is the coextensive discovery of aporia. Derrida states: "The singularity of the 'who' is not the individuality of a thing that would be identical to itself; it is not an atom. It is a singularity that discloses or divides itself in gathering itself together to answer to the other." (17)

According to Derrida, the self echoes the norm of differentiation and iteration. Iteration functions to form a connection of self to the more generalized idea of systems and laws. In the novel, Squeak (Mary Agnes) changes her self because of the demands of authorities on her. In discussing the self's singularity and the metaphysical generalities in which it is involved, Derrida applies Kafka's story, 'Before the Law' (261). This story is about a man who constantly tries to gain access to the law merely to be told at the end of his life by the gatekeeper: "no one else could ever be admitted here, since this gate was made only for you. I am now going to shut it." (Beardsworth 27) To Derrida the end of the story shows the aporia of the self and its decisions made in reaction to rules, discourses and laws. It is the generality of law which makes the singularity of the self possible, as the self cannot fold upon itself. Generality admits the self's selfness. However, generality makes singularity impossible, it restrains the purity of the self's singularity and the self makes the general possible. But it is impossible by the singular. Individuals know that the self is singular but its generality is attached to the law. 'Before the Law' depicts a man who consistently tries to gain access to the law. The law is something general and it is the individuals who give the law one singularity. Derrida implies:

> In order to be responsible and truly decisive, a decision should not limit itself to putting into operation a determinable or determining knowledge, the consequence of some pre-established order. But, conversely, who would call a decision that is without rule, without norm, without determinable or determined law, a decision? (17)

Individuals know that law is something general but in the novel individuals give the law one singularity which is defined as the result of their procedures. For instance, Sofia and her treatment toward law or law's treatment toward her is different from Squeak's. Derrida shows that the crisis and problem of the self is ontological, bound to problems of justice. Law does not exist in this society because there is no obvious justice in the novel. There is a chaotic situation by not having the correct means to narrate the laws and rules. The self is both the state line of the bounds of power, its boundary, and what makes the use of power possible and its possible transgression possible. The experiential aporia can simply be experienced as forming the connection between difference and repetition of Derrida's relating the self to itself with aporia.

According to Foucault, there is the general in the singular and the singular in the general. Foucault reveals in turning toward the action of the self in the manner he does, on aporia, on the form of possibility of decisions. Foucault's look at the self and the problematic of judgments and Foucault's view towards the self leads to pessimistic activism, and exemplifies aporetic judgments and concern about aporetic irreducibility and combination of legality and justice. A judgment must arise out of an aporia in order to be freeing irreducible to power. Aporia is the state of Foucault's examination whose possibility is assured by the ontological form of the self. But its success is temporary, so frequently untrustworthy, frequently based on the forward-looking guarantee. The selves are ontological and they do anything they have in mind without restraint on the bases of their own judgments. Therefore, they are involved in their own actions. It was seen in the novel that Mister and Harpo are each separately deciding what to do and they do not succeed in their actions and not succeed to achieve their ends.

Consequently, individuals decided to be what they aim to in their own approach. Although, individuals cannot arrive at aporia or the identification of it by turning toward the self in the manner Foucault does, as a care for self is a step in the way of justice. Individuals know that the care for self is both a consideration to a care for self as such and a care for others. The care for self is mediation between self and others as they exist in the arrangement of power and knowledge. Individuals cannot find justice outside the relation of self to self which does not occur outside power or relation of self to others. In the novel, the relationship of each self to self and to others is indicated. Justice was violated because in such society there is no authentic care for each other. When in *The*

Color Purple, Celie is raped by her stepfather Alphonso, he orders her to "not never tell nobody but God. It'd kill your mammy." (11) In this threat he imposes fear and guilt of possible maternal death on the young, superstitious and psychologically naïve Celie. Alphonso silences Celie's voice. Later, when he and Albert barter for her, Alphonso again silences Celie, but this time it is her credibility, for he tells Albert, "[s]he tell lies" (18) (Bloom 164), in the novel, Alphonso thought of profit than helping her daughter out of trouble.

Foucault's essential ontological concerns are subject, power or knowledge, and truth. Ideas of justice serve to connect these three axes. Foucault (1994) argues, "My problem has always been the problem of the relationship between subject and truth." (24) His problem is concerned for justice and games of truth. Foucault is not merely speaking of the self but he speaks of the ontology of justice. The reality of law assumes the justice of any judgment. Foucault believes his problem is the connection between subject whose ontological problematic is attached to the problematic of evaluative justice and truth. Foucault's care for self is a course of impression and communication whereby the self moves loser to comprehension. His care for self is an encounter with the aporia of law and justice. Self is the core of knowledge and power. It is the central part in deciding what is to be done next. In the novel, Celie chooses to leave Mister's house and furthermore comes to understanding how to live life on her own and how to take care of others. Sofia willingly decides to punch the Mayor; however, she knows what is expecting her.

Individuals cannot remove the self from the actions in which every one tries his own separate life in a way he or she likes. People may respect rules or violate rules. Finally, they come to the understanding as they witness the results.

Thus we find that there is a chaotic situation in which people are wandering around and have no specific values to stick to. In such kind of society, identity is defined according to various discourses in different places. Postmodernism has destroyed traditional identity and the notion of identity has differed a lot in postmodernism. Consequently, nothing makes sense within such community and people are lost and have no values to live for.

Works Cited

Beardsworth, Richard. (1996) *Derrida and the Political*, London: Routledge.

Derrida, Jacques. (1992) *Acts of Literature*, ed. Derek Attridge, London: Routledge.

Derrida, Jacques. (1993) *Aporias*, trans. Thomas Dutoit, Stanford UP.

Foucault, Michel. (1982) *The Subject and Power: Beyond Structuralism and Hermeneutics*, University of Chicago Press.

______.. (1994) *The Ethic of Care for the Self as a Practice of Freedom*, trans. J.D. Gauthier, Rasmussen, London: MIT.

Grenz, Stanly, J. (1996) *A Primer on Postmodernism*, Cambridge: Eerdmans.

Huntington, Samuel. (1997) *The Clash of Civilizations and the Remaking of World Order*, South CA Publication.

Kellner, Douglas. (1992) *Popular Culture and the Construction of Identities*, Oxford: Blackwell.

Middleton, J.R. (1995) *Truth is Stranger than it used to be*, London: SPCK.

Schrang, Calvin. (1997) *The Self after Postmoderntiy*, Yale.

Simon, Jon. (1995) *Foucault and the Political*, London: Routledge.

Tucker, Lindsey. (1988). *Alice Walker's "The Color Purple": emergent woman, emergent text*. Black American Literature 22.1:81-95.

Walker, A. (1982). *The Color Purple*. New York: Pocket Books.

Narratives of the 'Silenced Women': Victims of Violence and Sexual Abuse A Study of Fiction of the Indian Subcontinent

TEJINDER KAUR
Punjabi University, Patiala

Violence against women manifesting itself in various forms such as rape, molestation, stripping, eve-teasing, abducting and kidnapping, trafficking in women, forced prostitution, domestic abuse, wife battering, harassment in the workplace and cruelties to them in various physical, emotional and psychological forms has been a global phenomenon leading to their oppression, suppression, repression, victimization and marginalization. Ann Duffy in a thought-provoking article, "The Feminist Challenge: Knowing and Ending the Violence" rightly states, "The lives of almost all women, regardless of class, caste and age, race and ethnicity, sexual orientation, ability or disability have been distorted by violence and the expectation of violence. Whether women are the actual targets of violence, live in fear of violence or live with a commitment to transcend the violence, violence permeates their life experience and sense of self" (Duffy152). Duffy further says, "Research indicates that regardless of the form that violence takes, it has a dramatic impact on its targets and leads sometimes to attempted suicide, often to withdrawal from a work situation and frequently to significant psychological effects such as depression, self-blame, and anxiety" (Duffy164).

The pain, humiliation and traumas especially of the experience of sexual violence have drastic impact not only on the material, emotional and psychic life of the victims, in social sphere too they suffer humiliation, neglect, segregation and marginalization and are treated as 'the fallen ones' though without any fault of theirs.

This victimization of women, which is "a historical reality" had not been taken "seriously for long" according to Wendy Kaminer (41) but it has drawn the attention of recent feminist analysis and action, the world over. A few literary writers too have dealt with the issue of women's sexual violence and abuse in different life experiences and have tried to peep into their inner pains and silences. In this paper I will focus on a few fictional narratives by Bhabani Bhattacharya, Kamala Markandaya, Kamala Das, Sadhu Singh Dhami, U.R. Anantha Murthy, Rohinton Mistry, Bapsi Sidhwa, Taslima Nasreen, Shobha Dè, and a few narratives on the Partition dealing with the female victims of sexual violence during Partition and communal riots, and as prostitutes, and the impact of sexual abuse on their lives and psyches.

First of all, I shall take up the narratives portraying the plight of the worst affected victims of sexual abuse, i.e., prostitutes, how they get forced to become prostitutes, the treatment meted out to them, sufferings, pain, humiliation and traumas they undergo, their status in society and their silent dreams and desires which never get materialized.

In certain life situations many young girls get compelled to go for prostitution due to hunger and poverty and to support their families. Sadhu Singh Dhami in his novel *Maluka* narrates the "heart-breaking, painful, self-destroying" woes of young girls who, during the Depression period in the USA, due to hunger went "with men just for a meal" (256). Maluka's girlfriend Doris Mitchel has to take recourse to prostitution "to provide relief to her sick mother and ageing father." In Kamala Das's story "Padmavati, the Harlot," Padmavati tells the reasons of selling her body for educating her brothers and marrying off her sisters, who now well settled have forgotten her and even do not write to her. Her silent pain and anger are given an outlet before the loafers teasing her around a temple in Tirupati. "But I am not complaining. Who can blame them? Who will want to consort with a woman like me? Only loafers like you bother to talk to me. Nobody loves me" (Das 1992:24). Ira, the daughter of Nathan and Rukmani, in Kamala Markandaya's *Nectar in a Sieve*, unable to see her child brother dying of starvation opts to earn money by selling her body "to-night, tomorrow and every night, so long as there is need" (Markandaya 99).

Bhabani Bhattacharya in his novel *So Many Hungers* projects the grim picture of the uprooted families of the villagers during the politically created Bengal famine and their young daughters being raped, molested and inducted into brothels of Calcutta for a few silver rupees. He shows the thriving of prostitution during this phase, brothels becoming "a big business" and brothel runners considering the availability and readiness of these destitute girls "a fine balance between demand and supply" since "a lot of moneyed people have a liking for these skinny girls fresh from countryside" (241). In Kamala Das's story "A Doll for the Child Prostitute" Rukmani, a twelve-year-old girl, is a new arrival in the brothel run in Bombay, who was first raped by her stepfather when her mother was away to a house in the neighbourhood and then she was sold by her own mother for "a few currency notes" when they were "practically starving at home" (1992: 68).

In many cases, the poor and orphaned girls are seduced by touts and pimps and sold to the brothels. Sita, in Das's same story, was brought to the brothel at the age of ten by a broker in the village after her parents had died of cholera and no relative took care of her. Chandar Lekha in Bhattacharya's *He who Rides a Tiger* is misled by a lady pimp on the pretext of her father's serious sickness in the city hospital where she goes to see him but where she actually lands is the brothel.

The abandoning of many girl children, because the birth of a female child is considered a burden in many Indian families, also leads to their entries into the Kothas. In Das's story "A Doll for the Child Prostitute," Mira, wrapped in an expensive silk saree, was found by Ayee, the owner of the brothel, nineteen years ago on the threshold of her door. As per the latest survey conducted by Jubilee Action, an NGO in the U.K., on the child prostitution in the world, India ranks at number one in the world, US being at number two in the number of child prostitutes where around

30,000 children are "suffering sexual abuse, which includes working in pornography."

In Shobha Dè's novel *Starry Nights*, we see how the mother of a popular film star, when her husband had left her with their three daughters and had gone to live with another woman, forced her twelve-year-old eldest daughter Vizi to first work in the blue films to get money to run the house and pay for children's fees. At the age of fifteen she makes her go to bed with every Tom, Dick and Harry in the film industry of Bombay who might help her become a film star but the daughter is shown sad and morose everytime she faces sexual assaults.

In Kamala Das's story "Kalyani," we are shown another situation where a married woman going alone in a car after dropping her husband at the office is kidnapped by goondas in the police uniform, drugged and forced to strip and sleep with a man in a dark room and made to change her name from Ammini to Kalyani. Her husband, who had been sent anonymous letters earlier informing about her immoral conduct, is called to see her with a man lying naked. She is deserted by her husband saying, "I never thought you were a prostitute" (1996: 50). The helpless woman thus gets entrapped into the fold of the mafia as Kalyani.

In many parts of India the evil of prostitution in the form of Devdasi custom still continues in spite of the ban on Devdasi system as per the Prohibition of Dedication Act of 1982. In the Hindu society, prostitutes are considered to be low-caste in the caste hierarchical order, though the upper caste men secretly and many a time openly visit them and keep them as keeps since they are only the sexual commodities to be enjoyed and not to be legally wedded. U.R. Anantha Murthy in his novel *Samskara* ironically exposes the assumed moral superiority of the upper caste Brahmins who claim to be the Samskari ones caste-wise but are actually depraved as human beings, by showing the low caste harlot Chandri as a kind-hearted human being as compared to the Brahmin men and women, but who, being the daughter of a prostitute has to continue suffering the plight of the women of her class "ever auspicious, daily-wedded, the one without widowhood," entertaining men perpetually (54).

Through these narratives of the victimized prostitutes, the writers have expressed their unease with the entire social system in which these prostitutes, pushed into sex trade because of various family and social compulsions, continue bearing exploitation, humiliation and abuse from their pimps, clients, police and local authorities. In the social set up, too many curses and stigma trail them. They are dubbed as "immoral women" without anybody caring to go back to the causes which forced them to transact their bodies, lead a pathetic life of silent suffering and humiliation day and night. These narratives of the silenced women also voice the hypocrisy and immorality of the custodians of the protection of morality of their nation, such as the religious and political leaders, police and men in power, who should be curbing the flesh trade, are, in fact the virtual owners and supporters of these brothels. It is surprising that our legal system too does not come to the relief of the prostitutes, as the prostitution law does not punish the users of prostitution service but only the service providers.

Ironically it is the brothels alone, whether they are The House of Cages in Bombay in Rohinton Mistry's *Such a Long Journey*, Hira Mandi in Lahore in Bapsi Sidhwa's *Ice-Candy Man* or the ones in Bombay and Calcutta in Das's and Bhattacharya's narratives, which emerge to be multi-ethnic, casteless and classless places where what the Ice-Candy man says "any man who has the money. . . . My cook, wrestler, Imam Din, the knife sharpener, merchants, peddlers, the governor, coolies" (24) can come to relax and enjoy by playing with women's bodies with "make-up on their faces and flowers in their hair." But that "using their bodies as rinds has killed their spirits" (Das 1992: 85) nobody cares to notice and feel. In many Hindi movies also such as 'Mandi,' 'Tawaif,' 'Mausam,' 'Umrao Jaan,' the problems and silences of the prostitutes have been highlighted.

These silenced women too have "a homing desire" and dreams to lead a settled and respectable life of love and dignity but most of them do not want to go back to their homes to which they once belonged because they know their families will not accept them. Sita in Das's story, who dies a premature death because of an unhygienic abortion performed on her, wished "to have a home of my own" "a plump baby to dandle on my knee" and "to smile at me and call me Ma" but she was so sick of the sexual assaults on her that she did not "want to have any man in my house" (Das 1992: 84). Rukmani looks for her "misplaced father" in the fifty-five old police inspector, the friend of the brothels, calling her "Papa" and asks him to take her away from here "otherwise she will die" while he remains busy fondling her body. Meera, the most beautiful girl of the brothel, runs away with her client, a college boy named Krishna, in the hope of settling down with him as a married woman but returns disillusioned after seven days after being exploited by him physically, emotionally and financially. Ayee too wants to leave everything in the hands of Saraswati or Mira and go to Benaras to the home of the Lord but what happens to such women at religious places we come to know through the fate of Padmavati, who can offer nothing but only her body to the lord of the temple. Doris Mitchel too finds her dreams "shattered" and feels, "in fact, no dream is left" but still she wants to cherish the fleeting moment of Maluka's love which would give her strength to "face the wilderness of life, where there is no love, no friend, no home" for the likes of her (Dhami 263). Chandri too wants to become a mother and educate her children, though she knows her fate is fixed in this caste order. Though these victimized and marginalized women have tender feelings, desires and dreams but they find themselves entrapped in the given life of rut and hurt from which there is no escape for them and they keep on suffering mutely.

Now a brief analysis of the narratives on Partition which reflect the pains and silences of women on whom violence and sexual abuse were inflicted during the Partition which Mushirul Hasan calls "an epic-human tragedy and a man-made catastrophe" (10) and the immediate post-Partition period when the two independent nations, India and Pakistan, were in the process of getting formed and reconstructing themselves. In fact, it was not only during this period in the history of the Indian subcontinent alone that women suffered sexual violence and humiliation, rather during all kinds of communal and ethnic riots all over the world the lot of women has remained the same: "in times of communal strife and violence, women essentially remain non-violent and are at the receiving end of violence as victims, and . . . they are left with the task of rebuilding the community" but their "stories of humiliation and horrific suffering" remain historically silent because of "familial silence" on these matters, says Urvashi Butalia (180 and199). "Society still enjoins upon them [the abducted women] the silence of the dead around an event that, to it, was shameful and humiliating in its consequences," comment Ritu Menon and Kamla Bhasin (234). During such times, women belonging to one religious community are abducted and molested by men folk of the rival religious and ethic groups.

"Not that men do not suffer during these upheavals but women, who are subjected to sexual and physical violence, suffer much more intensely and go through greater humiliation. This happens partly to punish their men folk and partly because they are the most vulnerable section of society," remarks Satya M. Rai (191). The analysis of historical records reveals that rape of women has been used as "a military strategy" and as "a weapon of domination" and "repression" with an overt goal "to extinguish" "the will" of the women of other races and communities "to resist" and "in the process to demoralize their men folk." Susan Brown Miller in her book *Against Our Will: Men, Women and Rape* observes that this kind of sexual violence is actually not about sexuality but it shows "a pattern of power and domination. . . . For centuries, in groups and in individuals, as soldiers and civilians, ordinary men have used rape to humiliate and subordinate women and to proclaim their masculine superiority and dominance to women and to other men" (193). But "the official records do not reflect the pain and agony, fear and afflictions, dismay and disillusionment" of such victims, "creative writing does," affirms Mushirul Hasan (9).

Almost all the narratives on Partition by the writers such as Khushwant Singh, Chaman Nahal, Khwaja Ahmad Abbas, Aziz Ahmad, Krishna Chandar, Saros Cowasjee, Kartar Singh Duggal, Intizar Hossain, Kamleshwar, Saadat Hassan Manto, Bapsi Sidhwa, Qudrat Ullan Shahab, Rajinder Singh Bedi and many others have highlighted the abduction and molestation of the Hindu and Sikh women by the Muslims and vice versa. "The victimized women characters in such narratives evoke the strongest revulsions for the perpetuators of such inhuman acts," avers Bodh Prakash (197). Most of the men from these communities dishonoured the women from the rival communities. Raghuvendra Tanwar, while recounting the disaster that befell the women of these communities, states, "the atrocities committed on Hindu and Sikh women were by no stretch greater than those that were committed on Muslim women—indeed, if there was any balance it was in the beastly behaviour of the men on both sides who tried to outdo each other in what they did to the women of the 'other side'" (433).

Another dimension of the sexual abuse of women during this period is presented in the two stories, "The Reunion" by Saadat Hassan Manto and "Ya Khuda" by Qudrat Ullah Shahab where during the post-partition period, no consideration is shown being given to the religious identity of women but the men of their own communities use them for their sexual pleasure. In "The Reunion," a group of volunteers in India is pictured acting for the retrieval of the abducted girls of their own community and they promise a father to find his daughter for him. But on locating her, they become her rapists and the daughter is ultimately found in the hospital in a state of delirium. "Ya Khuda," which has been hailed as "a very powerful tale of what befell Muslim women during partition," demonstrates the plight of a Muslim girl named Dilshad, who after having suffered every imaginable abuse at the hands of her Sikh captors in India, boards a train to her new home in her own nation Pakistan—with a new hope of being with the brothers and sisters from her our community who would welcome her and where honour will be safe. But on reaching there, her hopes are belied when she discovers that even her own countrymen stare at her with lustful eyes and pass lewd remarks on her. After reading this story, "the title 'Ya Khuda' reverberates in our mind and sums up our total experience as no other words can," observes Saros Cowasjee (xxi). Through both the narratives, the writers seem to convey that "A woman without clothes loses her religious identity." "Symbolically the abused naked body of a woman" reveals the emptiness of "the claims of identity acquired from cultural, national and religious names." In fact "a woman as a victim of this violence, as a marker of social and cultural subjugation of the other, and trophies of conquest" signifies that "the discourse of nation" or beyond is "not only meaningless but oppressive for her" rightly observes Sudip Minhas (11).

As said earlier, the humiliation and the molestation of women did not occur only during the Partition or post-Partition period. This, in fact, has been happening all over the world whenever communal riots break out. Taslima Nasreen in her novel *Lajja* (1994), which describes the aftermath in Bangladesh of Babri Masjid demolition in Ayodhya in India portrays the inter-communal violence and gang-rapes of girls and shows Maya, a 21-year-old girl belonging to a Bengali Hindu family, being kidnapped, gang-raped and silenced to death by the Muslim fanatics as an act of revenge on the Hindu families to teach them a lesson and to create terror in them. Urvashi Butalia, Ritu Menon and Kamla Bhasin have been witness to the heart-rending fate of women during the anti-Sikh riots in 1984, the accounts of which they have recorded in their scholarly studies along with the oral narratives of the women survivors of the trauma of Partition.

Now the question is what is the fate of the humiliated and molested women survivors of such violences. Many of them like Ayah in *Ice-Candy Man* land into brothels of the nations of other communities with their "radiance and animation gone," living bodies without souls "emptied of life," "despairing" (Sidhwa 260, 264). But they want to go back to their families. Many of them like Hamida (from Lahore), who had been abducted by the Sikhs and taken to Amritsar, after recovery are not taken back by their husbands or their families as they are considered "the fallen women." They become aliens in their own homelands and pass their time by doing menial jobs or spending their lives in refugee camps, facing humiliation and insult, ever yearning to go to their families. Most of them like Lajo in Rajinder Singh Bedi's story "Lajwanti" though on recovery are brought home by husbands who claim to be generous and sympathetic towards such women on the public platform, but these women are "rehabilitated materially" only and are not "accepted" by "heart" and they continue sulking in isolation and wailing in silence. "By shifting focus away from the 'materiality' of the event to the consciousness of the victim, such stories . . . [deal with] an examination of their impact on the inner selves and the consciousness of individuals," comments Bodh Prakash (198).

In some cases where women are rescued from prostitution, restored and accepted by the benevolent men who offer themselves to marry them, as we see in Manohar Malgonkar's *A Bend in the Ganges* and Shiv K. Kumar's *A River with Three Banks,* these women feel highly obliged for their redressal and remain supplicants, but the memories of assaults of rape keep their inner wounds raw and alive. Mehr Nigar Masroor in *Shadows of Time* has shown the female protagonist, Shanti, a sufferer of the mental trauma of rape during partition, adopting a different survival strategy. Instead of committing suicide, she gathers her strength, plunges herself into studies and after becoming a successful lawyer supports her mother, gives shelter and motherly love to an orphan girl Nirmala and rears a Muslim male infant, a victim of partition riot whom she calls a victim of "men's rapacity." But the hatred for men for what they had done to her is shown brimming in her heart to the full. Though she is vocal in her arguments in every situation but the suppressed silence of the shock of her sexual abuse keeps surfacing in her painful memories and sarcastic comments on males.

An analysis of these few narratives thus not only reveals the sexual victimization of women and its impact on their material, emotional and psychic life, they do leave certain questions before us to be seriously pondered over:

i. Will woman, being a female body, continue to remain as commodity of sexual pleasure and uphold man's sexual power over the powerless?

ii. Will her body as an object of sexual pleasure continue to be transacted in any nation for satisfying the hunger of the belly and meeting other material needs of the family without caring for her dignity and self-respect and then dubbed as 'the immoral one'?

iii. Will woman's body remain as a sign through which "the violent dialogue between rival men" in the name of politics of race and ethnicity, nation formation and beyond, continue being conducted and then she to be labelled as "the fallen one"?

iv. Does women's empowerment help their being spared from sexual violence during communal frenzy and even in peaceful times, anywhere in the world?

v. Can women's subjectivity ever remain free from the sexual violence even in their own nation? Can their silences of the pain and trauma be fully opened up or erased from their psychic space?

These and many more issues are still question marks before the civilized and civilizing nations of the world to be seriously thought over and sorted out.

Works Cited

Bhabani Bhattacharya, *So Many Hungers* (Bombay: Hind Kitab, 1947).

Bhabani Bhattacharya, *He who Rides a Tiger* (1954; New Delhi: Arnold Heinemann, 1977).

Urvashi Butalia, "Community, State, and Gender: Some Reflections on the Partition of India," *Inventing Boundaries: Gender, Politics and the Partition of India*, ed. Mushirul Hasan (Oxford University Press, 2000).

Saros Cowasjee and K.S. Duggal, ed. *Orphans of the Storm: Stories on the Partition of India* (New Delhi: UBS, 1995).

Kamala Das, *Padmavati, the Harlot and Other Stories* (Sterling, 1992).

Kamala Das, *The Sandal Trees and Other Stories* (Orient Longman, 1995).

Shobha Dè, *Starry Nights* (Delhi: Penguin, 1991).

Sadhu Singh Dhami, *Maluka* (a novel) (Patiala: Punjabi University Publications, 1997).

Ann Duffy, "The Feminist Challenge: Knowing and Ending the Violence," *Feminist Issues: Race, Class and Sexuality*, ed. Nancy Mandell (Ontario, Scarborough, Prentice Mall, Canada, 1995).

Mushirul Hasan, ed. *India Partitioned: The Other Face of Freedom*. Vol II (New Delhi: Roli, 1997).

Wendy Kaminer, "Feminism's Identity Crisis," *Span*, Vol. XXXV, No. 12, Dec. 1994.

Kamala Markandaya, *Nectar in a Sieve* (1954: New Delhi: Sagar, 1968).

Mehr Nigar Masroor, *Shadows of Time* (Delhi: Chanakya, 1987).

Ritu Menon and Kamla Bhasin, "Recovery, Rupture, Resistance: The Indian State and the Abduction of Women during Partition," *Inventing Boundaries: Gender, Politics and the Partition of India* ed. Mushirul Hasan (OUP, 2000).

Brown Miller. *Against Our Will: Men, Women and Rape* (1975).

Sudip Minhas, "Narratives of the Silence: An Analysis of the Partition Narratives," *English Journal*, Vol. 6, No. 1. June 2005, pp. 1-13.

U.R. Anantha Murthy, *Samskara* (OUP, 1978).

Taslima Nasreen, *Lajja* (New Delhi: Penguin, 1994).

Bodh Prakash, "The Woman Protagonist in Partition Literature," *Translating Partition*, ed Ravikant and Tarun K Saint (Katha: 2001).

Satya M. Rai, "Partition and Women: The Case of Punjab," *The Partition in Retrospect*, ed. Amrik Singh (New Delhi: Anamika, 2000).

Bapsi Sidhwa, *Ice-Candy Man* (Penguin, 1988)

Raghuvendra Tanwar, *Reporting the Partition of Punjab 1947: Press, Public and Other Opinions* (New Delhi: Manohar, 2006).

The Changing Position of Woman in Society: Shashi Deshpande's *That Long Silence* and Chandani Lokuge's *If the Moon Smiled*

SEEMA SUNEEL
S.B.S. College, University of Delhi

Literature reveals principally three sets of relationships—human beings in relation to the universe, individual in relation to society, and man in relation to woman. In other words, literature may be considered a document of social criticism. Let us discuss the position of woman in Indian society.

Indian fiction, since its origin more than a hundred years ago, has dealt with the position of women in society. This is true of the very first novel in Urdu, *The Bride's Mirror (Mirat-Ul-Arus): A Tale of Life in Delhi a Hundred Years Ago*, written by Nazir Ahmed. The novel sold over 100,000 copies within a few years of its release in 1869. It was translated into English by G.E. Ward in 1903. It has been recently re-issued by Permanent Book and has gripped readers' imagination as a novel which raises the question of gender as early as the nineteenth century. The novel vividly portrays two girls—Asghari and Akbari. They are sisters, married to two brothers in Delhi. And the social locale pertains to the Delhi of the 1860s.

In the nineteenth century, social reformers like Raja Ram Mohun Roy and Jyotiba Phooley succeeded in eradicating several of the social evils like the tonsuring of widows, child marriage and 'sati,' and great thinkers like Rabindranath Tagore, Swami Vivekananda and Mahatma Gandhi encouraged women to participate in the national freedom struggle. This period is popularly known as the Indian Renaissance. However, both Tagore and

Gandhi believed also in the polarization of the social roles of men and women seeing them merely as supplementing and complementing each other's labours. Swami Vivekananda, in particular, was radical in his views on women. He wondered why there was distinction between the genders, because the *Vedanta* itself declared that one and the same conscious-self is present in all beings. Vivekananda did not see women as 'mere manufacturing machines.' In fact, he upbraided the irresponsible and indifferent Indian men who had contributed little towards the upliftment of women but sought to subject them under more and more stringent rules.

In the early decades of the twentieth century, the women's movement was marked by some special features: (a) it was led by women; (b) it raised questions from the standpoint of women; (c) women's own organizations and groups became active and sharply criticized the self-centred egotistic behaviour of men, their privileged position in which their disparaging attitude towards women and their tendency to exploit and rule over women; (d) several leading figures like Pandita Ramabai, Ramabai Ranade, Anandibai Joshi and Rukmabai, and magazines including *Madhuri* and *Nirmala* took up the women's cause.

With the Western impact on India, the position of woman started undergoing a change. India acquired an identity of her own in 1947, and there dawned an awareness in all walks of life and woman too made efforts to acquire her own identity. In the post-Independence India, a great stress has been laid on the education of women and redefining their role in family and society. The imparting of higher education inculcated a feeling of confidence in women and they started asserting themselves in various walks of life.

The concept of women in the present-day India has undergone several changes. In particular, a new set of writers deeply concerned with the social and psychological problems of the middle-class Indian women has come up. In the past, women in Indian fiction remained always on the periphery, even as their works glorified in unison the stereotypical virtues like endurance, devotion, self-sacrifice and total submission. However, in recent decades, novel writing in India has entered a refreshingly new phase, and the 'new woman' increasingly aspires to realize her proper position under the sun, be it in her own family or the society at large.

Fiction written during the last three decades provides a glimpse into female psyche and deals with the full range of female experience. The Indian society which had been so conventional and tradition-bound could not remain impervious to the new forces that had started slowly influencing it through education and social awareness. This brought about a change in the prevalent attitudes and beliefs and accelerated a tendency which favoured a new order in place of the old. In fact, the modern literature is making attempts at redressing the age-old imbalance, at creating and reflecting a new social order which no longer wishes to downgrade women but rather considers them autonomous and transcendent. Fiction today is seriously concerned with changing perceptions of man-woman relationship. This is true not only of Indian fiction but also of Sri Lankan fiction, as both the countries have similar cultural situation.

Shashi Deshpande is one of the most accomplished contemporary Indian women writers in English. She shot into prominence when her novel, *That Long Silence* was published by the British Feminist Publishing House, Virgo. It won the Sahitya Akademi Award in 1990. The novel looks at social history from the perspective of the family. While exploring man-woman relationship in Indian society, Deshpande in this novel offers reader an intimate and domestic chronicle of the subtle tyrannies suffered by woman and the pain of coming to self-knowledge. It is the story of personal journey; the heroine learns as she undergoes the mental torture and suffering at the hands of her husband.

The smooth course of Jaya's life is disrupted due to her husband's business problem. The novel opens with Jaya and her husband shifting from a cosy, comfortable house to their unfashionable, old apartment at Dadar, Bombay. They shift house at a time when Mohan has been caught in some business malpractice and an inquiry is in progress. Here, in a small old flat, Jaya gets confined and becomes an introvert. She broods over the situation and fondly recalls her past. She remembers having adjusted herself to the more cosmopolitan city of Bombay after leaving her earlier surroundings of Saptagiri.

Jaya is essentially a modern woman rooted in tradition, whereas her husband, Mohan, is a traditionalist rooted in age-old customs. The difference between their outlook is so marked that they fail, time and again, to understand each other. This greatly affects their marital life. It becomes more of a compromise than a relationship based on love or mutual understanding. There grows a silence between the husband and the wife. It creates a tension between them. Mohan had left home without a word after Jaya unconsciously laughed at him. His absence shatters Jaya and she thinks that the world would fall apart. She feels utterly helpless; a sense of vacuum, a feeling of ennui engulfs Jaya.

Then the situation changes. Mohan sends a telegram informing her that all is well, implying that the corruption case involving him has been settled without any harm to him. And finally Jaya goes back home. Her protest ends in futility. With the "All Well" news from Mohan, she finds herself slipping into the grooves of her marital life again. But a change has been wrought in her situation. By giving expression to her story, she has achieved articulation of her predicament and thereby broken her silence. Though Jaya makes a compromise with Mohan but she does assert her identity. The novel thus seeks to portray a woman who becomes aware of the biased attitude of her husband. Jaya, who stands for the modern emancipated woman, has asserted her individuality by challenging the taboos and destructive social norms.

Like Shashi Deshpande, Chandani Lokuge focuses on women's issues. She teaches in the Department of Postcolonial Studies at Monash University. Her first novel *If the Moon Smiled* was published in 2000 by Penguin. Like her protagonist Manthri in *If the Moon Smiled*, Lokuge is a Sri Lankan emigrant living in Australia but her novel is only in a very limited sense autobiographical in that she is weaving her own experiences in her fiction.

Chandani Lokuge's debut novel *If the Moon Smiled* presents the life of a Sri Lankan migrant living in Adelaide. It is a story of sadness and loss. Manthri, the central character, starts with a sense of nostalgia for her childhood in Sri Lanka. She daydreams about her parents' hillside village and a youthful unrequited love. She repeatedly returns to the memories of her childhood life which is perhaps the most beautiful part of the book. She remembers the different treatment given to male and female children in Indian society.

Right in the beginning, we are made conscious of the subordinate position of woman. Manthri's mother tells her that one day she will be happily married: "Yes, Manthri, you will. And like a floral offering to a deity, you will blossom for your husband and derive value from him." (7) The child Manthri empathizes with her parents who are sad because they have no son. She has also felt her mother's distress and understands that nothing and no one can "compensate for that loss." (10) Later, when Manthri's marriage is discussed, it is said: "She comes from a fertile family. Her horoscope predicts a son. It will be a fortunate marriage for her." (26)

It is amazing that the onset of menstruation is treated almost like an illness. When Manthri starts menstruating, her mother instructs her: "Lie down, Manthri. You must not be seen these days." (17) Manthri's marriage is no bed of roses. Her travails begin when Mahendra does not find bloodstains on the crushed white sheet after their marriage is consummated. He has a doubt that another man has shared her before him and demands incredulously: "You have been with another man?" (35) He feels that the woman he has married and who would be mother of his children was not a virgin. Manthri falls at his feet and pleads her innocence. But Mahendra is not convinced. Their marriage, thus, is a kind of failure. It is a pathetic beginning of the married life.

Manthri's problems escalate when Mahendra announces his decision to go to Australia. It may be stressed here that the decision to migrate to Australia is made by her husband despite Manthri's reluctance. Manthri does not want to go there since it will affect the education of their children. Nor does she want to leave her home or her parents. Mahendra calls Australia "a land of opportunity" (44) and that she would like it better than Colombo. When Mahendra refuses to change his decision, she submits by saying, "This must be my karma." (44) She believes in the Buddhist philosophy of being born with one's destiny written on one's palms.

The decision to migrate to Australia is made by her husband. In the foreign land, she finds herself in a loveless marriage and is increasingly estranged from her two Australian children. Torn between an idyllic past to which she cannot return and a present that breaks her heart, she never loses touch with dreams, nor abandons her passionate enchantment with life. When they migrate to Australia, the family faces desperate problems in Adelaide. Manthri comes from a very conservative Buddhist background and is not able to change with the changing circumstances. She becomes estranged from her Australianised children. She is caught between the two cultures and fails to adjust to the change.

The novel presents convincingly the conflict between the mindset of traditional people and the new generation. While the parents are steeped in tradition, the children are products of Australia's liberal cultural environment. Mahendra has great expectations from his son Devake. He wants him to get a very high score in his exams and become a doctor. Devake, on the other hand, wants to learn music but Mahendra is unhappy about this: "Music? What music? . . . Do you want the whole world to laugh at us? No, you're going to be a doctor. . . . I have arranged for you to have tuition in Chemistry and Maths." (73) He accuses Manthri of spoiling their son: "You have brought him up all wrong. It is your job to bring up the children. Why can't you control them?" (72) It is his wife who becomes the target of his attack for being lenient to children. When Devake shaves off his hair and becomes a skinhead, Mahendra is upset. He stops talking to Devake when the latter starts smoking and taking drugs. He rages when the school suspends Devake for three weeks. Later Devake takes up a part-time job in a pizza bar. For Mahendra, he ceases to exist.

Lokuge clearly brings out the difference between sons and daughters. In this novel, Mahendra's expectations from his daughter Nelum are also not met. He wants Nelum to marry a nice boy back home and puts the following advertisement in Sri Lanka: "Govigama Buddhist parents permanently resident in Australia seek a doctor, engineer or lawyer, willing to reside overseas, for their only daughter, medical student, 5 ft. 4 inches height, fair-complexioned, beautiful. Substantial dowry with a house in Australia. Please send horoscope and details of caste, religion, etc." (117) Initially Nelum protests vehemently but then agrees to marry a high-caste science lecturer from Ratnapura. She is supposed to give up her career, her dreams of specializing in surgery and settling down to being a wife and mother. However, all this does not happen. She escapes all this and fulfils Manthri's inner wish to create her own destiny. She breaks the tradition of arranged marriages and rejects the demands made by Mahendra. She becomes a successful surgeon and travels round the world. It is she who looks after Manthri when she ends up in the hospital. At the end, we are told that Manthri finds that Nelum has found her identity as a woman and can face the world on her own. Addressing her daughter, she says:

> Dearest Nelum, My child, my daughter. So young and confident, so cool and elegant. Unlike me, all knotted and tangled. . . . You want to be yourself, as always. . . . No, just go your way, my lovely blossom. Across oceans, ride the crests of waves. (222)

A study of the two novels, Shashi Deshpande's *That Long Sikence* and Chandani Lokuge's *If the Moon Smiled* reveals that there is a significant change in the society. Social awareness, education, economic independence and globalization have led to the emergence of the 'new woman' in the present century.

Works Cited

Deshpande, Shashi, *That Long Silence*, New Delhi: Penguin India, 1989.
Lokuge, Chandani, *If the Moon Smiled*, New Delhi: Penguin, 2000.

Gita Mehta's *A River Sutra*: A Quest for Love and Redemption

NANDA KISHORE MISHRA
G.M. College, (Auto), Orissa

Love is an essential urge, an inner force in all living beings. It is a free expression of one's inner joy based on a relation of mutuality. In reality, the gravitating values that govern life and motive in the modern world are money, sex, power, and fulfillment of one's egoistic desires. But these in excess have deleterious effects on life. The psychological problem resulting from a clash of egos has created for man a separate spatial and mental existence. At times, man is forced to lead a life of broken love with shattered dreams. In our contemporary society human relation is propped on a contractual basis involving commercial motives. In the midst of all such commercial behaviour, the soul of man becomes morbid and suppressed.

Love involves reciprocity in behaviour. It is dovetailed with a sense of sacrifice in life. Gita Mehta's novels have attracted the attention of international readers for the cultural ethos she creates. Her *A River Sutra* weaves various stories around a single thread of love and redemption. She has arranged such stories of love that show the deep secret of human heart that throb the multicultural society of India. These stories about the Hindus, the Muslims, the Jain ascetics, courtesans, minstrels, diamond merchants, tea executives, music lovers, tribals, and anthropologists people the pageant gallery of the novel and enrich its multicultural texture.

The narrator shows that love tends to assume a strong bond of attachment, but redemption in love comes through pain, suffering and sacrifice. As everyone knows attachment to another person is undeniably a sign of love. Hubert Benoit analyses the psychological urge for making love to someone:

> No human deed is done unless the doer finds in it some affirmation of himself; a completely disinterested action would be meaningless, because it could present itself as an effect without a cause. That man is prone to see himself as God; it is his weakness. . . . I willingly concede that we never nourish others without deriving nourishment ourselves at the same time in one way or another. (4)

Benoit further explains that any pleasure that one procures by means of another being; every affirmation of oneself that another being affords one is a kind of nourishment.

Gita Mehta culled typical India stories that undeniably urge readers to make philosophical speculations about life. Threading the different stories of love, she stresses the two ways of existence of life: to get fully involved in life through love and attachment, in other words to get involved in cosmic illusion. The other way is to escape from this illusion by accepting the path of renunciation of all worldly desires as in Jain monks. The narrator in the novel comes to know these stories on the bank of the river Narmada. The river in a way glorifies the mysteries of Indian mind and love that regulates man's élan vital. Making a reference to Gita Mehta's novel K. Venkata Reddy records the rich heritage of the Narmada River which is revered by generations of Indians as a sacred river that expresses the life-affirming impulses of people in the novel: "The novel is a celebration of life and life-affirming impulses struggling against death and life-negating forces. The river is seen as an eternal principle of life." (145)

Stories of love in this novel begin in a mysterious situation but end with a tragic note. Love is not confined between man and woman only; it arises out of sympathy or a strong sense of attachment for something or somebody. The rich tapestry of life throbbing impulses in *A River Sutra* is appreciated by C.J.S. Walia, one of the reviewers of the book: "The stories leave the reader with the sense that things are richer and more meaningful than they seem, that the beauty and the horror of this world are both irreducible and inexplicable."

The *sutradhar* or the unnamed narrator of these stories, an ex-bureaucrat, in order to lead a sequestered life after the death of his wife accepts a lower position to his rank in a government guest-house on the bank of the Narmada river. He identifies himself with a *vanaprasthi,* one who seeks enlightenment to acquire more philosophical knowledge about mystery of life. Some of the pilgrims he comes across in this place narrate strange stories to him about man's capacity to love, to make sacrifice and mystery that shrouds human heart.

The first one, "The Monk's Story," is based on the principle of renunciation in life by stripping oneself of all worldly comforts and attachment. One can say that in this story it is spiritual love that impels the son of a billionaire to renounce the rich inheritance of his father and adopt the life of a Jain ascetic. The young man's decision is based on the philosophical view of love for suffering in life, which is essential for attainment of salvation. Ashok, a young ascetic, weighs the worth of life in terms of one's capacity to suffer, to accept poverty, hunger and hardship. The world of riches no more fascinates his life. During the ceremony of his conversion to a monk, he is repeatedly reminded of the arduous and painful life of a Jain ascetic:

> You will be a social outcast.
> You will be insulted.
> You will depend on strangers for your most basic needs.
> You will experience cold, hunger, heat, thirst, and sickness.
> You will suffer loneliness.
> You will be deprived of the ministrations any woman lest she arouse your desire. (37-38)

Through self-mortification that includes accepting a life of poverty, begging food, detaching all ties with family, friends and relatives, a Jain monk seeks enlightenment and love for salvation in earthly life. The story presents a pattern of love for life beyond the earth that is not confined to man and woman. Love for salvation is sought for spiritual redemption from mundane life.

Love for music plays a vital role in man's life. A music teacher's compassionate love for a blind boy presents a heart touching story. Love for art is not less strong than the intimate relationship between lover and beloved. Compassionate love is based upon an ardent desire to do well to others without caring for apathetic attitude of others. Master Mohan's determination to help Imrat, a blind boy, overcomes the obdurate demand of his wife to throw him out on the street. She becomes highly jealous of her husband's deep love for Imrat's sweet voice. After his failure in reaching the acme of perfection in music, Master Mohan finds a sense of compensation and fulfillment in fostering the melodious voice of Imrat. In fact, Master Mohan feels self-affirmation in helping the unusual gift of God, in the sweetness of the voice of the blind boy: "He was convinced God was giving him a second voice, greater than he had ever heard, greater than his own could ever had been. He was certain such a voice must only be used to praise God, lest fate exact second revenge by robbing him of it." (72)

Bent upon taking revenge on her husband's excessive love for the blind singer, Master Mohan's irate wife arranges a contract with a rich man for the boy's musical performance against the opposition of her husband, fully aware that her husband had declined such an offer: "What will happen to music if this be the standard by which God judges us?" He muses to himself for the mundane joy the rich man derives from music.

Overwhelmed with joy the great *sahib* slits the boy's throat after the musical concert is over. He assassinates him because he does not want any one else in this world to enjoy the superb devotional song of the blind boy and share the divine joy like him. Out of an egoistic estimate the great *sahib* kills Imrat for he rationalizes: "the object of worship no one but himself can enjoy it." Being bereft of the most lovable musician in life, Master Mohan makes a pilgrimage to Amir Rumi's tomb with a broken heart and offers the boy's recorded music since the latter had never been able to fulfill his dream of singing at the shrine. Instead of returning to his family, he thinks his life is worthless without Imrat and commits suicide. In him he had found a kindred soul. Borrowing the term from Hubert Benoit one can say that Master Mohan shows benevolent love to Imrat. Hubert Benoit emphatically asserts that man never nourishes without deriving nourishment at the same time in one way or another. In taking care of the blind boy's well-being, Master Mohan derives self-satisfaction by creating his noble image in the boy's mind. Tariq Mia ascribes reason to Master Mohan's suicide: "perhaps he could not exist without loving some one as he had loved the blind child."

Study of books at times affects greatly the life of a reader. In the mind of Nitin Bose, a tea executive, reading books about Kamarupa hills, the "Kingdom of God of Love" subconsciously arouses love for a snake-woman (*nāga kanyā*). Stories about serpent women as enchantresses and sorceresses make deep imprint on his sub-consciousness. Surprisingly, in real life he falls passionately in love with a coolie's wife presuming her a snake woman. His passionate love for the snake woman regulates mind. Robert A. Baron and Don Byrne (1992) in Social *Psychology* view passionate love as a sudden, overwhelming and all consuming reaction towards a woman of which Nitin Bose seems to be a victim: "Passionate love seems to be a mixture of sexual attraction, physiological arousal, the desire to be physically close, an intense need to be loved as much as you love, and the constant that the relationship might end." (292)

The image of Rima as conjured up in his mind by coming across lady labourers in the tea estate of Assam wholly possesses Nitin Bose. The narrator too explains Nitin's desire to possess Rima on the backdrop of a mythological reading:

> If even the Great ascetic could not withstand the weapons unleashed from Kama's sugarcane bow strung with honeybees, how could poor Nitin Bose survive as Kama's arrows found their mark, piercing him with enchantment, inflaming with lust, parching him with desire rendering him helpless with the paroxysms of his own longing, until

> he was wounded with that fifth and fatal arrow the carrier of Death? (139-40)

Every night the serpent woman visits the bed of Nitin Bose. She catches mysteriously his soul between two halves of a coconut shell. These activities psychologically affect his mind. As a possessed being, he roves in the forest in search of Rima. Finally, to get cured of his mental sickness he comes over to the bank of Narmada River in search of a tribal shrine. The healing power of the shrine helps him to cast off his evil spirit—his love for a snake woman.

Forced love instead of ennobling the spirit of a woman is considered to defile her body. A courtesan's daughter to divest herself of a bandit's forced love in "The Courtesan's Story" sacrifices her life in order to purify her soul and jumps into the Narmada river. Being herself trained in the art of love, a courtesan imparts training to her daughter to protect her from the amorous advances of customers since it is her profession. Despite her best care and protective measures a notorious criminal, Rahul Singh, kidnaps the courtesan's daughter. Since he happens to be a dreaded bandit in the region, the courtesan fails to rescue her daughter from the clutches of Rahul Singh. He had unwittingly become enamoured of the lady having a preconception. He thinks that he lived with her for many lives. Such a preconceived notion prohibits him to touch her body without her consent. Knowing from other women that he will not touch her without her consent, the kidnapped lady cunningly punishes him by intensely 'inflaming his longing' for her. Strangely he endures her hatred and swallows her insults. She perceives his attachment for her never diminishing: "Each time he went on a raid he returned with a gift for me, although his men told him he had risked his safety in some bazaar to do so. And when he was in the camp he sat outside my cave like a dumb brute enduring my worst cruelties." (183)

The captive lady employs all art of love to dissimulate him and escape from him. She fails miserably in her attempts and finally she gives in. Many years after his death in an encounter with police and the lady comes to the bank of Narmada with a defile body in search of her mother to meet her for the last time in life. Having led a carnal life with a notorious bandit, she does not want to resume a different life in her society. To be "purified of all her sins," she jumps off a cliff into the Narmada river with a faith in its sacred power to cleanse her defiled body.

A reader finds in "The Musician's Story" human love turning to love for music. An ugly daughter of a famous musician fails to convince a young man to accept her as life partner but in turn develops a deep love for music and realizes: "Through music he [her father] tried to free me of my own image, so I could love beauty wherever it was to be found, even it was present in my mirror." (211)

Not for any human being but love for music redeems her life; she learns the music of the natural and spiritual world. Her father, a music teacher bargains a deal with a young music learner who comes to him to take music lessons. As per the deal after establishing himself as a perfect musician under his tutelage the young learner should marry the teacher's ugly daughter. The music teacher teaches both his daughter and the young man in a devoted way that their musical harmony transcends their physical existence and unites them as if in a spiritual world of sound. Through the musical lessons of her father, the ugly girl is gradually drawn to the beauty of the natural world.

The ugly lady's father teaches her that a musical instrument, *veena,* is like the body of a woman. She recounts her memory how both were taught by her father: "He taught me the subtleties of tenderness, how to gentle anger, how to seduce and sigh and caress through my music." (215). She learns to convey her pain through the strings of *sitar*, the inner feelings of a woman pleading for young man's attention. The silences between their notes grow electric with desire. While reciting songs, she sometimes notices the eyes of the young man lingering on some parts of her body left exposed by her garment. She senses the young learner becoming gradually enamoured of her. But the young musician violates the deal, abandons her to marry elsewhere. From that day she leaves music in disgust. As a measure of redemption for her attachment with the young man, her father advises her to meditate on the bank of the Narmada river to become the bride of music and not of a musician's: "He says that I must meditate on the waters of the Narmada, the symbol of Shiva's penance, until I have cured myself of my attachment to what has passed and can become again the ragini to every raga." (225)

In the "Minstrel's Story" readers come across a bond of spiritual love of a Naga Baba for a brothel girl. He rescues her cursed life from the profession of a prostitute. The Naga Baba for celebration of the night of Lord Shiva and to break his fast goes on begging at the doors of the lowliest of the low in the society. While begging at the door of a brothel, he chances upon a girl who was considered an unfortunate child and sold by her father to the brothel owner. Being repeatedly exploited by people, she becomes frightened at the sight of any male member. The Naga Baba takes pity on the child and rescues her from the ill-reputed house. He renames her as Uma. This name has a mythological significance. Goddess Uma was born from the penance of Lord Shiva. The Naga Baba teaches Uma the song of the Narmada river to adopt the life of a minstrel. In due course he leaves the girl to herself and journeys further in search of higher enlightenment. Uma becomes a roaming minstrel and keeps the legend of the river alive by leading a renewed life on the riverbank.

Weaving the various stories of love in the novel, Gita Mehta's central motive is to show that "the human heart has only one secret, the capacity to love." Each of the stories relates to man's love of something in life that shows an excessive sense of attachment. Attachment is aligned with the fear of losing the loved one, in other words it is a sense of possessiveness. It is an egoistic state of need for other person to some one for his nourishment. Haridas Chaudhury in *The Philosophy of Love* diagnoses how man's mind gets enmeshed in a strong bond of attachment, which leads to suffering: "Attachment clouds over our judgment and understanding, robs us of our true perspective and causing suffering and disturbance." (19) In some of the stories, attachment for the object of love is so strong that man in desperation puts an end to his life. Music teacher Master Mohan can no more bear the separation from the blind singer and commits suicide as if "perhaps he could not exist without loving some one as he had loved the blind child."

Falling in love is an act of focusing one's attention beyond the self on a loved one. One cannot love if one has no interest in the other. Master Mohan's interest centres on the blind boy's melodious voice and God has given him the opportunity to support such a voice: "Hearing the clear notes pierce through the night, Master Mohan knew he had been made guardian of something rare, as if his own life had only been a purification to ready him for the task of tending this voice for the world." (67-68)

Structurally, the novel comprises seven wonderful stories that evoke readers' sympathy towards the characters and reveal the secret of man's capacity to love, suffer and make sacrifice in life. The river sends out a distinct message—the lesson of man's attachment to an object of love as well as his capacity to make supreme sacrifice in life. The unnamed narrator describes the tales of various pilgrims encapsulating a mythical and artistic dimension of the river with the humanistic tradition. In narrating various stories of diverse creeds, faith, and religions, Gita Mehta makes an indigenous study of Indian culture, customs and traditions that have largely remained unaffected by the onrush of European influences. The indigenous culture of India takes into account myths, music, religion, art, folk beliefs, orthodox belief, and necromancy that have been found well blended in this novel.

Works Cited

Gita Mehta, *A River Sutra*, New Delhi: Penguin, 1993.

Haridas Chaudhury, *The Philosophy of Love*, New York: Routledge & Kegan Paul, 1987.

Hubert Benoit, *The Many Faces of Love*, London: Routledge & Kegan Paul, 1952.

K. Venkata Reddy, *et al*, ed. *The Indian Novel with a Social Purpose*, New Delhi: Atlantic, 1999.

Robert A. Baron and Don Byrne, *Social Psychology*, New Delhi: Prentice Hall of India, 1999.

Nergis Dalal's *The Nude*: A Bonanza of Themes

MALTI AGARWAL
N.A.S. College, Meerut

The Indian short story in English emerged quite late on the literary scene as an offshoot of fiction but gradually it dug a place for itself and appeared as a distinct literary genre for providing an astonishing range of subject-matter and techniques. It, needless to say, has maintained its national character. Shiv K. Kumar rightly observes, "Though often considered a derivative of its western counterpart, it is not a hot-house plant but manifests a striking resemblance in its genius to the story written in any Indian language" (1).

Today Indian English literature abounds in short stories. The writers like Mulk Raj Anand, R.K. Narayan, K.A. Abbas, Khushwant Singh, Manohar Malgonkar, Chaman Nahal and many others excelled in giving a shape to the English language to suit the Indian sensibility. Among the female short story writers, the names of Shashi Deshpande, Nayantara Sahgal, Anita Desai, Manju Kak, Gauri Deshpande and many others are worthy of mention. The stories by these Indian authors are vibrant with many Indian themes.

Among the modern Indian writers writing in English, Nergis Dalal occupies a prominent place. Till date she has five novels, a short story collection and one children story book to her credit. The present paper is a modest attempt to discuss her latest story collection *The Nude* which consists of twenty stories.

Nergis Dalal has infused the Indian "tempo" into English expressions. *The Nude* is a bonanza of themes, relating to the most basic and most intricate aspects of human nature. While the stories such as "Once for the Asking," "The Sacrifice" and "The Exile" study in detail the clash between the Eastern values and the Western ethos, some other stories, on the other hand, peer into woman's heart to learn what an Indian woman feels. Dalal in some other stories has tried to analyze man-woman relationship in Indian context. These twenty stories cover various aspects of Indian experience. The author has tried to explore even some grey areas of pain which always remain inarticulated or unheeded in the Indian society.

The first story in entitled "The French Wife" brings into light the paradigm of Indian culture where a widow or a widower is not supposed to marry soon after the demise of his/her spouse. It is considered a sign of insincerity, lovelessness or ungratefulness of the living spouse. In the present story the male protagonist Mr. Kapoor remarries a young French girl just after the death of his wife, Mrs. Kapoor. To Mr. Kapoor's friends, it sounds horribly incredulous as Mrs. Sharma comments, "How could he be married?" she asked. "His wife just died" (4). Falling in love at first sight seemed obscene to Mr. Kapoor's friends. His friends and their wives begin to picture this young French wife of Mr. Kapoor with a red mouth and shining blonde hair. Dalal minutely studies the socio-psycho dialectics of human thoughts. While, on the one hand, the news of Mr. Kapoor's bringing a new wife seemed horrible to all his friends for they considered it the violation of the social norms, they, on the other, grew jealous of him and regarded him lucky for they were all fascinated by the beauty of the French woman. They began to compare their wives to Yvonne. They criticized their own wives and perhaps wished to have foreign wives. Mr. Sharma asked his wife, "Why are you so fat?" Mrs. Sharma burst into tears. Mr. Singh said to his wife, "I didn't realize how much weight you had put on. Perhaps you should go on a diet?" (9). This enraged Mrs. Singh and she in a fit of temper slapped her husband. Their husbands' fascination for Yvonne, made the three wives "feel not only ugly but ignorant and stupid as well" (10). One day a news came that Yvonne had gone back to Paris. The theme here diverts to the dichotomy which exists between east and west. Yvonne could not stay any longer in India as she had no access to plays, music and intellectual stimulus nor Mr. Kapoor could think of going to Paris. He could not speak French and also he had no interest in plays, theatre or ballet. Mr. and Mrs. Kapoor (Yvonne) are culturally so different from each other that they could not live together. The story ends on a note of consolation when "Mr. Mehra looked at his wife—fat, comfortable, always there for him" (11). It is an Indian wife who believes in self-denial and sacrifices her pleasures for her husband—always ready with a cup of tea for him. This dichotomy of the Eastern and Western ethos touches the reader's heart.

Another story that brings into light the ambivalence of the east and west is "Once for the Asking." The male protagonist stayed with a European girl in England for two years. Both—the man and the girl—made a very good pair so much so that she like an ideal Indian wife "had a habit of walking a little behind" (25) the hero of the story. The narrator says, "I teased her about it and she said it was because I walked so fast, but I think she liked to walk like his, as though I sheltered her from stares or perhaps from that mysterious past" (25). At last, at the expiry of his tenure in England, the narrator decided to go back to India. He felt very confused and helpless to realize that he couldn't take the girl to India and marry her. The girl, on the contrary, took everything very calmly and naturally. To his astonishment, he found the lady walking away with the narrator's friend. It was unbelievable. "It was like seeing a film unrolling backwards, and I was not certain for a moment, whether it was I or him, walking away with her into the night" (27). The story reasserts the fact that the Indians are emotional beings whereas the Europeans are pragmatic.

"The Sacrifice," another story in this collection, confirms Nergis Dalal's belief in the polarities between the east and west. The story details Mr. Triana's visit to India who wanted to see the lush pastures, the green hills, the sloping tea estates, ruins and temples in India. His curiosity to know the real India took him to the tribals so that he could have "pictures of starved women with thin, hanging breasts and children with rickety limbs and swollen bellies" (28). His reaction to Indian manners and beliefs show how the westerners react to Indian manners. India's inability to feed her people becomes a butt of ridicule. "An excellent country," he sneered, "Independent but unable to feed itself. Without foreign food aid, famine would spread over the country like a rash" (31). He adds, "Floods, famine, corruption, greed and overpopulation. And there is nothing you can do about it without foreign aid. And yet you have the nerve to call yourself independent" (31).

Pritam Singh, the guide, described them an old Indian tradition, prevalent in that part of the country when people used to make human sacrifices to please rain-god so that the lives of many could be saved. He said, "Life is expendable here. It means one man's life to save hundreds. They would consider it barbarous to send men to kill each other in wars" (32). Pritam's justification enraged Mr. Triana and he said furiously, "Do you mean to compare the savage ritual of an illiterate tribe with the planned campaign of civilized nations?" (32). Mr. Triana went to the tribals and the sight of the children moving like skeletons with huge distended bellies filled him with glee and he cried, "Good, good, I'll get some wonderful pictures tomorrow" (33). Mr. Triana went to a hut and found a young woman lying half naked with a baby who looked like a foetus at her breast. When Mr. Triana touched the shoulder of the woman to move her out of shadows, all tribals attacked him and killed him. Mr. Triana was doing nothing but his touching the tribal woman made these people furious. Once again Dalal reflects on the difference which exists between eastern and western thoughts. To the westerners touching a woman is not significant or unethical while to these innocent tribals it is like violating the social code of conduct.

The story "The Exiles" depicts the ebb and flow of emotions in the hearts of the Wains—the wife and husband. The story proves how appearances are indeed deceptive. Mr. Wain, an English, after twenty-five years of stay in India said good-bye to his many English friends, staying in India. All these friends were exiles like Mr. and Mrs. Wain—Dalal beautifully depicts the psyche of the English. She writes, "They had nothing in common with each other except this delicate, tenuous thread of nationality. In England they would probably have neither liked each other nor been excessively friendly, but here they were all in the same boat. Their talk was always the same—the nostalgic dreaming of the exile, forced to live away from home. There was not one among them who did not regret the passing away of the great British Empire, or feel that they were infinitely superior to the natives in the manner of government. . . . They had only one thing in common—the desire to save up enough money to return and live forever in England" (118-19). Mrs. Wain is overwhelmed with the idea of going back to England. She happily dreamed herself back in England again, "no longer an exile, condemned to live forever in an alien land" (114). When someone asked her how she would manage there without servants, she cheerfully answered, "I shall really enjoy the climate and I like to do my own work. It is not the same as this you know. Everything there is quite different. There is so little dust for one thing, and all the fruit and vegetables come cleaned and packaged. I shall manage very well, I expect" (114). But soon Mrs. Wain found it difficult to leave India after such a long stay. She began to feel a little depressed. She knew she would miss the morning tea, the beautiful garden and despite of having many labour-saving devices which were there in England, she would still have to dust and clean and wash up. To return to England after In twenty-five years of service in India and make do without servants and remain in complete obscurity is not a pleasing project for Mrs. Wain. India has now become her home—her second home. Till now she had been talking of England, her home, and longed to be there, but now she "fell lost at the thought of leaving India. She realized that this was her home, here in India. She did not want to go home (England)" (120). The marigold flowers which earlier caused a sudden shudder of distaste in her suddenly became a symbol of the colour and gaiety of India and she couldn't dislike them. Eventually the time of departure came and the same Evelyn Wain who used to criticize Indians for being sentimental had tears in her eyes. "A tear trickled slowly down Evelyn Wain's face which she wiped away carefully" (122).

Another important theme dealt in by Nergis Dalal is the man-woman relationship. Diverse shades and nuances of this relationship have warmly been discussed by the author along with some other important issues such as a woman's longing for autonomy, her urge for motherhood. The story "A Taste of Blood" portrays a husband who wants to give to his young boy a taste of blood so that he may grow as a real boy. He says, "I don't want my son to grow up a namby-pamby. I've told you before I won't have him tied to your apron strings. I want him to be a real boy" (13). Perhaps it was his jealousy that he couldn't bear the closeness of the mother and son. Seemingly he excuses, "Mothers must be careful not to be over-possessive of their sons or they would emasculate them. Specially with an only son one has to be very careful" (14). But in reality there was a struggle going on for possession which was hidden earlier but was now open. Gradually the lady felt that all was finished and her arms were empty.

One day the family went on a picnic where the father trained the boy how to shoot little birds. The lady resented vehemently, "You are corrupting my child, teaching him the taste of blood. It is a corruption worse than that of sex—more perverse than any person" (17). Then suddenly a wonderful though shocking thing happened. The father went in darkness to see if there was any duck further up. The boy saw a deer and shot him dead. The mother and son, both were shocked to find the father lying in a pool of blood. The boy sobbed and the mother consoled him as the fault was not his. She said, "Little boys shouldn't be given guns" (19). The woman got consoled since the boy was hers now, all hers. It was bliss to have boy back again. The story indirectly conveys a message that a woman is not always wrong or mug headed.

Another eye-catching story in the collection is "The Alabaster Goddess" which opens with a memorable statement that the heart finds peace anywhere, in the market or in the hills, it makes no difference where the body is, if the heart is tranquil. The protagonist in the story is an old monk who relates his past to the narrator. Before he became a monk, he was an engineer. But his main passion in life was history. He devoted himself to writing history of the

Móghul Empire which his wife didn't like. Temperamentally, the wife and husband were poles apart—she a big woman, tall and broad and subject to the terrible fits of anger and he a quiet man, afraid of his wife. This ill-matched marriage resulted in a havoc. One evening he opened the door and found his wife holding the servant boy by his hair and shaking him violently. He pushed his wife and saved the boy. From that day she was puffed up with her victory, passed taunts which he accepted all in silence. But somewhere his manly pride got hurt and one night he crushed two sleeping pills into her milk and suffocated her to death. He, along with the servant boy, reached Mussoorie and got shelter in the temple of Alabaster goddess. The smile of the goddess was a solace to his troubled soul since "it has an extra-ordinary purity about it—she has all the loveliness, the warmth and tender beauty that I have never found in a woman" (50). See how one woman led him to murder and another to the life of sanctity and relief.

The title story "The Nude" brings forth some subtle nuances of marital relationship when a lady is matched with a drunken husband and the family suffers from poverty. The story seems to confirm that beauty lies in the eyes of the beholder. The opening words in the story are, "Some woman should never wear clothes—clothes which hide the shape and colour of their flesh and skin" (51). Robie Desilver came to this conclusion when he saw Mrs. Oliver. Mrs. Oliver posed only for one hundred rupees a morning for Robie who wanted to paint a large nude for an industrialist. Soon Robie discovered that her nudity was immense and disturbing. It roused a desire so elemental and physical that he plunged into it. To him she was the best model. The same best model appeared 'a bag of old clothes' to her husband. He felt ashamed for being married to 'a woman with fat legs and a body like a tub of lard' (58). How ironic it sounds that to Robie and the art critics her nude body in the painting struck 'physical excitement of the skin and flesh tones.'

Nergis Dalal broke new ground in Indian English literature through her stories. Highly innovative and experimental, she is an adept re-inventor of tradition. Her stories encompass a wide variety of themes and styles and no one story is like the other. "The Beautiful One," another story in the collection, explores the unfathomable recesses of human mind and heart. Nina, the female protagonist in the story, a twenty-year old girl, was the student in the college and her husband, Dr. Chander, was the Head of the Department of History. Dr. Chander was a scholarly-looking man always absorbed in his studies. He never paid any attention to his young wife. A young student, Suresh, fell in love with her to the extent of craziness. Dalal describes, "He was in love, as only the very young can be in love. There is nothing stranger than the condition of love—the weight, the strain, the anxiety, is a heavy load to bear, if only because among those confused passions and emotions loom dreadful possibilities like suicide and murder. It shakes one's own grasp of reality, and one realizes, under great emotional stress, how precarious is one's hold on reason. When one loves madly, one's hold on sanity is indeed provisional and insecure" (61-62). When on the advice of some of his colleagues, the Professor asked Nina to meet Suresh not so frequently, she burst out in resentment at the neglect she had suffered. She said, "I will go out with whoever I please and do exactly what I want to. Just because I don't exist for you doesn't mean other men don't find me desirable" (65). She continued, "You are not a man, you are just a machine, dry and filled with straw instead of blood. I'm a woman, and I'm beautiful. Do you think I want to spend my life alone with neither passion nor friendship given to me? Why did you marry me? You are happy with your books and your work. You could have kept a housekeeper instead. You don't need a wife" (65). Dr. Chander's belief that Nina also loved him was shattered. Nina accused him of being in love with his books. "You and your books," she spat out, "You are only half alive. I refuse to stay with you and grow mouldy and stuffy. I'm leaving" (65-66). Nina, to settle the score, eloped with Suresh. But soon her infatuation came to an end when she found Suresh crazily jealous. Eventually she revolted and married the managing director of a firm who was also madly jealous. The story ends on a note of compassion when Nina regrets for deserting Dr. Chander, her first husband, who truly loved her.

She admitted, "You know, I made a great mistake when I left the professor if I had any sense I should have stayed on. But I was very young. I didn't realize that he was the only man with whom I could be happy" (69-70). This realization came to her too late and what was done could not be undone.

The story "Christmas Means Love" narrates the experiences of a young boy who was in trauma because of the separation of his mother and father. He felt as if there was no sunshine anywhere in his world. His mother, Meera, assured him, "Daddy will be here for Christmas. We will wait for him and do the tree together" (75). Arun, the boy, missed his father whom he considered a wonderful being. It didn't mean that he didn't love his mother. But without his father he felt that his life, his whole small world was threatened. One day Meera received a telegram of her husband, "Arriving Christmas eve—love." This filled both—the mother and son—with a new vigour. They waited anxiously for Christmas eve. Meera, at this juncture, realized, "nothing was more important than his happiness, his sense of security. A little boy needed his father" (78). Dalal asserts and reasserts her belief in age-old Indian tradition—in the institution of marriage—marriage a seat of perennial bliss and the broken marriages as cause of unhappiness in the home.

The story "The Intruder" also deals with the theme of marital discord. The primary reason of this discordant relationship was the wide disparity between the husband, Mr. Vale and his young wife, Mrs. Vale. Mrs. Vale, the second wife of Mr. Vale, was a young, firm figured, robust woman. Mr. Vale, on the other hand, was "a thin stooped man, something of a recluse, with a brilliant reputation as a historian" (100). Mr. Vale remained devoted to his books and Mrs. Vale felt bored and lonely for "she longed for the comfort of human companionship" (102). She loved her husband dearly and did her best to win him but she failed. Like his first wife Helen, Mrs. Vale couldn't help Mr. Vale in his work. The story has a tragic ending when one morning Mrs. Vale was found suffocated and strangled. Her little self was liberated. The story conveys a message that two people who are incompatible are different from each other and so are not able to live or work happily together. Thus lack of capability between Mr. and Mrs. Vale led to unhappy marriage.

Another story which has x-rayed the on-goings of the mind and heart of an Indian husband and his Indian wife is "Ranjit's Wife." One day Ranjit asked his wife for a divorce since Ranjit has some extra-marital relationship. Lila had been married to Ranjit for ten years. She did whatever Ranjit liked her to do. Keeping herself close to his liking, she never painted her lips and eyes, reddened her nails or shortened her hair. She always wore a plain cotton sari and blouse with a round high neck and small sleeves. She brooded, "She had done what he wanted for ten years and this was the result. I've given him the best years of my life" (127). But now she didn't subdue herself. She was bold enough to face this crisis. She said to her husband, "I'd like two months in which to think about things. After that, if you still want this divorce, you can go ahead" (125). Lila suddenly shook off her old appearance of a meek, weak Indian woman and emerged a rough, tough self who could challenge the odds that threatened her very existence. The author comments, "But a streak of stubbornness inside, a hard core which she had not expected to find, was now asserting itself" (127). She went to Ranjit's solicitor to know about the money she would receive in the event of divorce from her husband. Out of this spineless creature, a dauntless self was emerging that was incredulous for those who knew Lila. Mr. Shah shrieked in excitement, "Women you never knew how they would react—even the quiet ones" (129).

Without any break in her composure, anger or distress, Lila now decided to live life on her own terms. She said, "I've been married to Ranjit for ten years and in all that time I have never really done anything to please myself" (130) and now he had found someone else. She decided not to be a polite doormat. She went to the beauty parlour to let her hair trimmed and curled, purchased pants, tops and kaftans. Now she was a transformed self. One evening, she event out for dinner with one Kamal Bhat where she met her husband with his new love—a young girl—Vanita.

Ranjit was taken aback at the total transformation of Lila and looked at her like a hypnotized rabbit. Back home, Lila found Ranjit waiting for her who shouted at her, "How dare you go out looking like a painted strumpet?" Lila at once retorted, "I'm free, thank heavens. Free to do what I like, say what I like, dress as I like. After ten years it feels wonderful" (140).

No ideal Indian woman can even be faithless if she remains assured that her husband is hers and she is the most beautiful woman for him upon this earth. Now Ranjit regretted his rude behaviour and begged pardon. But Lila, a woman of indomitable sprit, replied, "I'm sorry Ranjit. I don't think I want to forget about the divorce. I find it very enjoyable to do as I please, to dress as I please, to go out dancing and to find that others think I am beautiful. After all these years, it's intoxicating. I don't want to come back to you and the same dreary routine" (141).

The story "The Silver Ringlets" exhibits another aspect of man-woman relationship where Bhima, the wife, cheats her devoted husband—Madhu.

The story "Roses, Roses, All the Way" displays another shade of the diverse themes of the present collection. The story portrays a wide spectrum of human emotions through roses. This ecological element helps the author to communicate her feelings more eloquently. The story opens with a photogenic description of the beautiful rose garden in its full March blossoming, mesmerizing colours and fragrance. At this time of enjoyment, the narrator was suddenly taken aback by a stranger's demand for some lovely roses. The stranger, Miss Malik, wanted the flowers for the Swamiji's birthday. The narrator offered her a cup of tea which she sipped with a feeling of guilt since she had given a word to Swamiji to be away from all sorts of addiction. Miss Malik was an elderly spinster who devoted herself to looking after her ailing mother. After the death of her mother, she felt lonely and later came to an ashram. Miss Malik took the narrator to the Ashram and both of them were out of their wits when they found the clean shaved Swamiji, reclining on a diwan and sipping a mug of hot tea. Dalal once again shows how appearances are often deceptive.

Miss Malik at once left the Ashram and ran back to the hotel to enjoy sumptuous lunch. The lonely creature who was earlier in depression now was full of spirit. She had a rose into her hair and said, "in fact, you might say, it is going to be roses, roses, all the way for me" (90). Now her life was as sweet and full of fragrance as was the rose garden.

Like the story "Roses, Roses, All the Way," "The Silver Stallion" is also based on the ecological element which establishes the relation of man and animal. It relates the story of a hill boy, Bishen who loved his horse Moti and didn't like to sell him in order to get money for the water pump. Bishen Singh's and his father's happiness knew no bounds when Rajendra Singh told them that they needn't sell their house because father Kerry had a scheme to bring water to all the villages around that area. He planned to install tubewell and pumps so that there would be a green island. The story throws light on Dalal's amazing power of characterization as she studies minutely the ongoings of a child's mind and heart.

"The Temple Bells" focuses on two villagers'—Akhtar Singh's and Dilip Singh's—efforts to steal the jewels which decorated the statue of the deity of the temple. Akhtar Singh had some fear in his heart. He told Dilip of people's belief in the sacredness of the jewels and also how the bells went on ringing clamorously if ever anybody tried to steal those jewels. The story ends on confirming this belief of the villagers. Dilip Singh and Akhtar removed the jewels and when they were about to leave, suddenly the bells began to clang, awaking up the villagers. Akhtar reiterated the story of the bells but the reality was that the bells clanged because of Akhtar's stumbling over the ropes. But Akhtar paid no attention to this explanation of Dilip. He felt relieved because he was saved from committing a sin. Did the bells ring because of the ropes trailing loose or was it the divine will? However, the author, on the one hand, shows reverence towards the divine will but, on the other, hints to the illogical, blind faith of the innocent Indians.

The story "The Temple of Shiva" has similar undertones. It's about the attack of dacoits and the courage of an old man who saved the entire village. The villagers thought that it was Shiva who saved them since they all took shelter in the temple of Lord Shiva. But the truth was that neither the guns nor Shiva saved them, it was the courage of the old man and the intelligence and presence of mind of the young boy that saved the villagers. The boy hid the villagers in the temple and the old man applied nettle plant to his body which produced red angry spot, the exact replica of small-pox. Small-pox though eradicated from the whole world terrified the foolish dacoits and they left.

"The Selling of Mantras" is another story of this sequence, describing Rishikesh as "one of those places that could exist in India, a town dedicated to the salvation of souls" (205). The author comments, "Pilgrims sought here an adjustment between reality and dreams, secure in the knowledge that no matter what they did, a plunge in the holy water washed clean of all sins" (205-6). The story revolves around the agony of an unemployed young boy who after trying his luck in Delhi, Mathura, Ghaziabad and Meerut reached Rishikesh. He spent his last five-rupee note on purchasing a book of mantras. He sat down under a tree and read the mantras. Suddenly he heard somebody speaking to him, "Sir, please Sir, Maharaj, huzoor, saintly one. Give me a mantra" (207). He wanted a mantra to appear strong, virile and handsome to his young wife. The young boy uttered a few words into the ears of this old fellow. He stood up and slipped the young man a five-rupee note. From here started the young man's profession of selling the mantras. He played upon people's weakness. "He was selling dreams and sometimes dreams came true" (211). He gave people the ability to think positively with conviction. So it was not the power of mantras which made people happy but it was their own conviction that dreams would come true that made them happy.

The story, "Happiness is a Box of Fudge," describes an old man's practice of deriving sadistic pleasure by teasing a young boy and girl, reading him the newspaper with minutest details. For a twelve-year-old, it was not interesting at all. Sometimes the old man pressed a hot spoon against the inside of the young girl's arm. One day their mother told them that the old man was dead. Later, the gift of vanilla fudge, sent by the old man's daughter, and the news of the old man's death were the great causes of much jubilation for these young children.

The story, "The Red Pavilion," describes an elderly spinster of forty-five who arrived in a small Indian hill station and settled there. Miss Turner, that old spinster, had a mystical aura around her as nobody could ever know anything about her personal life nor anybody could know about her engagements and pastimes. One evening people in the club were talking in excitement about a book *The Red Pavilion* by some W.H. Travers. The anonymity of the author caused a lot of curiosity which ended with Mrs. Peter's getting an autographed copy of the book. She discovered that the letters H and T of the autograph in the book and in the signed invitation by Mrs. Turner were identical. Mrs. Peter made a promise to Miss Turner never to tell anyone what she had just learnt.

The story, "The Connoisseur," provides a glimpse of Dalal's sense of humour when she called Miss Krishna, a kleptomaniac, a connoisseur. Miss Krishna's real name was Maya and she was deprived of her mother's love that was solely won by her younger sister. She in that state of mind developed an awful love for beautiful things. She satisfied this craving by stealing the art objects or precious items of crockery from the house of her acquaintances. The story tells how cause of perversion is deprivation of something essential in one's life.

The stories in *The Nude* vibrate with some deep explorations of human relationships. Nevertheless, they unravel the many layers of marital and mysterious human relationships. The following words, written on the blurb of the text sum up the very spirit of the book. "Written in lucid prose and set in the most ordinary situations, the nineteen stories in *The Nude* are fascinating snapshots of life that chart some of the most basic and most intricate human emotions."

Works Cited

Dalal, Nergis. *The Nude*. India: Penguin, 2007

Kumar, Shiv K. *Contemporary Indian Short Stories in English*. New Delhi: Sahitya Akademi, 2007

Theme of Rape in Shashi Deshpande's Novels

SUNALINI KONDAPALLY
Ramappa Engineering College. Warangal

Violence against women, children and the weak is a Human Rights issue. Violence does not mean only physical violence; it denotes mental or verbal torture also. The 1991 Convention of Women and Violence categorically states that violence includes "any act, omission or conduct by means of which physical, sexual or mental suffering is inflicted, directly or indirectly, through deceit, seduction, threat, harassment, coercion, or any other means"

Deshpande's maiden novel *The Dark Holds No Terrors* opens with Sarita, the protagonist of the novel returning to her father's house, after fifteen years, a place she had once sworn never to return to—unable to bear the sexual sadism of her husband. Her rapid academic and social climb evokes inferiority complex in Manohar, her husband. The unhealthy male ego poisons his mind. The lover in him dies. He is metamorphosed into a mean loathsome individual. The first incident that shatters Manohar's peace and tranquillity happens when Sarita suddenly becomes the darling of the slum dwellers by attending to the wounded in a factory explosion. Sarita's overnight success as a lady doctor leaves "nothing" for Manohar who feels "totally ignored" (42). He begins to get "rough and abrupt" with her in love-making. It is thus that the terrors of the night begin. The second disruptive incident happens when a girl, interviewing Sarita for a women's magazine, asks Manohar, "How does it feel when your wife earns not only the butter but most of the bread as well?" (200) Manohar turns an animal at night and attacks Sarita. Thus begin the nightmares. Unable to come to terms with the fact that he is a failure in life, Manu lets his wounded pride manifest itself in the form of sexual sadism, "the hurting hands, the savage teeth, the monstrous assault of a horribly familiar body." (102) Bed is the only place where he can assert his animal power over her. Manu becomes a mean, despicable fellow and a rapist of his own wife. His ferocity and sadism are so violent that she feels, "this is not to be death by strangulation, it [is] a monstrous invasion of my body" (11-12).

One theme that recurs in many of Deshpande's books is rape—both as a random violent act and one within marriage. As Adrienne Rich puts it, rape does not deal with the rape of the body alone but with the rape of the mind as well. Viewing rape through the feminist angle, we find it a significant issue for feminists because it denies the woman the right to her body. It is a subject which society prefers not to discuss. Rape has been defined as a "forcible ravishment of a woman by a man. It is one of the manifestations of her oppression and an expression of male chauvinism," says P.D. Mathew in his book *The Law on Rape*. The Law Commission in its report on rape regarded it as the "ultimate violation of the self." It is a humiliating event in a woman's life, which leads to fear for existence and a sense of powerlessness. Sarita cannot talk in public about the pain that her body has embodied. She considers herself to be a victim of 'legalized rape.' Deshpande underlines the pain of a woman who is destined to die in pain. To Sarita it is not the cruelty of her husband that fills her with grief, but "the thing she knew she has lost forever . . . the eternal female dream of finding happiness through a man. It would never come alive for her again and it was like silent mourning wail inside her" (124). The framework of the novel provides good acoustics for woman's voice and establishes that woman, too, has choices in life. But Shashi Deshpande does not glorify women's sufferings. Though she enlists a sufficient amount of sympathy for her protagonist, it is not on the grounds of her being a female sufferer or a martyr in patriarchy. Throughout the novel, Shashi Deshpande maintains commendable objectivity and avoids generalisations and partial views. Deshpande, in depicting Manu, seems to show how the stronghold of tradition makes scapegoats of men and turns them into victimizers. In fact, the novel explores questions like, "Who is the victim and who is the predator? Are the roles so distinct, so separate? Or are we, each of us both?" (144) Saru analyses further:

> there is something in the male that is whittled down and ultimately destroyed by female domination. It is not so with a female. She can be dominated, she can submit, and yet hold something of herself in reserve. As if there is something in her that prevents erosion and self-destruction. . . . Does the sword of domination become lethal only when a woman holds it over a man? (77)

Shashi Deshpande recounts in one of her interviews that when she was in Bangalore where her husband was a doctor, she learnt about the rape case of a nurse who was in a coma. She wrote it for *Femina*. The incident stayed with her and she used the incident with appropriate changes and wove the story in her novel, *The Binding Vine*. As she tells in the interview with Lakshmi Holmstrom, "The theme came to me suddenly. I was actually working on another novel, and one day, suddenly realized that this was what I had to write" (Pathak 250).

The attempt to map out 'strategies of resistance' in an Indian and deconstruct the binaries, Deshpande's work could also be read as a 'metaphorical critique' of the demands of a postcolonial terminology itself (Siva Ram 179), which release constructs such as the center in the margin, the dominant/ hegemonic and the silenced/ subaltern. In the light of this analysis, Deshpande's work can be read as falling within a broadly postcolonial-feminist framework. But while she does attempt to examine various ideologically encoded binaries such as speech/silence, modernity, tradition, male/female, oppressor/ victim, dominant/ resistant, central/ marginal, majority/minority etc.

The Binding Vine, similar to *The Dark Holds No Terrors*, is the story of rape but the canvas is vast. Urmi, the middle-class, educated narrator in *The Binding Vine*, leads Shakutai, the poor, illiterate woman, to an understanding that rape is never 'deserved,' that her daughter has not 'shamed' the family by 'asking for it.' Kalpana, daughter of Shakutai, is brutally raped by her stepfather and lies in the hospital like a living corpse. Yet there is another example of rape here. Urmi, the protagonist, discovers the story of her own mother-in-law through reading her diaries and poetry. She learns that Mira was trapped in a marriage without love and raped by her husband. Urmila realises, "what has happened to Kalpana happened to Mira too" (63). Mira was raped by her husband while Kalpana by a man who was like her father. What pains is that such things are never reported to police. They are often treated as accidents for the sake of family reputation and so are never made public. By writing about rape, Deshpande was breaking the silence on an issue which was rarely discussed—a silence which was intended to protect the honour of the males in the family. Shashi Deshpande talks to B.B.C.:

> 30 years ago it would never be talked about and I think that to me was the worst thing that it's so bound up with the honour of the family. It's the men in the family who are wronged not the woman and the disgrace is the woman's. I think this is what *The Binding Vine* is really about: why is the mother afraid to speak? The disgrace is not the girl's—the disgrace is the criminal's. But that is not how it is—because she thinks that it will hurt her family. It's really the dilemma which Urmi, the narrator, faces because if she makes its public, it's possible the family is going to be affected and if she doesn't, you know it's like saying the woman is the one who is in disgrace, who has done wrong, and I find a lot of activists in India also face this problem. It's a very true problem.

Shakutai, the uneducated dependent mother of Kalpana, the girl who was raped, fears the consequences of proclaiming rape on her daughter. She gives an analysis of societal attitude towards victims of rape: "If a girl's honour is lost, what's left? The girl doesn't have to do anything wrong, people will always point a finger at her" (59). She has another daughter who will be victimised because of the rape of her sister.

Urmila is the voice of resistance in the novel that registers a protest against the patriarchal attitude to the issue of rape. We find two forms of gender violence juxtaposed here in the case of Kalpana and Mira. Kalpana's unconscious state represents the silenced subaltern whereas poems and diaries of Mira become a mode of resistance. The note of authenticity that the diaries bare has been shattered by the most unexpected behaviour of Akka, the second wife of Mira's husband. After Mira's death, he married Akka only because he wanted a mother for his son. It is interesting to note that Urmila, the narrator "becomes caught up in the discovery of her long-dead mother-in-law's poetry, written when she was a young woman subjected to rape in her marriage." This gives rise to many questions: Why has Mira been granted this higher position of being a martyr/victim? Urmila does concede that after Akka breaks down it is not Mira's story which occupies but her Akka's act, her breaking down—an unprecedented act, according to Urmila. Akka, who did not cry, when her crying would have been termed natural cries now and the narrator is left with an unanswerable question: "Why had she broken now?" It is this mute question which makes it clear that Mira has been selected because of her ability to articulate, to write poetry, to write confidential diaries. It is through this act of writing that the story of Mira gets preference over the story of Akka, who had worse marriage because her husband married her to get a mother for her son. Why is there no talk about 'rape in marriage' in the case of Akka? Rape has always been a horrible indignity heaped on woman by the male species merely on the strength of brute force. This violence and denigration becomes worse when it occurs within the sanctity of a marriage. And this is what Mira's poetry is all about. Urmila's account of the incident of Kalpana's rape is loaded with ideological undertones. Shakutai's insistence that the police should not be informed as it will lead to Kalpana's disgrace and exposure is, in reality, an exposure of the societal attitude towards the rape victim and the patriarchal ideology of the rape which disgraces the victim rather than the culprit. When Shakutai laments it was Kalpana's fault, Urmila subverts the patriarchal logic exploding: "Are you blind? It's not her fault, no, not her fault at all. . . . The man, the man who did this to her. Don't you see, can't you see he is the wrong-doer" (148).

The feeling of being victorious and gloating over the act makes the rapist even more detestable. To Urmila comes the shocking revelation that everyone wants to hush up a rape case and in the process the rapist is able to get away scot free. The general attitude is, "Okay, she was raped. But publicizing it isn't going to do anyone good. It's going to mean trouble for everyone, the girl, her family" (88-89). Even the police whose job is to ensure that the culprit is brought to book prefer to hush it up:

> Why make it a case of rape? . . . She's going to die, anyway, so what difference does it make whether, on paper, she dies the victim of an accident or a rape? We don't like rape cases. . . . They are messy and troublesome, never straightforward . . . think of the girl and her family. Do you think it'll do them any good to have it known the girl was raped? She's unmarried, people are bound to talk, her name would be smeared. (88)

This feeling is so deeply ingrained in society that even the mother of the victim does not want a case to be registered, does not want to ensure justice for her daughter, "You people are trying to blacken my daughter's name . . . don't tell any one. I'll never be able to hold up my head again, who'll marry the girls, we're decent people . . . even if it's true, keep it to yourself, doctor, don't let anyone know of it. I have another daughter, what will become of her?" (58-59)

In society's attitude towards rape, the dividing line between the criminal and the victim, the attacker and the prey becomes blurred and almost non-existent. Instead of pointing a finger at the bestiality and violence perpetrated by the rapist, most people, including Kalpana's mother, find it easier to blame the girl. "And if you paint and flaunt yourself, do you think they'll leave you alone?" (146) A little later, she laments; "She's shamed us, we can never wipe off this blot. . . . It's all her fault, Urmila, all her fault." (147) Prasanna Sree observes: "Shakutai's outburst brings to light the partisan attitude prevalent in the patriarchal society. If a girl is raped, for no fault of hers, she alone is censured, and victimized. Thus Shakutai, in spite of all her motherly love and sympathy for her daughter, sees the Kalpana's bold independence as real reason for this catastrophe" (128).

Shashi Deshpande's third novel *Come up and Be Dead* has several instances of rape within marriage as in the case of Sonali's mother, who having had a terrible experience on her wedding night could not accept such sexual act as a part of marriage. The experience she had that night left her mentally scarred for the rest of her life. She felt violated when her husband touched her, "And yet, she bore it silently. Something had told her it was just between the two of them. She knew you couldn't scream 'rape' . . . not when it was your own husband. And even if she did, who would hear" (141).

Mridula, the girl who committed suicide, was another victim of 'rape.' The young trusting and innocent school-girl was lured by the murderers to become a part of a call-girl racket. They got Mridula drunk and she was raped by a 'customer.' She was unaware of what she was being forced to do, and ended up getting pregnant. Unable to cope with the situation, unable to get out of it and unwilling to confide in her parents, she committed suicide, or rather she was induced into doing so by the murderers.

Small Remedies, the eighth novel of Deshpande, voices the story of Madhu, a lonely daughter, a sensitive and able woman. The novel unravels the struggle of the protagonist as a motherless child brought up by her father. Madhu is raped by the friend of her father at the time of her father's death. As a child she conceals the fact of rape. Knowledge of this truth makes Som, her husband, a savage. Madhu confesses to Som, "He slept with me, I was only fifteen then. I don't think he meant it, but it happened. And that's why he—that's why he died. He killed himself because of what he did to me (262)

Madhu tries to understand the reason of Som's violence against her. He wants to know whether she was a virgin when he had married her. She trustingly shares the memory of the incident in which she had sex with a man who was old enough to be her father; an incident which later drove the man to suicide. In Madhu's words, "I know what the truth is that Som wants from me: that it has not happened, that I was a virgin when he married me. I begin to understand the truth that truth he could, perhaps, have borne: that I had been raped, forced into the act, that I was a victim, not a participant" (260).

Madhu cannot help thinking of the episode of her single act of pre-marital sex as neither rape nor love because she doesn't reject him at the time of rape. The incident is a mnemonic repetition of her life at Neemagaon as Munni's friend, as Doctor Saab's daughter. It was Munni who first mentioned "it" (sex) to Madhu. One could retrospectively interpret it as a cathartic release for her but the physical sensations were there too. Madhu recollects the incident of her rape:

> There is a moment of strangeness, of fear, when I realize he is fumbling at my clothes, at his own, but at the contact of bare skin, the fear is immediately overlaid by a sense of shock, like plunging into cold water. There is the joy of feeling the cold water against my bare skin, its ripples teasing my body, caressing my skin. Pleasure runs swiftly along my nerves, through my body. I am conscious of my body, of the rich sap within it, rushing to meet and mingle with him. Nothing is unknown, nothing is strange (268)

Deshpande's treatment of the theme of rape is different in this novel. Though Madhu is a child of 15 years, still she enjoys it as an event of sex but doesn't consider it rape. Perhaps, the secret gossip of sex with Munni in her childhood subconsciously induced her to participate rather than reject. Madhu recollects:

> An ancient memory, waiting to be released all these years, is directing my body's responses, making me aware of the pleasure, the pleasure that reaches a climax despite the pain, the agonizing pain, when my body accepts him, when it mingles with his. (268)

Madhu is not a victim of rape because her body responds to it positively whereas she becomes a victim at the hands of her premarital husband after revealing the truth of her sex. This causes the death of their only son. Thus Deshpande picturizes the consequences of rape. The incident which tortures her in the form of nightmare. It is Munni's "it" which is at the centre of "the nightmare, the nightmare that is the beginning of the nightmare of our own lives" (259). The incident that Madhu wants to exclude from her life involves a fait accompli, a sexual encounter that she had with a friend of her father in the immediate aftermath of her father's death, long before she met Som. She is constantly reminded of the dead person who had committed suicide on account of rape: "And there was a face looking at me, a man's face, his mouth open, tongue hanging out, weals round the neck. Marks of a rape. And even as I stared in horror at the face, the face came alive, the eyes opened, they looked at me, they saw me" (261). Madhu's son Adit and husband Som are intertwined with this story of unarticulated violence. Som thinks this was an act of betrayal and is tormented by the thought of his wife's sexuality. It is the single act of sex that Som holds onto. It is this fact that he can't let go of as if it has been welded into his palm. Purity, chastity, an intact hymen—these are the truths that matter to Som. Readers cannot help admiring Shashi Deshpande for her probing into the psyches of women and exploring their unexplainable agony caught in a helpless condition under male domination.

Bibliography

Deshpande, Shashi. *The Dark Holds No Terrors* N Delhi: Vikas, 1980.

_____. *Come Up and Be Dead.* New Delhi: Vikas, 1983.

_____. *The Binding Vine.* New Delhi: Penguin India, 1993.

_____. *Small Remedies.* New Delhi: Penguin India, 2000.

Holmstrom, Lakshmi. "Shashi Deshpande Talks to Lakshmi Holmstrom," *The Fiction of Shashi Deshpande*, ed. R.S. Pathak. New Delhi: Creative, 1998.

Sree, Prasanna S. *Woman in the Novels of Shashi Deshpande: A Study.* [Dissertation]: Tirupati: Sri Padmavathi Mahila University, 2001

Reconstruction of a Powerful Myth: Feminist Intervention in Githa Hariharan's *When Dreams Travel*

KEISHAM RAGINI DEVI
Res. Sch., Manipur University

"Myth" has turned out to be the most distinguished term of the present day while discovering the general principles of literature of the present times. The word "myth" is derived from the classical Greek word "mythos" that denotes any true or untrue story or plot. The principal modern meaning of a "myth" is that it is a story in mythology which is a system of hereditary stories which were once believed to be true by a particular cultural group, and which served to explain (in terms of the intentions and actions of supernatural beings) why the world is as it is and things happen as they do, and to establish the rationale for social customs and observances and the sanctions for the rules by which men conduct their lives. (Abrams)

Most of the myths are concerned with rituals which are forms laid down as rules of the holy ceremonials. We can also categorize mythology as any religion that we no longer have a feeling of its truthfulness. In spite of the fact that poets do not accept the authenticity of myths, they still employ the myths of Jupiter, Venus, Prometheus, Wotan, Adam and Eve, and Jonah for the construction of their writings. The very term also indicates supernatural tales that have been created in a very careful manner by authors. As for example, just for the cause of setting philosophical conjectures before the mind far from one's understanding, myths were used by Plato in his "Myth of Err" in Book X of *The Republic*.

In this regard what Northrop Frye says about myth is worth quoting: the typical forms of myth become the conventions and genres of literature. (Abrams 103) Referring to Frye's theory, we find four main narrative genres namely comedy, romance, tragedy and irony or satire which are substitutes of the four fundamental forms of myths that are connected with the seasons of spring, summer, autumn and winter.

For a woman writer in the contemporary literary world, mythology appears an unpleasant field. Over and above the discovery of gods and goddesses having superior position than Mother Nature, there are also the sexually evil Venus, Circe, Pandora, Medea, Eve etc. By the time a figure or story that has been acknowledged earlier and described exactly by a culture is used by an artist, myth will be employed or accompanied by the possibility that its purpose will be revisionary.

However, there is also the probability of cultural change. On the part of women writers, myth-making develops from a hidden belief of female "self-projection and self-exploration." (Kottiswari 106) The critic adds: "Myths are, moreover, retrieved images of what women have collectively and historically suffered and in some cases they are instructions for survival." (106)

In the story of *The Arabian Nights*, we find a King called Sharyar who made a solemn promise of marrying a virgin every night only to be killed the next morning. This is because once he found his wife, the queen committed adultery and on seeing this he killed her as a legal punishment and then made the above promise. A vizier or the councillor of the state was given the responsibility of finding out virgin girls for marrying the Sultan only for the purpose. But it became a terribly hard task on the part of the vizier to find out virgin girls everyday. And finally, one girl among the two daughters of the vizier, Scheherazade by name took a firm decision of offering herself as a bride to the King. Her main purpose was to save the girls of the kingdom from the hands of the evil King with anger and vindictive motive full of revenge. In spite of the father's advice and warning of stopping her from such an act, the girl remained firm in her determination and finally married the King.

Scheherazade's younger sister Dunyazad also accompanied her to the King's palace. One very interesting thing is that she could obtain the consent of the King for telling him a story on the wedding night. She kept the story uncompleted at dawn when the King had to rise and deal with the matters of the state. But he was more eager to hear the remaining part of the story and thereafter Shahryar, the King, determined to execute Scheherazade the next day so that he could hear the end of the story. But the following night also, the story could not be finished and the King had to postpone his wife's execution once again. In the stories which are connected in series, we find the universe as a whole with experiences of human beings. This thread of narration elongated for a period of one thousand and one nights. At last the King was totally fascinated by the magical power of Scheherazade in her act of untiring story-telling and he decided to make her his queen. King Shahryar finally perceives the meaning of forgiveness, justice and humanity after he is thoroughly delighted by the tales of *The Arabian Nights*.

When Dreams Travel (1999), the third novel of Githa Hariharan, can be placed as a modern parallel of *The Arabian Nights*. In this novel, the novelist employs the tales of *The Arabian Nights* as the interwoven subject of the writing.

The dimensional, authenticated narrative yields to conversational narrative where time is dealt in a new and distinct manner. The historical Arabian tale, *The Thousand and One Nights* is granted lesser significance than memory and interior life. Githa Hariharan not only unfolds the historical story in a new way of understanding, but she also deconstructs the story so as to display the inconsiderate and merciless pretension of patriarchy existing in the well-known story of *The Thousand and One Nights*. The novelist changes the normal course of action of the earlier book while making it a part of the whole.

As its scheme, *The Thousand and One Nights* or *The Arabian Nights* employs stories inside the range of stories. Scheherazade, the storyteller, used the stories as her weapon to prevent herself from death at the hands of the merciless King who married a virgin every night only to be killed the following morning. Despite the fact that the historical story is completely filled with adventure and fantasy, the underlying theme aims at the physical suffering and savagery that remain concealed in it. Githa Hariharan keeps the supposition of patriarchy that we find in the stories of *The Arabian Nights*, in a prominent position through intertext and magic realism. The novelist revives the early storytelling with a view to challenging the male-centred mental conception.

Sultan Shahryar is introduced to the readers as a person who obtained sexual pleasure by making women suffer and at the same time his 'harem' is filled with women. But all these women are looked at by the Sultan as a group of greedy women. Hariharan indirectly states that the stories of *The Arabian Nights* consider deeply the extravagant pride of male as the stories were composed when women had no expression of resistance. Over and above this, the novelist indirectly introduces Shahrzad, a lady with a creative power who, by her remarkable mental ability can make the Sultan stay in a state of anxiety. But, regardless of this, the Sultan is unwilling to accept and recognise her natural skill.

Shahrzad's deed of storytelling could be perceived as an extremely serious and dangerous conflict of the genius that was being confined to convey its power of production. This was only for the purpose of accomplishing a healthy consciousness of self whereas the stories narrated by her did not convey that perception; on the contrary, they frequently suggested the unpleasant and extravagant pride of male. Further, the Sultan approved and admired Shahrzad for her pure female virtue but he did not consider her imaginative natural skill. A thing to be noticed is that the storytelling method that was taken up by Shahrzad is an extremely dangerous trial of the creative or confined imaginative power in order to accomplish a healthy perception of self, whereas, no such idea was found in the original tales which frequently hinted at the brutal pride of male.

The Thousand and One Nights is presented in a new style by Shahrzad's sister Dunyazad and her accomplice Dilshad in the novel *When Dreams Travel*. The two women characters who remained speechless in the first part of the story, narrate stories to each other for seven days and nights which is equivalent to "one thousand and one nights." The stories of these two women are related to one person only and telling them again in a different way is terribly unpleasant, ridiculous and also strange.

The story of the novel opens when Dunyazad engaged herself on a journey after learning about the death of her elder sister after many years. In the course of her travelling to Shahabad in a false appearance, she only created the existence of her sister who remained quiet, her mother, the mother of Sultan Shahryar, the slave girls and female servants of the palace whereby reviving the past and also telling the story again with a contrast. For seven days and nights both Dunyazad and Dilshad narrated stories to each other and thus the part played by the storyteller and listener alters. The role taken up by the storyteller and listener was a very important method of releasing the women from the confinement of rules carried out by patriarchy. When the story concludes, Shahrzad is portrayed as an old woman projecting her voice firmly as a challenge and caution to the young girls: "I fought for myself and yes, for you as well. And you—what will you do when your turn comes? When the drums roll and the sword blunted with age, the rusty axe, wake up to be freshly sharpened? (276)

Githa Hariharan makes a fresh dimension in an original way inside the range of the previous treatise that revives modern courses of life where women have risen as the operators of their unavoidable fate and not as those crumpled under pressure. These women state clearly with force that one cannot get away, prevent or restrain the past but one should come to an agreement with it. The portrayal of the past events cannot be avoided; rather it can be utilized and at the same time observed and explained critically, with the use of irony and parody. In the novel, there is a twist of a single narrative of apparently different stories by emphasising the several methods of telling the stories that are contemporary and traditional and at the same time oral and written. Both the ancient and contemporary literary stories and patterns are combined together, thereby producing a critical parody.

The significance of the novel lies not in the incidents but in the set of ideas that constitute the happenings of the past into the realities of present history. The fact is made more authentic by the following lines:

> But Shahrzad, like her own story, is a survivor. The travelling tale undergoes a change of costume, language and setting at each serai on its way. It adapts itself to local conditions, to this century or that, a permanent fugitive from its officious parent, legitimate history. And Shahrzad—she too has learnt the lessons of the tales she told. She is now a myth that must be sought in many places, fleshed in different bodies, before her dreams let go of Dunyazad or her descendants. (25)

Woman, the biologically weaker of the two sexes, has been oppressed since ancient times by the malefolk. It became a tradition that seemed hard to alter. But time has changed now. Tyrannical cruelty or injustice done towards women has become an unwanted tradition that has been discarded by many. But, in the story of the novel, *When Dreams Travel*, we find a King called Sultan Shahryar or friend of the city of the Kingdom of Shahabad who is depicted as a very suspicious and insecure King. Once, Sultan Shahryar and his brother Shahazaman, the ruler of Samarkand were confronted by their queens who were committing adultery with their slaves. As they were being fooled and betrayed by their wives, they considered themselves unfit to rule their kingdoms. The attitudes and manners of the queens could un-man the most influential of Kings and they resorted to violence by killing those responsible for their sinful act. Then, as a new plan for his harem, he created a perfect scheme to fulfil his sexual desire for which he needed a woman if she could be called a wife or queen. Every day a fresh virgin would be found out and married at night only to be killed the following morning. The scheme worked effectively for three long years. New and fresh virgin brides started entering the palace and before anybody inside the palace was aware of their names or faces, they were killed by the executioner.

Sultan Shahryar could overcome his sexual desire in this manner. He was filled with pride that his name would be recorded permanently in myth and history in the generations to come. Thousands of girls had been beheaded just one night after marriage and there came a time when there was scarcity of virgin girls. Then, the Wazir or deputy ruler of the state was given the responsibility and made in-charge of finding out virgin girls from the city. He took his responsibility faithfully and tried to search the desired girls. But he only heard fathers telling that their daughters had lost their virginity or learnt of hiding their daughters at a far away place. Thus, he was unsuccessful in his venture. While other faithful subjects of the city refused to give up their daughters, the Wazir turned his attention towards his elder daughter Shahrzad, only to show his loyalty to his ruler. She volunteered herself to be the bride of the Sultan and with the help of her sister Dunyazad, she started playing her role of telling stories in series. She was a splendid lady who did not admit defeat, fully aware that she possessed the fate of many other women in her tongue. Her life was full of risk and she suffered intensely even during childbirth. But, the Sultan, who was to be the father of the yet to born child had no consideration of the woman's suffering. She still managed to continue her performance perfectly and after a thousand and one nights, the Sultan was truly fascinated by her stories and cancelled Shahrzad's execution. At the end Shahryar resented. This is a great example of the tyrannical nature of a man.

Through the stories in the novel one can witness the severe appearance of a cruel and harsh treatment done by patriarchy towards women. Rama Kundu says about Githa Hariharan's writing competency: "With remarkable skill she evokes the grim "faces" of the thousand (plus one) nights; at the same time she uses it deconstructively to bring out the terror, the terrible oppression and injustice, the inherent chauvinism of the comfortable patriarchal assumptions often blunt-insensitive-irrational that she reads between the lines of the world famous legend." (180)

Shahrzad whose name means "born of the city" was "clever, ambitious and quick-tongued." (16) Shahrzad had entered the palace of Shahabad of her own will though knowing quite well that all other women could not escape their fate from the sword of the executioner, the next morning after marriage. She became the wife of Sultan Shahryar or "master of the city" who was a cruel ruler of great power whom people hated greatly. Standing in opposition to Shahryar was Shahrzad who had a great concern for the city and the lives of the dwellers of the city and other virgin girls. But during the course of performing the role of a saviour, she had to undergo many (54) hardships. One such incident was her unromantic pregnancy. For nine months, there was "the brain-bending rehearsal to be got through before nightfall." (122)

Shahrzad was habituated to remaining visible to the spectators. She took the role of a narrator having the knowledge of everything and thereby pacified the Sultan in every manner. But, she remained unnoticed to the spectators and went behind the soul in its journey to life after death. Regardless of the fact that she did not achieve complete victory, she could prevent the severe and unpleasant killings by the Sultan for nine months. She might die as the one who did not admit defeat but one who tried hard to overcome the problems till her last breath but she had firm determination that she should live. She believed in an existence following death and for that moment, she had a desire to live for her own sake and also for her child too, though her life was surrounded by the "harem, dungeons, palaces, its forbidding walls and shrouds." She could hear the angry cry of the baby and immediately the child was handed over to Sabiha to take its care.

In a number of stories, Shahrzad spoke of both sexually virtuous and modest wives and the other most probably to indicate that all types of men could turn out to be cuckolds. Ultimately, in a serene manner, Dunyazad exposed her wish to murder the King while he was listening to the story. She expressed her intolerance of seeing her sister's great and frightful attempt night after night. As the new King of Shahabad was sleeping in the arms of Sabiha unharmed, that night was the perfect time for the purpose and it was a time of poetic justice to some extent. But Shahrzad believed firmly that "righteous power waits at the end."

In the palace she hated bloodshed. Thus, both the sisters in company would use up their severe mental and physical suffering every night that was linked with delightful but hazardous telling of truths. Shahrzad and her unfair cruel husband were more strictly confined than other clearly evident connections of man and wife, also ruler and ruled. The situation remained alive for a thousand and one nights. In the still and quiet atmosphere created by the authority, three babies were born. After a number of nights, the day for a solemn ceremony came. The influential and energetic, the honest and brave, that was acting under false beliefs (131) Though she was a captive, she had apprehended the facts. "He has been brought to his senses by a woman; and with, of all things, her stories; her ready tongue, her cleverness." (21)

Shahrzad did not remain a typical sufferer struggling for her existence but she was rather an actively courageous woman instigated by the hazards of the circumstances. Shahrzad, who was given out to be dead, was all of a sudden shown as an old woman who led sleepless nights and remained in expectation of death. But she had a wish to tell young girls that she, Shahrzad, rescued their grandmothers, their mothers and all of them from the cruel hands of the Sultan. But they would have to make great efforts to fight for themselves when a moment of change came in their life. In the story finally, Shahrzad made this remark: "When the drums roll, and the sword blunted with age, the rusty axe, wake up to be freshly sharpened?" (276)

NOTES

Abrams, M.H. 1978. *A Glossary of Literary Terms*, Third Edition, Madras: Macmillan India.

Hariharan, Githa. 2008. When Dreams Travel, India: Penguin Books.

Kottiswari, W.S. 2008. "Postmodern Feminist Writers: A Study of Selected Works of Shashi Deshpande and Githa Hariharan," *New Lights on Indian Women Novelists in English*, Vol. IV, ed. Amar Nath Prasad. New Delhi: Sarup.

Kundu, Rama. 2001. "Githa Hariharan: Intertext, Metafiction and 'Her Story,'" *Post-Independence Indian English Fiction*, ed. Rajeshwar Mittapalli.

The Arabian Nights, Introduction. The Arabian Nightshttp:// www .enotes.com/classical-medieval-criticism/arabian-nights

An Interview with Manju Kapur

DEEPA DIDDI
Maitreyi College, University of Delhi

DD: Critics call you a feminist writer. Do you agree with their assessment of your works?

MK: Yes. I am a feminist writer in the sense that my works are woman-centric. My novels focus on the needs and desires of women from different backgrounds and in different situations. Women yearn for recognition for their work, particularly since domestic labour so often goes unappreciated. They want concern and a sharing of responsibilities.

DD: Why did you choose fiction as a mode to write?

MK: Fiction provides a lot of imaginative space.

DD: Who are your favourite authors? What is it that you like in their works?

MK: I always have a problem with this question as I thresh through various books/ authors in my mind, trying to decide which is my 'favourite,' only to decide I don't have a favourite. I like reading what is known as literary fiction, then I like reading biography, memoir, etc.

DD: How do you conceive your characters?

MK: My characters evolve as the writing goes on. I do not have a pre-conceived character. I like to create characters who behave consistently and plausibly in the given circumstances. I think of the theme first and then create the characters.

DD: Talking about *Difficult Daughters*, set in the Forties, what made you write a character like Virmati, who defies tradition? How ahead are you of time?

MK: Virmati's character is loosely based on my mother's story. The broad fact that she married a man who was already married is the same—the details are mine.

In general if you look at the three novels, *Difficult Daughters*, *A Married Woman* and *Home*, and the three protagonists, you realise that Astha and Nisha are a little less inclined to step outside the home. It's not that Virmati is very daring—she is—but you have to consider the background she came from, the political struggle, the socio-economic factors. The thirties and forties was a period of tremendous change and emancipation—particularly for women of her community, and all this made it possible for her to leave the house whether to study or to work. Women were involved in the freedom movement; they had access to education, social reforms; they were involved in teaching, spreading awareness. This did in some ways affect their personal lives. I write about women in the house and I do believe there are no water-tight compartments between domestic fiction and that plays itself in the larger world. Women live their lives at home with children, more than men do. The realities of day-to-day life may be filtered through men who face the world, but they affect women as well. In *Home*, even though the women live in a joint family and do not work, their lives are affected by what goes around and outside their home. Microcosm and macrocosm are intertwined.

DD: Why have you projected Indian mothers as being very harsh to their daughters?

MK: Mothers! Well I think sometimes parents can be very harsh in the belief that children particularly daughters should not get wayward and spoilt. It is all about conditioning. A huge concern, be it a girl or a boy, is marriage.

DD: Had Kasturi been considerate, would Virmati's future,be different?

MK: Why yes, had Kasturi been open and affectionate towards Virmati, she might not have fallen in love with the professor.

DD: Is it your way of telling the parents, especially mothers to wake up and treat daughters with love?

MK: Girls are treated differently, yes, even today, but if you look at children as individuals rather than as representatives of you, your family, your samaj, things would certainly be different. The Arya Samaj concept of female education was big in Punjab. Virmati, deviating from tradition and falling in love, was not just about the family getting a bad name. The Samaj would get a bad name, education for girls would get a bad name and so in their eyes her crime was doubly unforgivable. Moreover you find this psyche in the Indian family which is specifically addressed to women: 'You are just thinking of yourself.' That's a crime! The woman immediately becomes defensive: 'No, I am not!' So there is lot of defence, accusation around these things. This thinking is embedded in the discourse going on between parents and daughters.

DD: What prompted Virmati to marry Professor?

MK: It's hard to say—indeed the whole book is devoted to this issue. But Virmati is conditioned to look after, to nurture, and to care for. Harish appeals to her emotions, even to her sense of responsibility as he assures her he will die without her. Besides this he opens windows for her, through his conversation, his ideas, his interest in her reading, his encouragement of her studies.

DD: This is heady stuff.

MK: Virmati was also not taught to look out for herself—the family was going to do this for her. She is innocent and unexposed, as so many young girls who come from protective backgrounds tend to be. The reason that my stories are set within such strong social family contexts, is because all this goes into making you who you are.

DD: The grandfathers in your works are bestowed with feminine qualities and you have voiced very strong messages through them. Any special reason for this?

MK: The whole thing about girls being ill-treated in a family is not a universal phenomenon. There are families who are very fond of their daughters. It was easy to illustrate this through grandfathers.

In *Home*, the same family will both protect the daughter and cause her distress. Nisha's father for example cannot go beyond a point—he has to keep the larger interest of the family in mind. He could not agree to Nisha's marrying Suresh because that would be against everything he had stood for. He feels bad and realizes what his daughter is going through. He tries to then help her in every possible way.

DD: Is it guilt feeling that makes Nisha's father do things for her or genuine feminity?

MK: It is a mixture, he feels sorry for the necessary suffering Nisha had to undergo. He goes out of his comfort zone for his daughter. She is permitted to work, in fact it is Nisha's father who facilitates her business; it is a big step, she is allowed to work when no woman in the family could even think about it.

DD: Why your men have been bestowed with feminine qualities as against women?

MK: Men have more power and say in the family. Standing comes with economic independence. Men have social standing, money and power both in the house and out. In certain situations, this makes it easier for them to express caring and concern.

DD: You have raised the issue of sexual abuse in a girl child in *Home*. Don't you agree that it is the duty of the father to protect and fight against such a crime?

MK: It is, but often this is not done. Such issues are brushed under the carpet.

DD: Again the same issue, how can a mother and grandmother or to generalize a woman be blind and insensitive to Nisha's trauma?

MK: Often in families, one does not see and acknowledge what one does not want to. Statistics show that sexual abuse is often committed by a member of the family. Normally people tend to ignore and take a preventive measure—as in this case—sending Nisha to her aunt's house. I have tried to pinpoint this 'silence.'

DD: There is a stark contrast between the two sisters—Rupa and Sona. Coming from the same background, they have a different approach towards life!

MK: The way of approaching life stems from your circumstances. Sona came from a poor family and was treated as an outsider by her in-laws. She tries to adjust in the joint family. When the children grow, she tries to prove herself through her children. Rupa, on the other hand did not have to prove herself to anyone.

DD: Your views on the Indian psyche of equating love and sex with marriage.

MK: I have tried to bring these facts out in *Home*. A great deal of shame is associated with sex. Equating sex with marriage is one of the causes of Nisha's skin condition. She lives with the guilt regarding the moments spent with Suresh.

DD: What made Astha turn to Peepilika in *A Married Woman*?

MK: Astha is dissatisfied with her marriage. She is too timid to actually go all out and have an affair with a man. A woman makes it easier for her—the intimacy involved also comes about gradually, without the danger signposts there would have been, had a man been involved.

DD: I read on the net that since Astha and Peepilika do not get Aijaz, they fall for each other. What would you like to say?

MK: I am not comfortable saying which is the right reading or interpretation. There are as many versions as there are readers.

DD: Do critical reviews distract your focus?

MK: Good or bad, I do not read them.

DD: Looking back at your works, would you like to change the development of any of your protagonists?

MK: I do not think about them once the final drafts are done. I have been with the work so long and so intensely, that I do not like going back once I am through.

DD: Nina in *The Immigrant* wants to get married, and when the proposal of Ananda comes, she is sceptical!

MK: Nina is an example of a modern woman, who wants to settle down, yet is independent. She needs to be sure before committing herself to a relationship, especially one which involves going abroad and leaving her old mother behind.

DD: "One is not born a woman." You quoted this line in your novel three times. Any specific reason for this?

MK: Once Nina goes to Canada, she starts thinking about female identity from a different, more political perspective. She starts questioning Indian norms regarding gender bias. She realizes the ways in which she had been socialized and tries to break free from those ways.

DD: *The Immigrant* is a drastic change from your earlier novels. To whom do you attribute this change?

MK: The idea had been simmering at the back of my mind for a relatively long time. I have lived abroad and know the problems faced by immigrants, their thought patterns. It is very different from staying in your own country.

DD: Your comments on your journey as a writer till date.

MK: I always hope to write better and better books. My aim has been to improve and polish my craft. In fact writing has become more difficult and not easier with each novel. I devote a lot of time to style and ways of presenting my story.

DD: Are you working on another novel?

MK: Yes, I am. I have been writing it since 2004. I hope to complete it by this year.

DD: What would the theme be this time?

MK: Adoption, custody, marriage break-ups.

DD: The Indian woman has realized that she has been subjugated for centuries. Now she is ready to cross all lines and boundaries. Do you advocate this change?

MK: I wonder whether by pushing for equality, women can be said to cross all lines and boundaries—probably not. We do not live by ourselves. I would not advocate something for women which I would not advocate for men, who live within their own constraints. Women should be allowed to express themselves. They should have a sense of autonomy. Moreover, we should certainly not live in a climate where female fetuses are murdered. They should be respected, should be seen as valuable creatures of society who have a lot to offer, given a chance. I do not know what is wrong with our society that treats its women in such a manner. Women are in a difficult position in our country. Class rescues you to a certain extent but being a woman you have to struggle and push the negative energies away from you.

Manju Kapur's *A Married Woman*: A Feminist Study

KAMAL KUMAR RAUL
Res. Sch., I.I.T., Roorkee

'Feminism' is a literary movement that raises women issues relating to their equality, exploitation, liberty, socio-economic-cultural and familial rights in every walk of life. This term was first discussed by Alice Rossin, an American writer, in his book *The Athenaeum* on 27 April 1895. The female writers began to think that they had same talent and wisdom as male to write, expressing their claims of equality and emancipation in every sphere of life. Virginia Woolf's *A Room of One's Own* is an example of the feminist approach. It is an extended essay on the women issues. Published on 24 October 1929, the essay is based on a series of lectures she delivered at Newnham College and Garton College. The essay is generally seen as a feminist text, and is noted for its argument for literal and figural space for women writers in the literary tradition, dominated by patriarchy. The title of the essay comes from Woolf's conception that a woman must have a room of her own if she is to write fiction. The 'room,' here, is symbolic and significant. The title also refers to author's need for poetic license and the personal liberty to create art. In the essay, Woolf constructs a critical and historical account of women writers so far. Woolf examines the careers of several female authors, like Aphra Behn, Jane Austen, the Bronte sisters and George Eliot. The male patriarchy limits the creative power of women, imposing upon her domestic duties within the four walls of the house. In this context, one may quote Chaman Nahal who defines "feminism" as a mode of existence pertaining women emancipation in all respects: "I define feminism as a mode of existence in which the woman is free of the dependence syndrome. . . . There is dependence syndrome, whether it is the father or the community, whether it is religious group or ethnic group." (14) Again R.K. Dhawan writes: "feminism is to be used as a socio-cultural movement to secure a complete equality of women with men in enjoyment of all rights—moral, religious, social, political, educational, legal, and economic." (1)

Feminist writers give top priority to the maximization of freedom of women or minimization of patriarchal priority. This may cover the issues of identity, inequality factors, gender discrimination and exploitation as the second sex. Feminist movement fabulously focuses on female freedom in social, legal and the cultural areas. Further, it means the things relating to women issues or women consciousness. The feminist writers aggrandize their aggressive phallic selves to degrade the spirit of women as source of submissive sexual object.

Since Margaret Fuller's *Women in the Nineteenth Century* (1845), Kate Chopin's *The Story of an Hour*, Sarah Orne's *A Country Doctor* to Virginia Woolf's *A Room of One's Own* (1929) and Norwegian writer Henrik Ibsen's *A Doll's House*, the freedom plight of women has seriously been taken into account by feminist writers. In the modern frame of gynocentricism, various women write against male chauvinism and socio-political inequality.

Women's identity consciousness and quest for self-hood, search for place and person, claim for justice and equality in all respects without any discrimination of sex and gender have become popular objective-correlatives in the works of feminist Indian writers. They are also supplemented by their integrity of individuality, social and economic freedom as well as mental and emotional independence. The women writers like Ruth Prawer Jhabvala, Nayantara Sahgal, Nargis Dalal, Shashi Deshpande, Manju Kapur, Mahasweta Devi, Bharati Mukherjee, Anita Desai, Rama Mehta, Geeta Mehta, Shobha De, Arundhati Roy and others who portray their plight and fight for their rights. Identity crisis in the marginalized class seems to be one of the major concerns. It emerges as a major momentum against inequality, exploitation and otherness. The spread of education and western influence have inspired them to speak of other than traditional images of 'wife' and 'mother.'

Women writers begin to articulate their passions and plights in order to project them to be equal to man. In the holistic approaches of Hinduism, women are considered as images of sacrifice and sufferings. They are considered to be like Nora in *A Doll's House* in the hands of their parents before their marriage and after their marriage in the hands of their husbands and sons. A woman is considered to be an embodiment of sacrifice, suffering and faith. In our religious and national epics the *Ramayana* and the *Mahabharata*, they have been projected as victims and sufferers. Sita was kidnapped by Ravana and kept in the Ashok forest with countless suffering and ultimately went through an ordeal to prove her chastity. Draupadi, too, is made naked in the royal court in the presence of all by Dushasan as it is described in the *Mahabharata*. The biological difference between the male and female is misinterpreted as gender-biased cultural difference which is presented by feminist writers.

This present paper aims at discussing the feminist approach to Manju Kapur's second novel *A Married Woman*, where the female protagonist named Astha appears as silent Ibsenite voice and votary of women's emancipation.

Kapur's first novel *Difficult Daughters* has received a wide international acclaim and been awarded the commonwealth writers' prize. The book was in the bestseller's list. Her second novel *A Married Woman* is an epoch-making literary work that claims and carries two major feminist issues. One is radical feminism and another one is Marxist feminism. Before analyzing the novel, I would like to define these two terms: Radical feminism and Marxist feminism. Radical feminism is a philosophy emphasizing the patriarchal roots of inequality between men and women, or, more specifically, social dominance of women by men. Radical feminism views patriarchy as dividing rights, privileges and power primarily by gender. The radical formula of male superiority is heart-felt. Radical feminism opposes existing political and social organization in general because it is inherently tied to patriarchy. Radical feminism opposes patriarchy. To equate radical feminism to man-hating is to assume that patriarchy and men are inseparable, philosophically and politically. Gerda Lerner has summarized the radical feminism thus: "Reforms and legal changes, while ameliorating the condition of woman and an essential part of the process of emancipating them, will not basically change patriarchy. Such reforms need to be integrated within a vast cultural revolution in order to transform patriarchy and this abolishes it" (3).

Marxist feminism arises out of the doctrines of Karl Marx, whose theory is centred less on the material aspects of life than on the more broadly defined social ones. Simone Weil in *Oppression and Liberty* describes Marxism as a theory quite incomplete so far as its application is concerned, yet very relevant in describing the mechanisms of economic growth. Central to Marxism is the idea of the division of labour, which is central in the capitalist system. Marxist feminists base their arguments on the moral right with reference to the corruption of wage and labour. That is reported in the expression of class distinctions.

What appears to have gone unnoticed in Marxism is the perception that in the capitalist system there is a stripping away of the spiritual qualities of life as a person is reduced to being a mere cog in a machine. There is a tendency in some feminist writings to discuss the relationship between feminism and prostitution in much the same terms, thus stripping away the transcendent and spiritual qualities of prostitutes and leaving only a mechanistic view of prostitutes within prostitution. Kapur carefully articulates and emulates the Radical and Marxist feminism in various sequences and motivating motions of female characters relating to Astha, the protagonist. Her picture in the fiction seems to be more of a man than a mere character in the novel since it is mostly seen 'art and artists are inseparable.' Virtually liberal feminists are not more reactionary than the radical feminists. They apply liberal principles of freedom, equality and justice to women. But radical feminists are committed to bring a basic change to the women emancipation without any compromise.

The novel *A Married Woman* centers round a middle class Delhi-based Hindu family. Hemant, an America-returned Delhi business man, married Astha Bhadra, a middle-class educated Hindu girl. Initially their married life runs smooth and they have two children, a son Himanshu and a daughter Anuradha. Astha teaches in a college. Their conventional marriage is smooth, sound and healthy till Astha meets Aijaz Khan, a secular Muslim involved in Militant left wing theatre group. Their nascent friendship is cruelly brought to an end when Aijaz meets his lamentable doom in communal riots over Babri Masjid in Ayodhya. Then Astha is encountered with Pipeelika, the widow of Aijaz. Pipeelika is a qualified Hindu girl from mother's side. She is M.A. in economics and sociology. Astha and Pipeelika is a lesbian couple. Their love relationship reaches a climax when Pipeelika flies to US for her Ph.D. Astha again gets back to her emotional family attachment.

The two feminist theories mentioned above may be applied to this novel. The social institution of marriage and the role of woman relating to social and traditional affairs are tactfully articulated by Kapur. It is a story of the young Astha, who is born and brought up in Delhi in a typical middle class family. She has an arranged marriage where she is happy to see her husband and other relatives perfect in domestic and social attachment. She takes the role of a childbearing mother and housekeeping woman. She silently does all her work. Her mother, a conservative and orthodox traditionalist, says: "when you are married our responsibility will be over. Do you know *Sastras* say it without getting their daughter married; they will be condemned to perpetual rebirth" (1). Astha strongly objects: "I don't believe in all that stuff and I think an educated person neither should you."

This protest may be a strong feminist voice against traditionalists who suppress women freedom. This may be a version of radical feminism. Astha strongly reacts to her mother in challenging the inequality of gender and sex. This gender discrimination may be a strong foothold of radical feminism; "Ma did not you have a son to look after you when you are old. You can not take any thing from a daughter? Why did you stay with me?"

Socialist feministic attitude is reflected in the character of Astha. Astha's mother sells her plots and gives the money to Hemant to re-invest it. It is the feeling of Astha's mother that they cannot manage it since they are women. Astha challenges it; "Really Ma, don't you think women are responsible for their investment?"(97)

The socialist feminist's concept is sexual division of labour which may be an integral part of political economic theory having major connection between politics and economy. This political economy is the Marxist theory which aims at classless society. In crude form, it is known as democratic socialism. This concept is reflected in the character of Astha when she finds faults in her father and mother-in-law for bringing up of Hemant to never regard women as beings to be consulted in their own lives. (98)

When Hemant comes back from America, he finds his wife Astha pregnant. He happily says that his mother is very fond of a grandson. This irritates Astha and she speaks rebelliously to erase gender discrimination: "But Ma I want a daughter; in America there is no difference boys and girls." (67)

The claim of motherhood in India is a great craze for woman because metaphysically, they have a strong belief that bearing a child in her womb is a great blessing of god. A woman without child is unlucky. Society ill-treats her. It is believed that if one looks at her face, that day will end in fiasco. Even our ancestors do not receive a drop of water from her hand. She is absolutely secluded. The society is so patriarchal that if a woman gives birth to a female child, she is hated by her kith and kin. Hemant desires a son in Astha's second pregnancy and gives the derogatory remark: "You just go and talk to some children about poems and stories, organize few clubs and come back." (68) This comment certainly criticizes male dominance. Manju Kapur says in an interview with Ira Pandey, "I am exploring the space that women occupy in domestic relationships. It is a world I know . . . she is a wife, a mother, a daughter in-law in fact" (*The Hindu*, 5 Jan. 2003). The world of Manju Kapur is full of marriage and familial ties. There are two major dimensions: cultural confrontation and lesbian relationships. Kapur considers lesbianism better than male chauvinism. The plot of the novel revolves around this theme.

Thus, Kapur presents feminist concept in various forms and folds in the novel *A Married Woman* that places her among the front-ranking feminist writers parading the cause of women emancipation in all respects.

Works Cited

Betty, Friedan. *The Feminine Mystique*. Harmondsworth: Penguin, 1982.

Beauvoir, Simon de. *The Second Sex*. Harmondsworth: Penguin, 1972.

Dhawan, R.K. ed. *The Commonwealth Review*, vol. XVII, No. 1.

Devi, Mahasweta. *Women Writing in India*, vol. II, New York: The Feminist Press, 1993.

Figes, Eva. *Patriarchal Attitude: Women in the Society*. London, 1986.

Kapur, Manju. *A Married Woman*. New Delhi: Faber and Faber, 2002.

Lerner, Gerda. *The Creation of Patriarchy*.

Sue, Allen. *Feminism and Theatre*. New York: Routledge, 1984.

Spivak Chakravorty, Gayatri. *Can the Subaltern Speak?* 1985.

The World Book of Encyclopedia, Volume VII, London, 1992.

Feminism and the Societal Set up: A Study of Manju Kapur's *Difficult Daughters*

SANTWANA HALDAR
F.M. University, Balasore

In the beginning of the twenty-first century, the use of 'feminism' has been replaced by that of 'feminisms,' as it is agreed, almost unanimously, that there are many feminisms of concerns with the inferior social status of women that varies according to the economic, political, cultural, racial and such other differences. Women's biological difference mattered most with the feminists of the first generation. Gradually the focus of attention was shifted to the social construction of femininity; and as societies differ, so does differ the nature of that construction. Recent classification of feminism includes postmodern feminism, post-Structuralist feminism,[1] black feminism,[2] third world feminism[3] and such others. The present article intends to discuss Manju Kapur's *Difficult Daughters*[4] in the light of the author's presentation of women choosing them from different sectors of the Indian society in the backdrop of the Indian freedom movement and the Independence of India. Kapur presents women characters not from a fixed standpoint, but from different perspectives as she finds that there cannot be any feasible category called Indian women simply because the problems of Indian women vary from one family to the other. An educated and cultured family, often inspired by the thoughts of enlightened society such as Arya Samaj, allowed their daughters to get higher education even during the colonial period. Gandhiji's non-violent movement also shook the shackles that had tied the women to their homes since ages. Yet there were families where women were illiterate. Even in an enlightened family, marriage was accepted as the ultimate goal of a woman and education, only a stop-gap arrangement before marriage. *Difficult Daughters* renders a variety of women, but focuses on Virmati, a daughter in an enlightened family, who is in conflict more with her own self than with the society.

Virmati, the central character in the novel, was the eldest daughter of her parents who was under the protection of her grandfather Lala Diwan Chand, a respectable member of Arya Samaj. Shakuntala, the only daughter of Lala Diwan Chand's first son Chander Prakash, was older than Virmati and after her M.A. in Lahore she was engaged as a lecturer in a prestigious college. So, apparently Virmati had no major problem to face at home if she wanted to complete her studies and be engaged. But the emotional void she had within her and the magnetic charm of the married professor that constantly drew her close to him created problems for her which were aggravated by her incapacity for making choice. While focusing on Virmati's psychic area, Manju Kapur has also laid emphasis on the setting, the changing scenario during nineteen thirties and forties. The Indian freedom movement and, in particular Gandhiji's call for a non-violent struggle against the British domination, brought an overwhelming change in the Indian society, making issues other than freedom movement almost insignificant. The Indian cities and towns, if not the villages, were greatly influenced by this change. The partition of the two provinces, Punjab and Bengal, rudely shocked the people of the areas and it was difficult for them to forget the trauma. To quote A.V. Krishna Rao in this context, "Almost all the Indian English novels [set in nineteen forties] have one or more of the following nuclear ideas predominant in them: the evil of partition; the cult of 'Quit India' and the Gandhian myth."[5] Yet, an over-all emphasis on the private and personal concerns has always been predominant in all these novels.[6] Manju Kapur's *Difficult Daughters* justifies the above observations. It tells a story of women of three generations, though the focus is mainly on Virmati who emerges as a rebel, a New Woman of India during 1940s and 50s, but is misled in several ways. Blessed with the opportunity of receiving education, she is able to be financially independent and is appreciated in her circle for her contribution to the outer world; but the problems of her private world are rendered through the digging out of the past by Virmati's daughter Ida after Virmati's death.

Virmati is presented as opposed to her mother Kasturi who had the opportunity to receive primary education in school—her father considered her schooling a prudent and innocuous step towards modernity—and who was married at the age of seventeen in an enlightened family in Amritsar and yet who had to bear the pangs of repeated pregnancy at the risk of her life. After the birth of her eleventh child when she was almost in her death bed, Kasturi's father-in-law arranged for a change of climate for her in the hill of Dalhousie where she stayed for several months. She had no grudge against the existing norm meant for women inside home. When she had desperately sought for an abortion with the help of a quack and failed in her attempt, she "wondered at the punishment meted out to her for trying to interfere with the design of God" (8). She should have been grateful, she felt, for being blessed with the capacity of breeding so many issues. As she could not think independently, she accepted the norm that marriage should be the only goal in a girl's life. She said to her niece Shakuntala who was working in a women's college in Lahore, "What is the need to do a job? A woman's *shaan* is in her home. Now you have studied and worked enough. *Shaddi*" (16). She did not understand why Shakuntala avoided marriage and why Virmati was so keen on study for passing the examination. "It hardly made a difference to the real business of her life, which was getting married and looking after her own home" (22). Virmati's first cousin Shakuntala is introduced as a New Woman who enjoys the freedom of living single life. She said to Virmati when the latter was accompanying her sick mother in Dalhousie, "These people don't really understand . . . how much satisfaction there can be in leading your own life, in being independent. Here we are fighting for the nation, but women are still supposed to marry, and nothing else. . . . We travel, entertain ourselves in the evenings, follow each other's work, read papers, attend seminars. One of them is even going abroad for higher studies" (17). Virmati was greatly impressed by Shakuntala's way of life: she could ride horses, play cards and badminton, act without her mother's advice and could buy anything she wanted. Virmati liked to follow her cousin, but her life was not smooth. The peculiar bent of her mind also contributed to the complexities of her life. Manju Kapur focuses on this complexity through the revelation of the facts of her life.

Virmati's marriage with a canal engineer was fixed when she was seventeen, but it was postponed due to a death in the groom's family, enabling Virmati to study for her graduation degree in the meantime. The canal engineer ensured that the study would be good for her and her mother could not therefore object. However, Virmati had to struggle hard with her mother for getting time and space for her study in the midst of her ten younger siblings. At this time she came in contact with Harish, a professor of English in Arya Samaj College, who came as tenant in Virmati's aunt's house, adjacent to the house of her parents. Harish had come back from Cambridge and brought with him a taste for western music, painting and literature. Her wife being illiterate, he could not share his feelings with her and desperately tried to get her educated, though he was impatient and angry at any instance of carelessly managed household. It was almost fated that Virmati attended the Professor's class with much seriousness and the Professor "drank in the symbolism of her posture greedily" and was deeply moved. Virmati was naturally attracted towards the Professor's knowledge and his way of teaching, but unless and until the professor announced that he needed her, she had not replaced the thoughts of the canal engineer with the thoughts of the Professor. "That he looked at her, she knew. That she paid attention to her, she was aware. But to think of him was impossible, given the gulf between them, until he bridged it by crying out his need. Eldest and a girl, she was firmly tuned to neediness, it called to her blood and bones. She spread his anguish at her feet, and demanded that she do with him as she pleased" (54).

Virmati's moral conflict preceding her decision whether she should be loyal to the canal engineer, her family-approved fiancé, or should respond to the love-call of the Professor, a married man, who was capable of enchanting her young mind, is clear in the following sentences: "The Professor looked crushed and Virmati thought again how it was not his fault, how could he help it if he had been married off at the age of three? Her arms closed around him, and she cushioned his head against her young shoulder . . . on her stealthy way home, she felt as usual tainted by her moments with the Professor. The thought of her wedding was always at the back of her mind, splitting her into two socially unacceptable pieces" (55). At last when she could tell her mother that she would not like to marry, her mother was crestfallen. Virmati insisted on her further study in Lahore and her mother, unable to bear her daughter's foolishness any longer, "grabbed her by the hair and banged her head against the wall" (59). When she felt the difficulty of keeping any further relationship with the Professor, she told him that they would have to forget all about the affair. The Professor thought otherwise and tried to convince her that one day they would be together. "Virmati could not imagine how things were going to become all right, and she noticed that the Professor made no suggestions either . . . it was clear to her that she could not depend upon the Professor to sort out any domestic situation. It was up to her" (67-68).

Virmati faced a moral crisis at this point: she could not marry the canal engineer, she felt, when the Professor "needed" her so much. She framed her duty in this way that she was to be useful to someone who needed her. This type of thinking was quite new at that time; it is equally new at present. If her sense of duty is taken for her 'love' for the Professor, her love is prompted by no selfish interest. It is selfless love that ignores everything materialistic and that is why she was not much disturbed with her social status when she had secret relation with the professor. Aware that she was unable to avoid her marriage with the engineer, Virmati made a futile attempt to commit suicide. She had left her suicidal note to the Professor who made it known to others and as a result her relation with the Professor was no more a secret. After she was rescued and brought back home, she was forced to explain why she wanted to commit suicide. Her only reply was that she would not like to marry as she wanted further study. Finally, Virmati was locked in the godown and arrangements were made for her sister Indu to marry the canal engineer. In one of her letters to the Professor sent secretly, she wrote, "As for me I know I have failed my duty and I will be punished one day. Nobody can escape their karma. Maybe what is happening to me now is part of it, and there is no use protesting. My fate is cast, and I am free now. I feel far more peaceful in the godown than I did in the days before I went to the river. Then the confusion in my mind was terrible. I couldn't think, and all I heard around me was talk of my marriage . . . taught us about Sydney Carton, and how noble and fine he seemed at the moment of his death. His last words echoed in my ears all that day. So you of all people should understand my actions!" (92)

Virmati's suffering owes much to her idealistic mind set and to her clinging to knowledge and wisdom. Thanks to the Professor's unique knowledge, she could not keep herself aloof from the thought of marrying the Professor and was, at the same time, deeply moved by the plight of his wife. The Professor actually wanted to trap her with the help of his eloquence. He tried to convince her that theirs was an intellectual-spiritual relationship, something utterly different from what the common people call 'love.' He wrote in a letter, "Do you know how an earthworm lives? It inhabits an extremely limited space, its whole life is spent within the darkness of the soil. It can neither feel nor see. Uneducated people are like that. We are being murderers towards ourselves if we do not develop our intellect. Any part of us that is not used will atrophy and die—the same is true of our minds. Remember, it was through your desire to learn that we were first drawn to each other" (102-3). And Virmati supported his logic wholeheartedly. But soon she was greatly disturbed. When she was kept confined in the godown, she was not only informed that the Professor's wife became pregnant again, and this time for a son, but was forced to meet her. In what she thought was her last letter to the Professor, she referred to that meeting: "She blushed, and smiled, and I knew that the place next to you was rightfully hers"

(105). She naturally felt shattered and requested the Professor to stop sending secret letters to her. But the Professor continued to do what may be called "emotional blackmail" so that she could be trapped. He wrote,

> Will you brusquely cut me off, will you really condemn me without a word from my side? Day and night I move with your invisible presence next to me, my love for you quickening my heartbeat with life and vitality. . . . It was not because I wished to reaffirm the physical bond between my wife and me. My love, what can you understand of these things? You who are so innocent and inexperienced. Picture to yourself a man so in love, he cannot call his soul his own. . . . The man needs to be left in peace. What has happened to his beloved one has so shattered him he finds it difficult to think coherently, finds it difficult to resist the relentless appeal to what was made out to be his moral responsibilities. He does what he can to bring back domestic harmony. He feels guilty about ignoring the suffering of one who is also in a way blameless. An act is performed mechanically. (105-6)

This time Virmati stuck to her point that she should have no relationship with him and that she would study for B.T. in Lahore. She wrote to him, "What has happened has happened for the good. In which world was I living, to be so caught up in the illusion of your love? Just as you must do your duty to your family, and your wife, so too I must do my duty to mine" (107). She went to Lahore to stay in the hostel of RBSL School and College. She felt that her mother would never understand her attempt to live within a moral code. On the evening before leaving Amritsar she had burnt all the letters sent to her by the Professor and she wanted to close that chapter of her life. In the hostel she liked her room-mate Swarna Lata, who was doing her M.A. in Lahore. She was an active member of the Congress party and was very clear that she wanted to do something besides getting married. She had told her parents that if they would support her for two more years, she would be grateful. Otherwise she would be forced to offer Satyagraha along with other Congress workers against the British and be taken into jail.

Swarna Lata's straight-forward manner and her courage impressed Virmati and helped her to make a fresh start.

But this time she was trapped again by the Professor whose friend Syed lured him to come to his home in Lahore and start a fresh relationship with Virmati. At first Virmati refused strongly. The Professor wrote to her, taking the precaution of signing himself as a female. Yet, Virmati was extremely annoyed, writing back only once and asking him not to try to get her expelled. Syed advised him to develop persistence, and following the advice he continued writing letters. The first time he called, he posed as one of her brothers. The second time he asked Syed's lady-friend to call her out of the hostel. "Virmati, embarrassed by a strange woman's appeals, came, but she only spoke a few words, cold, confused and tentative. She refused to go out with them, but the reproachful glances out of her large eyes left the Professor full of joy" (124). His fourth visit was successful and he managed to tell her that she was everything to him. "Virmati was sure she should not believe him. Even allowing for the fact that he might be telling the truth, was it desirable for a man to abandon his children for the love of a woman?" (122) The Professor argued that co-wives were part of their social tradition. Moreover, he was not living a meaningful life with his wife. "There is a void in my heart and in my home that you alone can feel," he said. And Virmati melted. Before touching her, he announced, "Aren't you mine? And I yours, body and soul, heart and mind? I worship you, Viru, I want to express it, that's all." (125) "She cried afterwards, but not much. He dried those tears while she thought, he was right, she was meant to be his, what was the point in foolishly denying it on the basis of an outmoded morality?" (125) Whatever followed was obvious: they began to move together and stayed for some time in Syed's house. Virmati was excited when the Professor proposed to take her to the Roerich exhibition, the major cultural event of Lahore in 1940.[7] Virmati listened, looked, wondered as the Professor told her just what to look for, what to admire and what to criticize. "Of course, all that the Professor was saying must be true, he was older and so much more refined and civilized. He knew" (130). Virmati was soon mesmerized by the Professor and shut the door of the outer world opened in front of her by Swarna Lata. "Virmati stared at Swarna. What a girl! Her opinions seemed to come from inside herself, her thoughts, ideas and feelings blended without any horrible sense of dislocation. She was committed, articulate. Would the Professor want her like Swarna? She didn't want to do anything that would alter the Professor's undying love for her. Maybe she could be like Swarna from the inside, secretly" (135). Virmati had the scope to establish herself in the outer world in the way Swarna did. But she failed to exercise her freedom of will and liked to behave as per the Professor's will. Later, she even doubted if her relationship with him was prompted by her free will. The portrait of Swarna is sketched after the popular image of New Woman in India, one who responded to the clarion call of Gandhiji and devoted herself to the work for the country.[8] She told Virmati, "Marriage is not the only thing in life, Viru. The war—the Satyagraha movement—because of these things, women are coming out of their homes. Taking jobs, fighting, going to jail. Wake up from your stale dream. . . . So here we are. Responsible for our own futures" (151). Settlement through marriage was not her choice, but she was not against the institution of marriage. That is why after getting the job of a college teacher she married a person who accepted all her conditions. After her marriage she continued her other activities; she remained treasurer of the Women's Conference and went on working for the Party. Virmati is portrayed as opposed to Swarna: though she had already fought more fiercely than Swarna at the home front, that fight was for a personal cause and she had no goal as such; hence she was denied any glory for her fighting. She could very well assert her individuality in the world outside, once she had come out of her home for further study—she had the capacity of selfless love and to be useful in others' need—but she chose to spend her life as per the will of the Professor who only promised to marry her in spite of having a wife and two children. While other women were suffering under the dominance of their husbands and in-laws, Virmati suffered under the dominance of the Professor who used her for his selfish desire—the desire of enjoying a close companionship of an intelligent and educated girl, the kind of which was not available to him.

After the Professor had renewed his relationship with Virmati in Lahore, Swarna Lata took her to a meeting for the women where celebrities of the Congress party delivered lectures. Virmati was amazed to see that all the women had such strong opinions on strike, academic freedom, the war, peace, rural upliftment, mass consciousness and such others. "They were talking in a language she had yet to learn. She began to feel stifled. . . . She felt out of place, an outcaste amongst all these women. She thought of Harish who loved her. She must be satisfied with that. These larger spaces were not for her" (144). Virmati got ill after attending the meeting on a rainy day. Harish scolded her lovingly in letters after he got the news of her illness. "Why was Virmati so careless of her health? And what was she doing going to women's meeting any way? She was in Lahore to study, not fritter away her energies. Though it was important that Virmati be exposed to the latest in political and social trends, she must not overdo it" (148). This is the typical male voice that had been controlling the women folk, dictating them how much they should know and where to keep them within the circle. The illiterate voiceless women had so long been dictated by the male members of their families. Now it was the turn of an educated and intelligent lady to be guided by the whims of the male. Harish liked to have full control over her without taking care of her honour in the public. That is why he did not think of marrying her, but suggested that she should be in service after her study. Virmati spoke out in despair, "I break my engagement because of you, blacken my family's name, am locked up inside my house, get sent to Lahore because no one knows what to do with me. Here I am in the position of your secret wife, full of shame, wondering what people will say if they find out, not being able to live in peace, study in peace . . . and why? Because I am an idiot. . . . Now you want to prolong the situation. Why don't we get married?" (149) Still Harish continued to harp on his problems at home which had become a hell for him with every body antagonistic towards him. He came to Virmati as a haven and she, too, behaved like others, extending the hell of his life, he complained. "Virmati felt trapped. What had she been saying, was it so unreasonable? Why was he looking so sad? How could she leave him like this? Slowly she moved towards Harish, and slowly she took him in her arms" (150). Here is a perfect analysis of Virmati's psyche—her lack of resistance and her tendency to be captured by someone having superior intellect. It is interesting to note that Virmati does not lack self-analysis. Comparing herself with Swarna, she admitted that Swarna had actually exercised her power of choice. She chose her political leanings, her friends in college and the most important of all, she chose the course of studies for M.A. in Lahore, though her parents wanted her to go home and get married. Virmati could not explain her own actions as the result of her independent choice. She even wondered how much actual choosing had gone into her relationship with the Professor. Swarna had the clarity of vision to observe that if Virmati could keep herself out of the Professor's way and join the freedom movement, her family would be thankful to Gandhiji. But Virmati could not do so. Thinking of a life for herself without marriage was strange for her, and not quite right.

The complexity of Virmati's mind and her fear for a single life stood in the way of her emerging as a New Woman, independent and courageous to face life alone. Hence she had to face unwanted pregnancy and the sufferings of the termination of pregnancy. Everything was arranged by Swarna, as the Professor could not be traced. He was then in his village for the ritual of 'mundan' to be performed for his new-born son. When he came to know of the pregnancy, it was all over. Unlike a New Woman who must turn her back after this incident, Virmati felt that she was his for life, whether he ever married her or not. Her body being marked by him, she could never look elsewhere, she thought. With this state of mind she completed her B.T. and went back home. Her family found her a real difficult daughter, not knowing what to do with her. An opportunity of the job of a headmistress in a girls' school in the hill state of Sirmaur brought some relief for her as well as her family. Joining as headmistress, Virmati sensed her singleness and her power. Her qualifications, B.A. and B.T. from Lahore, were so impressive that she did not have to undergo usual interview prior to the appointment. The minister of the small kingdom was her self-appointed guardian there. The Professor's letters that came at regular interval—the letters fired with imagination as ever—did not allow her to accept her life as principal as the beginning of a career. Rather, she looked upon her stay there as a period of waiting. As it is usual for all lovers, the Professor could not be content with words alone. He liked to meet her there and in spite of Virmati's objection reached her quarter one day. Very much aware that there is an eye in every leaf, Virmati made arrangements for her guest in the minister's house. But later on, when the Professor came to meet her at night and she had no time for making arrangement for his stay elsewhere, Virmati had to face indignation and her job was gone. Thanks to the Professor's friend who took initiative in the marriage of Virmati and the Professor despite the latter's plea that everybody would condemn him and that the marriage would not be accepted by his children and wife, Virmati could ever get the status of a second wife. Her stay in the Professor's house was humiliating and nerve-breaking. She became pregnant again, and this time it was a miscarriage. During her stay in the Professor's home as his second wife, her father was unfortunately killed in a communal riot and her grandfather died of heart attack. When she went to her maternal home to pay the last visit to her father, she was insulted. To get relieved of the situation she went to do her M.A in Philosophy in Lahore, the subject of her study being chosen by her husband. "She hated philosophy, although Harish called it a noble subject. It was dull, abstract and meaningless, but studying it was her only means of escape. She wished Harish had thought another subject suitable for her. She also wished it was not such an uphill task, being worthy of him" (257). Virmati spent her summer vacation in Harish's home against her will and after that she did not like to spend her holidays there. During the communal riot preceding India's independence, people in Amritsar were scared and Harish's mother along with his first wife Ganga and her two children went to their village. Virmati, then, felt that, with the unrest in both cities, the most practical solution was to stay with her husband. After reaching her husband's home in Amritsar, the first thing she did was to shift everything belonging to Ganga to the dressing room and occupy the main bedroom. All summer long, she lay under the fan when the city burnt. The college being shut, Harish spent much of the time anxiously listening to the news bulletins. "Virmati had never had so much space around her. Maybe this was really what she fought for all along, space to be" (274). She conceived again. It was the horrible time of partition of India. Refugees having nothing but clothes on their back were coming in long processions. "Master Tara Singh had given away half his clothing and begged the inhabitants of the city to do the same" (275). Such a spirit possessed Virmati that she gave away all her clothes keeping only a few and also gave the clothes belonging to Ganga and her children. After a few days, she gave birth to a girl child and wanted to name her 'Bharati.' But Harish did not want their daughter to be tainted with the birth of their country. "What birth is this? With so much hatred? We haven't been born. We have moved back into the dark ages. Fighting, killing over religion. Religion of all things. Even the educated. This is madness, not freedom. And I never ever wish to be reminded of it" (276), he said. He gave instead the name 'Ida' which meant, for them, a new slate, and a blank beginning.

The 'Epilogue' of the novel informs the readers that after Independence, Harish was offered the post of the principal in one of the new colleges of Delhi University and Harish along with Virmati moved to Delhi. Ganga's two children came to live with them when their schooling demanded it. Unlike her two half-siblings, Ida refused to show any signs of intellectual brightness. She told her mother that there are other things in life like 'living.' She also protested when her mother told her that her father would be disappointed. It was not so important to please him, she told her mother. Later, she tried to bridge the contradictions in her life by marrying a man who was also academic. But the marriage was disastrous and she got divorced against her mother's will. As it is recorded by Ida, "My mother spent the period after my divorce coating the air I breathed with sadness and disapproval. 'What will happen to you after I am gone?' was her favourite lament. I was nothing, husbandless, childless. I felt myself hovering like a pencil notation on the margins of society" (279). Ida took some time to be herself after the divorce. Then she was able to come out of her mother's influence and be happy with her own life. Until she was totally free of her mother's hold, she could not adjust to her single life. She was filled up with melancholy, depression and despair. It is only after Virmati's death—as she ceased to be physically present before Ida—that Ida started a detached analysis of her mother's life, investigating the past thoroughly and trying thereby to piece together the scattered images taken from memory. This reconstruction of her mother's life made through interviews with her relatives and friends, verifications of the actual places she stayed at during the various phases of her life, a delving into the political condition of the time as well as imagined histories, helped Ida to sink into her mother's past and make that her own. To quote the concluding part of the Epilogue,

> In searching for a woman I could know, I have pieced together material from memories that were muddled, partial and contradictory. The places I visited, the stuff I read tantalized me with fragments that I knew I would not be able fully to reconstruct. Instead, I imagined histories, rejecting the material that didn't fit, moulding ruthlessly the material that did. All through I felt the excitement of discovery, the pleasure of fitting narratives into a discernible inheritance. This book weaves a connection between my mother and me, each word a brick in a mansion I made with my head and my heart. Now live in it, Mama, and leave me be. Do not haunt me any more. (280)

The concluding remark of the narrator is a clear indication that the narrator, Ida, consciously rejects her mother Virmati's ideologies and emerges as a New Woman who chooses to live life on her own. In some of her approaches to life, however, Virmati is a New Woman who has little faith in traditional moral codes. Sexual involvement before marriage was not a taboo for her. Nor was she troubled with any moral dilemma at the time of her abortion while studying for her B.T. degree. The point is, does the violation of a code alone make one the New Woman? When maintenance of co-wives was the social norm, at least in some sectors, it may not be said that Virmati violated the social code. Again, she might have faced the existential dilemma, but was, in no way, a free person as per an existentialist's view. She could not properly choose, but was guided by her emotions and some preconceived notions nurtured through ages. "A woman's happiness lies in giving her husband happiness" remarked Virmati, in a language she had learnt long ago (227). She had her doubts in regard to her choice. The narrator hints at this lacuna in her while describing her reactions at the professor's praise of the natural beauty of Nahan. "Virmati followed. Was it charming? She supposed it was. He usually had an eye for the charming, beautiful, lovely, quaint, picturesque. She tried to see through his eyes when he pointed things out to her. After all these years she was getting quite good at the exercise" (190). After Virmati was united with the professor in her quarter of the headmistress and expressed her intolerance for her unmarried status, the professor felt insulted instead of being sorry for her. Virmati's thought process clearly expresses her helplessness caused by her indecision:

> Virmati could not understand what was happening to her. Last night had been so wonderful; she wanted that bliss to continue. While he was with her, it seemed her life as a teacher was insubstantial, but she wanted more material to their togetherness. . . . Virmati realized—and thought how stupid she was not to have realized earlier—that to have a man stay with you is to invite certain consequences. (193-94)

When after her marriage she met Swarna and the latter asked her to join the Freedom Movement, she thought, "Hands like hers, should they be raised in sloganeering? Would Harish like it?" (252) Though Harish was much excited at the thought of free India, he had little concern for the women's liberation in general and Virmati's freedom to live with honour in particular. "There will be pressure put on her [Britain] to recognize our sovereignty. After all, a fifth of the world's population is still in chains, groaning under its yoke, condemned to servitude. . . . And me, thought Virmati, what about me? The war, or the end of it, rather, seems to have gone to his head. Suddenly he is transformed. He becomes visionary. His eyes are sparkling, his hair is flung about with passion. I feel so utterly left out, so utterly cold. Will there be any change in my life, I wonder?" (255) In her own comment on her mother, Ida makes an assessment of her mother's approaches to life: Virmati preferred staying with Leela's family, where she stayed as a paying guest in Lahore while studying for M.A. degree, even during her holidays to remaining in Harish's house in Amritsar; but she failed to act according to her will. Ida says,

> I play with the idea that she must have refused. That she would have said, I'm my own mistress. I will relate to you with dignity or not at all. None of this hiding and whispering and keeping my voice down and struggle over who is going to wash your underwear and who is going to clean your shoes. None of this for me. . . . Perhaps the words were at the back of her mind, teasing her tongue with their shadowy sounds. She looked for an opening, but she looked timidly, for though she had escaped the marital home, an essential part of it, the marital bed she carried inside her head, and its burden was heavy. Its rumpled sheets and tell-tale stains did much to ensure that her voice remained soft when she spoke. In the end, my mother couldn't have mentioned that she had more of a home with Leela than she did with him. . . . That is what she tried to give me. Adjust, compromise, adapt. (256)

Ida vehemently opposes this female inheritance of "adjust, compromise, adapt" and chooses a life of honour through her separation from her husband.

In *Difficult Daughters*, Manju Kapur presents her women characters not as stereotyped but as intertwined with different issues such as social, moral and political as well as existential dilemma. Shakuntala is projected as a New Woman from social angle—one who is financially independent and enjoys the glamour of single life that a married woman of the Forties could hardly dream of. Swarnalata is rendered as the ideal New Woman of the time who listened to Gandhiji's call and devoted herself to the cause of the country and at the same time maintained a married life. With all the potential of the New Woman during the time of Independence, Virmati faced existential dilemma but her self-analysis was not up to the mark and she failed to make a perfect choice of her own.[9] As she said to Swarnalata, "she briefly wondered how much actual choosing had gone into her relationship with the Professor" (151).

Ida, of all the women characters in the novel, emerges as the New Woman in post-Independence India, one who wants to live her own life and this decision reflects her capacity to come out of the existing code of conduct, nurtured for the women by the society since ages. Harish's first wife Ganga, who is a perfect housewife without literacy, is a typical example of Indian woman during the Forties who were married in their childhood and silently suffered humiliation and torture. Her desperate manner to keep control over Harish's household and to wash his underwear even after he had remarried, points to the pitiable condition of the Indian women who had no way to live independently or assert their individuality. Her problem was obviously different from that of Virmati. Manju Kapur has delved deep beneath the surface to reflect on the variety of problems faced by Indian women. The historical events have often intruded into the lives of her characters, changing the shape of their lives. When Virmati was in Lahore studying for her M.A, leaving Harish at Amritsar where he stayed with Ganga and others, the Hindu-Muslim riot broke in. During mid-August, 1946, the killings of Calcutta started. "The drops of blood in the distance come nearer. Only now it is not drops, but floods. The sewers of Calcutta are clotted with corpses, they float down the Hooghly, they lie scattered in the streets. . . . People die—roasted, quartered, chopped, mutilated, turning, turning, meat on a spit—are raped and converted in rampages gone mad, and leave a legacy of thousands of tales of sorrow, thousands of more episodes shrouded in silence" (263). The fear was spread all over the country. Ordinary events assumed an ugly communal hue. Harish's mother suggested that it was high time for the family to leave Amritsar and go back to their own place in United Provinces. Harish was not ready to leave his job. Finally, it was decided that every body except Harish would leave first and Harish, accompanied by Virmati, could follow once the house was wound up. Things did not turn up accordingly, and Virmati came to stay with Harish in Amritsar, and after independence they settled in Delhi. Ganga's leaving home, in the pressures and tensions of the moment, was meant to be a temporary affair. But she could never return. "She wept, begged, and stormed indirectly through her mother-in-law, but circumstances did not favour her" (278). Earlier, Virmati's father was killed during the riot and her grandfather failed to resist the shock. Gandhiji's direct influence changed Swarnalata's life altogether. Even when historical events do not control individual lives, those events are introduced, mostly through the professor's letters and his conversation with Virmati. Towards the end of the novel reactions of the witnesses of the riots are recorded by Ida.

NOTES

1. The postmodernist and post-Structuralist theories of feminism are almost same in the context of the feminist movements. They focus on specific aspects of sex in terms of race, geography, culture and the like. To quote Chris Weedon in this context, "post-Structuralist feminism . . . committed as it is to the principle of difference and deferral never fixes meaning once and for all. For post-Structuralism femininity and masculinity are constantly in process and subjectivity, which most discourses seek to fix, is constantly subject to dispersal" (*Feminist Practice and Post-Structuralist Theory*, Oxford, Blackwell, 1987: 99).
2. Black feminism developed out of a protest against mainstream feminism represented by a dominant, white, middle-class group of women. These women are criticized to have overlooked the working class Blacks in America.
3. Reacting against the popular view that feminism is a Western ideology, a group of feminists argue that real feminism was born in the Third World, responding to the particular and real problems of the

Third World women. Uma Narayan writes, "Issues that feminist group in India have politically engaged with include problems of dowry-murder and dowry-related harassment of women, police rape of women in custody; issues related to women's poverty, health and reproduction; and issues of ecology and communalism that affect women's lives. . . . I am arguing that Third World feminism is not a mindless mimicking of 'Western agendas' in one clear and simple sense" (*Dislocating Cultures: Identities, Traditions and Third World Feminism,* New York, Routledge, 1997, p. 13)

4. Manju Kapur: *Difficult Daughters* (Faber and Faber, London, 1999 paperback edition)
5. *The Indo-Anglian Novel and the Changing Tradition* (Delhi, 1982), p. 6.
6. Meenakshi Mukherjee writes in this context, "One might say that in spite of the fact that some Indian English novelists are still attempting to recapture a recent historical past, the majority of writers since 1950 have turned inwards to more private and personál concerns" *Twice-Born Fiction* (Delhi, 1971), p. 206.
7. Manju Kapur describes in detail the background of the exhibition. "December, 1940. Congress leaders in the Satyagraha movement are arrested on a daily basis. Their names appear in the papers, and if their prison centers are changed their names appear again. Various Muslims, Hindus and Sikhs continue to declare the Partition scheme fantastic and un-Nationalistic, while the Muslim League presses on with its demands. Food adulteration in Lahore persists without check, think the bitter inhabitants, while the city is declared to be the most expensive in the whole of Punjab. German efforts to bury London under mountains of rubble continue, and money, goods. arms, men flow out of India to support the war.

   That year, the Roerich exhibition was one of the major culture events of the season. Its inauguration by Sir Douglas Young, Chief Justice of Punjab, specially attended by the Punjab premier, Sir Sikander Hyatt Khan, provided a mingling ground for Indian and British celebrities. The exhibition, in a wing of the Lahore Museum, was a father-son affair, with both Professor Roerich and his son Svetoslav displaying paintings on opposite walls. Comparisons, contrasts, and an occasion for a wealth of commentary by art lovers. Of course the Professor made it a point to come to Lahore while it was on, and of course he took Virmati to see it with him" (129). Here is an attempt to link the National affair with personal ones.

8. Swarna Lata revealed her experiences to Ida when she went to the old freedom fighter to dig out the past of her mother. She expressed how she came out of the banner of Congress to fight for the people: "As 1947 drew near . . . the divisions of Hindus and Muslims were exploited by both the Congress and the Muslim League. I threw myself into my work. . . . After Rameswari Nehru was arrested in 1942, she handed over charge to Perin Bharucha and her girls. I was one of them. . . . That was the time when people were very aware of what was happening around them. I got involved with IPTA, we agitated against rising prices, we organized singing squads with songs based on folk songs to arouse awareness, . . . we wanted more equality between men and women, and we were against, totally against, segregation on religious lines" (136-37)
9. "That man is a free agent is the fundamental doctrine of existentialism. But the existence of freedom is not a doctrine to be questioned; it is taken to be a natural fact, which, if we are not corrupted by fear or prejudice, we can simply experience as true in our own lives. . . . That a man is free means that he is free to choose what to do." M. Warnock's *Existential Ethics* (Macmillan, London, 1967), p. 53 Virmati was corrupted by fear and prejudice and so she was unable to make free choice. Ida has neither fear nor prejudice to corrupt her and so she can act freely.

Feminism in Sujata Parashar's *In Pursuit of Infidelity*

ARCHANA SINGH
Govt. Bilasa Girls P.G. Auto. College, Bilaspur

> In childhood a woman should be under her father's control. In youth under her husband's, and when her husband is dead under her sons.' She should not have independence. (Manu, *Manusmriti*, 5148)

In Pursuit of Infidelity is a novel written by Sujata Parashar, a freelance consultant on social projects related to marginalized children and women. This is the story of a busy professional, Sheena's life, who is living with her husband Gaurav and one-year son Krish. Like a typical Indian wife, she leads her life by fulfilling her duties towards her family, without questioning anything. She doesn't even think about her personal happiness because she knows that being an Indian woman she doesn't have the right to think about it. One of the common characteristics shared by the female characters is that most of them have forgotten to be women. Some of them are wives, mothers, widows, spinsters but not women. They tend to repress their womanliness because of social or personal pressure. Sujata Parashar writes in the words of Sheena;

> Girl child is born . . . she is a good daughter . . . the good daughter has an arranged marriage . . . becomes a dutiful wife . . . then the wife becomes a responsible mother . . . and then the rest of her life remains a good daughter, a dutiful wife and a responsible mother who keeps struggling with life for something or the other.
>
> And mostly her fights are for others. She loses sight of her own self, her own likes, needs, desires.[1]

Before marriage Sheena considers herself the exact opposite of the 'conventional Indian girl,' outspoken, who only prayed during emergency but after marriage in the words of Sheena, "In fact staying with Gaurav I have also changed so much that I hardly smile or laugh now-a-days." (4) Like a typical Indian woman, she has accepted everything without questioning. Sometimes she introspects and thinks of her marriage, "I married him because marriage is a necessity to be counted as a respectable member of this society and feel secure, and settled in life." (4) Sujata Parashar portrays the realistic picture of an Indian married woman in the form of Sheena. Though Sheena is well-educated and self-dependant but yet she doesn't have freedom of choice i.e. freedom to a life of her own. Sheena says, "I can't be written off! She remembered laughing wildly long ago, of dancing, of being called pretty, of a young man who still comes in her dreams." (5)

A lot of things have been said and written about in favour of woman freedom but they all are "full of sound and fury, signifying nothing." The ultimate goal of feminism should be to enable woman to achieve self-realisation, self-definition, self-actualisation, self-emancipation and self-fulfillment by having freedom of choice—i.e. freedom to live a life of her own. Sheena's life takes a turn when the classmate of her college life Nikhil comes in her life. He discloses that he was in love with Sheena when they were in the college and that he is still in love with her. Suddenly Sheena's life is totally changed and everything becomes so beautiful for her. All the time there is a huge smile on her face. She starts caring about herself, "I must do my Yoga tomorrow. Gitanjali is right; it won't help me if I do it half-heartedly." (17) She starts questioning her married life, "Why did I marry Gaurav? I am only human and like to enjoy myself. He hardly takes me out except for the movies and that only because he likes to watch them too." (20)

Feminism is actually the consequence of the society and the social structures shaped by men to suit their needs. Women who are physically weak and tender cannot work hard on all days due to menstruation, pregnancy and the responsibilities of children, were forced to depend on men. All the social rules and regulations are made only for women. So-called care-takers of the society never bother for woman's basic needs and happiness. Even literature showed such a trend. Great literature focuses on the male protagonists providing secondary role to females. According to Simone de Beauvoir, "One is born, but rather becomes a woman. It is civilization as a whole that produces this creature."[2]

In this context, Ellen Morgan draws our attention to a new type of feminism which she names neo-feminism which considers woman as a person: "Neo-feminism means to achieve authentic selfhood and to experience what it is like to live as free and fully HUMAN FEMALE BEING."[3] Sheena's suppressed feelings pop up when she meets Nikhil. Being an Indian woman, the feeling of loyalty for her husband is deeply rooted in her and the sacred vows are strong enough against the carnal pull. Thus, she is in a state of dilemma and thinks, "Do I have the strength to face other people and tell them I want to break away from my stable marriage just because an old friend has walked back into my life saying he loves me." (52) Her better sense always keeps telling her that this is wrong but she finds herself unable to stop the nagging voice. Thus caught between the temptations of infidelity and the need for loyalty, Sheena is torn within and from here her psychological self-probing begins;

> My heart wants something and my conscience says the opposite. Eve must have felt the same way about the forbidden apple and then, unable to control herself, must have finally given in to her strong desire. But I am not Eve and my predicament is not as simple as whether to eat an apple or not. (52)

Sujata Parashar portrays the character of Sheena very close to life, in fact too close to reality. Sheena's heart says that she loves Nikhil but her conscience stops her and she pleads to Nikhil, "It would be completely dishonesty and sheer selfishness on my part if I continue this" (80) but heart wins over the conscience and Sheena surrenders herself to Nikhil.

Marriage in India is the most important aspect of life and from her childhood a girl is made to believe that her husband would be her god. She is a true wife who knows none but her lord. And this deep-rooted belief cannot be eliminated so easily. Sheena cannot dare to break her marriage, though Nikhil insisted a lot. Many questions arise in her mind;

> Can I experiment with my life? What if the experiment goes horribly wrong? Will I be able to take it? What about Gaurav and Krish? Will they be able to forgive me ever? Do I really love Nikhil? Does he really love me? (71)

When she is going through this mental conflict, her life takes another turn. She has to face a harsh reality: her husband is also having a relationship with another woman, Anita. This is a feminine quality that a woman cannot bear another woman in her husband's life; no matter she is doing the same. Knowing this, she puts a lot of questions on her husband:

> Inside her mind all sorts of thoughts were mocking her at the turn of events; she could not believe that instead of Gaurav, it was she asking all these questions. She was the culprit. . . . She was having an affair. And ironically it was she who was accusing her husband of the same. What a turn of fate. (146)

Now Sheena has a valid reason to leave her husband's house though it sounds worse than before. She goes to her mother's house and tells only partial truth; she cannot dare telling about herself and Nikhil. Her mother, like a typical old mother, starts giving her advice every day, "The wife needs to keep patience and be there for him always. If she leaves him alone or shows she does not care much for her man, then the straying man will go away and leave her for sure." (153) Sheena does not want to be a burden on her parents and comes back to Delhi but not to her husband's house and hires another house for living with Krish. Now she realizes that Gaurav has done the same with her what she has done to him, "God had punished her. Punished her well and proper. She had committed a grave crime by falling in love outside her marriage and he had given her back tit for tat." (158)

At this stage, she can understand that her love for Nikhil is momentary; it is just an attraction. She realizes that dissatisfaction is not a license to be unfaithful. She realizes that Gaurav has been a good husband and friend to her and an extremely loving father. She realizes that what he has done is unforgivable and painful, yet she feels like forgiving him as she is trying to forgive herself and she feels if she forgives him, she may be able to forgive herself as well. With this realization, she goes back to her husband Gaurav. Parashar writes,

> But, on the whole, things were calmer and happier. Gaurav left no stone unturned to make her feel wanted and loved. The efforts bore fruit and Sheena slowly but surely grew close to her husband again. They had gone through an extremely painful time, which also made them more mature and more understanding towards each other. (176)

Feminism does not call for a westernized sexually liberated woman with no respect for tradition. A new kind of feminism is needed, one that creates change from the inside out, the change that needs to sustain ourselves with self-respect and not just represent a violent clash.

NOTES

1. Sujata Parashar, *In Pursuit of Infidelity* (Roopa, New Delhi, 2009), p. 6.
2. Simone de Beauvoir, *The Second Sex* (Penguin, 1979), p. 295.
3. Ellen Morgan, "Humanbecoming: Form and Focus in the Neo-Feminist Novel," *Feminist Criticism*, p. 272.

Maya and Men in her Life: A Study of Anupa Mehta's *The Waiting Room*

SAGAR PANDYA
Gandhinagar

Maya, the protagonist of the novel *The Waiting Room* (New Delhi: Penguin, 2007), is a fragile little bird caught in the web of men. She willingly or unwillingly ends up having some very tender proximity with different men in the novel and that fills her life with some uncontrollable frustration, destruction and mistakes that she was unable to handle or correct. Her life turns upside down because of her varied relationships with them. Men befriended her, loved her, used her, molested her, disturbed her and ultimately forgot her as a part of their lives. In the end she was lucky enough to have Aniket Nair in her life to share her disturbing past and accompany her. And that was indeed some relief.

Maya is in constant search for the love that can heal her providing some serenity but every one back-stabs her except Aniket Nair, her college friend who loved her secretly once. She wants to fill the emptiness in her heart and longs for someone's uncompromising love but that remains out of her reach throughout all the actions of the play. The entire novel is about her longing, frustration, compromise, fight, hope and an ultimate defeat that leads her to death. Her tale begins as a 'Maya'—*an illusion* and ends also leaving the reader in an utter bewilderment, as it does not provide any outcome of Maya's fight.

Aniket Nair narrates the whole tale of Maya and through her diary uncovers every minute detail of her life to the readers. Handing over the diary Maya wrote, "Something to remember me by" (8).

It clearly shows that Maya herself wanted Aniket to know the story of her life. Her life story proved very painful for Aniket but he read it, as he was curious to know how she passed her life without him. He was secretly in love with her and that love was there from their college days. In those days he felt envious when Maya introduced him to someone who was more than friend for her, Sameer. She loved him from the depth of her heart and once she said to Aniket, "Oh, Ket, I love him like no other person in my life. He's so achingly good-looking with his light eyes and soft hair." (19) She marries Sameer afterwards and it meets a painful end. Maya's attraction to Sameer could be seen as young age infatuation and thus was destined to fade away soon; it lasted long enough to give Maya an unbearable blow that never healed.

It is notable that Maya's spirit, even after her death, was able to control and lead Aniket towards some things that belonged to her. While handing over her house, Aniket felt some vibes and sense of ownership. When he saw Mir's photograph, a person whom Maya called her soul mate, he "could only see Maya." (6) All the things and belongings of Maya held him back. At that time, Aniket felt sudden sexual urge too. When he got her diary, he saw a garment. He felt "as though I were holding Maya's body in my arms and a dark sepia nipple was gaping obscenely through the rip in her nightwear." (7)

But despite that, his love for Maya was very pure and full of respect. He accepts her daughter Sanjana with lot of grace and tries to understand her life with much sensitivity and compassion. While reading the life events of Maya, he was taking frequent pauses to be relaxed. This shows that the disturbed and troubled life of Maya was tearing his heart out. Considering the fact that Aniket had a deep love for Maya, it was a brave enough step for him to stand by her even after her death. Remembering her, he says, "Maya. She was never mine, and yet, so much mine." (9)

Aniket bore Maya in his heart throughout his life and that gives him ownership on her. It is not without reason that Maya shared all her joys and sorrows with him and that proves that she too had a very special corner for him in her heart. She informed about her love for Sameer and about her only abortion too. Reading of Maya's diary gave him pains and especially the agonizing experience of aborting the first child made him "sick in the gut." (26)

It is clear from the novel that Aniket knew Maya more than her own self and the relation that he shared with her was divine and ethereal. According to him, Maya was not that good-looking but she was very intelligent, wise and "a woman, enticing and alluring but entirely fallible." (8) She was capable to morph herself "from Aphrodite to Medusa in a split second." (8) He was attracted to Maya and in his heart wanted to establish physical relationship with her but somehow he was not able to take initiative. Maya also knew that deep in his heart Aniket loved her and she took him as more than a friend. Somehow she was sure that he would not try to defile her the way others have tried and that gave her confidence to remain with him. She was sure that in any situation Aniket would be ready to help her. Once she said, "I must have been a courtesan in a past life, and you, Ket, must have been my Ayesha, my eunuch handmaiden." (108) Maya in her heart always felt that she must have been a prostitute in her past life and that raises some questions regarding her actions in her life. The life that she was living in her mind was somewhere guiding her actual life and that led her to self-distortion.

In the novel, Maya tells about his family also in brief but it suggests many things to the readers. Her relationship with two men in the family also gives some clues to her falling apart. When she refers to his brother she just tells, "he exists. . . . I really don't know what really goes on in his mind." (14) This discloses that she was not really in tune with her brother and neither tries to know the matters of his life. We further get some knowledge that maybe her brother was interested in few illegal activities because from the childhood only he had the fascination towards "the lights twinkling on the sea" (14) and that would give him glitter in his eyes. Then on there is no mention of her brother and the author never mentions it again.

A brief reference is made to Maya's father also and that, after a research, provides the reason behind her fragile mentality. Speaking about her father, Maya says, "I dote on him. When I was little, he used to bathe me. . . . He would let me splash around a bit, then pull me out, wrap a rough towel round my body and dump me on their bed next to my mother." (16) This description does not sound very odd at the first time but when her psychoanalyst inquires further about this we can realize some hidden message in it. Here we can say that the writer suggests the possibility of child abuse and that is the reason why Maya feels uncomfortable in the room of her psychoanalyst. She tries to divert the topic and snaps off the conversation. In the novel, Maya seeks for some father figure who can embrace her and provide her a supporting shoulder. The search proves fruitless and by that time she breaks herself in pieces.

Her married life with Sameer turns out to be a failed attempt and further deepens the cuts on her psyche. Sameer was not successful in giving Maya sexual pleasures and that brought frustration in Maya. She was not able to understand the reason behind it and that made her more disturbed. Before marriage Sameer was very normal and their love life was pretty comfortable. When she got pregnant and went for abortion before few weeks of their marriage Sameer stood by her side and supported her completely. Here it is very important to note that, in spite of being the father of the child, Sameer indirectly favoured the act of aborting the child and tried to console her by reassuring his love for her. It is strange but if they were going to get married after six weeks of Maya's abortion then it could have been avoided. Actually Sameer was not ready to accept the child and his emotional manipulation helped him in getting the desired result. His love for Maya was a device to remain and function in normal acceptable lot of society. His lack of performance in bed poses some doubts about his potency and masculinity. As a reader we get a little hint that probably Sameer had gay relationship with some college friend with the nickname *Mynah*. Introducing Mynah to Maya, Sameer tells her, "he'd had the 'longest crush' on Mynah while at school." (19)

Maya was too naïve or in love to get anything out of that at that time. Sameer's love for Maya might have been just a way to appear normal in front of the world. After marriage, he accuses Maya of being incapable of arousing his sexual desires and in that manner he indirectly raises question about Maya's sexuality. His attitude to Maya changes and the proximity between them goes off. Maya despises the fact that Sameer ended up as a failure at the right time. She says; "I can not bear to see him feel like a failure—worse, to hear him say that I am 'tight.'" (30)

When she was referred as 'tight' she felt very ugly and to check on herself she even thought about sleeping with someone else whom she can trust. Her thinking was not result of her need to have a sexual experience with someone but an outcome to measure her own ability. Her desperation to know her own sexual power led her to a disastrous downfall. She had the inner feeling that told her the same thing while going for the first time to her psychoanalyst—*Nayan Parikh*. She wrote in her diary: "I was making the biggest mistake of my life and a surge of fear rose like bile along my gullet." (10) After some years of marriage too, Sameer did not earn enough money to run the house. He was not worthy as a life partner and in spite of being careless to some domestic duties, he tried to suppress Maya. He very often used foul language in front of their daughter Sanjana and that angered Maya a lot. When Nayan Parikh molested Maya, Sameer never tried to understand her and instead held her responsible for the whole act.

Nayan Parikh, a psychoanalyst, enters her life as a destroyer in disguise. Through his profession he used to read the psyche of his patients and he did the same with Maya too. When Maya met him for the first time, she was already unarmed and too tender to protect herself. Nayan took advantage of that situation and molested her physically. It seems that Maya presented herself to him but we can not forget that his deception was so smooth and gradual that even readers are misguided. As a reader we feel that Maya herself wanted to establish physical relationship with Nayan. Maya, like an easy target, was led towards him by his methodical manipulation. He carefully crafted his way to her inner self and then bit by bit defragmented her.

Nayan's motives were very clear from the beginning. His way of behaviour, manners, way of speaking, advancement to her—physically and mentally—all were means to achieve his goal. The warmth, openness, freedom, comfort provided by him were basically his tools to make his client defenceless as he did the same to many others. For Maya Nayan was not a healer and instead of boosting her mental strength he added more to demean her. She writes, "He had accidentally, or perhaps, wilfully, touched upon the throbbing nerve of my misapprehensions. He had the uncanny ability of zeroing in on the crack of an unsure thought." (25)

After series of meetings with Nayan, Maya gave him the license to rule her and perhaps that was the thing that she desired. Ironically she saw Nayan as her father, her mother; someone who was not judging her or arguing against her. She writes, "I've stopped thinking of him as a stranger. In fact, I felt like I was talking to a mirror." (15) While listening to Maya's family, her life, her love, her marriage; Nayan was plunged in her tale and that empowered him to capture her inner wishes. He got to know about her childhood, her longing to be cared and touched, her sexual experiences and first abortion. All those frank and pure revelations were like stepping stones for Nayan. After having involved with Nayan physically, she felt guilty and defiled but that proved fruitless. On his part it could have been "an assertion of power, or plain and simple lust." (31) Nayan, layer by layer, unwrapped the mystery called Maya and her complex personality. Nayan not only ruined her but also told Sameer, her husband, that she is not capable of arousing any interest in man. He described her as 'frigid' to her husband that devalued the status of both Nayan and Sameer in the eyes of Maya. She gradually understood the darker side of Nayan and felt an urge to fight against him. She starts investigating against him and collecting proofs to shatter the famous personality of Nayan. The author has not depicted her revenge completely but it seems that Maya was exhausted after all the frustration and trauma and she leaves her task in between. Somewhere she feels that all the efforts would go in vain and it was not worthy to clutch the threads of past life and she moves on to get destroyed further.

Maya's relationship with Murshid quite surprises her and the readers too. She was not able to find herself comfortable with him when they first met. When they spoke with each other earlier, Maya felt some kind of connection. Earlier "she developed a strong feeling that Murshid and she would be lovers in the truest sense of the word." (120) His power of commenting accurately on her life caught her fancy and pulled her to him. She was being dragged by Murshid's "quiet but powerful vortex" (120) and she says, "I could feel his energy coursing through my veins." (120)

Her mind was trapped by Murshid's charms but their first meeting gave some awkward vibrations to Maya. They sat "in stiff silence, despite having shared unimaginable intimacy, albeit without ever touching each other." (127) In fact she wanted to know what is going on in her daughter Sanjana's life and for that she was prepared "to do anything that was required to elicit an answer" (133). And it was too important for her.

Murshid, soon, started establishing a physical relationship with her and that frightened her. She found him too hard and overpowering. He believed that the union of man and woman was sado-masochistic. He took the union as one where there is a 'master' and a 'slave.' She said about Murshid: "I recognized in him an energy that could be just as malevolent as it was benign." (128)

But Murshid, actually, expressed her correctly when he said, "There is a tigress caged inside you, a beast whose hunger matches mine." (129) Murshid knew that Maya wanted someone to anchor her and control her. Maya was eager to give away her energy harboured in herself while Murshid was desperate to consume that in him. He used her as a tool to energize his own body and soul. His union with her was free from any lust or passion. Maya also realized at one point that she was "being used as a means to help him raise his energy." (131)

Even after offering all that Murshid wanted, Maya just ends up knowing that Sanjana had seen something that has "turned into a disturbing preoccupation." (133) This was not the answer or information that Maya craved and ultimately realized that Murshid had chosen not to reveal the truth to her which was so necessary for Maya to know. Her association with Murshid ended up resulting in nothing subtle. She was dissatisfied and also disillusioned. But one thing she realized was, she says, "I too harboured in my breast shades of the same beast that gallops through his body." (136)

Unable to understand the hidden desires of Murshid, Maya unconsciously gives him what he wanted from her. Maya realizes that perhaps, Murshid, being a tantric of certain power and capabilities, had taken something significant from her, an inner energy. In order to get some knowledge on Sanjana's life, she submits her body to the tactics of a tantric and when that realization comes it is too late for Maya. Maya falls without having the smallest hint about the person's background and intentions and her steps very often seem confused and irrational.

Maya's death was described by doctors as "a case of acute melancholia leading to premeditated self-abnegation" but Aniket says that "Maya died of tiredness. She collapsed under the burden of knowing yet not knowing." (epilogue) Maya lost her life in search of eternal love and peace that was somewhat heavenly and ideal. She died, perhaps, because of continuous failures and relentless struggle that life thrust upon her. Maya's inability to save her daughter from child abuse from her own husband—Sameer broke her psyche further. Maya at the end stops at the positive point and ensures her daughter's secure future by handing her over to Aniket. She established physical, mental, emotional and spiritual relationship with many men in her life and even then died with a vacuum in her heart. Her pining for true love and support diminished her ultimately. There were few moments in her life where it would have been possible for her to settle down but she missed all of them and when Aniket came in her life it was too hard to pull her from the abyss of exhaustion. Most of the men in her life were, directly or indirectly, messengers of devastation and performed her utter undoing.

Cyclone as Metaphor in Anita Nair's *Lessons in Forgetting*

AROONIMA SINHA
L.N. Mithila University, Darbhanga

Lessons in Forgetting is Nair's fourth novel published in 2010. She made her mark with her very first novel *The Better Man* (2000) but the novel that gave her immense popularity was *The Ladies' Coupe* (2001). The novel, the structure of which is similar to Chaucer's *Canterbury Tales,* was acclaimed for its unique portrayal of women belonging to different levels of society. Her third novel, *Mistress* (2005), is woven around the nine *rasas* of the Kathakali dance and established Nair's reputation as a writer who undertook extensive research before launching into the act of writing a new novel. *Mistress* and *The Ladies' Coupe* are both women centric novels, about ordinary women in extraordinary situations.

Lessons in Forgetting, however, is different from all the novels of Nair. As the title itself suggests, it's all about learning to forget and making fresh starts in life. It is undoubtedly a story of mid-life crisis and second chances which life offers only when we have learnt the valuable lesson of letting go of the past and let bygones be bygones. The novel has two protagonists instead of one and Nair has effectively used the metaphor of the cyclone to delineate the situation of both her protagonists who have been hit by sudden devastations and while fending for themselves they find succour in each other's company. The novel therefore, echoes the five stages of the cyclone beginning from the 'cyclogenesis of despair,' 'the cirrus canopy of denial,' 'the spiral band of deceit,' 'the eye wall of devastation' and lastly 'the eye of calm.' The plot of the novel follows these five stages meticulously. The narrative too constantly sways between the past and the present lives of her protagonists but there are no loose ends. The book has a neat and compact structure.

In one of her interviews, when asked why the narrative in her present novel always switches between the past and present tense, Nair's reply is interesting:

> It all began with the metaphor that I used, that of the cyclone. The power of the cyclone is such that you have to experience it; talking about it thereafter, there's a distance between what happened and the complete imagery of it grinds to a halt when you talk about it in the past. Initially, the book was written in the past tense but I thought there was something that wasn't happening. I tried this method on an experimental basis with a chapter and it worked very well. It just swept me away like a cyclone should and I believe that when I work with metaphor, it shouldn't be restricted to the narrative,—it should find its way into the structure and the form as well.[1]

Nair, therefore, uses the two essential and opposite ingredients responsible for the formation of the cyclone to describe the vital nature of her protagonists. Cyclones are created when hot air meets cold and this basic scientific detail made it easy for Nair to represent the volatile nature of Prof. J.A. Krisnamurthy (condensed to 'Jak' by acquaintances). He is also called 'Kitcha,' his boyhood name, by his near and dear ones. Jak is in fact a cyclone expert in a prestigious American University and is presently in India for a purpose. A man in his late forties, he is one who thrives in chaos and relentlessly and tenaciously goes about to find out the actual cause behind the so-called accident of his teenage daughter due to which she has been reduced to a lifeless and comatose state. With his estranged wife and younger daughter away in the States, he undertakes to care for his daughter in the confines of his own home rather than committing her to an institution. With the help of Kala Chithi, his aunt and a nurse, his Smriti is well looked after but for Jak, the scientist, it is necessary to know what actually happened to his daughter in the small coastal town of Manjikapuram in Tamil Nadu. Though Smriti was born and brought up in

America it had been her desire to see the land her father grew up in. He had not foreseen that his daughter would volunteer and become intensely involved in the cause of 'save the girl child.'

The small town of Manjikapuram attracted many pregnant mothers of the region where they could find about the sex of the unborn and even have a discreet abortion if it was a female foetus. The local goons who ran the racket could be ruthless to intruders. Though the other four friends of Smriti back out fearing rough consequences, the naïve Smriti fights on. She is gangraped and wounded brutally. She is left lying naked on the beach. The shock of the event reduces her to a vegetable existence. The perpetrators of the crime are never brought to book and the whole incident is given the convenient name of accident. The guilt pangs that her father suffers are perhaps a heavier burden to him than caring for his invalid and senseless daughter. A man who prided in his powers of prediction of storms and cyclones, a man who was acknowledged as 'the guru of simulated cyclones'[2] had been hopelessly deserted of his intuitive powers 'when he didn't know that his child was being mauled and ravaged' (49) across the world. The guilt of his broken marriage and the consequent trauma that the children undergo also lies heavy on his heart. Some marriages he admits become most vulnerable during the middle phase. They are like a 'well developed wave, a cyclone full of promise,' (67) which will not grow into the mature one as predicted before.

Meera on the other hand is entirely different from Jak or Jaikrishnan. She does not have his volatile nature and is passive, unlike Nair's other female protagonists. A chic corporate wife and a writer of successful cookbooks, Meera is unlike Akhila (*Ladies' Coupe*) or Radha (*Mistress*). All through her life, she has been somebody's daughter, wife or mother and has been content to stand in the shadows. In fact a major part of her life has been spent in the Lilac house, her girlhood home. Perhaps it will not be an exaggeration to say that her marriage to Giri had been the most happening thing in her life. Reticent and withdrawn, she lives in her imaginary world and to her nothing matters but her family. She compares herself to the Greek mythical figure of Hera and Giri, her husband, to Zeus, the powerful Greek god and Hera's husband. Hera, the Greek goddess had tremendous powers but was averse to change and insecure in her relationship with her spouse, the chauvinistic Zeus. Meera's relationship with Giri runs on similar lines. Safe and smug in a marriage of many years, Meera does not let those little nagging doubts about her husband disturb her tranquillity. She is totally unprepared for the devastation that awaits her.

The paths of Jak and Meera cross at a Page three party, on the same day when Giri, Meera's corporate climbing husband abandons her for good, for another life in another city with another woman. To Meera, Giri's act is simply incomprehensible because unlike him she had been utterly satisfied with her life with him. Though she had perceived some signs of discontent in Giri, she had shoved it to the background thinking it to be a part of any marriage. Mother of a thirteen-year-old son and a teenage daughter who is frankly antagonistic towards her, Meera's life revolves around the Lilac House where she has always stayed with her mother Saro and her octogenarian grandmother Lily, the actress of off-beat cinema of yester years. The house plays a crucial role in Meera's life. It is this house, with its elegance and gracious living that attracts Giri to her in the first place and it is this house that becomes the cause of discord between the two, bringing about the collapse of their marriage. To the ambitious, calculating, and hailing from the lower middle class, the riches of the Lilac House are irresistible to Giri. The house with all its female inhabitants exuded 'upperclass-dom' (37) that he knew about but had never witnessed in his life.

> Giri had never known people like this before. . . . He needed to round off edges that still clung to him from the small town, lower middle class boy that he was. Meera would make it possible, he knew with certainty. Meera who exuded upper classdom like the L'air du temps she wore. Discreet, elegant and old money. (36-37)

Meera, Giri feels, would be an asset if he were to pursue his career in the corporate world. So with added fervour, he woos the hand of the 'goose girl of the lilac house.' However, Meera does have qualms in the beginning, unsure if Giri was in love with her for all the wrong reasons. There was no old money stashed away in lockers. The house was all they had and Meera knew very well that gracious living came at a price. All through her adult life she had had to rack her brains and use all her ingenuity and thrift to make ends meet at the Lilac house in order to keep up that thin veneer of elegance that it exuded. But when Giri assures her that 'just you in this house is all that I ask for,' (38) she sits back and relaxes. With Giri at her side and the coming of two children, Meera's world was complete. She had learnt to worship at the altar of enough' (41)

> Enough to keep the roof over their heads and food in their bellies. Enough to retain dignity and not have to ask reluctant relatives for a temporary handout. Enough to live as they did. (41)

It was Giri who was the 'god of her enough.' (41) For Giri however, Meera's 'enough' is simply not enough. Selling the house seems to be imperative to him because the fabulous price that he was getting from the developers was tempting and he could start something on his own. The pressures of keeping his place on the corporate ladder, the 'endless dents to his self-esteem' (41) make him long to make a fresh start in life, a life in which he could be his own boss. Meera had of course never fathomed the depth of Giri's longing. She did not know when the Lilac house had lost its charm for Giri. Strangely, Meera's vehement denial to sell the house in the face of Giri's persuasions is perhaps the only strong stance taken by her and it sounds the death-knell of her marriage.

It is not that Meera remains a passive spectator of her life throughout. Like Akhila (*Ladies' Coupe*), she too experiments with relationships. But they are rare and random. For example, her brief affair with Rishi Soman, a man younger to her and a small-time actor seems really out of place. Perhaps this uncharacteristic step by Meera, after Giri has left her, is to fulfill some deep yearning within her, to prove to her that she is still attractive to men. For Meera it is 'but a conduit for a need.' (223) It's like a 'pinch of salt safeguard herself from years of desolation,' (220) when Giri has left her all alone to fend for herself, her children, her mother, her grandmother and the Lilac house. It is financial need that makes Meera take up the job as temporary secretary of Jak. The closeness that eventually develops between the two is natural and inevitable and thankfully without guilt. When Saro, Meera's mother dies in an accident, it is Jak and not Giri who stands beside her as a pillar of strength. Though they find succour in each other's company, both have their individual and singular crosses to carry.

As the novel reaches its conclusion, the changes that come over Jak and Meera are easily discernible. Jak becomes calmer especially after getting to the end of his investigations about his daughter's 'accident.' Meera who had always been the submissive wife to Giri, now has a new sense of identity. More in control of her life, she knows when and how much to give. She had removed the 'scales from her eyes, her desires.' (332) She is not averse to change any longer. Meera is not afraid to question the new developing relationship between her and Jak. She does not demur when Jak and she get into a physical relationship but she is fully aware of the weight of what has transpired:

> He responded to her embrace and she matched his manic hunger with hers, entwining lips and desires. But Meera was struck by the very nature of their slaking of need: two desperate people clinging to each other. Is that all we shall ever have? Will it ever become something else? A more sustaining love. (225)

Meera with her new-found confidence and understanding of her situation is afraid to make any commitment right away though fully aware that life seldom offers second chances to men and women.

The novel ends on a note of hope, whether it is the case of Meera and Jak or the poor Smriti. After months of lying in a comatose state there is a flicker of a movement in Smriti that portends a full blown cyclone, not of devastation but of well being. Therefore, it will perhaps not be inappropriate to say that this novel is not just about middle age and mid-life crisis but it is also about new beginnings, of rebuilding over ashes.

NOTES

1. http://ww.businessworld.in//bw//woman and womanhood =interview, dated, 9.2.2010
2. Anita Nair, *Lessons in Forgetting* (HarperCollins India, 2010), p.49

The Unethical Politics in Sivakami's *The Grip of Change* and Arundhati Roy's *The God of Small Things*: A Comparative and Analytical Study

S. SRINIVAS
Sri Sai Aditya Inst. of Science & Technology, Surampalem

Sivakami's *The Grip of Change* and Arundhati Roy's *The God of Small Things* predominantly deal with unethical politics. Sivakami translated her Tamil *Pazhaiyana Kazhithalum* and *Asiriyar Kurippu* into English with a title *The Grip of Change and Author's Notes*. However the title which appears on the cover page is *The Grip of Change*. Sivakami depicts the social relations and grassroot level politics in two villages in Tamil Nadu in this novel. The narrative of *The God of Small Things* takes place in a provincial town of Kerala. The sequential setting in *The God of Small Things* shifts back and forth from 1969 to 1993. It mainly shows the socio-political turmoil that was prevalent during the late years of 1960s. The story of *The Grip of Change* is placed in 1980s while people were considering caste unity as a means of solution to their problems. The social matrix, in which the downtrodden are deceived by selfish political leaders, is mirrored in these two novels. The writers of the two novels sneer at the unethical politics in their novels, through their characters—Kathamuthu, a contemptuous and condescending leader of Dalits and K.N.M. Pillai, a pseudo-Marxist and an egocentric cunning politician. In order to make a comparative study of the unethical politics in these novels, the analytical discussion of characterization is essential.

Sivakami reveals her political views mainly by ridiculing the character of Kathamuthu and upholding the character of Chandran, a union leader of workers. Kathamuthu is an Ex. President of Panchayat Union of Athur. Thangam, the wife of Late Kaipillai, is deprived of property rights over her husband's share of land and so, she leads a lonely life (without any support from her husband's brothers who expropriated her share of land and force her to submit to them) working on the farm of Paranjothi Udayar who eyes her. One day he calls her to a side and rapes her in the sugarcane field itself. She keeps mum unable to resist her landlord and thereafter she bears torture, obeying Udayar whenever he needs her. "But Udayar took no notice of me. He raped me when I was working in his sugarcane field. I remained silent, after all, he is my paymaster." (7)

Her husband's relatives spread a story that Thangam is Udayar's concubine. Udayar's wife and her brothers thrash Thangam cruelly, calling her a 'whore' and threaten her to leave the village. Thangam leaves Puliyur for Athur and reaches Kathamuthu's house seeking protection and justice.

On hearing what had happened, Kathamuthu takes Thangam to the Police Station and makes her complain against Kamalam, Udayar's wife and her brothers. Policemen go to Puliyur to inquire. Udayar, having been advised by the two constables, lodges a counter-complaint that Thangam 'had stolen a transistor and two thousand rupees in cash.' Kathamuthu understands that the policemen were bribed by upper caste landlords. He spoils their plot but he does not think of fighting the corrupt pro-rich system. When upper caste people set ablaze the huts of Dalits in the 'Cheri,' he demands ten thousand rupees of compensation for each family but in this context also, he does not dare think of teaching a lesson to the landlords by mobilizing the victims against their atrocities. Furthermore, he subdues the justifiable rage of the victims.

> An elder of the community, Sellamuthu spoke up. 'We have suffered enough. Let each man grab a torch or a sickle, let us test our strength!' . . . 'We starve and die anyway,' said an old man in the

> crowd. 'Let us die fighting them, instead of living such shameful lives.' (62 and 65)

Kathamuthu's perspective is different. He wants to transform the situation in his favour. By this time the upper castes had already imposed social eviction on Dalits. No work in their fields is offered to them. Therefore he now decides to discuss this matter tactfully along with the huts-burning issue.

> He wanted to prevent the spark of violence from getting out of control. He wondered as to how to transform the situation and gain something productive from it. 'What is practical? We will bargain for better compensation for our losses. We will demand to go to work from tomorrow. Let us make sure they pay us better wages. We should make it expensive for them to crush us another time. Remember, we have to live in this village. The village and cheri have to coexist. We can't live as enemies and in fear. (65)

Even though Kathamuthu's way of dealing with problems seems beneficial instantly, it ultimately helps the dominant to keep Dalits at their feet as a second-rate human beings forever as his politics are not aimed at elimination of class oppression. Kathamuthu says, Dalits are to live in peace not in fear, but how come it is possible to establish true peace so long as there is an unjustifiable demarcation drawn between the village and the cheri. While exploitative antagonistic contradictory production relations exist in society, peaceful coexistence of exploiters and the exploited is impossible unless the exploitative production system is abolished and humane production (social) relations come into practice. However, Kathamuthu does not bother about all this.

Kathamuthu speaks about practical approach. The novelist seems to have supported this compensation approach as she doesn't pass on any sarcastic comments against this kind of settlement in this context. When viewed and analyzed in the light of valiant struggles of the downtrodden, this approach seems revisionist in nature. It is the responsibility of the government to compensate the burnt huts with new houses. It is also the constitutional right of every citizen to have a house to live in. Had Kathamuthu been a truly committed leader, he would have fought for self-respect against upper caste chauvinism. Being part of bourgeois politics, he inherits and indulges in power politics instead of demanding the imprisonment of Udayar and other culprits in addition to demanding 'new permanent houses' for the sufferers. The novelist does not express revolutionary political consciousness in this context, in fact in any context in the novel. The Keezhavenmani massacre of the Dalits and the Absence of Naxalite movement in Tamilnadu appear to be the main reasons for author's deliberate silence at monetary compensation approach.

However in another context, the novelist scoffs at the brokerage of Kathamuthu: "As usual Kathamuthu was busy, running between various government agencies, the police station and the court. Cases were won thanks to his help. He received his share of the spoils of victory." (112)

Kathamuthu expropriates Thangam's money. He arranges a meet in Athur and asks Paranjothi to make Thangam a part of his household at first. As Paranjothi Udayar disagrees, Kathamuthu demands monetary compensation. Paranjothi Udayar agrees to pay ten thousand rupees at last. She receives the amount and Paranjothi leaves, as the case is settled. That evening, after meal, Kathamuthu asks what she would like to do with the money. She replies, she does not know what to do and she requests him what she would have to do. Kathamuthu suggests that she should buy a cow or a buffalo and keep the rest of the money in the bank. She agrees to that. Later, he asks her to lend him five thousand rupees. Without any shilly-shallying, she agrees and pours the entire money into his hands and demonstrates her gratitude and faith. Later, she hesitantly asks whether she could get her share of land in Puliyur as she no longer wants to work in the farms of others. He assures that she could get it back by going to the court. She wants to go to the court by spending a part of her compensatory money while a major part of it is handed to Kathamuthu.

Thangam continues to live in his house. She is now in her thirties. Kathamuthu's eye falls upon her. One Sunday, Kathamuthu consumes brandy along with his two wives—Nagamani and Kanagavalli—and sends a glass of it to Thangam. She refuses to drink. Nagamani is unaware of the scheme; her husband convinces her to drink. Thangam drinks it and falls asleep. Having ascertained that his two wives can not awake, he enters the kitchen where Thangam lies unconscious and seduces her. "Kathamuthu bent down, intoxicated by the alcohol and her posture. 'Why don't you eat something?' he muttered into her ear. She did not answer him. He smoothed her hair. . . . She turned over and he fell on her." (93)

Thangam gets conscious and prevents him while her eyes remain shut! Later she gets compromised with circumstances and settles down in the house of Kathamuthu as his third wife. "Thangam swaggered with newly acquired power." (93) In course of time, she wins the case and gets her husband's share of land. Thangam along with her land is now in the possession of Kathamuthu.

Kathamuthu's personal aggrandizement and thirst for power and money continues unhindered. He never hesitates to live off the profits of others. Chandran, a thriving leader of workers, is his brother's son. Kathamuthu drives them away, a few years ago from home claiming all property rights over the house they live in. However, when Chandran becomes self-reliant and also a union leader, Kathamuthu tries to associate with him with a view to sharing Chandran's popularity. Furthermore, when Kathamuthu reads an item of news in *Dinamani* that a new party was going to be formed by a 'thespian,' he loses in 'speculation.' He imagines whether he could 'wangle' a ticket from that 'brand new party.' He also feels convinced that he could 'turn his fortunes' by exploiting Chandran's good fame as a workers' leader. He, of course suppresses Chandran after his getting elected as an MLA. "He would of course pulverize Chandran after he became an MLA." (25)

Sivakami satirizes Kathamuthu's character. In some contexts, she portrays him a clever leader who works for his fellow men. In some contexts, she mocks at him. In fact the novelist expresses her disgust in general, of the Dalit leaders who do not work for the unity among lower castes, as Kanshiram advocated.

Arundhati Roy rebukes hypocrisy and opportunism of a political leader who represents the ideology of Left-wing politics of the Communist Party of India (Marxist) which exercises enormous influence over the lives of the people in Kerala. She lays bare the selfishness-driven, backstabbing politics played by the leaders of the CPI (M), in the guise of Marxism.

Karl Marx and Frederick Engels say, "Communists have no interests separate and apart from those of the proletariat as a whole." Contrary to it as the author depicts in the novel, the political agenda of the CPI (M) is framed (keeping aside the people's agenda which can eliminate exploitation from society), so that the leaders of the same Party could become treacherous for the mere self-interests.

K.N.M. Pillai is a local leader of the CPI (M) of Ayemenem, a small town in Kottayam District. He is an ardent follower of E.M.S. Namboodiripad. He runs a printing Press for his livelihood. He is well-educated too. He makes Marxism a way which will fetch him bright political career and fortune. His every action is aimed at personal gains, not for the progress of revolution. Comrade J. Kattu Karan and Comrade Guhan Menon are pushed out of the Party 'as suspected Naxalites.' Till then, Comrade Guhan would be a prospective Party candidate in the by-election. Now, with the expulsion of Guhan, K.N.M. Pillai eyes the Party's candidature of Kottayam constituency. "Two local Party members, comrade J. Kattu Karan and Comrade Guhan Menon had been expelled from the Party as suspected Naxalites." (119)

Roy scorns at the petty-bourgeois politicians and their cheap tricks to achieve popularity through the character of Pillai. One day, Chacko visits Pillai's house to get the labels of 'Paradise Pickles and Preserves' printed. Comrade K.N.M. Pillai makes use of Chacko's visit—the visit of an owner of a factory—to impress local people and party workers and so he secretly informs his wife to call the people who had already waited for him at his house a few minutes ago, seeking some help. Comrade Pillai wants to be seen in his chosen constituency as a man of great influence having good relations with the dominant people like Chacko. "The more people that were seen waiting to meet him, the busier he would appear, the better the impression he would make." (273)

Instead of sincerely working for the masses and winning their hearts, and getting elected as their leader, Comrade K.N.M. Pillai wants to play tricks to grab power. These sneaky tactics are totally against Marxism. His thoughts are treacherous and cunning. He is not a Marxist in practice. He establishes good rapport with Chacko and at the same time he wants to 'bring in' a worker's union, not for worker's sake but for the sake of his political gains.

> To bring in a new labour union, however small, in what he hoped would be his future constituency, would be an excellent beginning for a journey to the legislative Assembly (120)

But it is known to everybody that the factory is wading through a lot of constraints. "if the stakes were raised . . . the factory, already steeped in debt, would be in trouble." (120)

In the evenings, after the factory shift is over, Comrade K.N.M. Pillai intercepts the workers of Paradise Pickles and shepherds them into his Printing Press. In his high and unpleasant voice, he urges them onto revolution with his speeches of a clever mix of relevant local issues and grand 'Maoist rhetoric.' "People of the world, . . . be courageous, dare to fight, defy difficulties and advance wave upon wave . . . you must demand what is rightfully yours. Yearly bonus. Provident fund. Accident insurance." (120)

But he never comes out openly against Chacko. Comrade Pillai never refers to him by name, in his speeches, but he always refers to him as 'the management.' Comrade K.N.M. Pillai does not like to damage his own private business dealing, with Chacko. His contract for printing the labels of Chacko's factory gives him an income that he badly needs and so he always cleverly makes a distinction between Chacko, the client and Chacko, the management.

The members of Ayemenem house come to know about the secret liaison of Ammu and Velutha. Mammachi threatens Velutha with dire consequences. Velutha doesn't talk anything except saying quietly, 'we'll see about that.' He directly goes to the house of Comrade K.N.M. Pillai—his ultimate hope—and tries to explain what had happened to seek protection. But Velutha becomes dumbstruck hearing the words of Pillai: "you should know that Party was not constituted to support workers' indiscipline in their private life." (287)

The only obstacle in Comrade K.N.M. Pillai's plan is Velutha, the only card-holding member of the Party, and that worries him: "that gave Comrade Pillai an ally he would rather have done without." (121) He knows that all the other workers in the factory resent Velutha. And his removal from the Party would endear him to them. So Comrade Pillai 'steps carefully around this wrinkle, waiting for a suitable opportunity to iron it out.' He waits for an opportunity to eliminate the obstacle in his way to Legislative Assembly and it knocks at his door when Baby Kochamma files a complaint in the Police Station on Velutha, accusing him of being a molester, an abductor and a murderer of Sophie Mol. When Inspector Thomas calls K.N.M. Pillai and enquires about Velutha, he wickedly does not tell him that Velutha is a member of the Party. He knows well that Velutha's life is in danger. In this context, Roy discloses the secret common socio-political ideological unity between bourgeois political parties like Congress and the pro-bourgeois Parliamentary Left Parties, through the characters of Inspector Thomas who is a congress man at heart and K.N.M. Pillai, the local leader of the CPI (M). In fact, the cadre of the CPI (M) was alleged to have joined hands with the Congressmen and helped the police kill the Naxalites in the early years. It is this historical truth that is reflected in the novel through these two characters. In another way, this shows, how state machinery is deployed against the downtrodden by the oppressors in unequal society.

> The two men had exchanged numbers not words. No explanation seemed necessary. They were not friends, Comrade Pillai and Inspector Thomas Mathew, and they didn't trust each other. But they understood each other perfectly. They were both men whom childhood abandoned without a trace. Men without curiosity. Without doubt. Both in their own way truly, terrifyingly adult. They looked out at the world and never wondered how it worked, because they knew. *They* worked it. They were mechanics who serviced different parts of the same machine.

Later Velutha is caught and crushed to death by the policemen. However Pillai never laments upon his part in the killing of Velutha, a sincere party worker.

> Though his part in the whole thing had by no means been a small one, Comrade Pillai didn't hold himself in any way personally responsible for what had happened. He dismissed the whole business as the Inevitable Consequence of Necessary Politics. (14)

Comrade K.N.M. Pillai does not hesitate to suppress others for his political gains. Had Comrade Pillai revealed the fact, Velutha would have been saved from being killed at the hands of the police and Ammu, along with her children, would not have become prey to adversity.

If the means of production are in the hands of a few, the society is mainly split up into two classes—exploiters and the exploited. Politics in these societies are controlled and directed by the dominant (exploiters)—feudal lords, bourgeoisie and petty bourgeois classes. They subjugate the latter in order to safeguard their class interests. Many political parties in India are unofficially owned like property, by a few families! Though all are equal by birth and law, the state machinery stands in support of the powerful. This is the reason why cases are not filed and culprits are not put behind the bars (unless the authorities are pressured by democratic forces) when the huts and hamlets are set ablaze, when the weaker sections are harassed and evicted from their lands by the landlords and capitalists, when the innocent are killed in fake encounters. Political parties obtain votes from the ordinary people (the exploited, who live on their labour) and serve the super rich.

K.N.M Pillai wears the mask of communism whereas Kathamuthu hates the same. However the ultimate aims of both are same i.e. getting elected as MLAs. Even though Kathamuthu does not belong to any political party, he plays the same tricks as other popular politicians always do. He demands monetary compensation, when the huts in the Cheri are set ablaze and when Thangam is beaten by the brothers-in-law of Udayar. These atrocities on Dalits are taken for granted even by Kathamuthu, the leader of his community!

Monetary compensation can not bring in secured lives for the downtrodden. It might give some relief but can not assure them peace as upper-caste chauvinism does not fear cost, when determined to sink the Dalits in the 'River of Blood.' The blood thirst of the oppressive class can be curbed only by class struggles but Kathamuthu does not dare to think of class struggles while K.N.M. Pillai betrays people in the guise of Marxism and class struggles.

Karl Marx and Engels stated, 'The proletarians have nothing to lose but their chains' if they fight. Kathamuthu and K.N.M. Pillai are not proletarians. They are just petty bourgeois leaders. They have so much to lose—land, house, printing press and so on. Therefore they can not fight and lead class struggles and can not bring in revolution! This social reality is reflected in these novels.

In other aspects, Kathamuthu always yells at the people who come for help and assists them and gets his commission whereas Pillai speaks cleverly and lectures on revolution but does nothing for anybody. K.N.M. Pillai is a beloved husband and a wise father whereas Kathamuthu is a harsh husband and an inconsiderate father.

Lenin says that politics begin where people live in. Politics is a part of culture which includes 'the customs and beliefs, art, way of life and social organization of a particular society.' Nothing in Nature remains unchanged. Human society is also a part of Nature. Hence, social relations, culture, politics etc. undergo change. The ideals and the course of politics too change over time. Politics in the mainstream society moves on in compliance with the existing mode of production. These are reflected in literature.

Various literary genres surface society with the emergence of socio-economic needs and demands (movements) in society, and in turn literary texts influence society. They sometimes abnormally cause transformation in the course of contemporary socio-political movements. Harriet Beecher Stowe's novel shook the then American society and ushered discussions and debates on slavery. When civil war started in 1861, President Abraham Lincoln commented that the civil war, in fact, started with the novel, *Uncle Tom's Cabin*.

The Keezhavenmani massacre of the Dalits is to be essentially discussed when Dalit movements are analyzed. Dalits fought against economic exploitation and social oppression of landlords at Keezhavenmani in Tanjavur district in 1968. Their demand for hiking farm wages caused a furore in feudal lords. The infuriated landlords massacred forty Dalits on 25 December 1968 and suppressed their movement. The then ruling party DMK too was not able to prevent this massacre. Press strategically did not evince interest in bringing these atrocities to light. Until Indira Parthasarathy wrote the novel *The River of Blood*, depicting this butchery, the civilized society did not come to know about it. This carnage sent a message to the downtrodden that they would not survive if they question the hegemony of the upper caste landlords.

Even though the Naxalbari upsurge took place in 1967, unlike Kerala, Tamil Nadu remained unaffected by Naxalite movement which basically aims to stand in support of the underdog. Therefore, the downtrodden had no support and protection to resist the oppression and maladministration of the State. Consequently, the counter agitation seemed impracticable for the weakest after this bloodbath and this outlook was prevalent in the oppressed even during 1980s when Sivakami wrote this novel in Tamil. The writer's deliberate silence at Kathamuthu's compensation method of solving problems is due to this socio-political environment.

Roy published her novel *The God of Small Things* in 1997. The decade of 1990s witnessed two major historic events—the downfall of the USSR and the process of Globalization. The imperialists, with the help of their corporate media propagandized that socialism was an illusion showing the collapse of the USSR as an example during this period. N. Venugopal, an eminent writer and critic in Telugu, aptly comments that postmodernist outlook was hailed and propagated by the exploitative and oppressive forces in India and the world when *The God of Small Things* was published in 1990s. Roy's criticism of revisionist politics of the CPI (M) was unduly attributed to the scientific socialism of Karl Marx by the prejudiced literary and non-literary critics in this socio-political environment. Of course, she also unjustifiably comments in a context that Marxism too has become a tool of oppression when K.N.M. Pillai refuses to protect Velutha. The bourgeois intellectuals who are the supporters of American imperialism made use of her postmodernist novel to support the American model of economy by propagating against people's liberation struggles.

A new change, a humane, civilized change is the need of the hour in India like a caste-stricken class society. Rulers do not respond to the problems of people unless they are put under pressure. In order to establish true Democracy, people should be made conscious of the root cause of the evils that persist in the society where exploitation of man by man is taken for granted de facto. Progressive literature which aims at social change serves this purpose. Varavara Rao, the eminent revolutionary poet and critic, aptly says that when we read either history or fiction, it should, in turn, propel us to create a new history. It should also instill confidence in us that we shall have our own history and culture in near future.

Even though Roy sympathizes with the revolutionary forces, her novel, which depicts the historical events i.e. socio-economic, political and religious problems of the day, does not impel the readers to create a new history. Sivakami supports relatively progressive right wing Dalit political ideology by describing the problems of the Dalits and their hypocritical leaders.

While Arundhati Roy does not suggest alternative politics, Sivakami, who drifts herself towards the ideology of Kanshiram, tries to uphold the political agenda of the Bahujan Samaj Party. She seeks unity among Dalits and the lower castes. "The Vanniyars and Dalits are the workers in this society. If they are united then the ensuing revolution would overturn the country." (156)

The unity between Vanniyars and Dalits might fetch them political power but the exploitation and oppression would not vanish from society. Because, unless the productive forces like land, machinery, natural resources etc. are nationalized and brought under peoples' collective authority, the exploitative production relations can not be replaced by humane social relations. That means, so long as the productive forces are not liberated from feudal lords and big bourgeoisie, the emancipation of working class, which comprises the Dalits and the lower caste people, from exploitation and repression is not possible. However neither Sivakami nor Arundhati Roy views the social reality from this perspective. They seem to have escaped from this social responsibility as writers (of course, Arundhati Roy after her debut novel embarked upon the campaign against imperialism.) Consequently, they were not able to bring out socialist realism in their novels.

The social problems, they illustrate in their novels, are the inevitable consequences of the contemporary exploitative production system. But, they have seen and shown that the problems of the oppressed are created by the aspects of the superstructure such as Casteism, male chauvinism, politics, morality, police, courts etc., of society, avoiding the discussion of the exploitative economic base (mode of production). They have not shown the cause and effect between the semi feudal, bourgeois production system and the exploitative production relations in contemporary society. Marx says, "The philosophers have only interpreted the world, in various ways; the point is, how to change it."

Literature can bring in such a change if it is aimed at elimination of exploitation. Therefore writers cannot confine themselves to the mere description of the problems of the suppressed in society. They ought to write to mobilize and motivate people to face the repression and fight it. However Sivakami and Arundhati Roy do not make such attempts in these novels. Both the novels have not contributed to fuel the anti-feudal and anti-capitalist movements. Hence the oppressed do not find any inspiration from these two novels.

However, Karl Marx stated that he learnt a great deal about the social conditions of France from the writings of Balzac (1799-1850) who had supported the bourgeois social order. Ranganayakamma says that unless, it is too reactionary, there would be something good in every writing. In this view, Roy's *The God of Small Things* and Sivakami's *The Grip of Change* help the people understand to some extent, the unethical politics of parties and leaders during 1960s and 1980s in two South Indian states.

Psychoanalytical Approach to the Character of Manjari in Shashi Deshpande's *Moving On*

BHAVANA DWIVEDI
Rewa

Moving On is an autobiographical narrative of Manjari (jiji). The novel is remarkable for its exploration of woman's psychology. The narrator is Manjari, a widow of Shyam, daughter of anatomist Baba Mai, a promising writer. Manjari had only one sister Malu suffering from asthma.

In the opening pages of the novel, we find Manjari debating herself to turn up the pages of the diaries written by her father. Discovering her father's diary after his death, she sets out to evaluate her life retrospectively in view of Baba's revelations that show past events in a new light. Her curiosity about what her father thinks about her compels her to go through the diaries.

The present paper aims at the psychoanalytic approach to Manjari's character. Her introspective nature, her relations with other characters, her dealing with various situations, her wishes, desires and demands can easily be evaluated from her character.

Manjari's character is flat. She remains the same throughout the novel. A number of misfortunes fall upon her and she faces them one by one. She neither commits suicide nor does she run away nor turns her back to the situation. She could have done that, as it was the easiest way to escape from the realities of life.

Manjari came back to Baba's house when Raja, her devoted cousin, informed her about Baba's illness. She was afraid as she went away with Shyam--Manjari's perfect lover but imperfect husband. Baba and Manjari had a student-teacher relationship. Baba was a doctor, humorous and tolerant and Manjari a medical student. Baba always maintained a distance from her. Manjari realizes through Baba's diaries that he wanted her to face the situations in life boldly and Manjari did that. Manjari loves her parents. They play a very important part in her life. She avers, "You need to know your parent. I thought I knew them. Baba and Mai were a book I'd read a million times. I knew every word of it. I could visualize each page clearly. But it was not true. The Baba and Maj of my childhood were figures I had for my own purposes, they were my childhood pacifiers, the comforters I hugged for security, figures I had to discard when I grew up."

"We need to know our parents without this knowledge we can't go on. We will always remain incomplete." Manjari can feel the pain of her father when he wrote his diaries at the end of his life. Living alone, his wife dead, his daughter died at an early age, another daughter (Manjari) gone away. Baba, so-called Haddi-Doctor whose presence in the house adds a little footnote to every account of his family life.

Comparing and contrasting Manjari's character to that of her mother we find that the two have divergent conceptions. Mai was an elegant woman, well-dressed, enjoyed the household authority whereas Manjari always untidy, hair coming out of her plaits. Manjari had a sense of failure to fit in the role of an obedient child of her parents. Mai was against love and Manjari had a perfect knowledge of love. She believes in love and this was the reason that she gave up her medical profession for the sake of Shyam's love. Manjari loves her parents too. To Manjari, Mai was *Amchi Mai*; she was the sun around which Baba, Malu and Manjari revolved. Mai was a reserved kind of woman who concealed her personal life. She was happiest at her home. She wrote a number of stories like "Manasi" and "Annapoorna"—the stories which forced Manjari to think how a petty shopkeeper's daughter wrote stories as she had not gone beyond school. An independent woman who hated to be questioned wrote of women who found happiness in submission not only to their husbands, but to their families as well.

Mai adores Malu more than Manjari. It is evident from so many incidents in the novel. Manjari knew that she had to work harder than Malu if she wanted to be loved. Mai's anger was her speechlessness, which was terrifying. When she says 'Khulli Pori, Silly Ghodi,' Manjari knows that Mai was not angry with her. Manjari suffers from a pain that being the elder she could not hold the position that should be hers. Manjari did not have the courage to speak in front of Mai or revolt except her marrying Shyam, and that strength was also not of Manjari it was Shyam's love.

"Desire is the cause of the grief," says Buddha. Manjari's desire to marry Shyam as he was the only person who introduced her to what is called passion, she wondered herself when Shyam proposed to her and praised her innocence rather than the beauty. Manjari's marriage to Shyam was not a happy one. Shyam was a savvy cinematographer who was in search of a good offer. His instability, his family atmosphere made Manjari quite uncomfortable. She was in dilemma because she could not go back to her parents, neither can she talk to Shyam as she was afraid of being critical to his family. Her marriage changed her from an open friendly girl to a suspicious one. Manjari's marriage was not a happy one. She played the role of the typical Indian wife who is afraid of talking about her husband's family. Her marriage changed her from an open friendly girl to a suspicious one. This change made Manjari long to be back with Baba, Mai and Malu — a happy family, she called it. Manjari and Malu were closer than casual siblings. Malu was always behind her like a shadow. Malu declares her enormous joy at being like Jiji. Malu's statement that the two of us marry brothers and always live together, became a family joke. That was the way the two sisters imagine their future. But Malu's illness changed everything for all and it was never the same after Malu's frequent asthmatic attacks. Baba was right: Mr. Bones is the most important person. It is the body that most often dictates events and changes in our lives. Malu was the important person in the family and Mai was the centre of it. Malu's death left an aching emptiness inside Manjari. Malu was a part and parcel of her life. Her death was like losing something of her own self.

There are two tragic incidents that frequently recur in Manjari's introspection in the last section of the novel. The first one is Shyam's raping Malu and her pregnancy and the second one is Shyam committing suicide. Shyam's early demise drove Manjari to struggle in life and left her as a single woman, the breadwinner for her children Anand and Sachi. She decides to work as a typist, to take lessons or to take yoga classes. To become economically independent was her prime concern. She told Raja to have a car turned into taxi to earn money. But these were only plans which evaporate like mist in sunshine. She felt that she need not struggle any longer as her needs were simple. Manjari's past appears to be picture perfect, her present is cradled with uncertainty. She struggles with the loneliness in the large house that Baba had bequeathed, to her grand-daughter Sachi (Shyam and Malu's daughter). Anand and Sachi away in school visit her in vacations. Sachi and Anand were ready to sell the house but Manjari was against it in spite of a number of phone calls by the property mafia. As Manjari battles real estate sharks in Bangalore, she remembers her underworld connections and promptly casts it aside. 'The story is forgotten, no one knows of it . . . no need for the story to intrude into my life.' It's as if Manjari could have moved on, it was only a matter of time "We were a happy family. And then it all came to an end." She was determined not to sell the house as it was not the house made up of bricks; it was the house with which her emotions were bricked. Her name, identity, childhood, Malu and Anand's birth, Baba, Mai and Malu's deaths are the incidents which happened under the roof of this house. Manjari was threatened by phone calls but it matters more to her that she didn't let the house go in wrong hands. Though it was not her house, Manjari undergoes a sense of greed. Desire for possession, for ownership. At a moment she felt betrayed, cheated at the hands of Baba: "Baba's gesture was like a slap on my face; not only was it a repudiation of me, it was directed specifically against me. Or so I thought at first. I've learnt to accept it since then. I've thought of many reasons for Baba doing what he did. But the sense of having been wronged remains. Having got the idea that it would be mine, it's hard to think that I have no right to it." How can she leave it and go away from her past. Her idyllic childhood is populated with extended family members including Baba's loving sister Gayatri, her husband R.K., Baba's best friend B.K. and above all Raja, B.K.'s son.

Raja was an architect and a widower who lived in Manjari's neighbourhood. Raja was a childhood companion. He was well acquainted with Manjari's likes, dislikes, agonies and pains. Every now and then, he put forth marriage proposals in front of Manjari. Manjari gets infuriated at this idea of his and did not agree to become his second wife or be called his keep. She cannot give a name to this relationship. At the age of forty, how can she start a new life with another man when her children need her the most in making their career? Manjari could not find any solid reason for not marrying Raja. The reason she herself did not know. The truth lies in the fact that she likes Raja but could not marry him. Ghodi--as Mai called her. Yes, she was. She was like a horse, an animal with a tunnel vision blind to Raja, to his feelings for her. She takes him lightly. Raja was still a childhood companion. In spite of the continuous efforts of proposing to her, Manjari realised the anger of rejected male, the grief of the lover but she was blinded by her feelings for Shyam. Manjari didn't think of marrying Raja and having a sexual relationship with him. Her feelings can be well expressed in these words by her, "I don't want to get married, Raja. I mind sex though. I can't think of sex with Raja, either. I know him so well that his body seems, somehow taboo."

Manjari was a perfect mother who struggles for her children and did not want any one in between her and her children. Manjari even struggles with the desires and demands of her body. Manjari made a sexual relationship with a man called Raman who stays in her neighbourhood. Her sexual desire and its fulfilment create number of questions in her mind. She thinks: "Nothing wrong with it and ye, why do I bathe three times a day. Why do I punish my body so angrily? How can you want the act and hate the idea so much, why am I ashamed of what I'm doing, hiding all traces of it as if I have committed a crime, as if I've murdered someone like a criminal washing away the blood stains." She felt no shame in having sexual relationship with Raman because she felt that it is not she but her body which demands the need of another body. An arrangement that works for both of them.

Another trait in Manjari's character was her forgiveness. She forgives Shyam for his unbelievable act and was ready to go with him. She suffers from guilt and humiliation. Even then she wishes to let Shyam know about his (Shyam and Malu) daughter Sachi's birth. In the meantime Shyam commits suicide and after sometime Malu also dies of meningitis. Manjari wanted to take the baby girl with her but she was frightened of her beloved sister's face as it haunts her all the time. She collects the strength and takes Sachi with her as her own daughter. Sachi who changed everyone's tortured lives especially Manjari and her son Anand, her cries, her demands, her loud howls of protest, her angelic goodness thrust her out of the dark tunnel that she inhabited after Shyam's death. Sachi made her laugh and made things possible.

Though *Moving On* is also an autobiography like *Small Remedies* yet it is a somewhat different novel from the other novels of Deshpande on account of projecting the human relationships and the psychological approach to the protagonist of the novel. The protagonist psychology is portrayed right from the childhood to forty-five years of age. I do not find dominating and submissive kind of relationship between husband and wife as being described in other novels through the characters of Manohar-Sarita, Jayant-Indu, Mohan-Jayant in *The Dark Holds No Terrors*, *Roots and Shadows*, *That Long Silence* respectively.

To sum up, we may say that Manjari very often feels that she was one of the unfortunate mothers who admits disappointment to her children. She also admits that she disappoints her parents as well and may be this is the reason that her children had higher standards than her. But it was not true because in the end we find that it is Manjari who stands as an important figure in the novel and as the title of the novel suggests she moves on in spite of her struggles, her distancing with her beloved parents, sister Malu and other casualties falling upon her one by one. She adheres to faith as Baba says: "Faith is the adhesive that holds things together." With this faith she moves on and on.

Works Cited

Shashi Deshpande, *Moving On* (New Delhi: Penguin India, 2004).

Sudipta Datta, *The Art of Living Alone*. Sunday Express. Aug. 29, 2004.

Equating Mythology with Emotion: Marginalization of Women in Githa Hariharan's *The Thousand Faces of Night*

MONIKA GUPTA
H.N.B. Garhwal Central University, Srinagar-Garhwal

Indian English fiction took its own pace to develop. Initially some writers imitated the plots that were admired by foreigners. Then others wrote about Indian themes but viewed them with a European viewpoint. Githa Hariharan had her own unique style of writing and portrayed Indian way of life in an Indian set ting and she wrote in English. *The Thousand Faces of Night* that she wrote in 1992 has categorised her into one of the most creative Indian English writers of today. She has been bestowed with the Commonwealth Writers' Prize for Best First Novel. She was nominated for the Booker Prize much earlier than Arundhati Roy. She has been an avid social worker and has been actively involved in advocating the cause of women. Githa Hariharan's academic accomplishments are truly global. She has been educated in Bombay, Manila and the U.S. She successfully won a case in 1995 about a mother's right to be a guardian of her progeny. Her voice can be heard in her latest work *In Times of Siege* where she battles with the fundamentalists and is against the politicization of history.

The Thousand Faces of Night is all about Devi who is the chief narrator who listens to her grandmother's stories. She reminisces about America and her lover Dan. She has to go back to Madras and her widowed mother comes back there from Africa. Devi is shown prospective grooms and eventually she agrees to wed Mahesh who is a regional manager in a multinational company. Devi realises that Mahesh, her would-be husband, is a stranger and no prince, as her grandmother had told her. She liked his honesty when he said, "'I will be in Bangalore only ten days of the month'" (22). She likes Mahesh once she marries him but disillusionment sets in gradually. The tragedy of marriage is not that, "it fails to assure woman the promised happiness—there is no such thing as assurance in regard to happiness—but that it mutilates her; it dooms her to repetition and routine" (Beauvoir 478).

A woman's identity is questionable in Indian society. Reaction against traditional Indian stereotyped norms whereby an Indian woman's life revolves around her husband is inevitable. "Women often feel that, though insignificant themselves they can gain recognition and a sense of substantial achievement by producing sons" (Caplan, 50). Devi concludes that the ultimate state of bliss and satisfaction is not derived from self-realisation. Devi comes to the conclusion that there is no reason whatsoever to evade life's contradictions and takes control of things and finds herself in a better position to face the challenges in her life. The realisation of "androgynous self and transgression into the male dominion without being subjected by it, blends resolution with resistance which is in itself imperative" (Oberai 77). The female characters in the novel express their resistance in many ways.

Devi calls her father-in-law Baba and it is secretly revealed that she does not have a mother-in-law. Her maid-servant also lives with her. Marriage leads to disillusionment but she feels greatly attached to her father-in-law who is a Sanskrit professor and her maid Mayamma, who tells her nice things about her mother-in-law. Devi reminisces about the time she spent in her grandmother's house in her childhood. She would tell her, "Listen my child . . . listen to these stories of men and women who loved, shed blood and met their deaths as ardently as they lived" (27). She asked her, "Do you know about Gandhari, my little one? Listen; listen and you will learn what it is to be a real woman" (28). Devi learnt that Gandhari was not welcomed by her bridegroom, the prince. She was like the proverbial golden bird in a cage with all the wealth and luxury but not an iota of privacy. Devi's grandmother told her, "a woman meets her fate alone" (28). "Gandhari," as Devi learnt, "tied a piece of thick red skirt and tied it tightly over her own eyes [and] groped towards her unseeing husband, her lips straight and thin with fury. Gandhari was not just another will-ful, proud woman. . . . She embraced her destiny—a blind hus-band—with a self-sacrifice worthy of her royal blood" (29).

Devi could not analyse how Gandhari's story and Amma's came together. She began to relate with Gandhari's anger that was close to hers. Devi realised that even in her parents' case it was like the blind leading the blind. Her grandmother told her how the whole house appreciated her mother's musical skills and adeptness at playing the veena. Her grandfather was enraged when he went to pray in the morning and found that "The flowers had not been picked, the floor had been swept" (30). And he roared, "'Are you a wife, a daughter-in-law?'" (30) She immediately pulled strings out of the wooden base, "They come apart with a discordant twang of protest" (30).

Devi went escorted by two maids to her maidservant Gauri's marriage. She learnt that her husband was "an animal" and treated her "like dirt" (32). Gauri chose her lover, her brother-in-law, "an albino turning freak" (32). She ran away with him and ten golden sovereigns. Devi told her about the beautiful lady who married a snake. She was only ten and tried to analyse how after endless prayers a childless couple had a hooded snake as an infant and how the mother, "fed the snake at her breast" (33). *The Thousand Faces of Night* is all about women who are consumed by their overwhelming ambitions and how they become victims of their ar-rogance, humility and submission. It is all about sufferings of women, their tragic lives and sufferings in a male dominated framework in a male-oriented social structure. Yet not a single woman is rebellious against patriarchal forces like a feminist. There is a contrast between the uneducated women like Gauri and Uma and Devi who is a modern, well-educated woman who does not have guts to rebel against her mother who is very conservative nor does she dare to rebel against her husband Mahesh. Uma, her cousin, married and returned to live with Devi's grandmother till the old woman died. Her husband, like his father, was a drunkard. The latter made sexual advances towards her and "kissed her roughly on the lips" (35). She was a victim of disaster.

Close to death, Devi's grandmother left her a gift of the ultimate fantasy; a woman avenger who could earn manhood through her penance. The difference between Amba, a mere mortal, a woman like Uma, lay in the strength to seize sorrow and uncertainty and pour the mixture into the sieve of penance. Whatever emerged, however bloody and vengeful, was a distilled position of good fortune? No heroine died without the powerful and destructive protest that left its ark "a memorial to a fighter, behind her" (40). Devi was terrified by Uma's marriage and by the vengeful Amba, whose story made a deep impression on her like an irresistible horror film. This made her day-dream more and more about the female avengers. Her grandmother's mythological stories made her ponder about the all-pervading power of gods and goddesses. It inadvertently made Devi a woman warrior, a heroine. She said, "I rode a tiger, and cut off evil, magical demons' heads" (41). Devi took to fantasies and Githa Hariharan has skilfully woven Devi's dreams and fantasies. Her vision about "a mountainous woman, beautiful, but with the strong limbs of an ox" (41) clearly indicates her psychological state of mind. Yet in her subconscious state, Devi accepts she is not beautiful but knows that her heart beats in a weak little body. Her mentor makes her tough and finally tells her, "Now, my faithful disciple, you are ready for your battles with men" (42). Her in-built anger is something to be reckoned with. She sees her enemy ungodly, fat, ignoble and greedy that imprisoned innocent girls in his harem, and sat on them crushing and killing them. She fantasizes, "I met him face to face as he came out of the harem, smirking with satisfaction. One lash with my faithful chain of iron and spear-like spikes, and his head rolled to the ground in front of me, spluttering with bloody agony" (42). She imagined herself to be 'an incarnation of Durga.' Her sexual awakening is gradual and in her fantasy she likes to be worshipped by a young and wise man from the mountains. She lived with him for ten years and a day and bore him strong sons and daughters. He was a loyal knight and the perfect mate who played his flute. When her youngest daughter pleaded with her to go to the valley with her brothers, she agreed but came back wounded. Devi's mother brought her back to reality and was not at all impressed by Indian mythology. She told Devi's father, "The girl is almost a woman, she must stop dreaming now" (45). Her grandmother died when she was sixteen. Devi went to America and her father died in Africa. Her mother shifted back to a house by the sea in Madras.

Devi called Mahesh "a polite stranger" (49). After her wedding, she realised, "As long as the lights are switched off, he is suave, sure, unashamed of his body's needs and desires" (49) and Devi is thrown into an acceptance of her nightly rituals. When Baba, her father-in-law, tells her stories, she is reminded of her grandmother, but his stories are centred on, "a woman, a wife" (51). He harped on the fact that Devi was a Brahmin. Her husband Mahesh favoured the learning of English translation and discouraged her from learning Sanskrit. He also did not bother when Devi told her that Mayamma was ill and told Devi, "If you fuss over her today, she'll do it more and more often" (53). He has a cruel streak and did not 'feel' for the poor or deprived. He is also a male chauvinist who says to Devi, "Why don't I pray to be born a woman in my next birth. Then I won't have to make a living at all" (54). For Devi, marriage was like a sacrificial knife that hung a few inches above her neck for years and she had learnt to covet her tormentor. Devi's frustration with Mahesh becomes inevitable and she asks him, "Why did you marry me?" (54) He answered "whatever people marry for" and says, "Thank God, Indians are not obsessed with love" (54-55). Devi learns from her father-in-law, "On the death of her husband, the chaste wife, established in contingence, reaches heaven, even if childless, like students who have practised self-control" (55).

Devi's dreams are symbolic and reveal her inner fears and struggles. She dreams in sequence and there is a kind of survival instinct that suffocates her and there are scratches, bites, stabs and twists and then in another dream she finds herself in the clutches of an accomplice, his open robes revealing a cruelly bare smooth ivory chest. Hariharan has vividly described the plight of women in Indian society since ages. Women are still not at an enviable state in spite of socio-economic advancement in society. Women are still in the barriers laid down by males. Gender bias is practised by parents and the elders in a family. A daughter is neglected because her in-laws would benefit when she enters into their house and she is neglected by them beyond measure and asked to do household chores and live a life of subjugation till she got married. Boys are given more access to education. Female subordination is evident and it carries on even after marriage by her husband and in-laws.

In *The Thousand Faces of Night*, women's suffering has been explicitly portrayed. Exploitation of Indian women of all ages has been shown in the novel. It revolves around three women Devi, Sita and Mayamma, whose life is a chasm of darkness. They differ in age and status but all are miserable and their sufferings are similar. Mayamma is the eldest female character whose childhood is miserable and after marriage her in-laws ill-treat her. She is called a barren witch by her mother-in-law who fed her stale rice since she was considered useless. For ten long years, Mayamma has to undergo all types of unimaginable torment and Diwali is auspicious for her, "She gets the results of penances, a son" (80). Her happiness is short-lived because after ten years her husband runs away with all her valuables. It is now her son's turn to torment her since he is a male. "A woman without a child [son], say the sages, goes to hell" (81). He threatens to beat up his mother when he is fourteen and sells the last pair of gold bangles. He hits Mayamma with an iron frying pan. Throughout her life, Mayamma is tormented by her husband, in-laws and her own son. Yet, she feels deserted and lonesome when he dies.

Sita who is younger than Mayamma is married to Madhavan at the age of twenty. She plays the Veena and her father-in-law cruelly taunts her whether she is a wife and daughter-in-law. She has to leave playing the Veena and suppresses her desires and habits, love likings and even food habits. Marriage meant leaving to eat rice which she relished beyond measure. Hariharan portrays the plight of Mayamma and Sita and shows how they have to be like sacrificial goats and ultimately they are no different from the mythological figure Gandhari in the *Mahabharata.* Devi, an educated woman, is equally exploited after marriage. Mahesh insults her at the drop of a hat and tries to establish male supremacy over her. He decries her educated state and tells her that she is not an ideal wife. She suffers in silence. Women have been victims of sexual crime. She regards marriage as a sacrificial knife. She is disenchanted. She falls for Gopal, "a flashy man in his forties who drank rum and chewed paan between sublime ragas" (75).

Hariharan's novel deals with the issue of women's exploitation and endless suffering. Women are always sacrificing but not given due respect. Women are left to fight their battles but they are not rebellious. They lack a feministic approach in that they are always suffering in silence. There is no feministic revolution. Githa Hariharan has tried to equate mythology with emotions. She has displayed her innate love for Indian tradition and heritage. Devi reminisces about her grandmother's stories. Once she watches little fish swim in the pond and she runs and tells Mayamma who tells her, "You had better rescue them quickly, Devi. The other fish will eat them up soon." (87)

Like James Joyce, Hariharan has used the stream-of-consciousness technique while doling out mythological tales. She has portrayed the blind superstition and tradition that envelops lives of women in India. They are interwoven into the day-to-day lives of Indian women. Her theme is age-old and a woman has to succumb to torturous living.

Devi elopes with Gopal but eventually returns to her mother. After all her mother's efforts at consulting astrologers, Devi is married off to Mahesh after her horoscope is settled. Hariharan wants to unearth the blind superstitious nature of Indian women who rely blindly on horoscopes. In Mayamma's marriage, she has portrayed the horrible practice of child marriage and how a child has to undergo a torturous existence at a young and tender age. Dowry is another issue that she has highlighted in her novel.

Gauri, Pati's maid-servant is endowed with such great beauty that she could have a *swayamvara* but she has to work hard to collect a dowry of gold. Even after having collected eighteen gold coins, she is unsure whether she will have twenty to get married. Ultimately she has to return to her home. Devi says:

> It is useful to remember that a husband is man. So is a father. He trembles if you climb a tree, a foolish, unaided girl. He holds you back from journeys, mistrustful of devils, snakes, younger boys' legs, books, anything at all. He ties a fine chain of beaten gold around your outstretched neck; he marks you with his name. He drags your hair by its bristly ends . . . he strips your breasts of those whorish veils of the goddess, their thousand disguises. He holds his teeth apart in mock kindness and sucks like a hungry serpent coiled around your upright nipple. You can feel the tingling of the sweet venom, racing thick and wet through the insatiable glands of your outraged heart. Do not believe them. (92)

Hariharan effectively portrays the ineffectiveness of education vis-à-vis Brahmanical way of thinking and morality. Even though people are educated, they cannot be set free from cattiest thinking. Though the Srinivasans are in highly placed jobs, they say their son wants a Brahmin wife. They also have preferences and want a South Indian Brahmin girl. Even Devi's father-in-law who is a professor keeps reminding her that she is a Brahmin. Brahmin blood was supposed to be pure and unadulterated. Along with it follows an orthodox and conservative mindset that has not changed for centuries. Hariharan has portrayed the way of thinking of educated women who are still enveloped by casteism by their thoughts. She has also highlighted the religiosity of Indians who have their own ways of pleasing their Gods: "Red roses for Shiva, white jasmine for Vishnu; lotus for Lakshmi, yellow frangipanii for Sarasvati; mango blossom for Kama, red lotus for the sun." (114)

Sita returned home in a taxi, "her neighbours on the seafront ran to their windows to watch the tearful homecoming of a widow" (99). She was an expert at managing things. She missed eating rice after her marriage. She went into labour without a twitch on her dark face. Devi on the other hand was a "secretive girl" (104). Mahadevan, Sita's husband, was a "sick old man in his filters" (106). She believed in the power of her own magic. She realized that after all her quarrels with her husband about discipline for a growing child, won through silent, ferocious struggles and sleepless nights, the best of possible lives had been offered to her daughter, "She spent her rage, her acrid bitterness, on the over-pruned plants, the sloppy, impertinent cook, the nosy neighbours and the old men dependent on her for their survival" (108).

A woman has to make compromises by suppressing her dreams and desires and Hariharan has highlighted man-woman relationships by intermingling myth and reality. Marriage shatters women's dreams and they have to sacrifice and be subservient as sexual objects. Devi is a living example who is eternally ridiculed by her husband. Devi, Gauri and Uma walk out of their marriages and are judged unfairly for it. Women are victims of their destiny, according to Hariharan's perception. Though Devi has lived in America, she has a half-hearted relationship with her mother.

Hariharan has shown in her novel how women have to make compromise at every level and suppress their dreams and desires. She has laid bare the husband-wife relationship. Gandhari and Sita are sacrificing type of women and manage to save their marriage. On the other hand Gauri, Uma and Devi refuse to be cowed down by the injustice meted out to them by their husbands and finally leave their husbands. Devi is equally disappointed by Gopal and reaches the conclusion that all men are the same. All these women are rejected by the society who has double standards. Women should not even dream of leaving their husbands but since according to the societal norms, it is a man's world, it is also his prerogative to 'dump a woman' and still be accepted in society. Sita's husband suffers from a sense of guilt due to ill-treating her. They are both attached to each other and she is fortunate. Devi's father-in-law, Baba, is supportive but he is orthodox in his own way. One realises that the problem of exploitation of women has been carried on through the ages. Devi and Mayamma are victims of the insensitivity of the men in their lives. The educated men have the same attitude towards their wives. Hariharan's novel is circumlocutory and the circle meets when Devi returns to her mother:

> And I, thought Devi, and faltered in her thoughts. My grandmother fed me fantasies, my father a secretive love. My mother sought me out with hope, and when disappointed, pushed me forward in the direction she chose. You could say I have been lucky, I have been well looked after, I have mimed the lesson they taught me, an obedient puppet whose strings they pulled and jerked with their love. (136-37)

Devi, Mayamma and Sita have been victims in their own way. Devi took to fantasies that she was a woman warrior who rode a tiger and cut off evil, magical demon's heads. She dreamt quite often about female avengers. For Devi her fantasies are cathartic and her role play in her dream world is her catharsis.

Mayamma, on the other hand, is the typical Indian woman taking recourse to prayer who has been subdued beyond realisation and her tolerance levels are high. She suffers silently even though she has been ill-treated and even after a bashing from her son, she grieves at his demise.

Devi married Mahesh and suffered from pre-marriage pangs. She was afraid of entering into an arranged marriage with a complete stranger. "Horror stories of perversion, blind, bestial lust and impotence frightened me equally," (49) said Devi to herself and she was a naïve girl then. When she married Mahesh and sat peeling onions, she consoled herself that she wasn't a mistress but Mahesh's wife. He could not be her ideal man but she accepted things as they were and began to enjoy gardening and listened to the oodles of wise words shelled out by her father-in-law and at times she sat all by herself on the "stone love seat by the wall, watching the sparrows build their nests" (75). Her loneliness became unbearable and that made her enter into an extra-marital relationship with Gopal. She also had an affair with Dan and was candid enough to tell Mahesh about it. Even though she looked feminine to Mahesh, she was not so in reality and shocked Mahesh who said, "It's hard to believe you don't want a child" (93).

Sita's idle mind strayed endlessly and aimlessly for years. She had her garden done up, patio laid out saw to it that the gardener neatly trimmed shrubs. She was also the proud owner of six bonsai trees. She enjoyed her luxurious living. She hated to think about the earlier days of her marriage when she had to eat left over and stale food. Only Sita knew what relentless self-discipline had gone into the making of a perfect housekeeper, a blameless wife. "Before she was married at the age of twenty, (late by her family's standards), she had poured all her energies into her hours of practice on the veena" (101). Mahadevan, her husband was overwhelmed by Sita's sacrificing attitude. Sita, however, felt that what he did not quite grasp, and when he did, it was too late, was that a pattern set early in a relationship congeals into a trap. You can't get out of it without causing pain either to yourself or the other person. And Mahadevan, Sita had meanwhile discovered, could not swat a fly without wincing. Her silent mode of resistance and anger at having to give up the love of her life—music—killed something inside her.

Hariharan has portrayed the plight of women, whether they are educated or not and it is ironical that the 21st century Indian woman is still in some way or the other tied to chains of subservience in spite of being emancipated enough to walk out of her threshold to work with male counterparts in all walks of life, "Women are conditioned, and few can escape it, to think that it is the duty of a woman, whether she be daughter, wife or mother, to put herself in the service of the male and not neglect the least of his needs" (Belotti 32). Women like Devi are few who made very few choices, but once or twice when a hand wavered, when a string was cut loose, they have stumbled on stage alone and refuse to be a puppet on a string anymore. Her plunges from America, Jacaranda Road, Mahesh and Gopal are of no consequence to her anymore. Devi has resisted everything and walks out on Gopal with whom her life is "a floating island detached from the solidarity of the mainland" (138). Hariharan has been able to arouse the women of today to a new awakening.

Githa Hariharan is quite a contrast to other Indian English writers in India. She differs from contemporary novelists and her protagonists are not rebellious but are tough enough to fight their own battles. Hariharan truly deserves the 'Commonwealth Writers' Prize' for her first novel. Her protagonists have great courage and resilience yet they are too subdued and not strong enough to fight for their rights. They have great tolerance levels and cannot be termed as feminists and their plight remains the same over generations and female subordination is very much prevalent. Patriarchal forms in Indian society support male dominance. Women are humiliated and suppressed at every level and the trauma they experience at every level of married life is horrifying. Societal ignorance about genetically giving birth to a girl child by a woman is really shocking since they blame women for giving birth to a girl child. Women are condemned for it instead of laying the blame on men. Hariharan has mirrored the male dominated behaviour of males and the tragedy that envelops the lives of women eternally. Women are in as fragile a condition today as they were in days of yore. It does not matter whether they are educated or uneducated, they are weighed on the same scale and men will be men and expect them to be subservient and sacrificing or they will show them the door to loneliness and unhappiness.

Works Cited

Beauvoir. Simone De. *The Second Sex*. rpt. New York. Vintage. 1989.

Belotti. Elena Gianini. *Little Girls*. London. Writers and Readers Publishing Co-Operative: 1975.

Caplin, Paula J. *Barriers between Women*. U.K., MTP. 1981

Hariharan, Githa. *The Thousand Faces of Night*. New Delhi: Penguin. 1992.

Dialectic of Possession in Kamala Markandaya's *Possession*

S.S. GILL
Panjab University, Chandigarh

In *Possession*, Kamala Markandaya tries "to concretize the invincibility of the spiritual power of the East confronted with the glamour of the materialistic society of the West."[1] The novelist views Indo-British racial and cultural contacts from the cultural perspective. Western culture can influence an Indian mind only for some time but it can not leave a lasting impression on a Britisher. Lady Caroline Bell, a prosperous English divorcee, a great lover and promoter of fine arts discovers Valmiki, the twentieth century shepherd boy. He used to draw on the rock walls of caves and is a poor peasant residing in one of the interior villages whom she immediately decides to take under her care and succeeds in transporting him to London. In London she provides him with opportunities for the pursuit of his art and tries to make something exotic of the East. Eventually he wins worldwide fame within a few years. The popularity of Val (Valmiki) amongst the Englishmen is actually inspired by their enthusiasm for all that is Indian: "Being Indian helped him generally and massively for India had come into fashion, fashionable to know of India, fashionable to know Indians, fashionable to admire its art, fashionable to welcome its women and even, at a pinch, its men."[2]

Lady Caroline Bell, who is a woman of insatiable possessive instincts has whisked away a humble Valmiki from his village and his rugged little family to London, taking him away as a lover and boasting, "I discovered him in a cave. Oh, yes, a real one. In India, hideously bare and uncomfortable, except for those superb walls"

(121). She wants to be the discoverer of new talent and wants to show that she has picked up and polished the nugget of Valmiki lying in a crevice in the rocks. She desires to exhibit Val's paintings in France, America and London and also wishes to be his inspiration.

In a foreign atmosphere and among strangers, Valmiki adjusts himself to an appreciable extent and becomes anglicized in his manner and tongue under the patronage of Lady Caroline. Her training makes him cultivated and refined on the one hand and he loses some of his virtues on the other. His honesty goes and he forgets his own motherland, though temporarily:

> His English was good, the accent cultivated—Caroline had clearly made him work at it. Most of the uncouthness was gone and some of the honesty. Did it make him more acceptable? In this polished western world, obviously yes. The East was too strident, too dissonant, too austere, too raw, it had to be muted, toned down, tarred up . . . its people taught to genuflect before understatement—before a measurement of acceptance came. Undiluted East had always been too much for West; and soulful East always came lap-long fashion to the West, mutely asking to be not too little and not too much, but just right. (106-7)

Caroline represents "the colonial and postcolonial attitudes and outlook."[3] She represents the British in almost all aspects of possessiveness. She feels that India needs England for an all-round development and is so possessive in her attitude that when she sees Valmiki, she decides to whisk him away to Britain in order to establish her full and firm hold upon him. In addition, she is resolute, haughty, materialistic and self-centred. From the very outset, she treats him as an object of art to be collected and preserved in a museum. She considers him to be her possession. "Caroline thinks Valmiki belongs to her, and in a way one's right. She won't let go. People don't easily give up what they think are their possessions. The English never have" (192). This strong sense of possessiveness in her is in keeping with the general British attitude towards India. On the contrary, the narrator notices a kind of detachment in Valmiki: "I was left with the feeling that he was not only ardent partaker but partly onlooker as well: that there still remained, for good augury, vestiges of a cold and watchful inner eye, as disdainful of others as of himself" (107).

Caroline fully interferes in the life of Valmiki. She adroitly eliminates other young women who try to win Valmiki's love. Ellie Annabel is a Jewish war refugee and is engaged as a housekeeper by Caroline. She becomes Val's inspiration, but Caroline cannot tolerate this and she succeeds in separating them and later in the novel, Val leaves Caroline, as he realizes that all she cares about is the attainment of her ends. She starts living with eighteen-year-old Annabel, but Caroline is so strong-willed that she will not surrender so easily and somehow, manages to inform Annabel that Ellie was once 'an obsession' of Val and that she committed suicide. As a result, Annabel recoils and Val is overcome with remorse. After this, Caroline quickly exploits racial prejudice and tells Annabel that Indians are "Emotional . . . unstable. Foreigners are—Dear Annabel that, you must realize, they are not like us, you would never be able to rely on one of them" (206). The relationship of Valmiki and Caroline cannot be described as more than flesh-deep, as the inner urges and aspirations of Val remain untouched. He may not hate her, but he does not love her either. He is rather loved by Caroline, a lady having no conscience.

> it would have been difficult with majestic exception, to have found much love lurking in the old relationship. Perhaps, indeed, relationship was not the word to describe forcible possessing which had established nothing so clearly as that there could not be no reasonable relationship—merely a straddling of one stranger by another with little of it for either. (69)

Though Caroline succeeds in making Val a well known artist, in becoming his mistress, teaching him her materialistic values—in spite of her resistance, yet she fails in dominating him spiritually, because Val, in every crisis, turns to his mentor the *Swamy*. So, Lady Caroline comes into conflict with the *Swamy*, a wise and spiritual man who also stakes his claim to possess his spiritual disciple, Valmiki. However, Valmiki becomes:

> a mere puppet without the freedom to choose for himself. Moreover, the exoticism inherent in the story of an Indian goatherd who is a genius and a western Jezebel who discovers his talent and transplants him into another soil, comes in the way of any significant exploration of either East-West relations or the impact of an alien culture on the life of an individual.[4]

Valmiki is so much under the influence of the *Swamy* that when Caroline asks him to leave the village for London, he is not ready to move even a step forward without seeking the permission of the *Swamy*. Similarly, he does not start to paint, in spite of Caroline's promptings. It seems that the alien surroundings have strangled his talent. Caroline shows him a letter, which she pretends, is from the *Swamy*, his friend and guide in India. This inspires him and he starts painting once more. Caroline, in no way, can become Valmiki's inspiration. She cannot attain the place in his life which *Swamy* has. When the *Swamy* visits London, Valmiki totally forgets about Caroline and starts spending most of his time with the ascetic. Caroline is not afraid of anyone in this world but the *Swamy:* "She was afraid of him, or if not of him, of the power he still wielded over the clay she had moulded and caressed to an image she could love." (139-40)

Caroline is unable to understand the true spirit of Valmiki. Though she proudly claims having profound influence on Val, his spirit remains in the forceful grip of the *Swamy*:

> Valmiki's attachment to the *Swamy* seemed undiminished, if less emotional than when he had been a child. It was to some extent certainly reciprocated; and perhaps, it was this human lie, tenuous though it was, that had led the *Swamy* to forsake his isolated life. . . . In all the year of their separation he had never once communicated with Valmiki, nor had there been any indirect enquiry; and his visit to London, though distantly connected with Valmiki, was only a matter of a few brief weeks. (140)

Even the process of Westernization slowly wears away and love for the motherland and the *Swamy* gets stronger day by day in Valmiki. The glamour of the comforts of the West could not bind him for long. When Caroline reminds him of the awful 'wilderness' of India, his reply: "No crime. . . . The Wilderness is mine, it is no longer terrible as it used to be: it is nothing" (220) shows his detachment with the West. So the crippling Western impact does not last long upon Val.

Caroline utterly fails to understand the true powers of spirituality and asceticism. She believes that Valmiki will, one day, come back to her. She believes that this stay in India is only temporary:

> Now it is not for ever. He has tasted other satisfaction that I have given and which he knew I can give on day he will crave them again and then. . . . Valmiki is yours now, but he has been one day he will want to be mine again. I shall take care to make him want me again and on that day I shall come back to claim him. (65)

The trip of Caroline to India, to bring back Val to England, proves to be a complete failure. He refuses to return with her for he does not want to be owned. She is surprised to discover that he is living in total peace and satisfaction and has returned to his caves. The Western impact has cracked up in the face of the Swamy's spiritual aura. So, he adopts a tough posture towards her and ultimately she has to return empty-handed and disappointed, proving that the Western culture may influence the eastern mind but cannot possess it.

In *Possession* the quest for authenticity is depicted through Valmiki's character as a violent expatriate who is showing shuttling across the continents in order to eke out an honourable place and living for himself. Valmiki shuttles between the *Swamy* and Lady Caroline, however, he has no identity of his own. He is quite influenced by the *Swamy* and does not move even a step without his permission. Lady Caroline, who has insatiable possession instincts, wants to dominate him completely so "Valmiki who forms the focal point of the conflict is a mere puppet without the freedom to choose for himself."[5]

Valmiki agreed to leave the village for London and then starts painting only after seeking permission of the *Swamy*. Caroline tries to change Valmiki according to her own liking, trying to refine him in spite of Valmiki's resistance. When Valmiki comes closer to Elle and she becomes his inspiration, Caroline tries to separate the two. She does not want to lose Valmiki. In case of Annabel also, Caroline very successfully creates a rift between Annabel and Valmiki. She treats him no better than her property and guards him "with zeal and efficiency as she might have a property—the necklace of diamonds round her throat." (81) She fails to understand the true spirit of Valmiki which is still in the forceful grip of the *Swamy*. This upsets and disillusions Valmiki who does not want to be owned, and who yearns to lead an independent life. That is why, when he returns to India to the patronage of the *Swamy*, he is fully satisfied and peaceful and does not want to go back to London and lead the life of slavery. Valmiki is able to overcome the Western impact with the help of the Swamy's spiritual influence on him, and he is able to experience emotional satiation when he returns to India, to the patronage of the *Swamy*. Valmiki's deep attachment to the *Swamy* and his living with the *Swamy* in total peace and satisfaction is a matter of surprise for Caroline. Initially Valmiki leads a suffocated life, where he has no identity and he is just a puppet in the hands of Caroline, but ultimately he reaches the place which he thinks fit for himself and attains peace of mind.

NOTES

1. H.M. Williams, *Indo-Anglian Literature 1800-1970: A Study* (Madras: Orient Longman, 1976), p. 87.
2. Kamala Markandaya, *Possession* (Bombay: Jaico, 1963), p. 120.
3. S.K. Aithal, "Indo-British Encounter in Kamala Markandaya's Novels," *The Literary Criterion*, 73 (Winter 1966), p. 12.
4. N. Meena Belliappa. "East-West Encounter: Indian Women Writers of Fiction in English," *Journal of Commonwealth Literature*, 6.1 (1971), pp. 65-78.
5. K.R.S. Iyengar, *Indian Writing in English* (Bombay: Asia, 1973), p. 445.

Bridging the Gap between the Two Cultures in Kamala Markandaya's *The Coffer Dams*

SANGITA MEHTA, HCTM, Kaithal
SUMAN GARG, SBIET, Pundri

The post-Independence era in the Indian English novel makes an obvious advancement upon the pre-Independence period in so far as it brings to the forefront some remarkable women novelists. Kamala Markandaya, Anita Desai, Ruth Prawer Jhabvala, Santha Rama Rau, Attia Hussain, Shashi Deshpande have made significant contribution during the early post-Independence period. Among these distinguished writers Kamala Markandaya stands out both chronologically and qualitatively. To quote William Walsh, "Kamala Markandaya is one of the most distinguished of the generation of Indian novelists in English who succeeded the big three—R.K. Narayan, Mulk Raj Anand and Raja Rao. Endowed with prodigious talent, Markandaya is undoubtedly a distinguished novelist on the contemporary Commonwealth literary scene."

If Jhabvala is an 'outsider-insider,' Kamala Markandaya is ipso facto an 'insider outsider' in that she is an expatriate. Markandaya's presentation of the putting together of the eastern and the western ways of life goes beyond the clichéd stereotypes. There is shown a direct relationship in multiple nuances between the Indian and the British characters. Besides the impact of the modern urban culture brought in by the British rule, traditional Indian life has been dealt with equally authentically.

Kamala Markandaya in her novels depicted a conflict between the western mode of living, which represents itself through modernism, and the eastern mode of living, which represents itself through traditional mode of conduct. Modernism tends to exploit the natural resources to the maximum extent and considers human being as an important part of the natural resources. On the other hand, the eastern mode of living believes in developing a harmonious relationship with both nature and human beings. The writers of the postcolonial India also depicted a kind of struggle between the eastern and western modes of living. To assert nationality, they tried to define their own culture by placing the British characters in contrast but Kamala Markandaya tried to depict the British characters as human beings instead of the carriers of colonialism. According to her, everybody has his/her own positive and negative traits and through her novel *The Coffer Dams*, she seems to suggest that the synthesis of the best traits of natives and non-natives could have produced a better race. Therefore, there is an excellent exposition of the love-hate relationship of Indians and British in her novel. By showing the love relationship between an Indian hero and a non-Indian heroine, she has also shown the possibility of bridging the gap between the two modes and cultures. At the same time she condemns capitalism, the new form of imperialism. She also condemns the British characters that exploit the poor natives in the name of progress. She also praises the British characters who attempt to come out of colonial framework.

The Coffer Dams is about the building of a great dam across a wild river in the Indian highlands. As the novel opens, the project has reached a critical stage at which work on the cofferdams must be completed before the monsoon begins. In the beginning it seems that the development projects taken up by the government of the developing countries will prove a boon for the people, but as the novel progresses, Kamala Markandaya shows that such projects are more of a bane than boon for the native people. The contract for the execution of this project is given to a large British Engineering firm, the Clinton, Mac Kendrick Co. The chief officials of this firm are Howard Clinton and Mac Kendrick. The labour employed in the construction of dam is Indian. Thus the dam construction project is a combination of the Indian brawn and the western technocrats. The firm has also raised a township for Indian labourers and engineers, which comes to be known as Clinton's lines and reminds the colonial establishment of the by-gone days.

In this novel Kamala Markandaya conducts a threadbare analysis of such diverse British characters as Howard Clinton Mac Kendrick, Helen Clinton, Bob Rawlings, Milli Rawlings, Bailey and Jackson. These British characters have been shown interacting with the Indian characters such as Bashiam, Gopal Rao, Krishanan, the tribal chief and others. Clinton represents the Britishers and Bashiam represents the Indians. But like the writers of post-colonial India, she does not just condemn the British characters but also appreciates them for their good traits. She also believes that in every race there are good as well as bad characters. Clinton, the in-charge of the construction project, under the influence of imperial ideology, considers the Indians as some Stone Age dwellers. He equates them with animals. He pursues his work with single-minded devotion. He gives top priority to the construction of the dam against all odds and pressures. He allows nothing to come in the way of his schedule. He is completely obsessed with his work as is clear from the novelist's comments in the novel: "'My work,' he said, from mounting conviction, which loomed tall as a mountain now, 'my dam, my business.'" (23)

He is a man who talks by his deeds rather than by his words. In the words of A.V Suresh Kumar, "He is an ambitious motivated individual for whom zealous perseverance transcends the materialistic desire." Clintons' obsession with work wipes off all his emotions and he proves to be a bad example of the western materialism. Therefore, the individuality of his personality has been reduced to nothing. Though Clinton stands for the worst aspect of the British society but Kamala Markandaya believes that he does not represent the whole of the British race. There are also the Britishers who have a humanitarian outlook. The novelist lived for a long time among the Britishers; therefore, she had a very intimate knowledge of their nature. That is why she portrays life-like British characters in her novels. She portrays Mac Kendrick as a synthesis of diligence and affection. Unlike Clinton, he is the messenger of humanity, who is more of a human being than most of the Britishers. Similarly Clinton's wife, Helen, does not imbibe the colonial ideology. She also builds bridges but between hearts. She has humanitarian outlook towards the tribals. To her they are not mere animals but alive and feeling men and women. Clinton and Helen echo the same sentiments for industry and hard work to get the Coffer Dam built. The end is same for them but the means are different. If Clinton is interested in adopting an intellectual approach to achieve the goals, Helen is interested in adopting an emotional approach. She misses the human element in Clinton. Ultimately, both of them draw away form each other. Comparing the characters of both Clinton and Helen, Uma Parameswaran comments: "Both are stray personalities; both hate superficialities, scorn formalities, ignore conventions, most important both are impelled by a sense of higher ambitions."

It is Bashiam who introduces Helen to the tribals. Once she comes in contact with them, she feels her identity with them. She realizes: "These people are not of different clay; they are like her, like her people. What is for her is for them, there is no other kind of yardstick that is worth anything." (49)

Helen, however, fulfils herself when she makes love with the tribal mechanic, Bashiam and offers her body to him. Though on the surface level, this relationship depicts Helen in a bad light but as Madhusudan Prasad writes: "it is not that Helen is a freak for when she gives herself to Bashiam. It is Clinton's inconsiderable behaviour, which drives her to Bashiam's arms.

This relationship between Helen and Bashiam indicates a new kind of relationship that is developing between the new generation Britishers and Indians. As M.P. Joseph says: "The union of Helen and Bashiam transcends the barriers of race and is the novelist's way of indicating a possible solution to the racial problem."

Through the characters of Helen and Bashiam, the novelist suggests a possible way to bring about the union of two diverse cultures. In addition to Clinton, the novelist has depicted many other characters that have all the traits of the colonial mentality. Millie Rawlings and her husband, Bob Rawlings do not enjoy cordial relationship. Millie suffers from superiority complex of a typical English memsahib. She finds India a "bloody country" where "They won't ever let you get drunk." Like Helen she also feels dissatisfied with her husband, so she forges a desultory affair with young Bailey. But unluckily Bailey dies in an accident and she is left shocked and distressed.

Krishnan, the leader of the engineers deputed by the Indian government on the site, feels very hurt/when Clinton does not want to delay the work at the death of forty-two Indians at one time and assigns a risky job to Bashiam, an Indian instead of any other Britisher as a result of which he becomes permanently crippled. He thinks in rage that Clinton:

> Brush them off like flies, hurt and insult like splinters his skin, despise them because they are experts and are just beginning, beginners, he repeated bitterly, barred from knowledge and power as from the secrets of a master guild and the memory of these neglectful years lay in deep accusing pools in his mind. But it's over now. He said to himself our day is coming. The day when they will listen to us. (19)

The statement made by Krishanan highlights new kind of consciousness that developed in the Indians during the days of struggle as now the educated Indians were not ready to accept the subordinate position. The novelist draws the attention towards the worst situation of the hill tribesman who was looked down upon by both the British and Indian officers. Through this, the novelist wants to show that the English as well as the Anglicized Indians have similar views about the tribals. They spurn even Bashiam. On the other hand, Bashiam thought that a tribal feels isolated from his fellows because of his comparative sophistication. Thus Kamala Markandaya shows that every race has good as well as bad characters and every character has his or her own good and bad traits. No race or nobody is perfect in this world; for example there are certain Britishers who have full sympathy for the native people. Mac Kendrick understands the reason behind Krishnan's bitterness: "The days of ostentation were over, gone with their proponents the British and their less copyists, the maharajas. It was the day of common man and the common man was done with slumbering." (62)

Therefore Mac Kendrick stands for the generation of the Britishers who sympathise with the Indians. The novelist is of firm view that a new culture is in the process of formation by the fusion of different cultures. In this way, Helen-Bashiam relationship in the novel is, in particular, a symbolic consummation of kindred spirits. It is a union of minds rather than bodies, of cross cultural human affinities rather promiscuous sexuality. In this way, Helen has been used as a space when two diverse cultures unite with each other.

Thus *The Coffer Dams* depicts the British characters as living and breathing characters. She is against each and every form of exploitation. She condemns the British characters that exploit the poor natives in the name of progress like Clinton who can make a comfortable place to live in but not a happier one. She also does not spare the Indians who consider themselves superior to their fellow Indians, who are poor and uneducated. The novelist appreciates Helen and Mac Kendrick, the representatives of those healthy forces, which are active in the present world to develop harmonious human relations. Through this novel, Kamala Markandaya shows that there is possibility of bridging a gap between two modes and cultures, and two cultures can co-exist and enrich each other without smothering each other's identity. Thus Kamala Markandaya uses fiction as a vehicle for communicating her vision of life. As a writer she has clear perception of life in rural as well as in urban centers. She differs from other Indian English novelists in many ways. She focuses on the family structure to establish her themes in different novels. She is different from her contemporaries in that she vividly and with a rare understanding depicts the reality of Indian life.

Bibliography

Margaret P. Joseph, *Kamala Markandaya* New Delhi: Arnold-

Heinemann, 1980.

Ramesh Chadha, *Cross-Cultural Interaction in Indian English Fiction: An Analysis of the Novels of Ruth Prawer Jhabvala and Kamala Markandaya*. New Delhi: National Book Organization, 1988.

Rekha Jha, *The Novels of Kamala Markandaya and Ruth Prawer Jhabvala*. New Delhi: Prestige, 1990;

Fawzia Afzal-Khan, *Cultural Imperialism and the Indo-English Novel: Genre and Ideology in R.K. Narayan, Anita Desai, Kamala Markandaya, and Salman Rushdie*.

Usha Pathania, *Human Bonds and Bondages: The Fiction of Anita Desai and Kamala Markandaya*. Delhi: Kanishka, 1992;

Anil Kumar Bhatnagar, *Kamala Markandaya: A Thematic Study*. New Delhi: Sarup, 1995.

Sharad Shrivastava, *The New Woman in Indian English Fiction: A Study of Kamala Markandaya, Anita Desai, Namita Gokhale and Shobha De*. New Delhi: Creative, 1996.

A.V. Suresh Kumar, *Six Indian Novelists: Mulk Raj Anand, Raja Rao, R.K. Narayan, Balachandran Rajan, Kamala Markandaya, Anita Desai*. New Delhi: Creative, 1996.

A.V. Krishna Rao and K. Madhavi Menon, *Kamala Markandaya: A Critical Study of Her Novels, 1954-1982*. Delhi, B.R., 1997.

A.A. Sinha, *The Novels of Kamala Markandaya and Arun Joshi*. Jalandhar, India, ABS, 1998.

Ramesh K. Srivastava, *The Novels of Kamala Markandaya: A Critical Study*. Amritsar, India, Guru Nanak Dev University, 1998.

Uma Parameswaran, *Kamala Markandaya*. Jaipur: Rawat, 2000.

Quest for Authentic Existence in Anita Desai

JAGDISH BATRA
Hindu College, Sonepat

Anita Desai, the well-known Indian English novelist, has penned twelve novels and a collection of short stories for children over a creative career spanning six decades. What imparts individuality to her novels is the psychological depth of her characters brought out in a language that is equal to the task. Themes like alienation, inter-cultural relationship and individual/ family conflict have been taken up by her in her novels. When it comes to the exploration of the individual psyche, most studies underline the negative elements of existentialist thinking like alienation, rootlessness and normlessness highlighted by her. What is glossed over is a certain urge felt by her protagonists to lead an authentic life. The objective of this paper is to underline this dimension.

The focus on negative traits alone is, to my mind, due to a less than complete appraisal of the philosophy of existentialism, which is generally portrayed in negative colours. This philosophy also treats man as mature and powerful enough to stand on his own feet and decide his fate as also that of the entire human race with full responsibility. Anita Desai's protagonists like Maya, Nirode, Deven, Matteo or Eric show courage to taste the bitter fruit of life. Things may or may not go their way but a sincere struggle to lead an authentic existence cannot be denied.

According to the existentialists, who developed the concept of authentic existence, man is always found in a *situation*. This situation, often referred to as human predicament is fraught with anguish, anxiety, despair and dread. Normally this life is *inauthentic*.

Heidegger also talks of this as *Geworfenheit,* or 'thrown-ness'—the fact that one is born into a world which one did not make. This is the 'factivity' or the predicament of man. With a limitless mind imprisoned in a limited body, there is bound to be frustration and despair. Hence, existentialism talks of anguish, angst and nausea. There is no logic or rationale behind the phenomenon of this world. In fact, reason cannot cope with the particular or the contingent as it depends too much on the general and the universal. Therefore, meaninglessness and normlessness are dear to the existentialists.

Despite these odds, the concept of complete freedom is central to existentialism which means acting entirely according to one's own free will. It means freedom to choose but the existential choice is well-guarded against any nuance of compromise. The criteria of one's choice must be truly one's own. Mostly, we find some aesthetic or ethical considerations upheld by society or religion, influencing our choice of a particular course of action. Kierkegaard, therefore, says that when man "chooses from inward passion rather than external consequences, does he become truly an existential self" (Paul 234). Further, "He must turn to the inner voice, a voice that is a product neither of social conditioning nor of reason" (Paul 219). This "Self-conscious appropriation of the conditions of one's own existence and identity" is called authenticity in Existentialist jargon. (Indigo 44)

Anita Desai places an enlightened (read existentially conscious) individual in a predicament or situation. The search has different goals: the quest could be of self-identity, for the space to exist or for the freedom to lead life in a particular way. Maya, in the first novel *Cry, the Peacock,* locates her authentic life in marital bliss and compatible companionship. She demands life on her own terms, howsoever irrational it may appear to her husband. "Giving me an opal ring to wear on my finger, he did not notice the translucent skin beneath, the blue flashing veins that ran under and out of the bridge of gold and jolted me into smiling with pleasure each time I saw it" (14).

Maya justifies her decision: "The man who had no contact with the world, or with me. What would it matter to him if he died and lost even the possibility of contact? What would it matter to him?" In determining the authenticity of her life, she is surely her own judge and she must not be guided by any external yardstick of reason or duty or some transcendental entity. The argument advanced by her in arriving at the decision to do away with Gautama is fully hers and there is no hint of remorse on her face and she is cool as cucumber after the act is committed. What she forgets as an existentialist is that when she acts the way she does, she should expect others to follow her. In this lies the element of responsibility which is the other side of the coin of freedom in the existentialist philosophy. Existentialists hold man responsible for his actions because he has no guide either in God or in *a priori* realm of values. Comparing the philosophies of Sartre and Heidegger, it is found that both "believe that people must give themselves goals and meaning, and the more fully they realize this, the more authentic they become. For Sartre, this contingency is a cause for celebration because it means people are free to create the best lives they can, but this freedom sharply increases the burden of their responsibilities" (Shroeder 209).

The predicament in Nirode of *Voices in the City* can be summed up as a limitless mind imprisoned in a limited body. The world does not move according to his innermost urges known to the outside world as whims and desires. The initial partisan attitude of parents with regard to his brother Arun and later his mother's liaison with Major Chadha have jolted him. There is bound to be frustration and despair. His dream to become a successful playwright or continue the publication of the literary journal *Voice* is met with failure. Hence, existential anguish and angst as also the sense of alienation from society and self come his way. Nirode develops a personal value system that does not require social approval and in which success is "only one of their nets, this thing called success or reputation and when you hear it singing about your ears, the only thing to do is to drop everything and run" (94). He desires certitude in this world that is ever in a flux as is clear from his reference to Camus' observation: "In default of inexhaustible happiness, eternal suffering at least would give us a destiny. But we do not have even that consolation, and our worst agonies come to an end one day." He locates authentic life in "three drinks and a roof" (33) and in his journal *Voice* and for this he can cheat his aunt by selling a fake artifact to her, sponge his friends and can brashly tell Bose what he thinks of him. Neither success nor failure reveals to him the meaning of life. His quest culminates in a transcendental illusion—his mother merges with the goddess Kali, whereupon his search ceases. The existentialists, after all, do not merely value the mundane and the physical but also recognize that which appeals to our supra-mental personality called soul in the Indian philosophy.

Desai's characters have their own conception of life. There is no interference of intellect or worldly wisdom, literally speaking, here. The calling is received at the level of innermost recesses of consciousness and so cannot be analyzed. According to Kierkegaard, Abraham proved his faith by resolutely setting out to obey God's command to sacrifice his son Isaac, even though he could not understand it. This "suspension of the ethical," as he puts it, allows Abraham to achieve an authentic commitment to God. To avoid human despair, the individual must make a similar "leap of faith" (Shroeder 214) into a religious life, which is inherently paradoxical, mysterious and full of risk. One is called to it by the feeling of dread which is ultimately a fear of nothingness.

In *Bye-Bye, Blackbird*, the protagonist Adit, an Indian emigrant in England, after his marriage to an English girl Sarah, desires an identity which is denied since it falls outside the conceptual framework of society. For most people, this conception of existentialism is difficult to comprehend. What must be realized is that existentialism is against the universal. It lays stress on the individual. "Don't worry what the others say," is the clarion call. And it is this understanding of one's goals and values of life that Heidegger believes to be the only successful response to the experience of angst without falling into self-deception.

Most humans tend to live by "bad faith," i.e., they deceive themselves into thinking that their actions are determined by their circumstances or their own natures. Thus, they do not want to own their responsibility for their choices. To achieve an authentic human existence, individuals must overcome this tendency. They must recognize their freedom and own responsibility for the decisions that they make without holding society and traditional beliefs responsible. Even after encountering failure, Deven in *In Custody* does not complain against others, nor does he regret his own decision. He seeks his authentic existence in being able to achieve some distinction in his career and for this, hits upon the idea of interviewing a famous Urdu poet Nur for a friend's journal. His repeated meetings with the poet over a period of time, which are beset with unforeseen problems of logistics, disillusion him regarding the private life of that poet. Things do not occur the way he had envisioned but it is not a failed quest. He is satisfied as life has compensated him by revealing to him the secrets of celebrities.

Baumgartner, in *Baumgartner's Bombay*, is the picture of an individual, believing and acting in consonance with the basic tenet of existentialism which prizes existence over essence. For him, safe existence is what matters most, threatened as he is in India and in Germany. But he has seen death so near to him in the Nazi camps that he has recovered an authentic relationship to himself and his freedom, as Heidegger would put it.

Desai's later novels exhibit a pleasant change. Like Shakespeare's fourth phase of play-writing in which the dark clouds on his mental horizon had dissolved giving place to sunshine, Desai too shows success crowning the efforts of her characters, a far cry from earlier unsuccessful characters. In *Journey to Ithaca*, Matteo's quest is for the ultimate reality. "It is the spiritual experience," he tells Sophie, "for which you must search in India, nothing less" (36). His relentless pursuit of his self-ordained goal pays off:

> Then, as he continued to gaze at it, he saw that what was perfectly balanced there in a cleft in the tree was not a stone at all but a circle, and it contained within it another circle, and another, that there was

> no beginning and no end to them; they were infinite. . . . That circle was the universe itself, containing world within world, ring upon ring, sphere within sphere, and to his dazzled eyes they revolved within each other and yet remained perfectly static, maintaining a total balance and harmony that could be divine. The stone glowed now, became brilliant in Matteo's eyes, refulgent with what was he felt certain divine light. (68)

It is Matteo's body that fails to keep pace with his spirit even as he neglects responsibilities towards his family and loses contact with society. In the eyes of the world, he might be a failure, yet to his own self, he has been utterly sincere and has risen to his calling undertaking the arduous journey towards the ultimate reality.

Desai's engagement with the ideal of authentic life continues even in her latest novel *The Zigzag Way*, in which it takes the shape of roots search. For the first time, Desai endows her protagonist with an ultra-sensory experience as prize for his persistence. Eric and Em are live-in partners. Em lands in a Mexican town to carry on with her research and Eric hangs on to her. Eric is free and it enters his head to search for his roots since his grandfather had worked in the mines here in a nearby ghost town. He learns from an inn-keeper that people come on the occasion of the festival *Dia de los Muertos*, to pay homage to the dead relatives.

He sets out to visit the mining area. He has no idea of the grave of his grandmother but the intensity of his passion results in a mystical meeting with her apparition. Anita Desai is known for keeping the veil of mystery intact and so, contrary to the common belief in the omniscience of souls, this grandmother's apparition mistakes him for Paul (his father). The veracity of the apparition is supported by the author thus:

> A young woman was descending, with such ease and speed it was as though she did not notice the stones in her way, they were not impediments to her. She was preceded by a fragrance that was as fresh as the breeze that was blowing freely, not the heavy perfume of copal, tallow candles and funeral flowers but a much lighter, more natural one, of herbs like lavender, rosemary and thyme, mountain

> herbs *that seemed unlikely to be growing in that hostile rubble and stoniness but perhaps were since their essence was clearly present.*
>
> Seeing Eic standing by the low wall that ringed the cemetery, she lifted her hand, holding a small bunch of grey leaves and pale flowers, and to his amazement, waved to him. He could not imagine why she acknowledged him or who she might be or why she was there, *but his mind had ceased to pose questions*, they were all obliterated by the wave of her hand and the pure scent of the flowers. (175, my italics)

Excepting the words italicized here, there is no hint at this stage of any extra-terrestrial presence; the description of the scene is quite natural. "We're there. D'you know what they call it? Jews' Hill," the ghost tells him matter-of-factly. (177) Eric and the ghost of her grandmother have a lengthy discussion about sundry things, like the cactus plants, the Indian pilgrims visiting the place and Eric's grandfather's family origin. Finally, the unreality of the ghost is revealed when she beckons Eric to follow her but he cannot get through the wall like the ghost does and misses her trail altogether in the light of the dawn. Nevertheless, he has succeeded in paying homage to his ancestors and locating the missing link in building his identity.

Desai's characters, as such, pursue different goals—physical security, individual privacy, following a dream with the zeal of a zealot. Their conception of their authentic life is not conditioned by any social ideology, creed or religion. The calling comes from within. The obstacles en route their quest are aplenty and the end result is failure by worldly standards. But they have taken their own decisions and would not blame others. There is no whining and whimpering on their part. They are heroes and heroines of modern day epics called life.

It is in striving authentically, that is, with complete consciousness as being-for-itself that existentialism values most. One must live authentically even while acknowledging that there is no relief in this world. The reward that comes one's way is the enrichment of self-consciousness. Man is all the time projecting himself beyond himself. It is by pursuing transcendent aims or seeking to surpass the self that he is able to exist. Transcendence is constitutive of man.

Works Cited

Desai, Anita. *Baumgartner's Bombay.* London: Penguin, 1989.
_____. *Bye-Bye, Blackbird.* Delhi: Orient Paperbacks, 1985.
_____. *Cry, the Peacock.* Delhi: Orient Paperbacks. 1980. Reprint 2005.
_____. *In Custody.* London: William Heinemann, 1984.
_____. *Journey to Ithaca.* London: Heinemann, 1995.
_____. *The Zigzag Way.* London: Vintage (Chatto and Windus), 2004.
_____. *Voices in the City.* Delhi: Orient Paperbacks, 1965, Reprint 2001.
Indigo Dictionary of Philosophy. New Delhi: Genesis, 2002.
Paul, S.L., *Philosophical Background to Western Literature.* Karnal: Siddhartha, 1989.
Sinha, M.N. *Existentialism.* Delhi: Capital, 1982.
Shroeder, Y. *Existentialism and Philosophical Anthropology.* Cambridge: Cambridge University Press, 1987.

Psychoanalysis of Anita Desai's *Fasting, Feasting* in the Light of Humanism

MEENAKSHI CHOUBEY
Govt. Girls' College, Betul

Anita Desai as a novelist has imparted psychological depth to Indian English novel. In her *Fasting, Feasting*, she explores with a rare insight and observation the complexities and intricacies of human psyche. She is gifted with acutely keen imaginative faculty with prolific power of observation of human behaviour. Being purely subjective and a psychological writer, we can notice her often peeping in the inner recesses of the psyche rather than in outer spectacle of the world. Her favourite themes—man-woman relationship, alienation, East-West encounter, violence and death are all stuffed with psychological insight.

Anita Desai has close affinity with psychological novelists like James Joyce, Virginia Woolf and George Eliot in respect of theme and technique. Although Anita Desai does not write with specific purpose of creating awareness in the society yet her work contributed a lot in order to focus on the sensitive areas of human psyche. The very title of her first novel *Cry, the Peacock* is highly symbolic. The peacock crying, "Lover, lover, Mio, mio, I die," symbolically suggests the heroine's love of life and obsession with death which lead her to the final crack up. Maya's pet dog Toto represents warmth and faith, the qualities that Gautama lacks. Moon suggests death. It appears as a dramatic creature, 'the fierce dancer' and mad demon of Kathakali ballets, 'a phantom goes berserk.' *Voices in the City* symbolizes the varied voices of sensitive soul, which are futile and meaningless in the city (Calcutta) of death and despair. The island of Manori in *Where Shall Go This*

Summer? is an evocative symbol of an impending tragedy that occurs at the end of the novel. Thule and Bombay in *The Village by the Sea* symbolize agricultural rural life with magic cures and freedom and industrial urban life in metropolitan cities with science and medicine.

Anita Desai's imagery is derived from various sources like botany, zoology, colour and religion. Her imagery is central to her fictional strategy and spotlights her tragic vision of life. Anita Desai clarifies that she uses certain images again and again. Although real, they acquire the significant role of symbols. Each writer concludes by revealing his own mythology and that symbolizes his private morality and philosophy.

The language of Anita Desai very aptly depicts the mental states of her characters. Anita Desai's novels occupy a unique place in Indian English novel for their richness, psychological depth, sophistication, flawless style and technique. Anita Desai's *Fasting, Feasting* is an attempt to reveal the factors responsible for emotional deprivation which means lack of reasonable share of pleasant or desirable emotional experiences.

Human beings are rational but much of their behaviour is determined by the emotional support which they get from their family, friends, relations, society and ultimately from the belief system which assures them that someone is there to help during hard times and critical situations. Development of these emotions elevates man's character and undesirable or unpleasant emotions such as fear, jealousy, anger, hatred, grief and anxiety become the cause of emotional deprivation. Such is the case of Uma, the central figure in Anita Desai's novel *Fasting, Feasting*. Uma's emotional depression is the deprivation of reasonable share of pleasant or desirable emotional support and experience that a child wants from her family. After she fails in her examination, she stops going to school and is confined at home in order to look after her brother, Arun, the only heir of their family. Uma is smothered by the attitude of her overbearing parents and their so-called tradition. Due to their selfish interest, Uma's parents always deprive her of her basic right of getting education. Such attitude of any parent is harmful for the emotional development of a child and in Uma's case it has proved more harmful. Uma, an innocent child, tried very hard to convince her parents and teacher to help her: '"But I will work very hard,' she yelled, 'I will pass next time. Please tell him Mother I will pass next time!'"[1] But the teacher of that convent school advised her that whatever her father has suggested for her that is absolutely right and she said, 'Girls have to learn these things.' (28)

Although Anita Desai does not write with a conscious social purpose yet her work has unconsciously contributed to the feministic cause. *Fasting, Feasting* is an expression of inner preoccupation of women in our society and our illusion of the modern ideal of building a society free of male dominance. Uma's two time victimization by the dowry system and Anamika's death is an expression of onslaught of violence on the feminine sweetness and light all over the globe. The condition of Uma and Anamika reflects the unscrupulous frame of mind of our society which creates serious doubt about the thinking faculty of our so-called literate society.

In *Fasting, Feasting*, Anita Desai's attitude is deeply humanistic. An undercurrent of irony, satire, sarcasm which we can find in the episodes of her novel that speak about the genius of Anita Desai as an artist. Realization of God falls outside the purview of material sciences. Rationalism of Anita Desai examines religion and spirituality on logical ground and so through Uma, Mira Masi and Mother Agnes, Anita Desai tries to prove her rational attitude. According to Sigmund Freud, an Austrian psychoanalyst, "It does not lie within the scope of this inquiry to estimate the values of religious doctrines as truth. It suffices that we have recognized them, psychologically considered, as illusion."[2]

As in the case of Uma, these religious doctrines have proved an illusion. When Uma went to Mother Agnes in order to find some solution to her problems, for in so young age she finds herself incapable of handling a little brother like her mother. Instead of providing a solution, Mother Agnes gave her a picture of Virgin Mary and baby Jesus with following advice: "Pray for strength; pray to Virgin Mary for strength, never forget to pray." (29)

And by saying so Mother Agnes was not only dismissing her from her presence, her protection but it is also a sign of suggesting to her that she should leave the school. For an innocent girl like Uma, this was a shocking reply because, in general consideration, this is the ultimate place where people find solution of their problems. Through Uma, Anita Desai very dramatically conveys the pathetic condition of a girl whose basic desires are being smothered and its effect on that girl in the form of fits which leaves undesirable scar on her psyche. It is not just the religious ways of Mother Agnes but Mira Masi's way of roving to different pilgrimage cannot lighten the dark life of Uma. In one pilgrimage, Uma accompanied her and lived in an ashram in a remote place where Uma tried to find some solution of her problem and closely followed the rituals in the ashram. One day, when Uma was walking alongside the river, which she liked so much, thinking about sharing her problem with Mira Masi, suddenly Mira Masi appeared in front of her and whispered some words which was the cause of another fit for Uma. She said: "You are the lord's child, The Lord has chosen you, you bear his mark" (59)

Thus through both the incidents, Anita Desai wants to convey her humanistic approach of looking at the world. Sympathy for sorrowful and suffering soul is the characteristic of Anita Desai's humanistic approach and so Dr. Dutt's treatment looks more useful for Uma than the way of Mother Agnes and Mira Masi.

In her moral and psychological preoccupation, Anita Desai's talent comes close to that of George Eliot. Even the title of her novel *Fasting, Feasting* incorporates the central contradiction of human life where one gets more than his/her desire and the desire of survival of others remains unheard. Through the life of different characters like Uma, Aruna, Anamika and Arun, Anita Desai explores human psyche through their fulfilled and unfulfilled dreams and desires or how much they are capable of understanding their dreams and desires. Uma is the eldest of three siblings. In spite of the dictatorial attitude of her father, she is quite a normal child, though neither beautiful nor talented. We can see a kind of bond between mother and two girls before the birth of Arun—a precious son. The attention and affection of mother drifts away from the girls to the son, who becomes the central force in the family. The life of Uma is burdened with the responsibility of brother Arun. To make her life more horrible, her marriage fails and now she is confined to her home which is a kind of prison for her. Uma is expected to kill all her desires and to live for mamapapa who become all the more dependent on her as Uma is always there to take good care of everything about the house. In this way, a perfectly sane child is pushed into insanity by maternal indifference. "Uma is oppressed not so much by patriarch as by her mother. . . . Uma, a normal girl child grows into a dull, insipid shadow of a woman and going through various trials and tribulations finally attains a mental state which borders on insanity."[3]

The second daughter of mamapapa Aruna is very self-assertive, obsessive and arrogant girl from her childhood. She knows what she wants from her life and from others very well. She is smart, active and full of self-confidence. When mama was searching a husband for Uma, families were already asking about Aruna. "There were so many marriage proposals for Aruna that Uma's unmarried state was not only an embarrassment but an abstraction." (90) Ultimately Aruna married the wisest, most exciting of the suitors who presented themselves. In this way, for Aruna life is a kind of ceremony as Anita Desai asserted "Soon Aruna was whisked away to a life that she had said would be 'fantastic'" (91).

Arun, the third child of mamapapa, generates great excitement and joy in their life because he is a son, the only heir. Through the excitement and change in behaviour in mama papa's life, Anita Desai portrays the psyche of Indian parents who, despite being educated, want a boy/son in their life. Arun is a living example of such psychological disorder of Indian parents. Because of the birth of Arun, mama's position was raised and it was poor Uma who suffered the loss of her studies because she had to look after baby Arun. The whole concentration of mama papa was centred only on their son, Arun. In the eagerness to grow him up in the best possible way, the best health, the best education and the best life, they become over-possessive of the boy. Arun grow up according to his parents' desires, especially his papa's, without having his own dreams, desires and even decisions of his own life. From his childhood, the freedom, the selection, the choice of Arun had been smothered and he never enjoys life according to his own way. He is a puppet in the hands of his father who directs his every activity. Arun was exhausted with his tutors, studies, entrance exams and finally got admission in a foreign university. In the alien land, Arun stood bewildered. He had never seen so much freedom and so much stress in his own land. Through Arun, Anita Desai presents the psychological condition of an Indian student who is oppressed by the unexpected cultural condition of European people.

Human beings are considered a dignified centre of the universe and their sufferings and miseries are looked at as indignities and violation of the divinity of man. Anita Desai's novel, *Fasting, Feasting*, is a powerful attempt to throw light on the experiences of a disturbed and emotionally alienated mind. *Fasting, Feasting* is an indictment against all those people who considered themselves literate and in their own house girls like Uma and Anamika are being smothered. Above all *Fasting, Feasting* is an effort to give voice to humanity where so-called religious pursuits of men are looked at primarily as superfluities.

NOTES

1. Anita Desai, *Fasting, Feasting*, Vintage, 2000, p. 28.
2. Sigmund Freud, *The Future of an Illusion*, ed. Ernest Jones.
3. Asha Choubey, "A Feministic Perspective on Anita Desai," *Critical Response to Anita Desai*, ed. Shubha Tiwari.

De-masculinization of the Male in the Novels of Margaret Laurence and Anita Desai

SARITA VEERANGANA
Gaya College, Gaya

The ancient law-giver Manu was not in favour of extending absolute freedom to woman. In *Manusmriti*, there is a *sloka* which means: "A woman should not be free. In childhood, she should be controlled by her father, in youth by her husband, and in old age by her son." It was a primitive law, when the society was dominated by the male sex and the female sex had no say in any matter. Now the situation has changed. No woman would like to live in chains. Freedom is the cherished goal of all women irrespective of caste, creed, colour, community or nationality.

The oriental view of woman is that woman should be held in high esteem. In the *Rg Veda*, there is a *mantra* which means that when after marriage, the wife is brought to her husband's house, "she is escorted by the sun-god in his chariot by holding her hands."[2]

For centuries, however, women have been subjected to various types of atrocities, insults, and humiliations both in India and abroad. In such a circumstance reactions and repercussions were inevitable. The feminine writing is its natural outcome. A demand is raised by women for parity of status and the women have been agitating for liberty and right which has slowly and gradually precipitated into a disastrous situation almost to the point of volcanic eruption. The women have now become alive to their rights and they offer themselves to co-operate with men in all the walks of life. They say that duty and right go hand in hand. Right is the natural concomitant of duty and the modern society has done them great harm by extorting duty from them and depriving them of their rights.

Tracing the history of the feminist movement, particularly, in England, it may be recalled that around 1910, when D.H. Lawrence was still a young man, aged about twenty-five, the feminist movement was at its peak and seemed, by its nagging insistence on equality and even superiority of heaven, to be a further denial of the fundamental truth. D.H. Lawrence, in one way or the other, anticipated the synthesis between male and female, to be achieved by the next phase of civilization. As time passed, women became more and more conscious of their position, and the consciousness took within its grip all the countries of the world including India and this new consciousness has been a major preoccupation with the feminist writers. The feminist programme is a re-vision of women from the gynocentric point of view with the sole intention of counteracting the male supremacy and assert and validate the feminist discourse as different from and incompatible with the patriarchal discourse.

Coming to the novels of Margaret Laurence and Anita Desai, first of all, it is worth mentioning that the two novelists have entirely different social and cultural orientation and if they meet on certain points, it is by sheer coincidence.

Margaret Laurence is an eminent Canadian novelist. She is not recognized as an immoderate feminist in Canada. And yet, in her Manawaka writings, the male is wilfully marginalized and demasculinized. Her feminist bias redeems all her women characters. She has a predilection to portray women characters as paragons of virtue. On the contrary, her male characters are shown as eccentric, neurotic, deranged, evil, weak, pretentious, even of doubtful honesty. If they are redeemed, it is by way of pity or sympathy or contemptuous charity rather than by any ennobling emotion. Such a devastating, anti-male attitude is indeed very astonishing in a writer who writes within a predominantly humanist tradition and who herself advocates a more equitable attitude towards men outside her fiction. Referring to the Women's Lib movement, Margaret Laurence pronounces.

> I am 90% in agreement with Women's Lib. But I think we have to be careful here; for instance, I don't think enough attention has been paid to the problems men have and are going to have increasingly because of the changes taking place in women. Men have to be re-educated with the minimum damage to them. They are our husbands, our sons, our lovers . . . we can't live without them and we can't go to war against them. The change must liberate them as well.[1]

There are seven novels to the credit of Margaret Laurence. They are: *This Side Jordan* (1960), *The Tomorrow-Tamer* (1963), *The Stone Angel* (1964), *A Jest of God* (1966), *The Fire-Dwellers* (1969), *A Bird in the House* (1970) and *The Diviners* (1974). Out of these, at least four, *The Stone Angel*, *A Jest of God*, *The Fire-Dwellers* and *The Diviners* have positive and direct leaning on the subject of de-masculinization of the male and the superiority of women. Margaret Laurence died at Lakefield, Ontario, in 1987.

The fame of Anita Desai, the famous Indiàn English novelist, is on the decline. Her daughter Kiran Desai won Man Booker Prize in 2006 for her novel, *The Inheritance of Loss*. However, Anita Desai won Sahitya Akademi Award in 1978. Margaret Laurence also got Governor General's award twice, for the first time in 1966 for her novel *A Jest of God* and again in 1974 for the epic novel, *The Diviners*.

Among the major novels of Anita Desai, three novels are worth mentioning. They are *Voices in the City* (1982), *Cry the Peacock* (1986) and *Where Shall We Go This Summer?* (1988). What is common in Margaret Laurence and Anita Desai is that both are equally interested in dislodging the male and restoring the lost position of female. Like D.H. Lawrence, both are psychic mariners, both are subtle psychologists and both believe in the liberty of woman and both pity the image of modern woman distorted and tarnished at the cruel hands of man almost in a tyrannical manner. Although there is no evidence to show that Anita Desai belongs to the feminine group of writers or is actuated by male or female bias, it is manifest in her novels that she is in search of liberty of women and resents the indiscreet and supercilious demeanour of men.

Both Margaret Laurence and Anita Desai, in their novels, project a vision. Narration of story is secondary. The interest of their novels lies more in the manner of telling and the psychological exploration of characters rather than in mere plot construction. No less uncanny is the delineation of the female characters which are presented as seeking truth. They stand for self-actualization, self-renewal while their male counterparts are presented as weaklings, devoid of masculinity and vitality, uncommunicative, almost caricatures.

Like R.K. Narayan's Malgudi or Hardy's Wessex, Margaret Laurence's Manawaka has no geographical existence. It is a fictional name patterned after the birthplace of the novelist. In all the novels written by Margaret Laurence in Manawaka cycle, the male characters are presented as frigid, cold, insipid, apathetic, anaemic, bereft, of masculine vitality and to counterbalance them, the female characters are depicted as indomitable, boistorous, domineering and dauntless, not to be cowed down by threats. Hagar in *A Stone Angel*, Rachel in *A Jest of God*, Stacey in *The Fire-Dwellers* and Morag Gunn in *The Diviners* have been shown ruling the roost. Similarly, Sita in Anita Desai's *Where Shall We Go This Summer?* and Maya in *Cry, the Peacock* are presented as revolting women challenging the authority of men.

The question posed by Margaret Laurence in her novels has much to do with her personal life. She lost her mother in 1930 when she was hardly four years old. Her father passed away five years later. Thereafter, she along with her stepmother and step-brother shifted to the house of her autocratic grandfather who was so notorious and tyrannical that he did not allow any female member in the family to live in peace. This kind of subservience of the female sex created a sense of fear in her and at the same time a sense of hatred and abhorrence for the male sex which later shaped the theme of her novels. The female characters in her novels struggle for freedom. They assert themselves and fight for their independence. They stand against the egotism and self-conceit of men.

The theme of Margaret Laurence's *A Jest of God* is filial love, self-sacrifice, domestication and wish to be loved. The story of Rachel Cameron, the protagonist of the novel, is told in first person. She is a woman trapped in a prison of her own making. She lives all alone in her house. But it is worse than a prison. She is mother of four children. But she never feels that she owns them partly because of the vitiated atmosphere of the house which has told upon the mentality of the children who have virtually disowned their mother and partly because she falls a prey to desperation and ennui resulting from the nagging indifference of her professed lover. Despite perpetual tension, she does not like to wound the sentiments of others. Amid constant mental pressure, she finally decides to assert herself and turns rebellious. In the Afterword, appended to the novel, Atwood rightly observes: "desperation and courage are the two magnetic poles of this book, which begins with the first and arrives at the second."[2] Rachel is full of remorse because true mothering has been denied to her. At the age of thirty-four, she undergoes an acute mental crisis. With a heavy and penitent heart, she says: "Besides me sleeps my elderly child. What will happen? It may be that my children will always be temporary, never to be held. But so are everyone's." (208-9)

Rachel struggles to come to terms with death, with herself and her world. All her life, she runs after mirage. She runs after love as if it were true. She runs after lovers. But every time, her ambition is thwarted. She gets nothing save frustration and disappointment. She has children but she is hesitant to call them her own. There is a cleavage between the mother and the children. There is no one whom Rachel may call her husband. She languishes for love and sympathy. She feels that there is an impassable gulf between her and the world outside. From Nick Kazlik, her schoolmate from earlier days, she learns to reach out to another person. Nick Kazlick, who is thirty-five, seduces her and disappears never to come again. This further gives a serious jolt to her feelings and adds to the cracks of the already battered family life. Rachel, in a delirious mood, cries: "Where I am going, anything may happen. Maybe I will marry a middle-aged widower, or a long shore man or a cattle-hoof-trimmer, or a barrister, or a thief. And have my children in time. Or may be not. Most of the chances are against it. But not, I think, quite all." (208)

> I will be lonely, almost certainly. I will get annoyed at my sister. Her children will call me Aunt Rachel and I will resent it and find then that I've grown attached to them after all. I will walk myself on the shore of the sea and look at the sea gulls flying. Preposterous. I will take care to remember a vitamin pill each morning with my breakfast. I will be afraid. Sometimes I will feel light-hearted, sometimes light-headed. I may sing aloud, even in the dark. I will ask myself if I am going mad, but if I do, I won't know it. (209)

Rachel is well-nigh mad. She is no more than a shamble moving on the earth. The novel ends with the complimentary words spoken by Rachel in praise of the fools who have befooled her and tantalized her: "God's grace on fools. God's pity on God." (209) The tone is ironic but it well reflects the revolting ego of Rachel.

In Anita Desai's *Cry, the Peacock*, Gautama's wife Maya, is designed on a different model. She is not like Rachel to suffer silently nor is she torn from within and without. Maya is relatively shown as courageous, with an extraordinary power of endurance and forbearance. Maya is a young girl who was married to Gautama four years back. She is fed up with the high-sounding philosophy of her husband. She lives a life of complete abandonment, alienation, coercion and suffocation. Gautama is a busy lawyer. He has no time to look after his wife. Besides this, there is temperamental incompatibility between the two. The nuptial tie could be possible because Gautama was a friend of Maya's father. Maya shows resentment over her miserable predicament: "His anaemic skin stretched downward, currying bones of his cage-like ribs, his prominent shoulder blades made me pity his thinness, his appearance of being too flimsy attached to a world of solids, so ill-defended against it that is physically"[3] Whenever Maya remembers Gautama his frail image appears before her mind's eye. She often addresses him as "poor Gautama" (194) "Poor Gautama, my poor husband,'' (206) "poor dear Gautama," (208) "poor man, poor Gautama, my husband." (196) She looks upon her husband as a "somnambulist figure in opium white." (206) She thinks that "a gibbon would be defter" (199) than Gautama.

The protagonists of both Anita Desai and Margaret Laurence go through life in terrifying isolation because they find it difficult to reconcile the demands of their psyche with those of the world around them. The centrality of self in social interaction is established by both the novelists. Both are equally fascinated by the characters and the fact that human interaction is guided and modulated by internal processes. They believe that one's capability to adopt the new circumstances or heterogeneous personalities, and ability to interact warmly with others is closely linked with one's self-image.

In *Cry the Peacock*, Anita Desai focuses on the degenerative and crippling effect of an over-indulgent parental attention on the child. For Maya's father, loving a child means creating a world of sugar and candy; flowers and fairies; moonlight and star-studded dreams. Maya remembers that at her father's place: "the world is like a toy specially made for me. Gautama is, naturally, unhappy over the way Maya has been brought up, painted in my favourite colours, set moving to my favourite tunes." (36) He rebukes Maya: "Life is a fairy tale to you still. What have you learnt of the realities?" (115) He fixes the responsibility for her unreasonable expectation from him on her father: "What wickedness to raise a child like that" (115) Gautama and Maya are at loggerheads with each other. Both have grievances. But there is a limit to everything. There is a limit to tolerance also. Maya tolerates more than her husband does. The natural outcome of the conflict is that the disintegrated, neurotic and fearful Maya loses hold over her environment and fails to relate herself meaningfully to Gautama.

In *Voices in the City*, one comes across an exploration into the childhood experiences and nature of the primary ties in the case of Nirode, Monisha and Amla. The novel opens with a comparison between Nirode's failure and Arun's bright success. Arun leaves for England for higher studies whereas Nirode decides to live in "shadows, silence, stillness."[4] The childhood experiences of Monisha, Nirode's elder sister, and Amla are described in a telling manner. After the death of Nirode's father, his mother brings a social obloquy by developing affairs with Major Chaddha. Deprived of self-confidence, Nirode makes failure his creed. As a rootless drifter, he keeps on changing his goals one after another. His strong obsession with failure is revealed in his conversation with David: "I want to fail quickly." (7) Nirode's elder sister Monisha's predicament is all the more sad. The pernicious home environment robs her of the feelings of self-appraisal and self-image. Like Maya, Monisha also suffers from the conflict between the real and the ideal self.

Margaret Laurence's *The Fire-Dwellers*[5] adopts a theme which is rather uncommon. The image of fire has been derived from the flames of illicit sex. Stacey Cameron had two daughters, Katie and Jen who are fourteen and two and two sons Ian or Honey and Duncan who are ten and seven. Her husband Mac Aindra is a hardworking salesman. But he is wholly uncommunicative, like Gautama of *Cry, the Peacock*. Stacey aspires for a richer life. Her cage is too strong to be broken. When the story begins, we find Stacey repenting for her past youth. She is now a spent force. There was a time when she was nineteen and shook "the dust of Manawaka off." (7) In respect of education, she is much inferior to Mac. While Mac is a Ph.D., Stacey is only grade eleven. Stacey's grievance against her husband bursts out: "Damn him, snoring always so unconcernedly, I feel like giving him a sharp kick so he will wake up at least. We'll both be suffering." (27)

The traumatic indifference of Mac towards Stacey leads to estrangement. Stacey complains: "Four kids have altered me." (186) "Four kids have ruined me." (91) Mac admits that Stacey has a terrific will power." (193) She sits, as it were, on the crater of a volcano. A time comes when the situation becomes insufferable to her. She is not constrained to transgress the limit. In a mood of utter desperation, she says: "I could kill you, Mac. I could stab you . . . right this minute." (110) Quoting the saying of St. Paul, she stretches the saying to a funny excess: "What to do if you married and burnt." (193) It is a case not of loss of virtue but virtue gone sour. Stacey's doubts, misgivings and apprehensions are the outcome of her having a negative self-image. Her small town background and inadequate education are enough to make her feel inferior in a city like Vancouver. Burdened with the feeling of self-rejection she is sceptical about her relationship with her husband. When he is late in returning home, she imagines him enjoying his dinner somewhere else in the company of a more pleasant-looking person: "Click, well, c'mon Stacey, it's getting late. Yes, so it is." (120)

Purged of all inner conflicts, Stacey understands herself better and comes to admire Mac as she had done before. Formerly, Stacey felt uneasy when she was wedded to Mac sixteen years ago: "I wouldn't have minded about that except he doesn't talk any more, hardly at all, can you imagine what it's like to live in the same house with somebody who doesn't talk or who can't or else won't and I don't know which realm it could be." (181-82)

But after she traverses the thorny path of life, she learns what life is and then she is reconciled to her situation: "'I won't be twenty-one again. I'll never have a really decent-looking pair of hips again as long as I live. I don't claim that's any tragedy. I don't even claim it's anything except ludicrous.' . . . The house is quiet. The kids are asleep. Downstairs in the ex-study, Matthew has been asleep for hours, or if not asleep meditating. Beside her, she can already hear the steady breathing that means Mac is asleep. Temporarily, they are all more or less okay." (280-81) The novel ends on a note of poise and harmony.

The position of Sita in Anita Desai's novel, *Where Shall We Go This Summer?* is analogous to that of Stacey. Sita is also the mother of four children. When the story begins, Sita is in family way. She goes to Manori Island, the island of miracles, to give birth to the fifth baby. Sita, in great annoyance, hisses through her teeth: "I am not pleased, I am frightened."[6] The husband-wife relation is mysterious. There is no open confrontation between them. But they go on piling up fury to explode one day. The anti-male attitude of Sita is brought out when she calls her husband a "wizard." (100) She compares herself to a creature living in illusion. The story, however, ends happily. The children are nicely brought up and suitably placed. Sita gives birth to her fifth child. But this happiness comes after so much of ravages that it is no better than tragedy. Sita spends her last days in Bombay completely alienated from everybody around her. She cannot adjust with persons who live like animals in drudgery and self-aggrandizement. She says: "They are animals—nothing but appetite and sex .Only food, sex, money matters. Animals." (47) Sita is a woman of forty and displays distinct symptoms of a negative self-image. Lack of faith in her own self compels her to question everything and everyone around her. Her bitter relationship with her father who indulges in dubious clandestine activities while feigning as a saint also contributes to her low self-esteem. Things are made worse when her sister Rekha enjoys greater attention from her father. The mystery about her mother and the provocative information given to her by her brother Jivan make her all the more suspicious and doubtful. Long after everything is over at the island and when she lives in Bombay, she feels dissatisfied with the people around her. Like Monisha, she fails to accept them as they are. No one comes up to her expectation. Later she makes a compromise by adapting herself to the situation.

In the fictional world of Margaret Laurence also, one finds fearful and mentally sick protagonists striving hard for achieving harmony and fulfillment in their interaction with others. The male characters in her novels have been presented as perceived by women.[7] While reading the fictional narratives of Margaret Laurence, one gets an impression that the joy of living is possible only for those who not only understand themselves but have some knowledge of the human context also. Hagar Shipley in *The Stone Angel* is not really known by the people around her nor can Hagar really know them. When she realizes that she cannot convert Bram to her liking, she takes her younger son John along with her and goes out to live independently. For years together, she stubbornly refuses to communicate with her husband or with her elder son

Marvin. She is convinced that she can afford to live all alone at the age of ninety also. Despite her advancing age, she is not mellowed. She is proud of being fastidious. Her assertion is: "There is no one like me in this world."[8] Like Monisha and Sita, she too cannot accept people as they are and finds it difficult to appreciate and accommodate doing something unconventional. Then wisdom dawns upon her. She realizes that pride has led her to emotional wilderness. Sadly she muses that her principal aim in life was to enjoy it. But she lost the chance. It was her self-conceit that came in the way. After self-introspection, she admits: "This knowing comes upon me so forcefully, so shatteringly, and with such a bitterness as I have never felt before." (292) Hagar Shipley gives up pretensions in order to enjoy life and this is a great achievement on her part. In Hagar Shipley, the novelist creates one of the boldest and most memorable characters in Canadian fiction.

Margaret Laurence's Manawaka cycle reached its apex in her novel, *The Diviners*. The protagonist of this novel Morag Gunn is a professional writer. She is a constant fighter. Again and again, she is forced to test her strength. She is a symbol of courage and endurance. She was married to Brooke Skelton eight years back when she was only twenty. She is not afraid of anything in this wide world. She makes a bold declaration: "Forests can't hurt me because I have the power and the second sight and the good eye and strength of conviction."[9]

Morag Gunn has no family. She was brought up by some friends and acquaintances of her parents. But she refuses to be looked after as an object of pity. Her conviction is: "I can't bear pity." (210) Circumstance has made her revolutionary. Her husband has affairs with other girls. This is why he does not charge Morag with infidelity. Other male characters like Piper, Colin Gunn and Thor Buckler have been viewed with the same jaundiced eye.

It would appear that both Margaret Laurence and Anita Desai take a partisan view of man. A pertinent question arises whether or not an androgynous view is possible. Do we not have frail unscrupulous and turbulent women in our society? Both the novelists regard family as the psychic agency of society. Both are equally shocked at the bondage and servitude of women. This is why they plead for the liberty and rejuvenation of women in their fictions. Laurence gives us Hagar, Rachel, Stacey and Morag and Anita Desai gives us Maya, Monisha, Amla and Sita. These characters are trapped in an existentialist predicament. Their quest is for survival, freedom and self-actualization. The secondary women characters serve as foils to reinforce the quest motif of the protagonists. In contrast to the women characters, the male characters are shown as shadowy, devoid of masculine qualities. Thus, Nick Kazlik, Mac Aindra, Bram Shipley, Brooke-Skelton, the principal characters in the Manawaka fiction, play negative roles in their relations with Rachel, Stacey, Hagar and Morag . Similar is the case with Gautama in Anita Desai's *Cry, the Peacock*, who plays a negative role in relation to Maya. None but Gautama is responsible for the boredom of Maya. Both Margaret Laurence and Anita Desai attempt to reject and react against patriarchal misogynistic social structure. The view is however, lop-sided. There is no dearth of a Clytemnestra, a Madame Defarge and a Lady Macbeth in our society. It would be dangerous to take a parochial view of either man or a woman. The male female relationship can be truly assessed when we look at it with scientific detachment.

NOTES

1. Margaret Laurence, Face to face with Atwood Margaret (Woodcock, 1989), p. 23.
2. Margaret Atwood, "Afterword," *A Jest of God* (Toronto, 1966). p. 214.
3. Anita Desai, *Cry, the Peacock* (Orient, New Delhi, 1986), p. 200.
4. Anita Desai, *Voices in the City* (Delhi: Orient Paperbacks, 1982), p. 8
5. Margaret Laurence, *The Fire-Dwellers* (Toronto McClelland and Stewart, 1969), p. 11.
6. Anita Desai, *Where Shall We Go This Summer*? (Orient New Delhi, 1988), p. 33.

7. Michel Fabre, From *The Stone Angel* to *The Diviners*. An Interview with Margaret Laurence (Woodcock, 1989), pp. 193-209.
8. Margaret Laurence, *The Stone Angel* (Toronto: McClelland and Stewart 1968), p. 35
9. Margaret Laurence, *The Diviners* (Toronto, 1974), p. 61.

Doris Lessing's Feminist Concern: An Analysis of *The Grass is Singing* and *The Golden Notebook*

SANTWANA HALDAR
F.M. University, Balasore

During her literary career of more than fifty years, Doris Lessing (b. 1919) has been involved in issues ranging from the racial oppression of South Africa to the recurrent threat of nuclear war and has been tagged to almost all the major doctrines associated with literature in the twentieth century—doctrines such as postcolonialism, communism, feminism and mysticism—and her twenty-six full-length novels along with the volumes of short stories, poems and plays, reveal the changes in her attitude to those doctrines. Born in Persia to British parents, Lessing spent her early life in Rhodesia (now Zimbabwe) and then settled in London in 1949, gathering thereby vast experience from real life which is as much personal as universal. To quote Lessing in this context, "Writing about oneself one is writing about others, since your problems, pains, pleasure, emotions—and your extraordinary and remarkable ideas—cannot be your alone. The way to deal with the problem of 'subjectivity,' that shocking business of being preoccupied with the tiny individual who is at the same time caught up in such an explosion of terrible and marvellous possibilities, is to see him as a microcosm and in this way to break through the personal, the subjective, making the personal general, as indeed life always does." (Preface to *The Golden Notebook*, June 1971 version).

Though Lessing is recognized, almost universally, as the high priestess of Feminism, she denies that she had some readymade views on feminism to be delivered through her writings. Rather it is after handing the manuscript of a particular book to her friends and publishers that she learnt that she had written "a tract about the sex war." In fact, Lessing writes about her own observations and experiences in life as she is affected first by the turbulent climate of racial war in South Africa as well as her personal sufferings—she was twice divorced during her stay in South Africa—and then by her involvement into various movements in London, her powerful imagination and keenly observant eyes having enabled her all through to delve deep beneath the surface reality of the contemporary world. She is therefore a feminist, if at all, with difference; instead of projecting some fixed standpoint in regard to the patriarchal society and emancipation of women, she views women as human beings who may or may not be oppressed by the male-dominated society, but who get involved in all the significant issues they find around them and fight according to their might. While feminist writers lay stress on women's equal status in every sphere of life and draw the readers' attention towards the variety of tortures inflicted on women, Lessing focuses on those problems which women face in their encounter with their own minds as well as the outer world. The Nobel committee rightly praised her while bestowing on her the honour of 2007 Nobel Laureate for literature: Lessing is an "epicist of female experience who, with scepticism, fire and visionary power, has subjected a divided civilization to scrutiny." The present article takes into consideration two of her novels and intends to throw light on her concerns for issues which are typically feminist ones as well as others which are ignored by the feminists.

Lessing's first novel *The Grass is Singing* (1949), set in the backdrop of war-torn Rhodesia, is a powerful study in moral degeneration both of the colonials and the colonized. It was acclaimed, immediately after its publication, as a great success and the readers were attracted to the moving story of racial discrimination. Mary, the protagonist of the novel, spent thirty years of her life in a town in Rhodesia and developed typical colonial mind-set. She was denied a happy childhood—her father, a drunkard, could not provide the necessary money for maintaining his family and her mother was constantly in tussle with him—and had to cut short her education. She was however happy in her own ways, working as a typist in an office. She stayed in a girls' club and hardly bothered to present herself as a lady in front of others. She did not think of marriage until one day she overheard the discussions of her 'friends' in regard to her girl-like behaviour at the age of thirty and felt ashamed of herself. The innocence of her easy-going life being gone forever, she became a psychic patient and was asked by his employer to take long leave. After making some desperate attempts, she married the farmer Dick who loathed everything associated with town including the cinema which was Mary's favourite. Mary had earlier romanticized nature and did not oppose the prospect of living in a village with Dick. She had to pay a heavy price for her decision when she came to settle in the village: the unbearable heat, scarcity of water, lack of urban facilities and utter loneliness, thanks to Dick's devotion to land that even denied him profit, dragged her towards insanity. Her dealings with the natives—she had her native servant-cum-cook at home and during Dick's illness she had to go to the field to supervise the native labourers—made matters worse for her. She was unable to treat the black natives as human beings and misbehaved with them. She even slapped a native during her supervision of the farm work. Later when that native was appointed as house servant and Dick was firm that he must continue despite Mary's repeated demand to sack him, Mary developed fear psychosis in the presence of that native who kills her at the end. The novel starts with a newspaper report of this murder and the reaction of the local white men at this news. Mary's story is described in the following chapters, revealing her strength and weakness.

Mary's strength of character is revealed in her capacity to enjoy life on her own. She was extremely happy when she was sent to a boarding school. She was so happy that "she dreaded going home at holiday-times to her fuddled father, her bitter mother, and the fly-away little house that was like a small wooden box on stilts."[1] At sixteen she was forced to leave school and she took a job in a little town. "Again she was happy. She seemed born for shorthand and book-keeping and the comfortable routine of an office. She liked things to happen safely one after another in a pattern, and she liked, particularly, the friendly impersonality of it" (41). When she was twenty, she had a good job and also had a friend circle with which she was really happy. Her mother died at this time and she was virtually alone, because her father was five hundred miles away and she hardly took any interest in him. "Mary was pleased to be rid of him. Being alone in the world had no terrors for her at all, she liked it" (41). Mary's capacity to be happy, the positive quality of her character, was lost when she needed it most, because she did not know how to analyze her own mind and the minds of others. She was guided by her mother's blind rage for her father and never tried to understand his feelings. Her father, a male, was the 'other' for her as were the natives who belong to the 'other' race. Mary's mind was engrossed in her mother's feminist attitude and the typical attitude of a white man for whom a nigger is hardly a human being. Lessing has clearly pointed at this shortfall in Mary's character:

> It had never occurred to her that her father, too, might have suffered. 'About what?' she would have retorted, had anyone suggested it. 'He's a man, isn't he? He can do as he likes.' She had inherited from her mother an arid feminism, which had no meaning in her own life at all, for she was leading the comfortable carefree existence of a single woman in South Africa, and she did not know how fortunate she was. How could she know? She understood nothing of conditions in other countries, had no measuring rod to assess herself with. It had never occurred to her to think, for instance, that she, the daughter of a pretty railway official and a woman whose life had been so unhappy because of economic pressure that she had literally pined for death, was living in much the same way as the daughters of the wealthiest in South Africa, could do as she pleased—could marry, if she wished, anyone she wanted. These things did not enter her head. 'Class' is not a South African word: and its equivalent, 'race,' meant to her the office boy in the firm where she worked, other women's servants, and the amorphous mass of natives in the streets, whom she hardly noticed. She knew (the phrase was in the

> air) that the natives were getting 'cheeky.' But she had nothing to do with them really. They were outside her orbit. (42)

The shortfalls in Mary's character are clearly diagnosed in the paragraph quoted above. If she were not guided by her mother's "arid feminism," she could easily marry a young man of her choice in her early youth and there was likely to be no complication in her life. Again, if she were not influenced by a typical white man's attitude to the natives, she might treat the natives as normal human beings, who need food and rest, and then she could avoid the tragedy of her life. Lessing makes it clear that the problems faced by a woman are determined by the circumstances in which a woman finds herself and since circumstances vary, problems faced by women also vary and it is not proper to identify some problems as women's problems in general.

Lessing is not however blind to the fact that the existing social norms make a woman feminine.[2] As long as Mary was ignorant of what her companions were thinking about her, she was happy with herself. But the moment she overheard that they were discussing about her single status—they said, "She just is not like that . . . her skin is like sandpaper, and she's got so thin. . . . She'll never set the rivers on fire . . . she will marry someone old enough to be her father"—she was rudely shocked and tried to modify herself as per the norms settled by others. She began to feel that she must have married by then and desperately searched for a possible groom. Lessing discusses the changes in her mind clearly:

> She was stunned and outraged; but most of all deeply wounded that her friends could discuss her thus. . . . That little incident, apparently so unimportant, which would have no effect on a person who had the faintest idea of the kind of the world she lived in, had a profound effect on Mary. She who had never had time to think of herself, took to sitting in her room for hours at a time, wondering: 'Why did they say those things? . . . Turning over in her mind the words she had by accident listened to, she thought of ways to improve herself. She took the ribbon out of her hair, though with regret, . . . and brought herself tailor-made clothes, in which she felt ill at ease. . . . And for the first time in her life she was feeling uncomfortable with men. . . . And she

> began looking around for someone to marry. She did not put it to herself like that; but, after all, she was nothing if not a social being, though she had never thought of 'society,' the abstraction. (50)

Things became worse as she made herself ridiculous through her violent revulsion when the widower who had already proposed to her and was accepted, proceeded to kiss her. Mary's 'friends' laughed at her, for "in this age of scientific sex, nothing seems more ridiculous than sexual gaucherie" (51). It was obvious that Mary became more desperate than ever. While pointing at the causes of her despair, Lessing does not forget to mention that Mary was lacking in self-knowledge and that it was a terrible experience for a person if his/her self-image is destroyed in the interest of truth or some other abstraction.

> Mary's idea of herself was destroyed and she was not fitted to recreate herself. She could not exist without that impersonal, casual friendship from other people; and now it seemed to her there was pity in the way they looked at her. . . . She felt as she had never done before; she was hollow inside, empty, and into this emptiness would sweep from nowhere a vast panic, as if there were nothing in the world she could grasp hold of. . . . At the age of thirty, this woman who had had a 'good' State education, a thoroughly comfortable life enjoying herself in a civilized way, and access to all knowledge of her time (only she read nothing but bad novels) knew so little about herself that she was thrown completely off her balance because some gossiping women had said she ought to get married. (52)

The difference between Lessing's approach to a woman's problem and that of a popular feminist is clear: while the popular feminists accuse the patriarchal society of driving the woman towards insanity, Lessing makes other women as well as the woman concerned responsible for her nervous breakdown.

Lessing is also aware that the patriarchal society curbs the freedom of women in every walk of life. Once a woman makes a mistake, she is compelled to suffer. Mary might have done the great mistake of her life through her hasty decision of marriage. She had no idea about a farmer's life in Africa, and that too, of a farmer like Dick who neglects all sorts of homely comforts and even does not bother much to get the ceilings done in that scorching heat of South Africa. And when Mary expresses her inconvenience, he bluntly says that he has lived under that roof for six years and did not feel uncomfortable. Mary's real problem was not however the roof or the lack of good furniture and utensils; what she could not tolerate was the existence of the black servants in her home. Like any average male person, Dick imposed his own likings and dislikings on his wife, without trying to know what she wanted. After Mr. and Mrs. Slatter came to visit their home, Dick insisted on Mary's visiting their home. "Mary did not understand why he seemed alien and hostile to her, but she was piqued at this casual summing up of her needs. And she had no desire for Mrs. Slatter's company" (94).

But what was the most annoying and unthinkable for Mary was Dick's behaviour with the black servant who wanted to leave. Ignoring the unwritten rules, Dick told the servant that the new missus did not know much about running a house yet, and that she would learn and never misbehave with him again. "Speaking like this to a native, appealing to him, was contrary to Dick's ideas of the relationship between white and black, but he was furious with Mary for her lack of consideration and tact" (94). Mary was quite stupefied with rage at his taking the native's side against her. A quarrel followed, and it weighed heavily on her nerves as she was not habituated to quarrel in this way.

> Mary was beside herself. She said, wanting to hurt him, really wanting to hurt him for the first time, because of this new arrogance of his. 'You expect a lot from me, don't you?' On the brink of disaster, she pulled herself up, but could not stop completely, and after a hesitation went on. 'You expect such a lot! You expect me to live like a poor white in this pokey little place of yours. You expect me to cook myself everyday because you won't put on ceilings. . . ..' She was speaking in a new voice for her, a voice she has never used before in her life. It was taken direct from her mother when she had those scenes over money with her father. It was not the voice of Mary, the individual (who after all really did not care so much about the bath or whether the native stayed or went), but the voice of the suffering

> female, who wanted to show her husband she just would not be treated like that. In a moment she would begin to cry, as her mother had cried on these occasions, in a kind of dignified, martyred rage. (96)

Dick's reaction at this unexpected attack was a typical male reaction. White with fury, he just reminded her that he had explained to her before their marriage what she could expect from him and that there were farmers' wives all over the country living no better, and not making such a fuss. She gasped in astonishment as he had never spoken like that to her earlier. Inside, she went hard and cold against him. After supper when he went to bed, she felt "caged" and went out into the dark outside the house, and walked up and down the path, trying to catch a breath of cool air. She began to cry weakening into self-pity. The tension between them lasted for a week and then rains fell and the air grew cool and relaxed. He did not apologize; but the incident was not simply mentioned. "For the sake of their life together she had to smother her dislike of him because of the way he had behaved, but then, it was not so easy to smother; it was put against the account of the native who had left, and indirectly, against all natives" (97).

From this time on, Mary's intolerance with the ways of the natives began to eat into the very core of her life. She had to come in contact with more and more natives as she took charge of the store opened by Dick. "It was the store that finished Mary: the necessity of serving behind the counter, and the knowledge that it was there, always there, a burden on her" (117). Dick proved himself a novice in business. Whatever he stored in the shop was not purchased by the natives and things rotted, compelling them to face great loss. All the hopes of Mary that some day Dick would make some money and they might settle in town vanished and Mary had no other way but to allow herself to "dream about that beautiful lost time when she worked in an office and lived as she pleased, before 'people made her get married'" (118). She persuaded her into the belief that she should leave the village any way and once she reached the town, she would start a peaceful life. "The soil, the black labourers, always so close to their lives but also so cut off,

Dick in his farm clothes with his hands stained with oil—these things did not belong to her, they were not real. It was monstrous that they should have been imposed upon her" (119). She received the rudest shock of her life when she was denied a job in the office where she had served for a long time and was also denied lodging in the girls' club where married women were not allowed to stay. She was however brought back to the village by Dick who appealed to her not to leave him.

Lessing has often laid stress on this aspect of married life: the male partner, internally weak, depends on the female partner who is forced to accept his terms of life against her will. The shrewd male partner does not necessarily use physical force; in fact he need not appear to be rude even. The man's appeal is enough for the woman's resignation. Thus the malady lies in the very nature of the woman who is ready to be submissive. Mary, however, reached a dead end and had no option left but to go back to the village. "But when she got home, and she found herself back in her usual routine, with now not even day-dreams to sustain her, facing her future with a tired stoicism, she found she was exhausted. . . . This was the beginning of an inner disintegration in her. It began with this numbness, as if she could no longer feel or fight" (125).

During Dick's illness, Mary had to go to the field for supervising the work of the labourers. This time she got so much enraged with a native man that she "lifted her whip and brought it down across his face in a vicious swinging blow" (146). After the event she was terrified; the expression in the man's looks "turned her stomach liquid with fear" (147). She thought that the man might go to the police.[2] Her typical colonial mind-set could not tolerate the possibility of a native's complaining against a white person. She was also satisfied that she had won in the battle of wills. Mary had to pay a high price for this crime when that man named Moses, was recruited by Dick for house work. She could not reveal the truth to Dick and had to tolerate that black man's presence. A hysterical emotion overpowered her and her irrational anger along with a sense of terror squeezed her of the energy she still possessed. This time Dick's role is again that of a typical male in a patriarchal society. He found that Mary was not complaining against the servant but just was not at ease with him. He did not bother to know what was going on in her mind. He certified the black man as the best servant and insisted that he must continue. Mary, devoid of all energy by now, was totally submissive.

> He saw her reddened, crumpled face, and her blood-suffused eyes, and knew what was wrong. It was always because of rows with her servants that she cried. . . . He said, 'Mary, you must keep this boy. He is the best that we ever had.' She did not look up, even then, but remained quite still, apparently deaf. Dick saw that her thin, sun-crinkled hand was shaking. He said again, after a silence, his voice ugly with hostility: 'I can't stand any more changing of servants. I've had enough. I'm warning you Mary.' And again she did not reply; she was weak with the tears and anger of the morning. . . . Her continued silence, which was pure opposition, drove him to insist on an assent from her. 'Mary,' he said, like a superior to a subordinate, 'did you hear what I said?' 'Yes,' she said at last sullenly, with difficulty. (180-81)

Mary had not the vitality to face Dick's challenge and this awareness caused her to hold herself "like a taut-drawn thread, stretched between two immovable weights" (183). "She was letting everything slide, except what was forced on her attention. . . . Her mind, nine-tenths of the time, was a soft aching blank. She would begin a sentence and forget to finish it" (183). The next day, when she was giving out supplies from the kitchen cupboard, Moses told her that he wanted to leave at the end of the month. Her hand dropped from the door of the cupboard, and she was horrified with the thought of Dick's anger. She simply could not go through scenes with Dick. This time she had not said anything to the servant and yet he was leaving. Though she hated him and his presence was horrifying to her, she had tried her best to keep him. She felt helpless and weak and began to sob. Wild with panic, she told him that he must not go. She was filled with shame and mortification as she could not move herself and was helped by the black man to her bed. The touch of the black man's hand on her shoulder filled her with nausea and through her torment she could hear his voice, firm and kind, like father commanding her. Soon she was relieved from the torturing thought of Dick's anger and again started using sarcastic comments on the native's work. One day he turned to her in the kitchen and said that if she would behave in that way he would go. "She felt the usual anger rise within her, at the tone he used to her; at the same time she was fascinated, and out of her depth; she did not know what to do with this personal relation . . . she went away without replying." (189).

For the first time in her life, Mary began to take any black man seriously. She found that Moses was worried about the war. She learnt from Dick that he had a mission background. She felt that he forced her now to treat him as a human being. She realized daily that there was something in it that was dangerous, but she could not define it. This time Dick fell ill again and Moses voluntarily nursed him at night, strengthening thereby the new human relationship between them. One day when he asked if she was afraid of him, she laughed nervously and said, "'Don't be ridicu lous. I am not afraid of you.' She spoke as she might have done to a white man, with whom she was flirting a little. . . . She saw him give her a long, slow, imponderable look" (205). She noticed a change in his voice; the tone became familiar, half-insolent, domineering. She was undermined with fear. In the mean time, Dick's illness had aggravated the situation for him; he was on the verge of bankruptcy. Their neighbour, Mr. Slatter who had kept an eye on Dick's land, found an opportunity to persuade Dick to sell his land to him and work as his manager.[3] Dick was asked to go for a holiday with the money which was a need for both of them. By this time Mary became a "strange, silent, dried-out woman who seemed as if she had forgotten how to speak" (227). She became so much lethargic that Moses slipped her dress over her held out arms and even buttoned up the dress. The white man Tony, who stayed in a hut in the compound for some days, caught sight of Mary being dressed by the native and later asked her if that native always dressed her. She replied, "He has so little to do. He must earn his money." Tony retorted that it was not customary in that country and felt that the solidarity of white people in Africa meant nothing to her. Her utter indifference to her surroundings and to Dick was also apparent. "She had shut out everything that conflicted with her actions, that would revive the code she had been brought up to follow" (232). Suddenly she told Tony: 'They said I was not like that.'[4] Tony could not follow her and yet made an assessment of her: "She behaves simply as if she lives in a world of her own, where other people's standards don't count. She has forgotten what her own people are like. But then, what is madness, but a refuge, a retreating from the world?" (232) After a while, Mary muttered, "I don't know why I came. . . . Why is all this happening? I didn't mean to happen. But he won't go away, he won't go away" (232). Tony was full of pity and rose to go to her. At that time, Moses was seen standing on the doorway, his face "wickedly malevolent." Tony asked the native to go away and Mary too, in a desperate attempt to get back a command she had lost, ordered Moses to go away. Much to his anger and surprise, Tony heard Moses say to Mary, "Madame wants me to go because of this boss?" The way in which the words were spoken made Tony rise to his feet and stride to the door. He asked the native to get out and "after a long, slow, evil look," the native went. He again came back to ask if Mary was going out for ever and Tony would also accompany her. Mary replied in the negative and asked him to leave. And then Moses vanished. Mary's first reaction was that of relief and immediately she accused Tony of driving him away and lamented, "What shall I say to Turner?" Tony felt that all this was sheer madness and left the place.

Next day Mary's mind was obsessed with the thought of how the home would be destroyed after they would leave and also of her own death. She was mortally afraid of Moses and kept herself within closed doors when she was alone during the day. The heat of the little room with the tin roof overhead was so unbearable that she ran outside. Her instinct told her that Moses was waiting for her in the bush. "She walked straight into the bush, thinking: 'I will come across *him* and it will all be over.' . . . She reached up her hand; it brushed against a cluster of leaves, and something whirred away. With a little moan of horror she ran through the bushes and the grass, away back to the clearing. There she stood still, clutching at her throat" (243-44). She anticipated that Moses was there, but she saw it was another native carrying Dick's message that he would not come for lunch.

She came back home and slept through the day, her last day in the country. After getting up she wondered if Moses had come into the house looking for her. "She got to her feet in a rush of defiant courage and marched into the front room. It was empty. But she knew, without any doubt at all, that he had been there while she slept, had peered through the window to see her. The kitchen door was open: that proved it" (246). For a while it came to her mind that the young man Tony would save her. Sustained by the thought of his coming, she left the house by the back door and walked towards his hut. She entered the hut and admired the fashionable shoes and the books. Then she came out of the hut and approached the store that she hated so much. In a sudden violent hate, she banged the door of the store and it swung open. Much to her surprise, she saw that Moses stood behind the counter; looking at his puzzled face she felt that the young man could no more save her. She recalled that when she had been in trouble and wanted to be saved from herself by marrying a young man from a farm, she was denied the help: "There was nothing new even in her death; all this was familiar, even her feeling of helplessness" (248). With her "queerly appropriate dignity," she walked out the way alone and reached her room again. After Dick and Tony came back, she told them separately that 'he' was outside, but neither of the two took her seriously and interpreted her behaviour in terms of madness.

At night, propelled by fear and also by instinct, she rose out of her bed and came out of the room to the verandah. She saw Moses approaching and felt that if she would move forward to appeal, the fear would be dissolved: "She opened her mouth to speak; and she did so, saw his hand, which had a long curving shape, lifted above his head; and she knew it would be too late. All her past slid away, and her mouth, opened in appeal, let out the beginning of a scream, which was stopped by a black wedge of hand inserted between her jaws" (254). Moses first thought of posing innocence and then he changed his mind and was prepared to be caught by the pursuers: "Though what thoughts of regret, or pity, or perhaps even wounded human affection were compounded with the satisfaction of his completed revenge, it is impossible to say" (256).

Lessing has rendered Mary's death as a product of a complex situation: in spite of her dignity, Mary failed to have command over Moses who was attracted towards her in spite of his hatred and rage and who also became jealous of Tony who controlled Mary and drove him away. Guided by the age-old concept that a woman is to be protected by man in her crisis, Mary sought help from two men and she was denied. If she were not guided by those ideas, she might not be trapped. Her racial feelings, again, that she never bothered to analyze, stood in the way of her being a proper human being. Lessing puts emphasis on the capacity of analysis that must precede one's free choice; Mary's lack of analyzing skill led her to a trap and she could not exercise her free will and herein lies the root cause of her tragedy.

Lessing's best-known work *The Golden Notebook* (1962) projects a galaxy of free women—she excels in portraying the nebulous undercurrents in human relationships and raises the question of freedom as far as a 'free' woman is concerned—and explores the dilemmas of the independent, activist women in the society. Commenting on the daring technique of the novel, Lessing writes in the 1971 preface of the book, "There is a skeleton, or frame, called *Free Women*, which is a conventional short novel, about 60,000 words long and which could stand by itself. But it is divided into five sections and separated by stages of the four Notebooks, Black, Red, Yellow and Blue" (http:// thegoldennotebook.org/book/ p. 1). The central character Anna Wulf keeps the notebooks as she feels she must keep things separate from each other lest there be chaos and formlessness. In the notebooks, people have discussed, theorized and dogmatized in voices representative of the time, reflecting each other's thoughts and behaviour.

The book starts with Anna and her friend Molly, both separated from their husbands. Anna, a writer, lives with her daughter and Molly, an actor and also a painter and a dancer, lives with her son Tommy. After one year of their marriage, Molly got divorced from her husband Richard who married Marion and had three boys and became friend of Molly and Anna again. Molly and Anna are thus 'free' women, though their freedom is curtailed through the accusations brought against them. During Molly's Europe tour, she left her son Tommy alone in her flat and Anna looked after him during her absence. Though Tommy was 19 by then, Richard brought serious accusation against Molly for neglecting Tommy. He said, "Why don't you admit you had a whale of good time junketing all over Europe, without Tommy to tie you?" Molly retorted, "Of course I had a good time, why shouldn't I? I was glad to be for the first time since I had a baby. Why not? And what about you—you have Marion, the good little woman, tied hand and feet to the boys while you do as you like—and there is another thing. . . . I don't want him to grow up as one of these damned mother-ridden Englishmen" (27).

Molly also protests against the patriarchal norm of using the husband's surname. When Richard angrily says, "You call yourself Miss Jacobs. Miss. In the interest of your right to independence and your own identity—whatever that means. But Tommy has Miss Jacobs for a mother," Molly brings the accusation of racial feeling against Richard: "It's not the miss you object to. It's the Jacobs. Yes it is. You always were anti-Semitic" (29).

Lessing portrays Molly not just as a woman protesting against the norms of a male-dominated society, but as one belonging to a particular race that has to face atrocities arising out of racial feelings and also as one having faith in a particular political party that is criticized by others. A woman is thus seen from several perspectives and her problems therefore are more complex than those of one who demands only equal status for man and woman. Molly also brings in the charge of moral looseness against the men in general: "Now we free women know that the moments the wives of our male friends go into the nursing home, dear Tom, Dick and Harry come straight over, they always want to sleep with one of their wives' friends, God knows why, a fascinating psychological fact among so many, but it's a fact" (36). She also accuses Richard of neglecting his present wife Marion who is treated as a housewife and never as a human being and whom Richard thinks of sending to some home lest her addiction to wine affects the boys. Richard bluntly answers, "I've had half a dozen unimportant affairs. So do most of the men I know who have been married any length of time. Their wives don't take to drinks" (37).

Anna speaks about two writers, the American writer Nelson living in London for political purpose and the Sri Lankan writer De Silva settling in London, who abandoned their wives for no fault of theirs. Nelson simply told that his wife was a neurotic—a common charge against women—and then married a nice girl who was also abandoned for being neurotic and after that he married for the third time and his third wife has not yet been neurotic. De Silva was staying in London with his wife and suddenly he decided to settle in Ceylon—the marvellous place for poetry, he said—and took his unwilling wife with him there. He soon came back to London abandoning his wife who was stuck with two kids in Ceylon and no means. Anna's personal life, her ideas and ideals and also her emotions, along with those of the persons she came in contact with, are rendered in patches in the pages of her notebooks.

The first one, the Black Notebook, records among other things, Anna's experiments with novel-writing. *Frontiers of War* is the only novel she published and she expresses her dissatisfaction with it. She believes that a book must be powered with an intellectual or moral passion strong enough to create a new way of looking at life. But she has been unable to do so in her own writing and so she thinks that she won't write any more. According to her, novel is a sort of creature with its own life and therefore she expresses her disgust at the proposal of making a film based on her novel. Anna also feels that what she wrote in the novel is not the 'truth' of life. The straight, simple and formless account of life would not, however, be a novel, and would not have got published, Anna writes in her Notebook. But anyway, she has never been genuinely interested in 'being a writer' or in making money through writing.

Anna's attachment to Communism and her critical analysis of the members of the Communist Party occupy some place of this notebook. When she comes to express her views in regard to her husband Willi, she consciously avoids adjectives and wants to present a real picture of Willi through description of real events from which a reader can feel the reality about him. And it comes out from her description that in spite of his outwardly progressive views, he is basically a male who prescribes the proper behaviour of women, even if they are committed communists, from traditional point of view. For example, Willi does not approve of what he calls Anna's bohemianism. Criticizing Anna's idea of collective breakfast, he says that woman of her position needs extra dignity of behaviour. Anna gets angry because of the "trapped feelings" women get at such moments. Willi explains, "Yes, Anna, but things are different for men and for women. They always have been and they very likely always will be" (106). A quarrel is obvious at such points and Anna writes in her Notebook the nature of such quarrel: "We knew all the phrases either was likely to use—the weakness of women, the propriety sense of men, women in antiquity, etc. etc. etc. *ad nauseam.* We knew it was a clash of temperament so profound that no words could make any difference to either of us—the truth was that we shocked each other in our deepest feelings and instincts all the time" (106). Through Anna's description of George's behaviour, Doris Lessing reveals her power of psychological analysis: "George needed a woman to be under his spell physically. And men can no longer dominate women in this way without feeling guilty about it. Or very few of them. George looked at a woman he was imagining her as she would be when he had fucked her into insensibility. And he was afraid it would show on his eyes" (110). Anna has the capacity to analyze others' minds as well as her own. So she acknowledges that she was attracted to George and also that she was jealous of the black woman George was in love with. Anna's assessment of this first Notebook was that it is full of nostalgia.

The second Notebook, the Red one, reveals Anna's analysis of the ways of the Communist Party. An insider's criticism of the

Party is found in the Notebook. That the Party discourages the intellectuals from being its members is revealed in Anna's conversation with Comrade Bill who sarcastically says that because Anna is an intellectual, she will write against Communist Party in five years. Anna was angry and retorted that if she were not an old hand, she might be disillusioned by his attitude. Molly's experience of how she was forced to be a member of the Communist Party is also recorded by Anna and it reveals "the tight, defensive, sarcastic atmosphere of the inner circles" (134). The way the journalist Jack Briggs was harassed by the Party is another evidence of the Party's duplicity. Anna seriously thought of leaving the Party, but could not as she felt that the black side was not the only truth. She writes, "while most of the criticisms of the Soviet Union are true, there must be body of people biding their time there, waiting to reverse the present process back to real socialism" (137). Anna's analytic capacity compels her to admit that the Party failed to satisfy her hankering for wholeness; rather, joining the Party intensified the split.

The Yellow Notebook looked like a manuscript of a novel in which the central characters Julia and Ella are 'free' women with their independent views of the world around them. Julia is an actress who loves rehearsals and performances on the stage even when she abhors the role she is given to play, for she enjoys what she calls flaunting her personality around. Ella, who works for a woman's magazine, lives with her son Michael in Julia's flat. The journal for which Ella works introduced a medical column which is written by a doctor. Every week, several hundred letters come asking for medical advice and half of them being of personal nature, they have to be answered privately. Ella handles these letters. She has also written half a dozen short stories which she calls feminine and also part of a novel. While Julia always likes to go outside, Ella avoids parties. Julia asks her to attend parties so that she can marry again. This stand of Julia is strongly criticized by Ella who is basically an idealist and who believes that marriage is based on love and that love is not only physical. However, both of them considered themselves normal women without conventional, emotional reactions to matters. Their lives never run on usual track and so they were regarded by women with a mixture of envy and hostility and by men with emotions which were "depressingly banal"; their friends saw them as women who positively disdained ordinary morality.

Ella's husband had married the day the divorce was final. Ella was indifferent to this; she would have felt a traitor to her own self had she remained in a compromise marriage. For outsiders, the story went that Ella's husband George had left her for somebody else. She resented the pity she earned on this account, but did nothing to put things right because of her complicated pride. Ella could not imagine this future without a man and yet she has never been in a hurry to marry any man. She has been looking for a man who would understand her properly. Julia had working class parents and she is a communist though she has not joined the Party. Ella's work for the women's magazine—she has to read the letters sent for medical advice—brings her close to the problems of women which are often not physical problems but psychological ones. For example, one Mrs. Dorothy Brown wrote that she had rheumatism from the day her husband expired and now she was alone in her flat and was afraid that she would be suddenly attacked by rheumatism in her solitary flat. She asked for the doctor's advice and Dr. West, the physician in charge of the medical column, bluntly said that he had been engaged to write a medical column, not "to run an out-patients for neurotics." "Ella feels sorry for so many people simmering away in misery and no one cares" (145). Julia argued with Dr. West and criticized his inhuman attitude but failed to change his mentality.

Julia's relationship with the psychiatrist Paul brings out a real picture of a male who poses to be intellectual and sympathetic only to draw a woman's attention, but treats a woman only as a sex object. During her long conversation with him she found that "there was no trace in glance of a man assessing a woman for her sexual potentialities" (159) and also felt that he would be her lover "because of the quality of his voice which he trusted" (161); but soon she was disappointed when after making love with her he asked about her sexual habit and she noted "a hard ugly look in his eyes" as he said that she was much too thin. As her nature was, Ella "was shrinking away in spirit" (162) from this man and told him that she would never see him again.

After she came back angrily to Julia's flat, Paul called her on phone requesting her to go to a film with him. Though she refused the proposal in a humorous tone, she was again misled by his voice as she found that "his voice on the telephone had no connection at all with the hardness of his face in the field" (164). She started a relationship with him and was so much guided by her instinct that she began to think that he would marry her soon, leaving his wife. "His marriage must be no marriage at all, if he could stay with her, night after night, going home at dawn for a clean shirt" (166). Her "perfect trust in him" was soon gone when Paul advised her to remain unmarried. She felt completely rejected and after a discussion with Julia it was clear that he felt a stranger to his wife after he came back from war and probably had love affairs since then. Ella felt a cold hurt despair and Paul stopped coming to her at night. He bade her goodbye telling her with his small bitter grimace that she was now free to give time to her boyfriends. Ella wondered, "But what's that got to do with all these hours we've been together, when every look and move he's made told me he loved me?" (168)

Anna does not make the end of the affair between Ella and Paul at this stage. She lets the affair restart and brings Paul to sleep with Ella after two days. And Ella began to think that their being together started from that moment when "they had both tasted their responses to other people and found that what they felt for each other made other people irrelevant" (171). Again their relationship was disturbed: Paul instinctively stiffened whenever Michael came to him and he disliked Ella's relationship with Julia. He also began to accuse Ella of sleeping with other men and Ella tried to understand him using her intellect: "It occurs to her that Paul's shadow, his imagined third person is a self-hating rake. . . . Paul with me is using his 'positive self. I am using with my 'negative' self" (172). Anna comments on her characters, "Any intelligent person could have foreseen the end of this affair from the beginning. And yet, I Anna, like Ella and Paul refused to see it. Paul gives birth to Ella, the naïve Ella. He destroyed in her the knowing, doubting, sophisticated Ella and again and again he put her intelligence to sleep, and with her willing connivance, so that she floated darkly on her love for him, on her naivety, which is another word for a spontaneous creative faith. And when his own distrust of himself destroyed this woman-in-love, so that she began thinking, she would fight to return to naivety. . . . What Ella lost during those five years was the power to create through naivety" (175).

Instead of a sudden break of the relationship, Anna uses slow withdrawal so that some other motifs such as solidarity of women (Ella's relationship with Julia deepens in the face of Paul's opposition), the myth of maternal love (Ella's love for her son Michael strengthens in the process), the motif of Paul's attitude to his profession and such others may be introduced in her proposed novel. Anna also intends to introduce analysis of sexual relationship which has been a taboo subject for women writers. From a variety of problems faced by different types of women characters in the novel, it is evident that Lessing projects feminism from different perspectives.

The Blue Notebook begins with the sentence, "Tommy appeared to be accusing his mother." Anna thought of writing a short story on the topic as the theme would be true to life. After his first visit to his father's home, Tommy began to criticize his mother Molly for being a communist and a bohemian. Molly laughed it off. But after his second visit Tommy became hostile. Anna intervened and told Tommy the history of his parents. Tommy at first did not believe the ugly story about his father. Later he seemed to believe the story but argued that he should go for National Service. This became an attack on Molly's way of life, her politics, her friends—everything she is. After a long fight, he came to attack the militarism of Soviet Union and such other topics. It became clear that Tommy did not feel for his mother—her sacrifice of love, marriage, happiness for bringing him up. "If Tommy could feel that, he would stop resenting Molly for leaving his father" (190). Anna finds similarity between Molly's experience and hers: her husband Max wanted a baby and they were united for once and Janet was conceived; though they married the following weak, the man never touched her and they were divorced after a year.

Anna consulted the psychiatrist Mrs. Marks when she was depressed and had several sittings with her, some of which are recorded in the Notebook. But the day the psychiatrist suggested that she should maintain the habit of writing, Anna stopped writing personal documents in the Notebook which continued in the form of newspaper cuttings. There were cuttings reflecting Anna's concern for the threat from atom bomb, hydrogen bomb and such other means of destruction used in war. The war in South Korea, labour camps in Soviet Russia, mass deportation of unproductive people ordered by the communist government of Rumania, the hanging of 'Capitalist spies' in Prague, atrocities in Egypt and such other events are recorded in the newspaper cuttings. Anna comments on those cuttings, "Whenever anything happens anywhere that is terrible, I dream about it, as if I were involved in it personally" (205). And as a result, in the background of the "overwhelmingly terrible" situation the world over, whatever she writes has no point at all. Lessing's protagonist in *The Golden Notebook* is thus a woman who is above all a human being, seriously concerned with the deviations of human values all over the world, and her concern is, obviously, inclusive of the feminist's particular concern.

The following chapters of *The Golden Notebook* are continuations of the events described in the first two chapters as well as the Notebooks pinned to the pages of which are newspaper clippings. The exploitation in the British colonies and the miseries of the women there are included in these chapters. Ella, the protagonist in Anna's proposed novel, says dryly, "My dear Julia, we've chosen to be free women, and this is the price we pay, that's all. 'Free!,' says Julia, 'Free! What's the use of us being free if they aren't?' I answer to God that everyone of them, even the best of them, have the old idea of good women" (357). Lessing acknowledges that unless and until all the women of the world are free from their adherence to the standard of good women—the myth of good mother, the myth of good and faithful wife, for example—which had been appreciated in the patriarchal society since ages, the emancipation of women would remain only a concept.[5]

The novel ends with Marion's declaration that she cannot go back to Richard and she does not care for the children—she says, "we have children because we love a man" (400)—and with Anna's decision to join Labour Party and to do a job in Dr. North's marriage centre where aches and pains of people that come from marriage will be tackled. Her decision of leaving the Communist Party in favour of the Labour Party as well as of writing no further is disappointing to some critics for whom the novel ends tamely.[6] But Lessing's remarkable truthfulness in delineating characters and her clear-sighted observation of the dilemmas faced by those characters get the better of making the novel more interesting.

Lessing has created a variety of women characters in her novels who face their surroundings according to their intellectual capacity and mental make-up, revealing thereby the author's excellence in portraying the undercurrents in human relationships. The heroine Martha Quest in *The Children of Violence*, an ambitious series of five novels, is an allegorical parallel. Like the author, Martha was also brought up in South Africa that witnessed the ugly face of racism and joined the Communist Party. In *A Proper Marriage* (included in *The Children of Violence* sequence), Martha's feeling of claustrophobia within the space of marital experience prompts her to protest against the existing system. Desperate to express her ideas and to be free from the suffocating sensations of family life, Martha joins the Communist Party which was promising during the Fifties. Martha however feels that joining the Communist Party did not make one a communist. At the end of the novel she moves out of her marital home to be wholeheartedly devoted to social service.

The heroine Jane in *The Diaries of Jane Somers* is rich, smart and utterly self-absorbed. In her forties, when she has lost her mother and her husband, Jane starts writing diaries in a mood of introspection, questioning the existing value systems. Her sudden meeting with Maudie, frail but strong-willed even after she crossed ninety, brings a change in Jane's mind compelling her to be emotionally tied to the old woman.

In *The Child in Question,* Lessing concentrates on the problems of Shireen, a 10-year-old girl in a large Muslim family living in London. *The Grandmothers* is a narrative of two close friends who fall in love with each other's teenaged sons and the relationships continue till the two young men settle down to traditional family life. The two friends adjust themselves to the changed situations promising to be perfect mothers-in-law and then wonderful grandmothers. All these characters are unique in their own way and taken together, they reveal the contemporary reality with unparallelled honesty and percipience.

Lessing has not liked to be pigeon-holed as a feminist author because in that case the vast range of experiences that she revealed through her characters would have to be curtailed. She makes her position clear in an interview: "What the feminists want of me is something they haven't examined because it comes from religion. They want me to bear witness. What they really like me to say is 'Ha Sisters, I stand by you side by side in your struggle toward the golden dawn where all those beastly men are no more.' Do they really want people to make over simplified statements about men and women? In fact they do. I've come with great regret to this conclusion."[7] Lessing has made a thorough study of the history of human civilizations and comes to the conclusion that the mutual relationship of man and woman is not fixed and hence it is useless to devote oneself to the cause of feminist ideals. She writes, "men and women have taken infinite numbers of roles in the past, and do now in different societies . . . everything we now take for granted is going to be utterly swept away in the next decade" (Preface to *The Golden Notebook*, http://thegoldennotebook.org/book/p.2).

NOTES

1. *The Grass is Singing* (Heinemann, Johannesburg, 1973, 40.

2. In this respect Lessing almost echoes the French existentialist philosopher Simone de Beauvoir who is recognized as a precursor of modern feminist movement. Beauvoir observed that one is born with one's sex, and the gender is created by the society. She also wrote, "the terms masculine and feminine are used symmetrically only as a matter of form, as on legal papers. In actuality the relation of two sexes is not quite like that of two electrical poles." (*The Second Sex*, p. 15) For her, 'Feminine' and 'masculine' represent social constructs—patterns of sexuality and behaviour imposed by cultural and social norms. Lessing, however, does not share Beauvoir's ideas in regard to the femininity as a social construct. Rather, she comes close to Claude M. Steiner who finds the roots of social maladies in imperfect personalities.
3. Doris Lessing projects the colonial mind-set of Mary in such a way that shows the writer's hold on psychology. Lessing portrays a full picture of a white woman in South Africa, a woman who is oppressed in her own society by persons belonging to her own race and who again becomes the cause of torture of the persons belonging to the other race. Lessing's ironic presentation of Mary's mind-set is worth-quoting. "She thought: he will complain to the police that I struck him? This did not frighten her, it made her angry. The biggest grievance of the white farmer is that he is not allowed to strike his natives, and that if he does, they may—but seldom do—complain to the police. It made her furious to think that this black animal had the right to complain against her, against the behaviour of a white woman. But it is significant that she was not afraid for herself. If this native had gone to the police station, she might have been cautioned, since it was first offence, by a policeman who was a European. . . . She had behind her the police, the courts, the jails; he, nothing but patience. Yet she was maddened by the thought he had even the right to appeal; her greatest anger was directed against the sentimentalists and theoreticians, whom she thought of as 'They'—the law-makers and the Civil Service—who interfered with the natural right of a white farmer to treat his labour as he pleased" (*The Grass is Singing*, pp.147-48).
4. Lessing lays bare the rich men's process of oppression in South Africa. The white men exploit not only the black but also other white men who are financially weak. When Charlie Slatter occupied Dick's property, he argued that he was doing all that for the sake of

his community: "He spoke as there could be no question of a refusal; he had been shocked out of self-interest. It was not even pity for Dick that moved him. He was obeying the dictate of the first law of White South Africa, which is: 'Thou shalt not let you fellow whites sink lower than a certain point; because if you do, the nigger will see he is as good as you are.' The strongest emotion of a strongly organized society spoke in his voice, and it took the backbone out of Dick's resistance" (221).

5. Uttering these words Mary recalls how her friends assessed her as non-feminine because she remained happy with her single status, putting on frocks usually worn by girls and not trying to draw the attention of the male. Sushila Singh's observation may be quoted in this respect: "a woman who does not conform to the chosen standard is considered unfeminine and therefore unnatural. To make women believe that there is such a thing as essence of femaleness, called femininity, serves the interest of the patriarchy" (*Feminism: Theory, Criticism, Analysis*, Penecraft International, Delhi, 2004, p. 75). Lessing is not biased against the male and so she shows that not men, but the women become instrumental in spreading 'the essence of femaleness.'
6. Analyzing the causes behind the oppression of women in the society, feminist writers find that women in general try to live up to the standard of good women set by the society. The proverbial traits of women's behaviour—for example, a mother sacrifices her happiness for her child—gave rise to several myths. Paula Caplan's *The Myth of Women's Masochism*, for example, exposes the myth that "women enjoy their suffering." (New York: E.P. Dutton,1985, p.1) The myth of motherhood is one of the major themes explored in this book. In the myth of motherhood, the mother is wrong no matter whether she gives too little, or too much attention to her child. Caplan analyses the self-contradiction in these myths to point out the ideology behind them, that what is frequently judged masochistic in women is often that which most clearly indicates women's feelings of self-esteem.
7. Zerin Anklesaria writes, "it ends tamely when Anna, like Martha, joins a political party, not communist this time but Labour! Such a bald summary does little justice to a seminal novel, one of the most influential of the twentieth century." *The Hindu*, Literary Review, Nov.4, 2007.
8. *The New York Times*, 25 July 1982.

Doris Lessing's *The Cleft*: An Argument for Men by a Feminist

DHANANJAY TRIPATHI
University of Allahabad
&
KRISHAN RAI
National Institute of Technology, Durgapur

Different authors create different phantasmagoria to express their dormant ideas. In the continuation of this trend, Doris Lessing imagines an alternative mythical story of human origin in the Nobel Prize-winning fiction *The Cleft*. *The Cleft* is a typical example of the 20th century sensibility and writing; it touches tangentially the trend of science fiction tradition which we have since Mary Shelley's *Frankenstein* (1818) and which is one of the hallmarks of the 20th century literature.

Lessing has a wide range of experience as she moved from Iran to Rhodesia to Uganda to London. These recurrent shifts infuse her with the in-depth experience of different worlds. Consequently these shifts have a strong impact on her writing. She starts her career as an author who condemns the Apartheid system and soon moves on to the Communist theme (1954-1956) in the *Children of Violence* series. Then, she experiments with psychological themes (1956-1969) and finally she explores her writing skill in her science fiction series. This deliberate switch-over to science fiction is not appreciated in the earlier phase. For example, John Leonard wrote in the *New York Times* in 1982: "One of the many sins for which 20th century will be held accountable is that it has Mrs. Lessing. . . . She now propagandizes on behalf of our insignificance in the cosmic razzmatazz."[1] However the statement receives an apt reply as Lessing responds: "What they did not realize was that in science fiction is some of the best social fiction of our time. I also admire the classic sort of science fiction like *Blood Music* by Greg Bear."[2]

The Cleft is a science fiction based on the concept of the 'Pathogenesis,' a biological phenomenon in which a single sex can generate or multiply without the assistance of the opposite sex. Lessing publishes her first novel *The Grass is Singing* in 1949 which examines the relationship between a white farmer's wife and her black servant. The novel soon is followed by her magnum opus *The Golden Notebook* (1962) wherein she renders the multiple selves of contemporary women. *The Golden Notebook* is a story of Anna Wulf who strives for ruthless honesty as she aims to free herself from chaos, emotional numbness and hypocrisies. Even before *The Golden Notebook* she explores the growth of the consciousness of Martha Quest, the eponymous character of the *Children of Violence* series. These novels make the critics label Lessing as a Feminist. However Lessing does not like the idea of being pigeon-holed as a feminist author. She argues:

> What the feminist want of me is something they have not examined because it comes from religion. They want me to bear witness they would really like me to say is, 'ha sisters, I stand with you side by side in your struggle towards the golden dawn where all those beastly men are no more.' Do they really want people to make over-simplified statement about men and women? In.fact, they do, I hence come with great regret to this conclusion"[3]

In fact it can't be guaranteed for any author that he or she is of this or that particular mind-set, for literature is a creative process and it is highly sensitive to the socio-political and socio-economic evolution of the time. There is slow but constant shift in the world, in the thinking pattern, sensibility and in the writing of Lessing from 1949 to 2007. This shift of focus is natural and gets justified by the author herself when she says in an interview to Associate Press,

> when you look at my life, you can go back to the late 1930s, what I saw first of all Hitler, he was going to live forever. Mussolini was in

> for 10,000 years. You had the Soviet Union, which was by definition going to last forever. There was a British Empire—nobody imagined it could come to an end. So why should one believe in any kind of permanence?[4]

This shift from a feminist to an author who looks at things as they really are can be seen in her late science fiction. *The Cleft*, in this regard, is a mature work where she imagines a mythical land occupied by 'Clefts' that are women, the name derived from the essential part of female anatomy and argues that the primal human stock is female rather than male.

The Cleft acquaints us with a society free from sexual intrigues, free from jealousy even free from men. The novel is narrated by an old Roman Senator who tells the story of human creation. He describes the Cleft community living in a coastal valley surrounded by mountains; they have neither need nor knowledge of men. Childbirth is controlled and the children are always female by sex. But due to the birth of a strange child—a boy, the peace and harmony of the society is disturbed. As the number of the male infants increases they are nicknamed as 'squirts' who are thrown outside for death but rescued by eagles which are in fact sent to kill them. These eagles live on the other side of the mountain. One of the female characters goes beyond the geographical territory of the mountain and discovers the fact that 'the Clefts' are forced to share the world with their male counterparts.

However, through this mythical story Lessing, an accepted feminist, shows the shift that has taken place in her sensibility. Through *The Cleft* she seems to suggest that women are nothing without men and the life of Clefts is nothing but a dream: 'the coming of the Monsters not only shocked the first females out of their long dream but nearly ended it' (23). They were without the basic things of life; they 'had never seen a hut or any shelter because [they] had always had [their] caves' (15). It is the man who invents hunting and makes shelter which changes their lives. The Clefts accept it as well, "now can we not admire them for their daring and their cleverness? The river was wide, deep and rushed along. Yet they had to catch a fish in it. How did they shelter? . . .

They had seen the eagles' nests and they dragged sticks and then larger sticks and made piles of them, and crept in to them when dark came" (35-36).

In this way comes the concept of home and we witness the sense of creativity for the first time. The sense of identity is not present before the birth of 'deformed babies' and life is like a dream: "sometimes I think we lived in a kind of dream, a sleep, everything slow and easy and nothing ever happening" (11). There are no names in the community of Clefts. The word 'old shes' and the first proper name 'maire' take place only after the birth of the first 'squirt.'

These monsters (baby boys) are also responsible for the creation of language and words in the island. Even the word 'island' comes in existence with these 'monsters.' It was the male babies who "had the new words for tool and utensil" (49). It is evident to Cleft that two languages develop after the birth of the 'damaged males.' The life of Cleft fills with emotion and feelings because of the 'squirt,' "they felt the new emotion because of 'New one'" (86).

Lessing indirectly claims that the concepts of family, enmity and relationship are the result of the growing intimacy between the Cleft women and the newly-born 'damaged males.' This intimacy results in the feeling of togetherness which in turn results in the concept of family life which can be exemplified by Maronna's speech "Don't you care about us? Did she mean all of them, males and females, Cleft and once upon a time monster" (212). So monsters are no longer different for them and 'squirts' are now their children.

Lessing in her brilliant narrative points out that it is not only the good things for which the squirts are responsible but they are the progenitors of the negatives as well, "there is no record of any of us doing cruel things not until the monsters were born" (19). According to the narrator, the first murder in human history takes place because of squirts: "A squirt that had lost consciousness for a while up there on the platform picked up a stone and crashed it on her head." The first murder recorded in the "annals of the males" (131). It is because of the males that the Clefts are divided into two parts 'old shes' and the 'new clefts.' In fact the former live in a vacuum; there is nothing that can be related to the real life as they are extremely rigid male company, while the latter are accommodating and accepted their male partners.

The Cleft is not simply a narrative of 262 pages, it is a reflection of the journey of a feminist author's life in which consciously or unconsciously she comes to realize the importance and the contributions of the opposite sex. It is an assertion that the female or the male are nothing by themselves alone. She claims that some of the very basic concepts of life like anger, love, sorrow, happiness and even the sense of gender come into existence only with the existence of males: "when the first baby monster were born males and females was born too because before that were simply, the people" (78).

Lessing's science fiction may be regarded as the conscious or unconscious portrayal of a feminist authoress. Feminism does not always mean the degradation of male sex or the rejection of the fact that females are nothing without males. The argument of Lessing for men in this novel seems quite authentic and plausible. This recent novel of Lessing not only accentuates the ground reality of man-woman relationship but also clears the fog over the trendy concept that feminists believe in the degradation of the opposite sex. Keeping the status of woman intact, Lessing has shown the place and importance of man in this world. By reiterating these traditional concepts, she has substantiated the age-old notions of human existence as well. *The Cleft* is the author's pioneering attempt as a feminist to not only accept but also highlight the importance of man and in this sense she may be credited for giving a sense of completion to the concept of feminism.

NOTES

1. John Leonard, "The Spacing out of Doris Lessing," *The New York Times*.http://query.nytimes.com/gst/fullpage.

2. Harvey Blume, "Doris Lessing: Hot Dawns," interview, *Boston Book Review*. http://www.dorislessing.org/boston.html.
3. Lesley Hazelton, "Doris Lessing on Feminism, Communism and 'Space Fiction'." *The New York Times*. http://mural.uv.es/vemivein /feminismcommunism.html.
4. "U.K.'s Lessing wins Nobel Prize in Literature," Swedish Academy http://www.msnbc.msn.com/id/12784353.

Works Cited

Barry, Peter. *Beginning Theory: An Introduction to Literary and Cultural Theory*. Manchester: Manchester United Press, 2002.

Beasley, Chris. *What is Feminism*? London: Sage, 1999.

Lessing, Doris. *The Cleft*. New York: Harper Perennial, 2008.

_____. *The Golden Notebook: A Novel*. New York: Harper Perennial Modern Classic, 2008.

Walter, Margaret. *Feminism: A Very Short Introduction*. Oxford: Oxford University Press, 1999.

Gender Construction as an Emerging Trend in Margaret Atwood's *The Edible Woman* and Shashi Deshpande's *The Dark Holds No Terrors*

R.P. MAHTO
B.N.J. College, Sisai (Gumla)

It is said that the literature of a country is the storehouse of the cultural and sociological aspect of its people. But literature all along has been turned to the point of view of the male element or theme. Woman is often 'marginalized,' 'repressed,' or 'silenced' in literary works. The role of woman is restricted by her womanhood and therefore the experience of the muted female forming half of the society is not reflected in literature very clearly.

But with the rise of feminism, woman becomes aware of the fact that her inferiority is not ordained in heaven because it is a creation of patriarchy. It is a construct which should be deconstructed. Women realize that the system of patriarchy which has existed since time immemorial no longer serves the needs of the rapidly-changing society where women are trying to emancipate themselves and define their potential. Revolting against their marginalization, they have started questioning the sexual politics and gender arrangement or construction.

The emergence of women novelists has considerably influenced the change in attitude. The writing reflects a shift in the sensibility of the writer as well as reader. Margaret Atwood, a representative novelist of Canada and Shashi Deshpande, a famous Indian English novelist, portray the new women and their dilemmas. They concern themselves with the plight of the modern Canadian and Indian women trying to understand themselves and to preserve their identity as wife, mother and above all a human being. They consider childhood as an important period for the formation of characters of children especially girl children. This reflects both a literary and a social reality. Girls are a silent part of the family and society. What they think or feel about their social eclipse does not interest most writers or social thinkers. The most formative years of the woman's life—when she is growing up—remain by and large unexamined and unexplored. Margaret Atwood and Shashi Deshpande are perhaps the few English novelists who have portrayed girl children/ women.

Margaret Atwood has a concern for the predicament of woman because she is a feminist. Elizabeth Brady, a famous feminist critic, in her article entitled "Towards a Happier History: Women and Domination" rightly remarks: "Atwood's analysis of woman's predicament has been executed on several levels each of the worker divorced from her emotions: and as mother, wife whose capacity for maternity subverts everything that falls outside of her reproduction function."[1]

In patriarchal society women are given secondary treatment and they are deprived of the opportunities and assignments that are enjoyed by men. This discrimination pushes the fair sex into the background position and they fail to get the status equal to men. Margaret Atwood has this sort of experience in her own life. She discloses it in her Gerstin Lectures. Her Canadian professor had tried to dissuade her from completing her graduation. He had also advised Atwood that she may remain unmarried if she wanted to get higher education.

In her novel *The Edible Woman* Atwood presents this kind of discrimination meted out to women in the Sixties in Canada. During this decade, some specified fields were opened for women. Marian, the protagonist of the novel, has almost the same experience which the novelist had. Her parents hold the opinion that if Marian gets higher education she will change. They believe that the university education will have bad effect on the formation of her personality. She may avoid marriage and be very critical of the wedding. Marian narrates her parents' worries and anxieties in the following way: "They had probably been worried that she would turn into a high school teacher or a maiden aunt or a dope addict or a female executive or she would undergo some shocking physical transformation like developing muscles and a deep voice or growing moss. She could picture the anxious consultations over cups of tea."[2]

But her growing intimacy with Peter consoles them that she will marry Peter. And she will not change into which they have the sense of fear. Their satisfaction can be seen in the following words: "But now their approving eyes said, she was turning out right after all. They had not met Peter, but for them he seemed merely the necessary x-factor. They were curious though: they continued to urge her to bring him home for the weekend soon." (174)

They are prepared to solemnize Marian's wedding in their family church when they come to know about her engagement. Peter expresses the feelings of Marian's parents in the following way: "they had been pathetically eager to have the wedding in the family church. Their remote from her was less elated glee than a quiet rather smug satisfaction as though reactions she would estimate of people were now so their fears about the effects of her university education, never stated but always apparent had been calmed at last." (174) They upheld the traditional role of a woman i.e. to get married and lead a conventional life.

The novelist reveals the fact that during Sixties women had exclusive choice open to them. They could not opt for jobs which were especially for men. It means that women had limited options. In the novel Ainsley and Marian are asked why they have such "crummy" jobs. When Duncan has interviewed Marian on behalf of the Seymour Surveys, he asks Marian: "Hey, why do you have crummy job like this. I thought only fat, sloppy, housewives did that sort of thing." (55) In order to save her dignity she replies: "We all have to eat. Besides, what else you can do with a B.A. these days." (55) At the professional level, Marian is bound to opt for this kind of job because it is only for women during the Sixties. Though women may be equally educated, they are not given equal assignments of importance. This discrimination is the primary concern for the novelist.

The Edible Woman establishes Atwood's broad thematic pattern that she works out with suitable variations in her other novels too. This novel's central metaphor reinforced by the title is that of woman as food object and the theme is the woman's endeavour to attain humanity and a human identity. The protagonist Marian works for Seymour Surveys for consumer products. It seems a good job at the time she takes the job but "after four months its limits are still vaguely defined." (19) It becomes clear that Seymour Surveys is projected metaphorically as a trap. Marian realizes that she is literally and metaphorically trapped. The novelist expresses her views thus: "The company is layered like an ice-cream sandwich with three floors the upper, the lower crust and our department in the middle." (19)

In the first part of the novel, the novelist uses confessional mode of expression. The protagonist tells about herself in her own voice. She has got the job at the Seymour Surveys after her graduation. The company where she works is three-tiered like an ice-cream sandwich. She is in the middle. The upper floor is occupied by the executives and psychologists. They all are men and they arrange things with clients. They have expensive furniture and carpets. The lowest floor is peopled by machines who are only women. Their work is only counting, sorting and tabulating the information. In the middle floor Marian works with her colleagues. All are interviewers and her department deals with housewives. The only male person is the office boy. While working in this office, Marian realizes that she will have to stay on in the middle point of the office structure for her whole life. Marian is not allowed to go to the upper structure whereas she does not like to go to the bottom. She later on comes to know that she will get pension after her retirement. Even though she has already completed four months working there but still she has a feeling of depression because of the discrimination between men and women. Clear vision of future flashes before her eyes where she finds that women have to perform the role drawn by the patriarchal society. We can see her feelings presented by the novelist in the following manner: "Sometimes in front of me a self was waiting pre-formed, a self who had worked during numerable years for Seymour Surveys and was now receiving her reward. A pension foresaw a break room with a plug in electric heater. Perhaps I would have "a hearing aid, like one of my great aunts who would throw snowballs at me. I told myself not to be silly, the world would probably below between now and then. I reminded myself I could walk out of those the next day and get a different job if I would, but that didn't help." (21)

She becomes aware that this is the direct offshoot of the technological advanced society and advancement for as individuals into pre-fabricated roles of womanhood. She is afraid because she might turn into Mrs. Bogue or her assistant and finally becomes a traditional wife. She is worried also about her identity which perhaps she may lose.

Through the imagery of three layers, Atwood depicts a metaphoric parallel for the woman's place in patriarchal society. The three layers represent three levels: mind, body and matter. The men are mind, the woman is above the 'matter' but below the 'mind.' Marian as a woman is faced with a dilemma of what she is to 'be.' As she says: "I couldn't become one of the men upstairs, I couldn't become a machine or one of the questionnaire-making ladies as that would be a step-down." (20)

Marian's woman problem, therefore, is one of 'becoming' which is metaphysical and socio-political problem. At the metaphysical level Marian's quest is for a meaningful human identity i.e. she is conscious of her gender construction; and at socio-political level her quest is to become neither a man nor a machine but a woman with an absolute as against a relatively defined identity.

But when we discuss the theme of gender in Shashi Deshpande's novels we find that her female protagonists like their author hail from middle class families. Deshpande's women are cultural hybrids, in the sense that they struggle with the cultural conflict of native traditions mixed with an English education. She does not attempt to cover or conceal her class or gender identity. She says that her writing is very strongly gendered in the sense that her novels could have been written only by a woman: "As writing is born out of personal experience, the fact that I am a woman is bound to surface. Besides, only a woman could write my books—they are written from the inside, as it were."

Shashi Deshpande unveils the subtle process of oppression and gender differentiation of work in the family and in the male-dominated society. One of the features of their upbringing is their inculcation as girls into the socially defined roles as daughter, wife and mother. Deshpande shows great sensitivity and awareness of the ways and means through which a young girl is prepared for her future status in society. The factors that influence her include cultural aspects, social and psychological factors such as the family structure and woman's position in it.

Shashi Deshpande traces the quest for self-definition of women who are educated and modern but they cannot quite shake off their background and the manner in which they have been brought up in her major novels like *The Dark Holds No Terrors, Roots and Shadows* and *That Long Silence.*

Gender roles are conceived, enacted and learnt within a complex of relationships. Sarita, the protagonist of *The Dark Holds No Terrors*, grows up as a victim of her mother's sexist and gender-based bias. Even as a child, she remembers her mother's preference for her brother Dhruva and the importance attached to his birthdays. She is constantly reminded that she is a girl whose destiny is to get married and leave the house while her brother need not do so. The mother is concerned about her daughter's appearance particularly the colour of her skin. If she grows dark, it would be difficult to get her married: "Do not go out in the sun you'll get even darker. Who cares? We have to care even if you don't. We have to get you married."[3]

Here in this context we are reminded of Kamala Das who in her *My Story* recounts how worried her grandmother was about the duskiness of her skin and rubbed raw turmeric every Tuesday and Friday before her oil bath. "One is not born but rather becomes a woman—it is civilization as a whole that produce this creature . . . described as feminine" (45) becomes relevant when one sees the methods through which a girl is brought into femininity. Even daily household works are set aside for girls—such as setting the table, cleaning up after meals, helping in the kitchen and doing other odd jobs. Boys are discouraged to do this sort of household chores.

Although this process of preparing the girl towards her 'otherness' beings in her early childhood, it is intensified from the moment she attains puberty. As a girl grows up, she is made to feel different from her male counterpart, made to feel conscious about revealing her femininity to the male members of the family. Deshpande depicts this in the present novel in a beautiful manner: "You should be careful now about how you behave. Don't come out in your petticoat like that. Not even if it's only your father who's around." (55)

Deshpande's novels explore the search for selfhood undertaken by women who come from such environment. They are caught between a traditional upbringing and the longing for freedom in the modern sense. A quest for identity or gender construction forms the theme of *The Dark Holds No Terrors*. The protagonist Sarita revolts against her mother's aggressive dictates, becomes a doctor and marries a man of her choice. She felt security and love in her marriage with Manohar at one stage. For her he is an ideal romantic hero who satisfies her hunger of love.

But Sarita's family life and happiness started declining as her popularity started increasing day by day. A conflict in her mind follows due to her achieved position and the ascribed position of her husband. The financial ascendance of Sarita renders Manohar less significant and impotent. He thinks to retain her potency and masculinity and for this he starts torturing Sarita mentally and physically. For both it becomes a psychological problem. The burden of a working housewife always ends up with the burden of double duties and conjugal relations. Unless the balance is maintained, the feeling of disenchantment and imbalance lead to separation which becomes a possible way out for mutual benefits and happiness.

But she realizes at last that she is a human being throbbing life with a reawakened individuality. That individuality is nothing but the reality which the individual has to face in order to overcome setbacks and set things right. When realization comes all other things that cause problems melt away because of the mental equilibrium attained through the realization. Sarita's all endeavours are now directed towards the only objective to live. Ultimately the expression and fulfillment of it can be called the purpose of life. It is further increased by the individual's attitude reflected through a prisoner of mind towards life assuming a social responsibility to tell other fellow beings how to live.

Sarita is not philosophizing anything here. She is not a philosopher either. But she says: "I am a realist. We are realists. We deal with the ultimate reality. Human body." (8) The understanding or reality which makes Sarita see for herself the whole world around her in distinct form. In consequence, she gets a new vigour which makes her to achieve wholeness and overcome her identity crisis or gender construction. Sarita, who had once tried to run away from this self because of the pain it had caused her, leaves the house as a doctor to attend a sick child. She, however, tells her father to receive Manu if he comes and tell him to wait. She says, "Baba, if Manu comes tell him to wait, I'll be back as soon as I can." (221) This gives us a clear cut hint of a possible reconciliation between the rebel protagonist Sarita and her husband Manu.

In this way we see in the novel that Sarita represents the middle-class working women in modern India. She rebels against the traditions but ultimately tries to compromise with the existing reality. The novel ends in the affirmative note of hope as against frustration and despair with which it had begun. It is also Sarita's freedom which she enjoys, gives her the courage to do what she wants and believes it is right and the determination and tenacity to adhere to it which paves way for harmony in life. Thus we see that Sarita is equally conscious of her identity and gender construction.

After discussing gender construction as an emerging trend in Margaret Atwood's *The Edible Woman* and Shashi Deshpande's *The Dark Holds No Terrors*, we find that the protagonist of Atwood's novel Marian's avoiding of food and preparation of cake can be interpreted through Indian practice of 'shudhikaran' (purification) for 'atmagyan' (self-knowledge). She achieves symbolic purification of herself by refusing to eat and her final act of baking the cake in the shape of a woman to offer Peter as a substitute symbolizes her having attained the necessary self-knowledge. Henceforth, it implies that she will not be Peter's or any man's consumable commodity. She is liberated from the notion that she is some kind of appetizing food. And hence Marian starts enjoying taking food. She has finally been able to refuse to be the edible woman and be instead just a woman which indicates her consciousness of gender construction and to achieve her identity. Shashi Deshpande's *The Dark Holds No Terrors*, on the other hand, exposes the absurdity of rituals and customs which only help to perpetuate the myth of male superiority. This shows how a woman grows from 'self-surrender' and 'self-abnegation' to assert her individuality with newly emerged gender construction and identity. The novel rejects the traditional concept that the sole purpose of wife's existence is to please her husband. It reveals a woman's capacity to assert her own rights and individuality and become fully aware of her potential as a human being.

NOTES

1. W.J. Keith, *Introducing Margaret Atwood's "The Edible Woman", A Literary Guide* (Ontario: ECW Press, Sydenham, 1989), p. 20.
2. Margaret Atwood, *The Edible Woman* (Toronto: McClelland and Stewart, 1969), p. 174.
3. Shashi Deshpande, *The Dark Holds No Terrors* (Delhi: Vikas, 1990), p. 45.

A Journey into the Self: A Study of Margaret Atwood's *The Edible Woman*

V. MADHAVI
S.K. University, Anantapur

The Edible Woman[1] is the first published novel of Margaret Atwood. It is a proto-feminist novel; it entertains and presents the most serious problems that women face. It depicts how women are objectified by conventional society as consumer products. Even though the novel was published even before the emergence of the feminist or women's liberation movement, it successfully exposes the ideological and gender differences, thus proving to be a pioneering novel. The novel focuses on how Marian McAlpin, the protagonist of the novel, first loses and then rediscovers herself.

Though the narrative language abounds in various symbols and metaphors, it is the "food metaphor" which is the chief vehicle that serves to put forward the feminist tendencies of the heroine that help her protest against the dehumanizing tendencies of the society and save herself by rejecting her authentic self. Dealing as it does with the patriarchal society which has become synonymous with consumerism of women especially, the novel presents "symbolic cannibalism" of women. The novel proves once for all that financial independence is no independence at all. The awareness of being subjugated and victimized has to come from within the self of an individual.

The first phase of the problem Marian has to face and overcome is at her workplace. The company Marian works for, 'Seymour Surveys,' has a highly stratified, three-tiered, hierarchic structure. The top floor is exclusively meant for the executives, the so-called 'men' who are capable of decision-making at the higher level. Bottom floor is occupied by the machines which are capable of functioning unceasingly. Marian can not become one with either one of the men in the top floor, as convention does not consider that women possess the same quality of mind as men do, or the machines in the bottom floor.

Marian shares her apartment with Ainsley, a radical feminist, who is placed in contrast with Marian. They are two extremes in their attitudes. Ainsley has strong views about the male-dominated 'consumer' society. She is against marriage but she desires to give birth to a child outside the marriage institution in order to fulfill her deepest sense of femininity. Wanting children "by choice" rather than as a natural consequence of a happy relationship in a marriage, she looks out for a perfect male specimen to father her child and finds one in Len, thus partially fulfilling her dream. It does not take her long to realize that such a role as she has chosen for herself would be a difficult one to perform in the patriarchal society and she changes her views regarding matrimony and accordingly gets married to provide the infant a father. Marian, repulsed by Ainsley's cold-blooded attitude to men and marriage, thinks it is all wrong: "I know Ainsley was wrong, but she sounded so rational. I thought I'd better go to bed before she had convinced me against my better judgment." (43)

Ainsley's movement towards conventionality ironically counterpoints Marian's growing rejection of it. Clara and Joe present Marian with another alternative—a different facet altogether of love and marriage. Theirs is a fairly good marriage and they have three children. Clara is quite content to remain within the bounds of family. But Marian is not unaware of Joe's condescending attitude towards women. "He tends any way to think of all unmarried girls as easily victimized and needing protection." (131)

Clara, impractical and non-assertive as she is, tends to be rather leaning on Joe always. In this regard Marian agrees with Ainsley that "the power of the wife declines as the number of children grows." Even though Clara does not admit it to herself, this seems to be perfectly true, for the children are unplanned. Despite

Marian's dreams as to their future, she also has her own doubts regarding Peter. Disturbed by Peter's casual attitude towards sex and general behaviour, she feels at times that "he was treating her as a stage-prop; silent but solid, a two-dimensional outline." (71)

Peter in turn is drawn to Marian because she is unlike the other women of his acquaintance. Undemanding and non-aggressive, she is a girl who wouldn't try to take over his life. When he proposes to her, Peter is trying to fit Marian into a "conventionalized, even stereotyped image of a woman passive and dependent."[3] He rationalizes his sudden surrender to marriage by saying: "A fellow can't keep running around indefinitely. It'll be a lot better in the long run for my practice too, the clients like to know you've got a wife, people get suspicious of a single man after a certain age, they start thinking you're a queer or something. . . . And there is one thing about you, Marian, I know I can always depend on you . . . you're such a sensible girl." (91) He considers Marian as a sensible girl because she leaves all the major and minor decisions to him. In fact, this can be seen immediately after she agrees to his proposal of marriage. When Peter asks her when she would like to marry, she wants to say 'Ground hog day' but instead she grants Peter the authority to take the decision.

Marian accepts the proposal of Peter and in spite of her unease at the acceptance, she tries to defend her choice. "I'd always assumed through high school and college that I was going to marry someone eventually and have children, everyone does. . . . I've never been silly about marriage the way Ainsley is . . . she is against it on principle, and life isn't by principles but by adjustments." (100)

Here Marian is accepting the role that is traditionally foisted upon women that "Marriage is the destiny traditionally offered to woman by society. . . . The celibate woman is explained and defined with reference to marriage whether she is frustrated, rebellious, or even indifferent in regard to that institution."[4] It is only after the acceptance of the marriage proposal that she is assailed by serious doubts as to whether she made the right choice. Her relationship with Peter seems to have undergone a sea change and

Marian realizes that "she had let herself be sold as some kind of a desirable commodity."[5]

She fails to identify the real Peter underneath all that sophistication and doubts her understanding of his true self. Disliking strongly Peter's manipulation of herself, she identifies him with an anonymous caller who introduced himself to ladies as a seller of underwear, but whose real identity was not known to anybody. "This was his true self, the core of his personality, the central Peter who had been occupying her mind more and more lately. Perhaps this was what lay under the surfaces, that secret identity which in spite of her many guesses and attempts and half-guesses she was aware she had still not uncovered: he was really the Underwear Man." (118)

But later she begins to recognize her sense of loss of identity. But first she ignores the demands of her subconscious mind, and thus the problem starts. At this point her body intervenes and makes her realize that marriage to Peter means more than protection, a socially acceptable suicide. It is her digestive system which carries the rebellion and makes her stop eating one thing after the other. It is in this sense that the significance of the "food metaphor" can be felt very strikingly in this novel.

The first symptoms of anorexia (loss of appetite) are seen in Marian immediately after she agrees to the marriage proposal made by Peter. First her body refuses anything that may at one time have been alive. It begins with meat when she goes to dinner with Peter. First, Marian finds it difficult to eat the steak because she feels it as a hunk of muscle. "Blood red part of a real cow that once moved and ate and was killed, knocked on the head as it stood in a queue like someone waiting for a street car. . . . She set down her knife and fork." (155) In contrast Peter chews and smiles pleasantly, conscious of his own superior capacity and control over Marian. After this, one after the other crosses out of her list of eatables.

As Marian stops eating certain things, she begins to view herself as powerless and weak, quite in line with Darwin's theory of survival of nature that says, if one is powerless and weak, one becomes edible. Thus she identifies herself with a consumer product. For sometime she relies on omelettes, pea-nuts and cheese which also slowly disappear from her list of eatables as she identifies herself with these things also: "The next morning . . . when she opened her soft-boiled egg and saw the yolk looking up at her with its one significant and accusing yellow eye, she found her mouth closing together like a frightened sea-anemone. It's living: It's alive, the muscles in her throat said, and tightened. She pushed the dish away." (165) This makes her stick on to 'salads' and vitamin pills for some time. But when her appetite for vegetables also goes, panic is clearly evident: "She was watching her own hands and the peeler and the curl or crisp orange skin. She becomes aware of the carrot. It's a root, she thought, it grows in the ground and sends up leaves. Then they come along and dig it up, maybe it even makes a sound, a scream too low for us to hear, but it doesn't die right away, it keeps on living, right now it's still alive. . . . She thought she felt it twist in her hands; she dropped it on the table. Oh, no, she said, almost crying. Not this too." (183)

Thus identifying herself with lower forms of life, she refuses to eat, which she equates with preying upon—first steak and all meats, then eggs, then carrots. She reaches a stage where she is unable to destroy the lowest forms of life. She finds herself unable to clean the used vessels and the kitchen sink. As Peter begins to gain control over her in every aspect, her identification with the hunted and the consumed reaches the precipitation point. She comes to the realization that she is powerless to control her own life. Marian's horror at the act of consuming flesh coincides with her alienation and detachment from society. She becomes a passive figure, just watching the society with shocking clarity and not playing any active role. She comes to view "eating" as a violent action concealed behind the social façade of dining which also reminds us of the sacrifice of the victim in the Moose Beer ads.

The unreality of her situation becomes more evident to Marian when she agrees to play the part of a meek and submissive fiancé as dictated by Peter. She decks herself out in all her fiery apparel, but when she looks up in the mirror she fails to see the rightness of it, as unable to recognize the true Marian behind the glittering façade. Nothing seems to be real any more: "What was it that lay beneath the surface these pieces were floating on, holding them together? She held both of her naked arms out towards the mirror. They were the only portion of her flesh that was without a cloth or nylon or varnish covering, but . . . boneless, flexible." (229)

As the impending engagement party approaches, Marian becomes more and more aware of her loss of free will and choice. Marian's presence in the beauty parlour reminds one of the preparations of animals for sacrifice. Her hair is decorated "like a cake something to be carefully iced and ornamented."[6] Marian is being 'packaged' out of all recognition and the scene in the hairdresser's shows Atwood at her most sharply satiric. The scene also brings together much of the telling imagery that Atwood has already employed. When all the technology is in place, Marian's head resembles 'a mutant hedgehog with a covering of rounded hairy appendages instead of spikes.' We are reminded perhaps of Duncan's image of the frenzied armadillo. More often, however, the imagery is drawn from the clinical, industrialized, 'air-conditioned nightmare' side of modern city life.

She recognizes her loss of identity and her "edibility" to Peter. Her sense of victimization becomes acute after she comes across Joe discussing the after-effects of university education on women. He says, "She gets the idea she has a mind, her professors pay attention to what she has to say, they treat her like a thinking human being, when she gets married, her core gets invaded. Her core . . . the centre of her personality, the thing she has built up, her image of herself. . . . Her feminine role and her core are really in opposition, her feminine role demand passivity from her." (235)

The conversation provides Marian with a flash of insight. She realizes what married life with Peter would be. She perceives that as Peter's wife she would be expected to don the mantle of a conventional woman, assuming the role of a meek and docile woman, dependent on her husband, allowing him to devour her relishing slowly.

Although Marian refuses to be an "edible woman" for Peter by running away from him, yet she falls a victim to male-dominance in the person of Duncan. He seduces her feigning ignorance and helplessness. Later on, it occurs to Marian that she has allowed the men in her life to use and consume her, thus actually helping the process of victimization.

This new awareness provides her a renewed strength and purpose in life. As in the Freudian theory of catharsis, when the neurosis is recognised, it should not only lose its power but also make way for the long-stifled element of the authentic self to grow. This pattern of increasingly conscious neurosis reduction and simplification of the neurotic action, followed by tentative new growth, is the true pattern of Atwood's novels. Marian's unconscious fear of being devoured comes to the 'surface' of her consciousness as an increasing aversion to food and culminates in her realization that 'what she really wanted . . . had been reduced to simple safety.' The realisation takes place in a snowy ravine which Duncan describes as 'close to absolute zero,' 'as near as possible to nothing' when she returns to her apartment and decides to take her first positive action in several days—to bake a woman-shaped cake for Peter, this marks a sense of new personal beginning.

Atwood says that by doing so Marian is trying to depict "an action, a preposterous one in a way, as all the pieces of symbolism in a realistic context are, but what she is obviously making is a substitute of herself."[7] She offers the cake to Peter who is affronted at the very sight of it. Denying the passive role as his fiancé, she tells him: "You've been trying to destroy me, haven't you, she said, you've been trying to assimilate me. But I've made a substitute, something you'll like much better. This is what you really wanted all along, isn't it? I'll get you a fork, she added somewhat prosaically." (271)

Marian realizes immediately that the spell of anorexia has been broken. Suddenly she feels hungry, 'extremely hungry.' As soon as she has broken off her engagement with Peter, her body reverts to normal responses. In addition, as soon as this appears, the cake ceases to be regarded as a symbol, failed or otherwise,

that it is historically rooted in power struggle both as a process of history in which there is always a war between the subjugated and the dominating group. Writing is politics because it occurs *against the grain*. "The principal objective of feminist criticism," says Toril Moi, "has always been political: it seeks to expose, not to perpetuate, patriarchal practices" (Moi xiv).

Before we proceed to the study of Emecheta's formidable feminist text, *The Joys of Motherhood*, I am to quote a substantive theoretical formulation of feminist criticism:

> Indeed, feminism and feminist literary criticism are often defined as a matter of what is absent rather than what is present. Unlike the other approaches . . . feminist literary criticism is often a political attack upon other modes of criticism and theory, and its social orientation moves beyond traditional literary criticism. In its diversity feminism is concerned with the marginalization of all women: that is, with their being relegated to a secondary position. Most feminists believe that our culture is a patriarchal culture: that is, one organized in favour of the interests of men. Feminist literary critics try to explain how power imbalances due to gender in a given culture are reflected in or challenged by literary texts. (Guerin 196)

However, feminism is culture specific despite the common experience of women the world over: the painful history of sexual domination and marginalization, women having been treated as inferior to men, denial of rights and privileges in all walks of life. Simone de Beauvoir demonstrates her insightful study of women in relation to man in culture: "A man is in the right of being a man; it is the woman who is in the wrong. . . . Woman has ovaries, a uterus: these peculiarities imprison her in her subjectivity, circumscribe her within the limits of her own nature" (15). Holy Scriptures (the *Bible*, the *Quran*) and thinkers are of the view that women are negative markers. "The female is a female by virtue of a certain lack of qualities" says Aristotle; St Thomas pronounced woman an "imperfect man," "and incidental" being (*ibid.* 15-16). Every culture accepts it: she is the Old Testament sinner. Probably, the commonality ends here, and the rest is the specificities of culture. Feminism does not have a single accepted definition; it is often to be true to the place and to the peculiarities of life and experience of a given culture.

As one of the most distinguished champions of the oppressed African women, Buchi Emecheta rejects the Western notion of elitist feminism based on women's suffrage, sexual autonomy and their conscious individuality. Western feminism is for the educated, [insert rich] middle class women whereas the Third World feminism in most cases is not an organized movement of conscious women. They are a class of women who are/were oppressed/ suppressed by colonialism and/or other social conditions which have kept them ignorant, uneducated, poor, malnutritious with many children to feed through strenuous labour, while at the same time they have to show their gift. Feminism being a Western term is inapplicable to the poor women of Africa and the Third World countries, non-Western feminists maintain. As mentioned above, it is for the West a struggle of the "privileged minority" for their equal rights and sexual freedom. Emecheta comments:

> Sex is part of life. It is not THE life. Listen to the Western feminists' claim about enjoying sex, they make me laugh. African feminism is free of the shackles of Western romantic illusions and tends to be much more pragmatic. (Petersen 177)

African feminism is collective, communal and racially bound and it sees both women and men as victims of all forms of colonialism, the Slave Trade and racial discrimination on the one hand. These women again bear the burden of sexual oppression within their culture on the other hand. Unlike the Western women African women have unique three-fold suffering inflicted by racism, colonialism and sexism. Therefore it is impossible for the educated and conscious Western women to recognize and empathise with the African women, who are tradition bound, poor and by and large uneducated. Since African human situations are entwined in social, historical and racial problems women as well as men are to get rid of such things. Liberation of one sex will not solve the deep-rooted social, cultural and historical problems. In her *In Search of Our Mothers' Garden: Womanist Prose*, Alice Walker being herself a coloured feminist and critic prefers the term "womanist" to "feminist" in as much as black women's movement is concerned because "a womanist does not turn her back on the men of her community" (Guerin 209). That is why African feminism is not integral to the mainstream feminism because freedom of the women alone does not guarantee solution to the impending social, racial and communal issues. Mieke Maerton observes:

> African women's activism cannot be seen separately from the larger context of repression and exploitation of both men and women. This has given rise to a feminism and activism primarily aimed at changing social and humanitarian conditions. ("Feminism in Africa," http://www. .rosadoc.be/site/rosa/english/blf/factsheets english/34.pdf Accessed 10 October 2009).

Not only do the African feminists fight against sexism of their own men but also they have to fight to save their image, their culture that has been falsely represented in the Western discourse. As for the African man he is quite unnerved when his masculine role is slightly changed such as fetching a child. He feels it is Western feminism that his wife is capable of asking him to do something he never did earlier. Miriam Tlali, a South African feminist, describes the kind of reaction the man would make: "Look, you are already a feminist. You are a white women [sic] and a feminist" (Petersen 185).

Again, on the other hand, the missionaries wrongly interpret the custom of dowry or bride prize as buying of the bride but it is far from true because in African society procreation is highly placed for that only ensures the lineage of a family. And it all depends on the fertility of the woman, and giving dowry to the bride's family is to facilitate that. Thus, African feminism implies a struggle for cultural self definition against the Western misconceptions about African tradition. But that distinguishes itself by siding with "the patriarchal power structure" (Guerin *et al.* 208), hence African feminism is more complex than it appears to be, and one needs to tread it cautiously. However, as an African feminist Emecheta writes:

> Being a woman, and African born, I see things through an African woman's eyes. I chronicle the little happenings in the lives of the African women I know. I did not know that by doing so I was going to be called a feminist. But if I am now a feminist then I am an African feminist with a small f. (Petersen 175)

African women are tradition bound in the sense that they try to retrieve the traditional values of motherhood. They make life, their homes and the future generation; they are mothers, wives and sisters too, a position one cannot think of in the Western context. Emecheta continues:

> In my books I write about families because I still believe in families. I write about women who try very hard to hold their family together until it becomes absolutely impossible. I have no sympathy for a woman who deserts her children, neither do I have sympathy for a woman who insists on staying in a marriage with a brute of a man, simply to be respectable. (*ibid.*)

In Africa, motherhood is a boon bestowed upon women. Whatever "seething experience" it may give, nothing in the life of a woman is as eventful as being a mother of children. Lauretta Ngçobo rightly says, "As elsewhere, marriage amongst Africans is mainly an institution for the control of procreation. Every woman is encouraged to marry and get children in order to express her womanhood to the full" (Petersen 141).

Taking a cue from Flora Nwapa whose novel *Efuru* ironically made a reference to the goddess of the lake, worshiped by women for beauty and wealth, who "had no child" of her own because she "had never experienced the joy of motherhood" (221) Emecheta has created a fertile woman in her novel, *The Joys of Motherhood,* but this woman with her children does not experience the joys of motherhood, too.

II

Being Africa's most acclaimed (expatriate/diasporic) novelist over the past few decades, Emecheta has received very serious critical attention the world over. Well-known critics like Lloyd Brown, Carole Davies and Florence Stratton have done commendable critical work to assess Emecheta as a novelist. Yet Emecheta criticism invites a serious thinking particularly at a time when literary studies conflate with cultural and historical perspectives. In this paper, an attempt is made to study *The Joys of Motherhood* pragmatically from the point of view of African culture and history vis-à-vis women's life and experience. Emecheta places her woman protagonist, Nnu Ego, in the midst of conflicting situations when the ground is fast shifting from the rural background to urban development before and after the Second World War. A simple village woman of Nigeria's Ibuza the central character is hooded by the myth of motherhood but actually in the process of mothering she has faced heavy odds, hardships and untold misery dragging her to her lonely death betraying her dream that when she is old she will be protected and looked after by her children. In the second half of this paper, my task is to uncover two cardinal points: firstly, to analyse woman as a victim in the context of African culture and colonial relations, and, second, to review Emecheta's critique of culture and history through a counter-discourse, ideologically grounded in feminist polemical discourse that interrogates the patriarchal culture and European construction of history.

As the 'Other' of patriarchy and colonial discourse, Emecheta rejects such concepts as nature, essence and fixity of woman's identity imposed on women's sexual body, body being the site of male oppression. The novelist finds it necessary to undo the cultural definition of African women by attaching her to a number of traditional roles because such roles continually change along with the process of modernization and urbanization. These are very complex central issues in Emecheta's work. The slave woman motif in the earlier novel, *The Slave Girl*, grows into its full form in *The Joys of Motherhood* offering a complex African vision of motherhood in the wake of socio-economic changes. It questions whether or not cultural valorization of motherhood specific to Africa is still valid in a complex context when modernization replaces the old values. Is it possible for motherhood to withstand the pressing need of existential problems? Isn't the much cherished African motherhood a shackle to woman? With all these questions Nnu Ego is put to the test.

The novel's structural binarism of centre/margin, man/woman, rural/urban, tradition/modernity, colonizer/colonized, black/white is crucial in our analysis. Apparently, Nnu Ego's suffering is rooted in her ignorance, backwardness, illiteracy, superstitious beliefs and traditionality with which she has been blindly bound up in a strangely hostile urban environment where she faces complete dislocation. The book, earlier dedicated to her daughter Chiago was later to be dedicated "to all mothers." Emecheta writes in her *Head above Water*:

> In *The Joys of Motherhood* I created a woman, Nnuego, who gave all her energy, all her money and everything she had to raise her kids. She chopped wood for sale, she dealt on the black market, she did everything except whore herself to raise money. She was so busy doing all this that she had no time to cultivate any friend among her own sex.
>
> The children grew up and left. They loved her still, but they were busy with their own lives—so much so that when she was ill they could not come to see her. When she became tired, she died alone by the wayside with none of her living eight [sic] children to hold her hand. (225)

When the book was done, her daughter, Chiago read it and commented: "But we love you, Mum, you must remember that. You'll never die like Nnuego, not when I'm living anyway" (*Head above Water*: 225-26). Providence, what it had in store for her daughter! She who had spoken so was not destined to live longer, for her own end came only a few years later in 1984. The dedication had to be changed. Was Nnu Ego's final death a model of death in perfect peace, an impression of the death of the old mother of her friend Clive Allison, "death can be peaceful and beautiful" (218). Irony, death could be worse. Whatever fetishism Emecheta may have, Nnu Ego's canonized death, however, reaffirms a mother's unfulfilled life. Anyway, her death is "peaceful" in the sense that it's quiet.

In her well-informed article "African Motherhood—Myth and Reality" Lauretta Ngcobo insists that African motherhood is given a special place of honour, but she adds:

> Women should not have to be martyrs to win the respect of their societies. We are looking for a self-defining image of women who win respect in their own right because they are strong and achieve things in their lives and triumph, not only because they are men's wives or mothers of sons but because they are valued members of their societies, outstanding in their societies as bread winners, teachers of their societies, nurses, politicians and whatever else. (Petersen 151)

Ngcobo's type of quality of a woman is seen in Nnu Ego for she is everything that African women are proud of. But then in her case cultural definition of motherhood and real existentialist problems are intimately bound up. In a swiftly changing society where money determines everything, human beings are defined by the success or defeat of their labour. Stratton writes: "complex social beings . . . are defined and destinies determined by their interaction with their environment" (Stratton 116). Emecheta's realistic portrayal of women characters in the novel has double function: to show Igbo women's allegiance to their tradition on the one hand, and to challenge the stereotyping of women on the other hand.

True, *The Joys of Motherhood* is a novel about female fertility, procreation and also about polygamy. Nnu Ego's first marriage to Amatokwu becomes luckless: she cannot fulfil the expectations of her husband. So, instead of wasting his "precious male seed on a woman who is infertile"[1] Amatokwu chooses another woman for his wife who bears him a son in the very first year. Soon after that Nnu Ego is divorced. But her second marriage to Nnaife is rewarding: she becomes a mother of children. Now, in her joy she cries "that her old age would be happy, that when she dies there would be someone left behind to refer to her as 'mother'" (54). Now she praises her husband whom she earlier called a "pregnant cow" (42) for making her a mother in spite of his big belly, short stature and ugliness. She reflects: "now with his son am I going to start loving this man. He has made me into a real woman—all I want to be, a woman and a mother. So why should I hate him now?" (53) But instead of praising her husband for his manhood, she should have rather congratulated herself on her being fertile. As a traditional woman, she conforms to the cultural valuation of male sex in her African society. Unlike her, Western feminists hail the rich potential of women's body and bodily capacity to create (not restricted to procreation only), enjoy bodily, spiritually and conceptually, the experience of *jouissance* (Humm 97). In her allegiance to her culture, Nnu Ego has self-esteem of being a mother of sons, a position she holds higher than that of a mother of daughters. Look at Adaku, Nnaife's co-wife, who has got a disadvantageous position as she has no son. In the creation of Nnu Ego Emecheta has cherished the African value system. "In most African societies," writes Emecheta, "the birth of a son enhances a woman's authority in the family" because a male child "will not be carried away, but will stay in the family home and look after his mother when she becomes weak and old" (Petersen 179). So, at such moments Emecheta falls into the trap of patriarchy, and her character is a helpless victim of cultural construct.

Emecheta's feminist politics is very vexed because at times her complicity with her culture is very evident, while at others she is a virulent critic of her culture. In Nnu Ego's dejected death, she questions the *modus operandi* of her culture. Nnu Ego's tragedy is caused by her excessive faith in her children, a kind of false conviction, her *hamartia*. She failed to understand that her children generation was flooded with open opportunities. They go catching the wind of change and are least concerned with parental bond. Children belonging to the post-war and post-colonial period are honed to self-actualization. Thus African cultural paradigm gives way to the coming of new prospects brought by cross and multicultural alliances. The novel bears witness to these cultural and historical phenomena.

Admittedly, Nnu Ego's life from start to finish is spun elaborately around the belief system of Africa. Her own birth is mysteriously connected with the *ogbanje* myth, which means the "myth of infant mortality," "a living dead" (Stratton in Umeh 101), a condition of life that appears and reappears several times to wreck family peace. Achebe writes about *ogbanje* as being "one of those mysterious, elusive and often highly talented beings who hurry to leave the world and to come again" (Achebe 113). Believably, Nnu Ego's *chi* is a slave girl, who was mercilessly buried alive along with the dead body of Agunwa, Nnu Ego's father's first wife. Thus slave girl's life entered Ona's pregnant body to appear as Nnu Ego with vengeance and make her life a "catalogue of disasters" (9). Another such story runs in *The Slave Girl* as Chiago relates. The novel is precisely a cultural metatext. Nnu Ego's sufferings are linked to it, that is why her life indicates that a woman is slave. Her inability to be pregnant in the first marriage, the death of the first son four weeks after his birth, resulting in her abortive suicide attempt, then the birth of many more children than she can feed, her hardships, poverty, starvation, the children's revolt, the husband's blame on her, casting her off and her final death are a metaphor of the slave. She dies unseen, unknown "with no child to hold her hand and no friend to talk to" (224).

Motherhood is rendered as nothing but perpetual servitude, not different from that of a slave, so that they become the cultural metaphors of female suppression and oppression inflicted by patriarchy. The slave girl's cry for mercy and Nnu Ego's lifelong struggle and final defeat relate to each other—slave and woman are conflated. Emecheta's deep understanding of the suffering of these two "makes the slave's life and woman's life parallel and, portrays Nnu Ego, the mother as living the life of a slave, slave to her child, slave to tradition" (Davies in Davies & Adams 253). So Nnu Ego, the slave and mother pays the price on two counts, first, for the crime her people had committed before her birth, like the *karma* theory in Hindu philosophy,[2] and, second for her own extreme faith in her femininity. In Nnu Ego's life and suffering, Emecheta's feminist critique of her culture and society is very explicit and her voice against cultural practices biased against gendered female class as male prerogative is quite revealing.

The Joys of Motherhood can be treated as a modern African saga of individual human suffering. Nnu Ego's quality is her endurance through odds and hardships without wavering. She continues to remain a benign mother stoically despite her being torn by circumstances beyond her control. Hope never deserts her nor does she disappoint her children. In her utter destitute, she goes on fighting for her children and for herself. Her presence is full in the entire book with or without her husband or children in her wrecked state. Her husband is always absent doing odd jobs elsewhere, at sea, in India, in Burma for a period of time fighting on the side of the British during the Second World War. Not only does she become the sole bread-earner in a family of many children but also she educates her children even when stark misery stares her in face. In an effort to make both ends meet, she chops firewood, sells cigarettes and matches, runs stalls in front of her house, at the railway station, deals on the black market, but still far from satisfying the demand. When her husband becomes bestial by inheriting Adaku, the young wife of his deceased brother, Nnu Ego resolves to work like a man lest she die. Thus a great deal of Nnu Ego's suffering is attributed to the patriarchal cultural practice that privileges man, even a brute of a man. Quoting Filomena Steady, Cynthia vanden Driesen writes: "Nnu Ego . . . could be regarded as the ultimate female victim of a patriarchal society which only valorizes her child-bearing capacity so as to perpetuate a society in which male privilege remains enshrined. Her capacity for survival, independent of the assistance of a token husband, establishes her as a symbol of female self-sufficiency. (26-27)

By no means, does Nnu Ego accept defeat; she takes blame and shares it with no one. It is her wish not to show a defeated face to anyone, even to her loving father. When her husbands in both the marriages become polygamous and she is denied sex, she has to accept polygamy as a way of life. Her father, who had several wives, asked her to make no complaint against the system. It is tradition and faith in it that cause Nnu Ego's suffering.

Emecheta interrogates her culture from the feminist angle, and addresses the evil social and cultural practices that are imposed on women so that women are perpetually imprisoned and put in place. For the liberation of women in Africa, what is necessary is to change social, political and economic environment through education of women. She writes: "I want very much to further the education of women in Africa, because I know that education really helps the women. It helps them to read and it helps them to rear a generation. It is true that if one educates a woman, one educates a community, whereas if one educates a man, one educates a man" (Petersen 175). True, education is a source of women's empowerment and without education women will live in ignorance and in darkness, hence their marginalization. Emecheta's feminism is grounded in women's collective awareness, a campaign for social and sexual equity.

In Nnu Ego Emecheta creates a strong woman character in *The Joys of Motherhood.* The *sarah* episode is an example, in which she is hurt emotionally as badly as her son Oshia but as a benign and sympathetic mother, she hides her emotion; she puffs up the morale of her hungry child, not by filling the stomach of her son but by the power of her words. She says that he will go to school like the Ibuza children, dressed in good clothes to look like an Arab or a Fulani and so on. But in actuality all this is an empty promise. On the other hand, look at Nnaife, the husband and father of many children: he escapes responsibility, squandering his money on drinking, loitering and playing guitar, and boasting of his virility—Adaku, Okpu are his new possessions, and he even impregnates his brother's wife Adankwu. He is a typical example of African patriarchy, a stereotype. What a difference, Nnu Ego fights single-handed for existence, for bringing up and educating her children. Credit goes to her when two of her sons distinguish themselves, are whisked off abroad on foreign scholarships, however painful it is for their ageing parents. African feminism claims that however painful and broken the life of a mother, she does not deter the growth of the potential of her children. Being a mother of five children on a foreign soil struggling as single parent for the well being of her children, Emecheta's creation of Nnu Ego is to express her concept of African feminism charged with family-oriented political ideology: that despite everything a mother is always creative and her role is both multiple and dynamic. She is the power ready to rise to the occasion. An African mother is family-oriented because family is the source of her power, and kitchen is where she creates. Emecheta writes:

> In our kitchens we raise all Reagans, all Nkrumahs, all Jesuses. In our kitchens we cook for them, we send them away from home to be grown men and women, and in our kitchens they learn to love and hate. What greater job is there? I asked. A mother with a family is an economist, a nurse, a painter, a diplomat and more. (Petersen 180)

The character of Nnu Ego is to demonstrate African feminism *per se* in the most vivid and realistic manner. Emecheta is not a radical feminist but she is one who believes in the positive aspects that can be achieved within her society and family. She is not heading for a world of women alone. She sees that women's problems are not always man-made, men need not be accused of what women are. There are woman-made issues in which woman imprisons herself. She wonders why women are "on the lowest rung. Men did not put us there, my sisters, I think sometimes we put ourselves there" (*ibid*).

Emecheta seems to emphasize that as members of a society, both men and women have equal sharing and equal responsibility, not to talk of equal rights. We can analyse the episode, that is, Kehinde's runaway marriage with a Yoruba Muslim butcher's son much to the anger of Nnaife. That is the case of a child's violent refusal of the parents. Now, the father who has remained all through a derelict husband accuses Nnu Ego of the failure of the children. In her tragic resignation, Nnu Ego cries: "When the children were good they belonged to the father; when they were bad, they belonged to the mother" (206). It is male hegemony, no less. He disowns her and the children whom he calls her brats. At this, Nnu Ego's profound motherhood, almost universal, comes out as she says, a man "can reject a bad son, a master . . . his evil servant, a wife can even leave a bad husband, but a mother can never, never reject her son. If he is damned, she is damned with him" (214). She forgives her children, Oshia, Kehinde, and prays for all.

To a woman, her children are a part of her body and for their welfare, she will make any amount of sacrifice. Stekel's remark may be quoted in this context:

> Children are not substitutes for one's disappointed love, they are not substitutes for one's thwarted ideal, children are not mere material to fill out an empty existence. Children are a responsibility and an opportunity. Children are the loftiest blossoms upon the tree of untrammelled love. . . . They are neither playthings, nor tools for the fulfilment of parental needs or ungratified ambitions. Children are obligations; they should be brought up so as to become happy human beings. (Beauvoir 537)

In her woman-centred novel, *The Joys of Motherhood*, Emecheta has spun the character of Nnu Ego as a fine model of motherhood, as distinguished from other feminist preoccupations with self-realization and self-fulfilment in public domain.

But thc ironic treatment of motherhood is another ploy used by the novelist. Women's future in the male-dominated society is unpredictable because she is grossly treated and her worth relegated to the secondary position. When Nnu Ego dies by the side of a village road, the much-cherished concept of motherhood is deeply flawed. Neither the urbanized city of Lagos nor her native Ibuza village gives her peace. The textual structure is paradoxical, allowing a reading against the text which produces the indeterminacy and undecidability of the euphoria of motherhood itself. Pragmatically speaking, motherhood itself is a complex social, cultural and emotional state. Emecheta rightly points out, "if you don't have children the longing for them will kill you, and if you do, the worrying about them will kill you" (212).

Motherhood is an enigma. About the time of her death, Nnu Ego becomes schizophrenic, and when she dies, she repudiates motherhood. Her death nullifies motherhood. She turns her back on her cultural women's prayer to be fertile and have children. People call her wicked, but this time she keeps mum. She weaves her life into *silence, exile,* and *cunning* in the Joycean fashion. Exile is the motif that casts its shadow on Nnu Ego from the very beginning. She has double exile, the first from her traditional Ibuza village to colonized city of Lagos (Fido in Nasta 333) following her second marriage, and, the latter, when her husband disowns her she returns with shame and defeat to her father's home, the completion of an exile's life in solitude. She adopts *cunning* as a strategy to keep herself to herself, and to keep the knowledge of fertility a secret to herself. Because as an African mother she knows what it is to be a mother in her culture. Her silence is the "silence of refusal"—not just silence, but a refusal to speak, yet it is capable of sending waves of communication in unspoken discourse. Emecheta employs this as a feminist strategy by which she returns to *semiotic chora* (Kristeva's phrase), the pre-symbolic order state where there is free play of signs, "made from within, of a woman's consciousness" which every reader aspires to reach. (Daymond in Umeh 279). Feminist texts abound in this characteristic mode of female silence.

Emecheta's feminist agenda is not to create free and independent women characters but that she is interested in the creation of women characters who are still cultural adherents. The point is substantiated when we look at the two fairly independent characters Adaku and Ona. Emecheta as a feminist seems to have lacked sustained interest in such independent characters primarily because she sees things from her culture, and African feminism tends to be tightly woven with the seething experience women face in African culture. This, however, is not true of her other novels. For instance, in *Kehinde* the heroine fights for her rights and independence. The strength of *The Joys of Motherhood* derives from the schematization of irony as a principle of novelistic structure. Emecheta's treatment of motherhood firmly rooted in oppressive male culture is ambiguous for the reason that she also shares with contemporary African women writers in "demystifying this traditional romanticization of motherhood" and rejects her culture's mythologization of the "tedia involved in motherhood" (Davies in Davies and Graves 6). All this is a part of the crucial agenda in the post-colonial feminist discourse which seeks to decolonize women through fissions and fissures of culture. The death of Nnu Ego alone, deserted and unnoticed points to the fact that much as the myth of motherhood beguiles all women into being mothers of children, in reality, motherhood for every woman is a ground for becoming a martyr to the family.

Another perspective the book offers is Emecheta's interrogation into the historical and political contexts of her society reflecting the colonial situation in Nigeria. Emecheta redefines the African men and women according to their new roles under colonialism. Women's lot, in particular, as Katrak says, was directly affected by the new changes in such spheres as: "the burdens of female roles in urban environment (instituted by colonialism), the rise of prostitution in cities, women's marginalization in actual political participation" (Ashcroft 257). For an uneducated woman like Nnu Ego the rapid changes that followed colonialism were too strong a blow to endure because she was ignorant of what was happening. Her simple logic why they are slaves to the white while they themselves abolish slavery is an unequivocal attack on post-colonial praxis. And then she asks why her husband is fighting against those who do not harm them. Such questions rework in the novel to upset the colonial agenda based on hierarchical structure of racial differences in which the relationship between Europe and the colonized subjects is that of master and slave. Under any circumstance, a slave has to serve his master. Anti-colonial discourse the text produces reveals feminist enquiry into the damage done by colonial process to women's lives in colonized societies.

As a colonized, traditional, conservative and religious woman, Nnu Ego's displacement in such an urban area as Lagos is thorough. The breakdown of rural farming economy leads a woman with many dependent children to hard living by hawking, trading in small items to earn a meagre income so as to pay house rent, feed many children. How hard her life as a wife is, one can see: "She had to work. She provided the food from her husband's meagre housekeeping money, but finding the money for clothes, for any kind of comforts, in some cases for the children's school fees, was on her shoulders" (52-53). War aggravates the situation, and women were to bear the entire burden alone when their husbands fought for the British on a foreign soil. Ignorant as she is, her entrenched faith in her tradition worsens still. Adaku, just the opposite of Nnu Ego in understanding, chides the latter for not seeing the changes taking place, and for her traditionality: "Nnaife does not own anybody [Nnu Ego thinks that she is owned by Nnaife]. . . . But, senior wife, don't worry. You believe in the tradition. You have . . . stood firm by your belief" (218).

Emecheta brings out the effect of social, political and economic changes during colonialism on women's lives in particular. The burden is more on a woman who is tradition-bound because her suffering is caused from lack of knowledge and ignorance of the mechanization of life. Nnu Ego's life and struggle are characteristically ascribed to a transitional period between village and urban development under colonialism. Idayi, Agbadi's friend, states very emphatically: "she was born in her own time. Things have changed a lot. This is the age of the white man" (37). In common parlance, it is the characteristic of a Third World woman. In the words of Chandra Mohanty: "This average third-world woman leads an essential truncated life based on her feminine gender (read: sexually constrained) and being 'third world' (read: ignorant, poor, uneducated, tradition-bound, religious, domesticated, family-oriented, victimized etc.)" (Mohanty 65). Colonization and its aftermath have seriously affected sexual relationship between man and woman. Women don't even consider it bad if they become sexually promiscuous. Even for the married couple, there is little room for romance. Nnu Ego's experience on the first night with Nnaife (44) contrasts with the one she got from Amatokwu.

With colonialism, role-change takes place. The African man who had enjoyed a higher gender status in his culture is in his nadir. Now he is subservient to the White man in whose home he cooks and washes, all traditionally reserved for women. The height of his humiliation corresponds to his loss of dignity and the symbolic emasculation. Now men have to work as grass-cutters, road builders, foundry workers, railway, ship and dock labourers, and jobs unthinkable for villagers like Agbadi—complete dependents on the new economic order introduced by colonialism. Thus they are reduced to the status of the slaves. Even women raise a voice of protest against the fall of their men's position. Nnu Ego protests Nnaife washing the smalls and nightie of Mrs. Meers, whom she calls a pig-like English lady. In her house, Nnaife is "a woman-made man" (50), who loses his manhood quite contrary to the heroic posture of the Igbo traditional man, who may be a chief, warrior, fighter, great farmer, hunter keeping the world at his command like Agbadi or Okonkwo in Achebe's *Things Fall Apart*. Here the appropriation of Western feminism by African "womanism" is guaranteed. Women deplore the attitude of Nnu Ego and Cordelia, the wife of Ubani, the cook, is quite significant. The latter says: "Men here are too busy being white men's servants to be men. We women mind home. Not our husbands. Their manhood has been taken away from them. The shame of it is that they don't know it. All they see is the money, shining white man's money" (51).

Thus, through the depiction of the brutalized colonized man Emecheta attacks the European imperialism's relentless inhumanity. So her subversive womanist/feminist discourse not only counters male discourse but also disturbs and contests the colonial discourse constructed along Eurocentric cultural superiority and false humanism. The horrendous effect of colonialism on women steals the genuine concerns of a realist feminist. She rewrites her story against the grain, bringing out sloppiness of colonialism as well as native culture where there is a flawed politics of domination. Emecheta's critical feminist politics challenges and exposes whatever form of oppression and injustice whether originated from her African myths and customs that prescribe for women rigid gender roles (Umeh xxvi) or from the Western-oriented social, political and racial discrimination. (Ezeigbo in Umeh 6)

As already pointed out, under colonial process, men were ruthlessly effeminized to the extent that their women felt pity for them. Nnaife threatens Nnu Ego for her searching eyes while he is eating for he knows such a look hints at his lost masculinity. Cordelia protests, "They stopped being men long ago. Now they are machines" (53). For the success of the colonial policy, matters are very complex that not only had the White man to propagate his cultural values and been warned against going native but also for the protection and security of their women folk, the native men were subjected to name-calling and jokes at their expense. In the colonized world, "'feminization' of colonized men" (Childs and Williams 199) continued and had to be complete, taking precedence over other things because that policy would prevent the natives from revolting against the colonial rule on the one hand and would tame them not to pose a potential threat to white women on the other hand.

In *The Joys of Motherhood* Nnaife is called a "baboon" by Dr. Meers, his white master much to the consternation of him, but he remains unaffected as long as he is paid, and simply calling him a baboon does not make him one, he thinks. The net effect of this kind of treatment on the native women is that they become the victims of their angry men's physical abuse. In his essay "The Fact of Blackness," Fanon writes, "The Negro is an animal, the Negro is bad, the Negro is mean, the Negro is ugly," and adds further, "I am the slave not of the 'idea' that others have of me but of my own appearance" (Ashcroft 324, 325). The colonizer's metaphor of the colonized "other" as inferior breed is related to the physical facts: skin colour, eye, nose, hair, body structure, race etc. The body of a Black is the very site of racial oppression and human denigration. Under the circumstances, African woman inevitably bears the burden of double colonization, of her own man and of the white rule. Ezeigbo writes:

> Women groaned under the burden of double oppressive structures—the Igbo patriarchal system and the alien patriarchal system introduced by the white man. It was, therefore, almost impossible for the women to remain afloat; and to survive they needed to devise new strategies to confront the new areas of oppression lined up against them. (Umeh 15-16)

Women in Emecheta's world are not to be taken as passive dependents on men. Within the given society they explore all possibilities for their existence by participating in the economic struggle. One can see Nnu Ego's struggle when she is faced with a grim reality as a result of Nnaife's loss of job at the Meers.' Leaving his family behind, Nnaife is in search of a job at sea. Meanwhile Nnu Ego and her children are forced to vacate their rent-free house by the army leaving her as if she were a fish out of water. Now, the question of survival for a large family with seven children is a daily ordeal for Nnu Ego. Molara Ogundipe Leslie has used Mao Tse Tung's metaphor, "mountains on the back" for Chinese women, to define African women's situation in the contexts of cultural oppression and colonial history. These mountains are six-fold: foreign oppression from colonization; the cultural oppression and slavery; women's own backwardness and underprivileged position as a result of colonial and neo-colonial practices resulting in their poverty and ignorance; African man's unchanged attitude of sexual domination; discrimination against women internationally as a race and a class; women's own failure (Davies 7) to assert their claim.

African women's road towards self-realization is rather long, because they have to decolonize themselves from internal and external forces of colonialism. Therefore their men are to be equally responsible by shedding sexism. Polygamy increases woman's suffering. As an African feminist, Emecheta in *The Joys of Motherhood* draws her attention to the prevailing social and cultural impediments towards women's emancipation although she is accused of supporting polygamy on grounds of women's sharing in farm work and bonding. Although Nnu Ego is shattered by Nnaife's continuous obsession with many more women, she cannot protest against this male excess mainly because she is still part of the system which was cherished by her father. Both man and woman are unable to free themselves of the age-old cultural traditions. There are two reasons for this: one, within the African culture itself, people look upon it as something absolute, unalterable and infallible, and second, such practices as polygamy and unrestricted production of children are in complete harmony with the African popular beliefs that already unborn children are awaiting rescue by mothers (Ngcobo in Petersen 142). To be an African feminist therefore is to walk on the razor's edge. Emecheta's own disapproval of such practices can be seen when Adim expresses his anguish over his parents' mindless breeding of more and more children which makes his future bleak. Emecheta says in an interview with Oladipo Joseph Ogundele that the objective of the novel is "population control" and adds, "Nnu Ego in *The Joys of Motherhood* is about population control. You have a vague idea that you want to use this woman to depict the fact that having so many children does not mean that you are going to be rich in your old age" (Umeh 453). This has indirectly refuted her own earlier comment on the practical use of polygamy in her essay, "Feminism with a small 'f'!"

The Joys of Motherhood is a novel about an African woman who is pitted against the patriarchal norms of her society that was increasingly worsened by the rapid changes in social and economic life of the people of Africa due to colonialism. The book not only records the suffering of women who are uneducated, superstitious, tradition-bound, poor and ignorant of what was happening around but also is a vigorous protest against "sexual inequality in both pre-colonial and postcolonial Africa," a shackle against women's freedom pronounced by African women novelists, Ama Ata Aidoo, Bessie Head and Buchi Emecheta (Brown 7). Emecheta sees that women's primary need is economic self-reliance without which a woman is an appendage to her husband. She maintains that sex is important for an African woman, and to please her man she has to be beautiful. As she said earlier, it is only "a part of life," "not THE life." She differs from the Western feminists in regard to the attitude towards sex. She does not hold that sex is pure and it should be preserved for only one man. No, she flatly refuses such an orthodox view but sex and life are both pragmatic no less. She admits an African woman can be promiscuous for economic reasons, to elevate and enlighten her position.

At last, in the novel, Adaku comes out against polygamy and sexism, "becoming a woman 'fulfilled in herself'" and "a dignified single woman" (Stratton in Umeh 112). Adaku realizes polygamy incurs nothing but jealousy, flexing of muscles over trifles, poverty and above all meanness and conspiracy all of which make life intolerably ugly. She escapes into prostitution as a means of freedom from sexual bondage under the traditional marriage institution, and of economic self-realization. Now, she educates her daughters at better schools, wears good clothes, gains an air of confidence, and best of all she has a separate *living room of her own*, a feminist prerequisite, as a space for women. Thus she emerges as a "role model" of a resilient, freedom-loving and self-conscious woman. Nnu Ego, however, cannot revolt, being herself an adherent to her tradition. In spite of her best efforts to become a successful mother with her children, she cannot fulfil her desire and dies in penury without any of her children by her side at the time of her death. In fact, Adaku is a new generation African woman. As Emecheta says: "the Yorubas have a saying that a woman must never allow a man to sleep with her if, at the end of the day she is going to be in debt. Few of our women go after sex *per se*" (Petersen 176). Therefore, Adaku is not going to die like Nnu Ego. Truly speaking, African feminism does not support Nnu Ego's idealization of marriage and motherhood *per se*: they "are unqualified routes to female fulfilment and redemption" (Brown 7). Nnu Ego's tragedy, in spite of our sympathy with her, is due to her blind faith in the myth of motherhood by which she fails to look at its disadvantages caused to women.

As a feminist, Emecheta is a social realist, wanting to dismantle the patriarchal norms that cripple women. She also sees the opportunities given by new social and economic order. Oshia and Adim choose to study and live abroad pursuing education as a life-long project. The colonial history's first phase of setback in terms of social, cultural dislocation, change in life style and economic restructuring that transformed societies beyond recognition, however, tended to give rise to the growth of cross-cultural pollination through migration. While taking this overall experience into consideration, Emecheta's feminist ideology is not only complex but also ambiguous when she embraces Western values, a point which other black feminists accuse her of European condescension. She is not one who tries to recuperate and retrieve her past culture. The gangrene of the past should be removed by incision because that impairs women's struggle for self-discovery, sexual identity, and war against inequality.

Thus, through the (de)construction of patriarchal culture and the colonial history of Africa as prevalent in the first half of the twentieth century, Buchi Emecheta in her *The Joys of Motherhood* tries to resituate women by the continual exposure of meaning constructed by patriarchy and the Western culture. To follow such constructs will amount to lending support to the victim syndrome with which women have been oppressed perpetually. The feminist sees that meaning (of role) is not transcendent, as Foucault admits, thereby the role given to women needs to be deconstructed, so also the myth of motherhood. There is nothing predetermined meaning (Sartre) and each individual, Foucault would say, is "free to create his own meaning through his own actions. . . . Any time we do not accept our essential freedom, we are acting in *bad faith*" (Fillingham 89). In all forms of feminist resistance what is central to Emecheta's feminist politics is that whatever aspect of culture and history that undermines women's self-respect and human dignity deserves erasure through guerrilla warfare, for politics (understood a form of war) can topple hierarchy. The collective strength of women needs to be mustered through women's consciousness, through knowledge and power. Will not it work to see, then, an era of women's millennium in the offing?

NOTES

1. Buchi Emecheta, *The Joys of Motherhood* (Rpt. 1994, Oxford: Heinemann, 32).
2. *Karma* theory: according to which one believes that what s/he gets in this transient life depends on what s/he did in the earlier life.

Works Cited

Achebe, Chinua. 1989. *Hopes and Impediments: Selected Essays*. New York: Anchor Books.

Ashcroft, Bill et al., ed. 1995, 1997. *The Post-Colonial Reader Studies.* London: Routledge.

Brown, Lloyd W. 1981. *Women Writers in Black Africa.* London: Greenwood Press.

Childs, Peter and R.J. Patrick Williams. 1997. *An Introduction to Post-Colonial Theory.* London: Prentice Hall.

Davies, Carole Boyce. "Motherhood in the Works of Male and Female Igbo Writers: Achebe, Emecheta, Nwapa and Nzekwu." Carole Boyce Davies and Anna Adams, ed. 1990. *Ngambika: Studies of Women in African Literature.* Trenton: African World Press.

Dayamond, M.J. "Buchi Emecheta, Laughter and Silence: Changes in the concepts 'Women,' 'Wife,' and 'Mother.' Marie Umeh, ed. 1996. *Emerging Perspectives on Buchi Emecheta.*

de Beauvoir, Simone. Rpt. 1997. *The Second Sex.* London: Vintage.

Driesen, Cynthia vanden. 1995. *Centering the Margins: Perspectives on Literatures in English from India, Africa, Australia.* New Delhi: Prestige.

Emecheta, Buchi. "Feminism with a Small 'f'!" Kirsten Holst Petersen, ed. 1988. *Criticism and Ideology.*

_____. Rpt. 1994. *Head above Water.* Oxford: Heinemann.

_____. Rpt. 1995. *The Joys of Motherhood.* Oxford: Heinemann.

Ezeigbo, Theodora Akachi. "Tradition and the African Female Writers: An Example of Buchi Emecheta." Marie Umeh, ed. 1996. *Emerging Perspectives on Buchi Emecheta.*

Fido, Elaine Savory. "Mother/lands: Self and Separation in the Work of Buchi Emecheta, Bessie Head and Jean Rhys." Susheila Nasta, ed. 1991. *Motherlands: Black Women's Writing from Africa, the Caribbean and South Asia.* London: The Women's Press.

Fanon, Frantz. "The Fact of Blackness." Bill Ashcroft et al., ed. 1997. *The Post-Colonial Studies Reader.*

Fillingham, Lydia Alix. 2000. *Foucault for Beginners.* Hyderabad: Orient Longman.

Guerin, Wilfred L. et al. 1999. *A Handbook of Critical Approaches to Literature.* New York: OUP.

Humm, Maggie. 1994. *A Reader's Guide to Contemporary Feminist Literary Criticism.* London: Harvester Wheatsheaf.

Katrak, Ketu H. "Decolonizing Culture: Toward a Theory for Postcolonial Women's Text," ed. Bill Ashcroft et al. 1997. *The Postcolonial Studies Reader.*

Maerton, Mike. "Feminism in Africa." <www.rosadoc.be/site/rosa/ English/blf/factsheetsenglish/34.pdf>. Accessed 10 October 2009.

McNay, Lois. 1997. *Foucault and Feminism*. Cambridge: Polity Press.

Mohanty, Chandra P. "Under Western Eyes: Feminist Scholarship and Colonial Discourse," *Feminist Review*, 30 Autumn 1988.

Moi, Toril. 1995. *Sexual/Textual Politics*. London: Routledge.

Ngcobo, Lauretta. "African Motherhood—Myth and Reality." Kirsten Holst Petersen, ed. 1988. *Criticism and Ideology*.

Nwapa, Flora. 1966, 1978. *Efuru*. Oxford: Heinemann.

Ogundele, Oladipo Joseph. "A Conversation with Dr. Buchi Emecheta." Marie Umeh, ed. *Emerging Perspectives on Buchi Emecheta*.

Petersen, Kirsten Holst, ed. 1988. *Criticism and Ideology*. Uppsala: Scandinavian Institute of African Studies.

Stratton, Florence. 1994. *Contemporary African Literature and the Politics of Gender*. London: Routledge.

_____. "The Shallow Grave: Archetypes of Female Experience in African Fiction." Marie Umeh, ed. *Emerging Perspectives on Buchi Emecheta*.

Tlali, Miriam. From the Discussion on Buchi Emecheta. "Feminism with a small 'f.'" Kirsten Holst Petersen, ed. 1988.

Umeh, Marie, ed. 1996. *Emerging Perspectives on Buchi Emecheta*. Trenton: African World Press.

Memoir as Literature: An Analysis of Fatima Bhutto's *Songs of Blood and Sword*

JYOTI DAHIYA
M.L.N. (Eve.) College, University of Delhi

Fatima Bhutto's *Songs of Blood and Sword,* though written as a memoir, resembles the framework of a potboiler with oversimplified, dramatic conflict between good and evil; mysteriously carried out murders; scheming aunt; girlfriends and wives; manipulations; vengeance; nemesis and family truths buried forever. The work is a memoir where the political history of Pakistan, till recent times, is perceived from the vantage point of personal experience and memory of the author.

The paper is a study of the said work by the author firstly as an illustration of much established narrativists'[1] position in the debate on historiography and secondly to review the author's politics of selection and representation in the memoir.

The memoir covers a span of almost fifty years with the first part looking at the entry and rise of Zulfikar Ali Bhutto in the active politics of Pakistan; formation of his party "PPP" with a socialist agenda; his rise to the position of first democratically elected prime minister of the country; and the military coup by general Zia-ul-Haq. The second part of the memoir deals with the efforts of his two sons Mir Murtaza Bhutto and Shahnawaz to reinstate democracy in Pakistan. They initially endeavour to generate world support through ideological forums like creating "Save Bhutto Committee" and post Zulfikar-execution they resort to coercive means by supporting an armed rebel against the regime. The third part takes us to the point in the family history where Shahnawaz had been mysteriously murdered, Benazir Bhutto has taken the control of PPP and the position of the prime minister of Pakistan at the age of thirty five. This section sees the ugliest fight over power between the two siblings—Benazir (Fatima's aunt) and Mir Murtaza (Fatima's father) and assassination of Mir for which Fatima openly accuses Benazir and Asif Zardari.

For the current study I would like to analyze Fatima's construction of the characters of Zulfikar, Benazir and Mir Murtaza Bhutto and her reading of some critical episodes in the history by selectively selecting her sources to validate her narrative. In the process, her politics of selection and emplotment,[2] to use Hayden White's term, gets reflected. White argues that history favours a particular mode of emplotment and may appear as a tragedy, romance, comedy and satire. The memoir here is part tragedy (in dealing with Zulfikar and Mir) and part satire (in sections on Benazir and Zardari). The problem with this historical account is that it is over-simplistic and the complexity of the characters and multifaceted nature of the episodes is conveniently ignored to validate her thesis.

Fatima is blindly uncritical of Zulfikar Ali Bhutto. An evidently feudal person whose first marriage to a girl, ten years his senior, brought him abundant wealth and his second marriage got the much-desired ticket to active politics, he is constructed as a socialist who believed in the solidarity of Muslim world and desired pan Asian unity. His coercive policies towards the innocent civilians of present-day Bangladesh and Baluchistan are heavily diluted in the narrative which, however, does not fail to highlight the possibility of glass shreds in the food given to him in jail during Zia's regime. Max Hastings,[3] among many other historians, has suggested his role in Bangladesh massacre. Nevertheless, Fatima, in Zulfi, creates an ideal democrat whose imagined legacy could have saved Pakistan from the current state of lawlessness, corruption and being a US satellite.

The memoir presents, in detail, Zulfikar's role in strengthening the ties between Pakistan and China. He was anti-American and pro-Muslim leader who did not pay heed to the warning that "the Americans would 'make a horrible example' out of him if he were to proceed with Pakistan's nuclear ambitions" (123). He withdrew from being a part of the Commonwealth nations which was later revoked by Benazir in her tenure as a Prime Minister. The atrocities meted out to the people of Bangladesh are blamed on the Pakistan Army and the role of Zulfikar is not explored in the same. It was "General Tikka Khan [who] led the assault on Dhaka University and various other points in the city's old quarters" (100) and the reports of over 400,000 women being raped in Bangladesh is analyzed as "a tactic of war" by the "Pakistani Army" (101). Zulfikar is presented as an Aristotelian well-meaning tragic hero whose *hamartia* is his socialist policies which led to a withdrawal of powerful feudal lords and big capitalist forces in Pakistan and his over-dependence on the Pakistani Army.

Benazir Bhutto, a dynamic leader, is portrayed in absolute negative terms in the memoir. Everything from her way of dressing to the choice of paint colour for her bedroom walls is immensely criticized. Mir has been constructed as rightful "political heir," a position Benazir steals from him. On the one hand, she is shown as politically naïve to have announced openly and incorrectly that her brothers were involved in the hijacking of PIA plane (228) and on the other hand she is the manipulative politician to have allied with CIA and got murdered both her brothers to claim her father's position. She is constructed, through various episodes, as a despotic leader with no patience for criticism and with a desire to be around sycophants (17). It is not her political wit but opportunism that she negotiates with the people, who were openly against her father, for retaining power. Fatima highlights Benazir's political opportunism when she mentions how "Mahmood Haroon, whose signature was on Zulfikar Ali Bhutto's death warrant, was appointed the Governor of Sindh" (302). The problem with Fatima's argument is that she ignores the fact that politics is about ideological and not personal differences.

Also, her "un-Islamic" way of life is highlighted and criticized. She enjoys her smoke and drink, has a string of admirers, does not know the Urdu language (her speeches were written in English, 290) and covers her head with a *hijab* as a political stunt.

She is shown to be a callous wife and daughter who spends time baking cake when her father is in jail and her brothers are in exile, to generate support to save the father. Years later when Zardari is in jail on corruption charges, she is busy buying jewellery worth $190,000 on Bond Street, London (387). Benazir's and Zardari's corruption is emphasized throughout the second half of the narrative. Fatima mentions how Shaheed Bhutto's '*roti, kapra aur makan*' was altered to "loot, plunder, steal" (389).

Throughout the narrative, Fatima is satirical of her every action. While Mir's affairs during his exile are romanticized, Benazir's exile is dismissed as "self-imposed" (293). She is portrayed as self-centred and power-hungry, who went to the extent of being instrumental in the murders of both her brothers. It is also suggested that the murder of both her brothers could also be seen as a part of the cold war between the capitalist and socialist super powers. It is an open secret that Benazir worked with the CIA whereas Zulfikar and the Bhutto brothers were of socialist temperament:

> 'It's clear that when Mir and Shah decided to take this action,' Verges said, referring to AZO, 'that Benazir would not approve. She was on another track—one with Western cooperation, especially with the USA. They were both against it, fighting it openly. I am not surprised that it would benefit her for one brother to be disposed of before the other.' . . . But why Shah first? . . . Verges calmly speculated. 'Among the two brothers, the strongest brother was Mir. Perhaps it was necessary to get Shah out of the way because he was the weaker one.' . . . 'She [Benazir] never opened an investigation into her brother's [Shah's] murder . . . perhaps she already knew.' (259-60)

Mir Murtaza, the writer's father, is fashioned as a compassionate, democratic, socialist, mass leader—a rightful political heir to Zulfikar's legacy—and antithetical to Benazir in every respect. The only aspect of his which Fatima is critical of is his smoking. The narrative supports the reading that he graciously accepts her sister taking away what belonged to him and comes back only when he realizes that Benazir is nothing like their father. What Fatima seems to have forgotten is that Pakistan is not their feudal family's *jagir* to be shared among siblings. Also, politics is about ideologies and in a democratic state also about numbers and not a commodity to be inherited. Throughout the narrative, though in principle she advocates democracy, she does not shy away from using phrases like "He [Mir] didn't return and demand his title" (311); he is "the heir to the Bhutto throne" (328); he gets a "prince's welcome" (357). The narrative voice fails to be critical of the dynasty politics and the author is feudal in her argument that male child is the rightful heir as opposed to the female child. While Mir's decision to enter politics is seen as altruistic, that of Benazir's is seen as selfish. While as a son he is in danger and in exile trying to "save Bhutto," Benazir is under 'comfortable' house arrest. Mir has passionate affairs during his exile (at least three are mentioned in the book) which are romanticized and idealized. The fact that he broke up with one only after he impregnated the second one is not criticized. Mir is absolved of any charges of terrorism, proved otherwise in many historical accounts. Also, his role in the PIA hijack is negated on the grounds that the Pakistan courts had acquitted him. Ironically, throughout the narrative, she has highlighted the corruption in judiciary and has mentioned over twenty high profile cases to validate that but uses the same to support her argument vis-à-vis Mir. Fatima also hints at a conspiracy by quoting Dr Ghulam Hussain, an elderly comrade of Zulfikar:

> 'The hijackers weren't PPP people,' Dr Hussain told me in his home in Islamabad. 'The whole thing was maneuvered by General Zia! He wanted an explosion in front of the world that would destroy the Bhutto boys.' (227)

Fatima conveniently forgets to mention that the source has been a faithful family friend and party worker. Also, this "revelation" by Hussain is neither elaborated nor followed. Fatima also suitably ignores the available narratives which ascertain her father's role in the said incident. Her politics of selection further highlights her agenda of presenting history in subjective terms to achieve her current purpose. Mir's role in the said hijacking has been established by many. (As qtd by Arifa Akbar[4]) "William Dalrymple has written that Murtaza was "alleged to have sentenced to death several former associates," and under the guidance of Yasser Arafat, he and Shahnawaz received arms and training. Bhutto argues that Murtaza attempted to drive the party back to the fine socialist principles on which it was founded by Zulfikar, but the latter cut a compromised figure by the time he was executed, having amended the constitution to enhance his powers." In Fatima Bhutto's memoir, Mir becomes a tragic hero interestingly without a real tragic flaw.

The memoir begins and ends with a detailed description of Murtaza's assassination, rendered in emotional terms. The Online pictures and videos[5] of the said incident reiterate Fatima's claim that Mir Murtaza was becoming a real political threat to Benazir. The gatherings at the public meetings held by him in his last days and the swarm of people at his funeral confirm the author's assertion. However Benazir's pain at the loss is also evident in the film clippings. Benazir's grief during her visit along with her mother at Mir's burial site, as captured by the cameras, is obvious. Fatima ignores the possibility of Benazir's sorrow in her narrative.

History is revisited not only to understand the past but more importantly to define the present and shape the future. So why does the author pen this memoir? Fatima Bhutto clearly uses the genre to get her nemesis and achieve her personal political agenda. Ghinwa and Fatima are politically active in Pakistan and are members of *Pakistan People's Party Shaheed Bhutto*. Ghinwa (Mir's second wife) is openly critical of Asif Zardari's politics.[6] She, perhaps, wants to set the record "right" and evidently—post Benazir Bhutto—intends to present her brother, Zulfikar Jr, as the real Bhutto as opposed to Benazir's children who have denounced their biological surname 'Zardari' and have legally adopted "Bhutto." Online sites authored and maintained by "Inqlaab" and "PPP Shaheed Bhutto" substantiate the argument. For instance, an online story titled *Bilawal Bhutto Zardari—The Cool Image—Party Boy*[7] presents a series of pictures of the chairpersons of PPP. The film starts with Zulfikar Ali Bhutto, followed by a dignified Nusrat Ali Bhutto. The third shot is that of a baffled Benazir followed by pictures of Bilawal. He is initially shown with his mother's picture and thereafter partying with white girls. He clearly appears as an irresponsible, young boy incapable of shouldering the given responsibility. Fatima, in a TV interview,[8] announces her disgust at Bilawal's adoption of family name by her statement, "By changing name as BHUTTO you can't be Bhutto."

However in her attempt to establish the only rightful Bhutto male heir, she ignores the criticism of dynasty politics. The non-linear plot presents a story where a daughter's grief is palpable on every page. Mir's callous murder by the authorities in Benazir's regime is rendered in emotional terms. In achieving her designed plan, she selectively uses quotes of pro-Murtaza political workers and sympathizers, old girl friends, university professors and friends. To conclude with Saba Imtiaz's[9] words, her rage at Benazir is understandable but "it is a niece's anger, not a historian's or a memoirist's."

NOTES

1. Theorists like Ronald Barthes (*The Discourse of History*); Foucault (who does not hide his distaste for "total history"); Hayden White (in works like Metahistory, Tropics of Discourse); Partha Chatterjee (*A Princely Imposter?: The Kumar of Bhawal & the Secret History of Indian Nationalism*); Rushdie (*Midnight's Children*); Linda Hutcheon (*The Politics of Postmodernism*).
2. "Figuring the nature of the times deceased': Literary Theory and Historical Writing," *The Future of Literary Theory*, ed. Ralph Cohen.
3. Max Hastings in http://entertainment.timesonline.co.uk/tol/ arts_ and_entertainment/books/non-fiction/article7082779.ece)
4. Arifa Akbar in (http://www.independent.co.uk/arts-entertainment/ books/reviews/songs-of-blood-and-sword-by-fatima-bhutto-1945756.html
5. A six-minute long film titled "Mir Murtaza Bhutto a tribute" on YouTube at the web address http://www.youtube.com/watch?v= SqWyQWKepHA presents images from the firing site and the funeral. Another three and a half minute long film titled "Real video of

Shaheed Mir Murtaza Bhutto by MZBhutto" at http://www.youtube.com/watch?v=iv5CU7Gkq3w&NR=1 depicts the incident. Over eleven such short films are available on YouTube.

6. YouTube at http://www.youtube.com/user/Inqilab2008 has videos of Ghinwa's political activities.
7. On YouTube at the address http://www.youtube.com/watch?v=TctexrTyGGs&feature=related
8. On YouTube at the address http://www.youtube.com/watch?v=rvEzg6I6KhQ&feature=related
9. http://afpak.foreignpolicy.com/posts/2010/04/26/the_bhuttos_and_their_books

Bibliography

Bhutto, Fatima. *Songs of Blood and Sword: A Daughter's Memoir*. London: Penguin, 2010.

White, Hayden, "'Figuring the nature of the times deceased': Literary Theory and Historical Writing," *The Future of Literary Theory,* ed. Ralph Cohen. New York and London: Routledge, 1989.

http://www.independent.co.uk/arts-entertainment/books/reviews/songs-of-blood-and-sword-by-fatima-bhutto-1945756.html

http://en.wikipedia.org/wiki/Memoir

http://www.answers.com/topic/memoir

http://entertainment.timesonline.co.uk/tol/arts_and_entertainment/books/non-fiction/article7082779.ece

http://www.youtube.com/watch?v=SqWyQWKepHA

http://www.youtube.com/watch?v=iv5CU7Gkq3w&NR=1

Incarcerated Women in Modern Indian Fiction

PUNITA JHA
M.R.M. College, Darbhanga

My paper aims at clarifying the concept of women liberation as it emerges from the pen of eminent Indian novelists in English. There were marked periods in history when fundamental changes took place. This century basically fosters a new world order, a world where women's lives are devoid of fear and brutalism, a world where her spirit is free, and she is allowed to live as a person, creatively contributing to her own growth and development of our society!

The part played by culture in moulding the manifestations of the female psyche in different countries and societies should also be taken into account. Female thought and their behaviour differs from place to place. Indian women are quite different from English women. In Indian writing in English, we find what is termed creative feminism, which examines the role and status of women in society through creative literature and does justice to her feminine identity as an individual. Indian novelists portray the feminine principle and the female virtues through a creative portrayal of women character. They project and sustain traditional values and extol traditional roles of women as wife, mother and caretaker.

There has always been a remarkable quantity of books on social reforms and the revival of past traditions, the search of identity, and the increasing awareness of the role by the individual in the society. All these socio-cultural factors are responsible for the birth of feminism and the concept of women liberation. This naturally led to a new look at the status of women in the Indian society. In fact, the whole burden of civilization is summed up in its feminine images.

Our modern society is torn between two extremes, one that glorifies and idealizes women and the other group portrays the incarcerated picture of an imprisoned women hovering in the dark to free herself from the prison.

In the present socio-cultural set-up, a woman feels deeply frustrated by her restricted and regimented life, the lack of privacy, the physical burden and the drabness of a family life. All these collectively impede the concept of liberation with the rapid progress in the field of education. Women are becoming alienated from their core self and their freedom of feminity. It's the educated women who have become discounted with their lot, especially their role as a housewife.

R.K. Narayan's Savitri in *The Dark Room* has a special urge for emancipation, even if it may be 'freedom at the cost of her life.'[1] Women like Savitri are economically so helpless that "they just have to lump what they do not like."

Rabindra Nath Tagore, on the other hand, in his novel *Binodini* portrays women as a passively and reluctantly ideal character, she can be hailed as the first novelist in Indian writing who subordinated women to the stereotyped socio-cultural values as well as to her male counterpart. He portrays the harrowing and stifling impact of traditional rules and regulations on the psyche of the character. As Tagore has said in one of his early songs:

> O Women, you are one-half women and one-half dream.

A young wife turned a widow, Binodini is exposed to all the miseries that are incidental. As a widow, all her rights and privileges as a woman are lost; she is exposed to the most stringent privations of widowhood and is often given to melancholic brooding, culminating in an unconscious protest against her stifled existence. Binodini is different. She lives in the world of erotic fantasies and sensations approximating the state of dreams. Mahendra and Binodini can not part from each other, though Binodini wants to avoid Mahindra, her deep desire does not permit her to live away from Mahendra. With a deep sigh she says to herself. "Where will he go? He must come back. He is mine."[2] Binodini still pines for love and doesn't like to spur the amorous advances of Mahendra. "I will wear it as a crown. I haven't had so much love in life that I can afford to reject what is offered" (71)

Despite the desire for love, she is not blind to her social status as widow: "Why must you merely drag me down into disgrace?" (67) she asks Mahindra. Through Binodini, Tagore is expressing his discomposure against all kinds of inhibitions that stunt the growth of one's individuality. Here as in almost all his other novels he rails against encumbrances of family, caste, ritual, set, group, party, nation and administration that divide men and dwarf their personalities. The novelist seems to[2] question the very foundation of our social and cultural order which has been a monopoly of men. "These men are cold-blooded libertines who unscrupulously use women as instruments of their lust."

Binodini's renunciation at the moment of her life's triumph comes as a sudden surprise to the readers. Did she back out of the love-deal because of her lack of courage or because she was scared of breaking the social taboo. Binodini conveys her message beautifully in the given lines when she declares at the end: "These words be my final reward, I want nothing more than what you have just affirmed. If I took more it would not last Religion and society would never tolerate it." (218)

Tagore has deliberately given such a conclusion. He wanted to make Binodini traditionally convincing and morally acceptable as an ideal feminine figure true to the demands of her social self. Marriage of widow at the end of the novel would be an outrageous theme defiling the sanctity of widows.

Virginia Woolf has rightly said: "Women and fiction remain unsolved problems." Binodini remains pure, though victimized. What she wants is to be nothing but a woman; she is the unravished bride of quietness. "My novel is about time as a destroyer. As preserver and about what the bondage of time does to people. I have tried to tunnel under the mundane surface of domesticity."[3] This is what Anita Desai says, it is her opinion of the present as the important section of past and future that makes her pursue her ambitions, despite the gloomy atmosphere at home, and the burden of responsibility.

Anita Desai's work represents a unique blending of the Indian and Western. Her novels catch the bewilderment of the individual psyche, confronted with the overbearing socio-cultural environment and the ever-beckoning modern promise of self-gratification and self-fulfillment. In the face of this dual onslaught, her female protagonists Maya, Sita, Monisha and Amla are seen poised tantalizingly at different junctures of the philosophic spectrum.

A common contemporary issue facing every country is the question of women. The women are seen launching themselves for their identity. The liberated women today challenges the traditional notions of "Angels in the house" and sexually voracious images. A liberated woman is essentially a woman of awareness and conscious of her low position in the family and society.

Anita Desai asserts that her protagonists are liberated and different. "I'm interested in characters who are not average but have retreated or been driven into some extremity of despair and so turned against the general current." It is for them a challenge to better their personal existence. Her protagonists, brought up to be different, weak and quiet in the face of exploitation are yet highly sensitive and intelligent and are desperate to find an outlet to their pangs. Their extreme sensitivity, however, channelises their mode of liberation in various directions. According to Anita Desai, that woman is new or liberated who in the dimension of time is a rebel against the general current of the patriarchal society and time to explore her potential, struggling to fulfill her urges and needs.[4]

In *Voices in the City* the house to Manisha is a prison, an object of intimidation. In the first few pages of the novel, the concept of her husband's house as a prison cage comes across very strongly, she does not belong to it, does not relate to it. In the privacy of her room, she is oppressed by a terrifying sound that repeats like a motif of a nightmare, from which there seemed no escape. The atmosphere in and around the house seemed to stifle her self-expression. She is encaged in the house. The house in Desai's novels is not only a symbol of shelter and protection but also of "*incarceration and laceration.*" It is the house that fails to house the houseless. "Man can think of himself without a woman. She cannot think of her self without man."[5]

According to Shobha De, the girls now feel that they could be and do whatever they wanted to do with the same freedom as boys. They have become so wild that they have gone to the extent of having boys as their toys. Shobha De's Karuna in *Socialite Evenings* gives us the picture of the marginalisation of Indian women at the hands of their husbands.

In *Socialite Evenings*, Shobha De plays different roles at different times to quench her emotional and psychic thirst. She is a model, a housewife, a society lady and an actor writer and a paramour. Marriage subjugates and enslaves women. It leads her to aimless days indefinitely repeated, life that slips away gently towards death without questioning its purpose. But not so with women like Karuna unlike other married women who have practically no choice left to them save what their husbands will and desire. Karuna has independent thoughts. She has her say and is free to choose her way and means. Karuna's is a life of instincts and urges. She unveils and unfurls herself to creative urge stifled within her self and this act of unburdening herself is a compromise with herself. Like Shashi Deshpande, Shobha De does not overdo women's suffering. She transforms it into a creative principle of art and beauty.

In Indian life and so in Indian fiction, role expectations are highly specific and institutionalised. Thus woman's role in the family has remained multifarious. Raja Rao has rightly said.

> Life is made for women,
> Man is a stranger to this earth.

Despite quite radical changes, the status of women, more than that of man, is bound up with the traditional wife and mother role. Ideal housewife is the favourite image, virtually moulded in the same fashion in all Indian novels. We find that service, sacrifice, submissiveness and tolerance are the qualities which come to them naturally. Excessive endurance and the list of adjustments she makes is endless. This was how women were portrayed by early Indian novelists like Tagore. Anita Desai and Shoba De protest against present time, against monotony, drabness and humiliation. Binodini and Manisha refuse to be taken for granted and do complain against this system. The liberated women as portrayed by 21st century Indian novelists try to protest but the psychological odds against which they fight are peculiar. It seems that the idea that a woman can be free and yet good at the same time is not acceptable.

Are they portrayed by modern novelists merely as vehicles to carry the writer's deliberate interpretation of the East and not as humans with real feelings?

NOTES

1. P.S. Sundaram, *R.K. Narayan* (New Delhi 1973), p. 48
2. Rabindra Nath Tagore, *Binodini* (Choker Bali), trans. Krishna Kriplani (New Delhi: Sahitya Akademi, 1982), p. 85.
3. Anita Desai, Tremendous changes interview by Sunil Sethi, *India Today*, Dec. 15, 1980) page 142.
4. Yashodhara Dalmia, An Interview with Anita Desai, *The Times of India*, April 29, 1999.
5. R. Selden, ed., "The Theory of Criticism," *From Plato to Present: A Reader*, 1988, p. 534.